AUTUMN OF THE BLACK SNAKE

"Hogeland breathes new life into a transformative conflict unknown to most modern Americans but decisive in shaping the future trajectory of the United States . . . He paints vivid portraits of leaders such as Blue Jacket (Shawnee) and Little Turtle (Miami), who were among the most formidable indigenous adversaries that U.S. forces ever faced . . . [and] convincingly argues the significance of Washington's decisions during this episode . . . Indeed, Mr. Hogeland's work invites reflection on why some of the most important (and darker) legacies of Washington's presidency—establishing federal supremacy over the west and its native inhabitants in a war of unbridled conquest—have also been the most readily forgotten."   —David Preston, *The Wall Street Journal*

"Compelling . . . Hogeland rescues some colorful key players from obscurity and restores them to the main narrative of the early American republic."   —Amy H. Sturgis, *Reason*

"[*Autumn of the Black Snake* is] narrative-driven; carefully constructed for maximum tension and dramatic payoff . . . [Hogeland] has situated himself as one of the foremost critics, outside academia, of the Founders Chic that—in the wake of *Hamilton*—remains a remarkably dominant paradigm . . . He also makes a sustained effort to include Native American perspectives . . . [and] grapple[s] with the possibilities and limitations of Native *strategy*—which is crucial to challenging assumptions about the inevitability of white conquest . . . Hogeland uses the stuff of archival texts, with all their idiosyncratic underlinings, deletions, and postscripts, to get into the head of enigmatic characters like 'Mad Anthony' Wayne . . . [He is] a storyteller of flare and ingenuity."   —Tom Cutterham, *The Junto*

"Hogeland does a fine job of bringing this untold tale of the U.S. Army's birth to life . . . It's an intriguing saga of double-dealing, limited diplomacy, and strong personalities on all sides . . . Hogeland's writing shines . . . For any reader interested in early American political or military history, *Autumn of the Black Snake* would be a good addition to their bookshelves."

—James A. Percoco, *Washington Independent Review of Books*

"Irresistible verve . . . To turn all this into a coherent story, with characters introduced and portrayed at precisely the right moment in the complexities of an ongoing plot, is extraordinarily difficult. It is done here so deftly and so inconspicuously that I do not hesitate to call *Autumn of the Black Snake* a masterpiece."

—William R. Everdell, *The Eighteenth-Century Intelligencer*

"Hogeland grippingly relates the battles over the Ohio Valley between the fledgling U.S. and a coalition of the Shawnee, Miami, and Delaware nations . . . Well-known Revolutionary characters (Washington and Hamilton, for instance) fill Hogeland's pages; so too do colorful, little-known, and impressively skilled British military figures and Native Americans . . . Stuffed with detail, Hogeland's solid and distinctive book fills a significant gap in the narrative history of the United States."

—*Publishers Weekly*

"Tightly focused . . . Hogeland vividly delineates these seminal personalities, such as the first commander of Washington's Western army, 'Mad Anthony' Wayne; the Indian leaders Blue Jacket and Little Turtle as well as the half-white Indian ally, Alexander McKee . . . An enlightening history of American westward expansion." —*Kirkus Reviews*

"[Hogeland] spreads a rich tale of land hunger, self-dealing, betrayal, and change as colonizers steadily migrated west, pushing Native tribes out of their traditional hunting and agricultural demesnes. Jeffersonian and Hamiltonian philosophies clashed while an unending stream of settlers trekked west. Detailed and . . . comprehensive."

—Edwin Burgess, *Library Journal*

"Hogeland relates . . . [this story] with eloquence and insight into the motives and actions of each side. This is a scrupulously balanced account of a formative period in westward expansion."

—Jay Freeman, *Booklist*

"[Hogeland's] story bristles with larger-than-life characters."

—Edward Morris, *BookPage*

"Superb . . . [Hogeland] is a masterful storyteller . . . Extraordinarily vivid accounts . . . I hope I am not belaboring the point here when I say how much I learned from and enjoyed this work."

—Peter Staffel, *The Eighteenth-Century Intelligencer*

"Like all great nonfiction, *Autumn of the Black Snake* takes the familiar and turns it upside down and inside out. With clear, muscular prose, William Hogeland sets the record straight on badly neglected early American history. He knows his stuff, and his point of view is fresh and sure-footed. My notion of the republic's narrative has been forever altered."

—Eric Bogosian, actor, Pulitzer Prize–nominated playwright, and author of *Operation Nemesis: The Assassination Plot That Avenged the Armenian Genocide*

"William Hogeland is one of the best historians of early America. His books are pulsating and thought-provoking, and in *Autumn of the Black Snake* he marshals his skills to recount a sweeping story of frontier turbulence. Relating this saga would have been sufficient for some historians, but Hogeland goes further and lays bare President Washington's hidden motives. This is history at its best. The gripping account Hogeland provides is must-reading."

—John Ferling, author of *Whirlwind: The American Revolution and the War That Won It* and *Jefferson and Hamilton: The Rivalry That Forged a Nation*

"*Autumn of the Black Snake* is an elegantly written and scrupulously balanced account of what is sometimes called President George Washington's Indian war, enhanced with a nuanced and intriguing recounting of the often dirty politics behind the formation of the United States Army. I highly recommend this important—and thoroughly enjoyable—book on these overlooked but crucial episodes."

—Peter Cozzens, author of *The Earth Is Weeping: The Epic Story of the Indian Wars for the American West*

"Some wars America remembers, some wars we work to forget. William Hogeland gives a dramatic telling of the war that we have never really talked about, despite being the war that made us the global military power we are today. It's a harrowing story, brilliantly told, and a radical relook at the ragged collective of colonies who fought for their own liberty and then, once getting it, set out on the warpath, an empire bent on taking its neighbors' liberty away."

—Robert Sullivan, author of *My American Revolution: A Modern Expedition Through History's Forgotten Battlegrounds* and *Rats: Observations on the History and Habitat of the City's Most Unwanted Inhabitants*

"In this page-turner, the bigger-than-life characters of Little Turtle, George Washington, Blue Jacket, and Mad Anthony Wayne clash over the future of the continent at a time when any of them might have prevailed. A rich and important book."

—Kathleen DuVal, author of *Independence Lost: Lives on the Edge of the American Revolution*

"William Hogeland's rare talent is turning books into conversation, and bloodless, impenetrable histories into compelling and strange narratives. Icons become flawed people who did all sorts of things for contradictory reasons. The author is a skeptic, political analyst, and truth teller. Which is all fine, but not nearly as important as being a brilliant and amusing storyteller."

—Paul Chaat Smith, author of *Everything You Know About Indians Is Wrong*

"If you think Custer's Last Stand was the biggest defeat inflicted on an American army by Native American forces, you should read William Hogeland's *Autumn of the Black Snake*. This book describes one of America's least-known but most important conflicts: the so-called Northwest Indian War. Hogeland shows how the annihilation of a large American force by a confederation of tribes caused the stoic George Washington to cry out in rage and led to the formation of the Legion of the United States, which became the foundation of the American army. He argues that this struggle is an ominous prequel to Imperial America, as greed, nationalism, and ambition swirl through a cast of amazing characters. In *Autumn of the Black Snake*, Hogeland once again manages to write rigorous, original history in wonderfully colloquial prose."   —John Dolan, a.k.a. Gary Brecher, the War Nerd

GAIL BROUSAL

WILLIAM HOGELAND

AUTUMN OF THE BLACK SNAKE

William Hogeland is the author of three books on founding-era U.S. history—*The Whiskey Rebellion*, *Declaration*, and *Founding Finance*— as well as a collection of essays, *Inventing American History*. Born in Virginia and raised in Brooklyn, he lives in New York City.

ALSO BY WILLIAM HOGELAND

Founding Finance

Declaration

Inventing American History

The Whiskey Rebellion

AUTUMN OF
THE BLACK SNAKE

AUTUMN OF THE BLACK SNAKE

George Washington, Mad Anthony Wayne,

and the Invasion That Opened the West

WILLIAM HOGELAND

Farrar, Straus and Giroux   New York

Farrar, Straus and Giroux
175 Varick Street, New York 10014

Copyright © 2017 by William Hogeland
Maps copyright © 2017 by Jeffrey L. Ward
All rights reserved
Printed in the United States of America
Published in 2017 by Farrar, Straus and Giroux
First paperback edition, 2018

The Library of Congress has cataloged the hardcover edition as follows:
Names: Hogeland, William, author.
Title: Autumn of the Black Snake : the creation of the U.S. Army and the
    invasion that opened the West / William Hogeland.
Description: First edition. | New York : Farrar, Straus and Giroux, 2017. |
    Includes bibliographical references and index.
Identifiers: LCCN 2016052193| ISBN 9780374107345 (hardcover) | ISBN
    9780374711580 (e-book)
Subjects: LCSH: Wayne's Campaign, 1794. | Wayne, Anthony, 1745–1796—
    Military leadership. | Indians of North America—Wars—1790–1794. |
    Indians of North America—Wars—Ohio.
Classification: LCC E83.794 .H64 2017 | DDC 970.004/97—dc23
LC record available at https://lccn.loc.gov/2016052193

Paperback ISBN: 978-0-374-53784-5

Designed by Jonathan D. Lippincott

Our books may be purchased in bulk for promotional, educational, or business
use. Please contact your local bookseller or the Macmillan Corporate and
Premium Sales Department at 1-800-221-7945, extension 5442, or by e-mail
at MacmillanSpecialMarkets@macmillan.com.

www.fsgbooks.com
www.twitter.com/fsgbooks • www.facebook.com/fsgbooks

1 3 5 7 9 10 8 6 4 2

E.W.H.
1929–2005

CONTENTS

LIST OF MAPS

AUTUMN OF
THE BLACK SNAKE

PROLOGUE: THE RUINS
OF AN OLD FRENCH FORT

Where the Mississippi River drains North America on the southward tilt, ceaselessly carving and enriching the bottomland, France once gave a name to an expanse fanning asymmetrically eastward and westward from that spine of moving sediment. Saying its name in rude mimicry of Cajun, Quebecois, or the Paris street—like a guttural "uhln-wah"—would parody how a New Frenchman might have pronounced what his trading partners, designated as savages, called that expanse. Of Europeans, it was traders, soldiers, villagers, and administrators of France who first came to know the Illinois Country. They knew it for a long time.

But unlike the English speakers who came later, the French never knew that region as an American West. They did go west. Early on, seeking inland passage from the St. Lawrence River to the Gulf of Mexico, they navigated Lake Superior before they even knew about Lake Erie. They would name the Platte and ascend the Missouri. French traders would lift their eyes to the white peaks of the Rockies. But that wasn't the main thing.

The main thing, once it was sorted out and made feasible, was to travel up the St. Lawrence River from the citadel Quebec into Lake Ontario, portage around the gigantic falls of the Niagara River into Lake Erie, embark upon rivers running down to wider rivers, cross more of the land bridges known as portages, and finally enter the Mississippi itself as it moved, so treacherously but steadily lower, to posts below sea level at New Orleans and Biloxi and emerge at last in the Gulf of Mexico. This empire wasn't western but transmarine. It stretched from the St. Lawrence's mouth at the Atlantic to the Mississippi's mouth at the gulf.

The imperial claim, it's true, extended for vast distances in all directions. The claimant was His Majesty by the Grace of God the most Christian King of France and Navarre, Count of Provence, Forcalquier, and lands adjacent, Dauphin of Viennois, and Count of Valentinois and of Diois. That monarch listed in his North American holdings everything east and west of the Mississippi, up to and including both the Appalachian Mountains and the Rocky Mountains, and everything north of the Great Lakes as far as the Hudson Bay. Yet he made actual use of a far more limited section of continent. His two great American seats were New France above and Louisiana below. Though often in tension, they participated in a constant imperial motion, undertaken on three types of peculiarly French boats, from the Atlantic to the gulf and back again. The Illinois Country, in between and pulled administratively both ways, serviced that motion, which had one purpose.

Like other people, Europeans had to wear hats. There was no imaginable alternative to covering the head, and a hat had become the standard means, so demand was ceaseless. Smooth, warm fur of the big beaver made the best felt for peltry hats, as well as for other garments, and the beaver had grown scarce in Europe, with a market nevertheless unsaturated thanks to price. Discovering the outlandish abundance of giant beavers in North America had been like discovering gold and silver, or a license to coin them. The supply was evidently inexhaustible, and obtaining it was easy: by the mid-seventeenth century, a host of indigenous cultures, expert in extracting the resource, had become eager for—dependent on—everything that Europe made in such high volume: metal, buttons, muskets, glass, tailoring, brandy, and more.

And forts. It was in service of getting beaver and other furs that the French became such great fort builders. Illinois Country Indians often sought protection from the powerful, aggressive Iroquois confederation to the east, and the French built forts, usually with the permission of their trading partners, on the high banks of the Mississippi itself; others they garrisoned near strategic confluences of the many tributaries. A few permanent settlers hugged the network in support, and the villages were nice, with houses standing gaily painted in rows along the riverbanks. While English speakers to the east thought of the region as remote, the more cosmopolitan forts were scenes of balls and soirees; villagers owned mirrors, billiard tables, and neat kitchen gardens. Many years later, American soldiers discovering the ruins of an old fort on the Great Miami River in the former Illinois Country would conclude that no Indian nation could have enjoyed sole hegemony there: the French had been there too.

New France villagers wore the latest Paris fashions. So they wore, of course, the American beaver. Of peltry from America, the hatters of France made thousands and thousands of hats, and French merchants and shippers sold some of them across the sea to the French Americans. That all went on for nearly one hundred years.

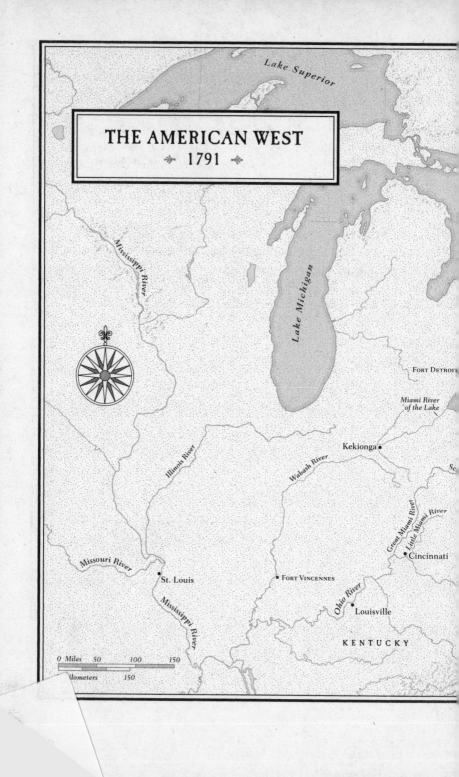

THE AMERICAN WEST
⚜ 1791 ⚜

Lake Superior

Lake Michigan

Mississippi River

Illinois River

Wabash River

Miami River of the Lake

FORT DETROIT

Kekionga

Missouri River

St. Louis

FORT VINCENNES

Great Miami River

Little Miami River

Cincinnati

Ohio River

Louisville

Mississippi River

KENTUCKY

0 Miles 50 100 150

ilometers 150

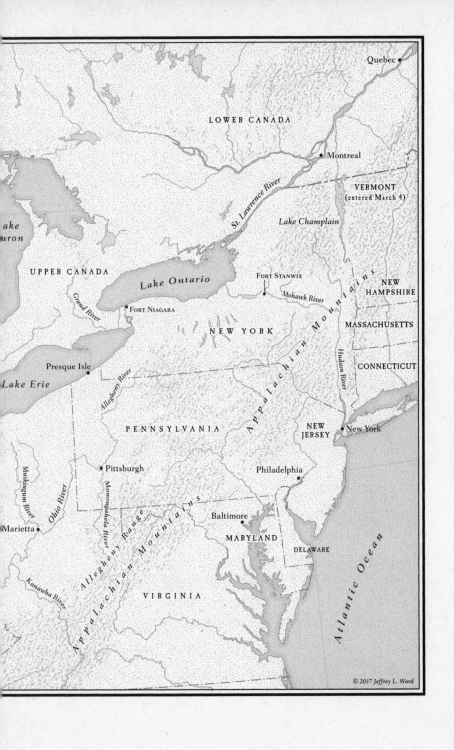

Quebec

LOWER CANADA

Montreal

VERMONT
(entered March 4)

St. Lawrence River

Lake Champlain

Lake Huron

UPPER CANADA

Lake Ontario

FORT STANWIX

NEW
HAMPSHIRE

Mohawk River

Grand River

FORT NIAGARA

NEW YORK

MASSACHUSETTS

Appalachian Mountains

CONNECTICUT

Presque Isle

Hudson River

Lake Erie

Allegheny River

PENNSYLVANIA

NEW
JERSEY

New York

Muskingum River

Pittsburgh

Ohio River

Monongahela River

Philadelphia

Marietta

Allegheny Range

Baltimore

Atlantic Ocean

MARYLAND

DELAWARE

Kanawha River

Appalachian Mountains

VIRGINIA

© 2017 Jeffrey L. Ward

PART I

SINCLAIR'S RETREAT

1

THE DEATH
OF GENERAL BUTLER

On a November morning in 1791, nearly thirty years after the French Crown abandoned its American empire, a man named Richard Butler sat against a mattress propped against the base of an oak, dying in pain near a bend of the upper Wabash River. Butler came from Pennsylvania, and to him this cold ground, once called the Illinois Country, lay indisputably in the American West, specifically in the Northwest Territory of the United States. Close by and in the distance, others were dying too, hundreds of them. Some screamed and some groaned, and through the smoke of exploded gunpowder came a sharp cacophony of musket and rifle fire, triumphant screams of the enemy, and orders yelled in English and being ignored.

Around the wounded Butler, a group of men and officers crouched in hurried conference. Butler started laughing. Evidently, he'd registered the shrieks of a cadet nearby and was struck by the sheer intensity of that noise. A beloved general, he'd been shot in the arm while trying to rally troops back from their outright flight in the face of a surprise attack from all sides. Getting his arm in a sling, he mounted a horse to take charge of the collapsing front line; shot again, he fell from the saddle. Four soldiers had lugged and carried him in a blanket to his tent in a row of tents, but he found his wound too painful to allow him to lie down, so they'd propped him against this oak, an especially huge, spreading tree, and stacked two knapsacks on either side to hold him up. Butler was a heavy man, and as he laughed, his sides shook his coat.

Some of the men around him were grieved to think he had no chance; others thought he might make it if they could only remove him from the scene, but it was becoming horribly clear that getting out of here at all, let alone lugging a large man, was more unlikely every second. Most of the officers were dead. The numb-fingered soldiers left alive had been firing as best they could, but as the enemy began to breach the perimeter, they gave up, collapsed their formations, and crowded by terrified instinct toward the center of the field of battle. There they were easy to shoot down en masse.

Now where Richard Butler sat propped, his youngest brother, Captain Edward Butler, appeared, carrying on his back another brother, Colonel Thomas Butler, both legs broken. In pain and with no time to spare—arrows were thrumming into the row of tents—the Butler brothers tried to confer.

Richard's corpse was sure to be a prize. The Indians who were destroying the Americans knew Butler. The fighters had seen him mount, with his arm in a sling. They'd picked him off.

And Butler knew them. He'd been at various times their translator, business partner, military ally and opponent, to some a boon companion, to some a lover and a spouse. Almost everybody of every race and nation in this contested zone was some kind of line crosser, but particularly good stories attached themselves to Richard Butler. He'd run his own fur-trading operation out of the rough village of Pittsburgh at the headwaters of the Ohio River. He'd fought for Pennsylvania against the French and Shawnee, against Virginia, and against the British while serving in multiple capacities in the government of the colony and then the state, as well as the Continental Congress and now the newly formed United States, in whose service he sat dying today. During his adventuring and moneymaking, he'd fathered a child with a Shawnee wife, or so it was said, or maybe children, under Shawnee wedlock rites. His purported Shawnee bride wasn't just any Shawnee. Nonhelema, called "Chieftess" and "the Grenadier Woman" by some whites, had a reputation as a fighter and war leader. She too made good stuff of legend. She was many years Butler's senior, and some people seemed to believe she stood six feet six. Maybe she did. Butler's Christian wife, Maria, living at posts and forts behind shaky lines, might or might not have known or presumed anything about all this, and the whole story might have been nothing but a cluster of rumors that Butler himself saw no percentage in denying.

Indisputable was his authorship of a Shawnee vocabulary and grammar. That project had come at the direct behest of General George Washington, so Butler had taken it up eagerly. Better yet, it was Washington's old war comrade the Marquis de Lafayette who had asked for something on Indian languages, and that request was made on behalf of none other than Lafayette's good friend the Austrian monarch Maria Theresa, a superstar among the crowned heads, known to many as the Great Reformer, with a name outdoing that of the king of France—it included, in a page-long host of titles, Dowager Empress of the Romans, Margravine of Moravia, and Lady of the Wendish Mark—and an interest in aboriginal languages. At his desk in a scruffy outpost village, fiddling with his words and phonetic equivalents, Butler might have imagined his work being professionally copied and ceremonially presented months or even years later at the court of Vienna, a curio from the savage American wilderness. That's the kind of job that made Butler happy.

Nonhelema the Shawnee war leader served as a consultant for another Indian vocabulary book. Maybe she and Butler shared nothing more than certain practical and intellectual interests. Maybe they were just good friends. Maybe that's what made Butler laugh as he sat propped amid the killing in the woods, while his friends and brothers grew frantic with desire to remove him, frantic for escape themselves. Who knows where Butler's mind ran or why he really laughed.

Somewhere in the smoke and noise and chill of that November morning were Little Turtle and Blue Jacket. Little Turtle would be leading Miami forces, Blue Jacket the Shawnee, and both were leading the whole thing. The scene so chaotic and horrific for American soldiers was for the Indians becoming a thrilling victory, thanks to precise planning, irreproachable execution, and full coordination of forces led mainly by those two men, along with the Delaware war leader Buckon-gahelas.

Little Turtle and Blue Jacket never agreed on much. Those who talked about them at the time and would write about them in the future—some praising Blue Jacket to the detriment of Little Turtle, others vice versa—never agreed either. But that November morning, as a man they'd come to see as their nemesis sat dying under an oak, they were in agreement on at least one thing: this was a war for the survival of their people, and they would work together to win it. The victory they were even now achiev-ing against U.S. forces represented a triumphant step forward in that war for survival.

Like those of the European monarchs, these leaders' names involved mystery and tradition. It was English speakers, of course, who called the Miami leader "Little Turtle," sometimes "the Little Turtle," some-times only "Turtle." In his language, he was called something English speakers phonetically approximated as "Mi-chi-kin-i-kwa," referring to the common painted turtle of North America. Blue Jacket's name had once been something sounding like "Se-pe-te-ke-na-te," which comes into this language as the "Big Rabbit," but he changed it to something that might be translated as "Whirlpool," and the handle Blue Jacket had nothing to do with either of his other names. There was a reason for it, but nobody remembered what it was.

You had to be there. Little Turtle was by no account little, and Blue Jacket wore scarlet. The Turtle stood over six feet tall, some said; others disagreed, but more important was his stature as a military leader. It was unexpected. He was about forty, his roots obscure, his connec-tions strange, and he was quiet, for a war leader, philosophical yet blunt, his attitudes enigmatic. Blue Jacket, about forty-five, was more flamboy-ant, and his people did have a reputation as brilliant, deadly fighters, and as leaders of other nations. The way many Shawnee like Blue Jacket looked at it, they'd been pushed out of the region north of the Ohio River long ago by the powerful Six Nations of the Iroquois, re-duced to wandering for generations in diaspora as far west as the grass-lands, as far south as the gulf. With Blue Jacket now in command for war, some hoped for a Shawnee return here, a whole people re-formed in an ancient homeland.

Today the Indians had encircled the Americans' camp in a crescent, with Blue Jacket's, Little Turtle's, and Buckongahelas's men making up the crescent's base and fighters from other nations on each horn. Then the crescent moved, synchronized: the leaders' base charged the camp's center, while the horns, not charging, ran all the way around the outside of the camp's perimeter. Caught in that net, the Americans never had a chance. That's what the men whom English speakers called Blue Jacket and Little Turtle were good at. It took collaboration.

Richard Butler was facing inevitability. The men around him at the tree, under fire now, began to shift into retreat mode, hoping to withdraw in some kind of order. And yet Thomas and Edward were refusing to leave their brother's side.

Richard took charge by pointing out the obvious. He was mortally wounded; there was no chance for his escape. As both elder brother and superior officer, he gave young Edward an order: leave Richard to his fate and save their wounded brother. Over protests, Richard began handing his sword, watch, and ring to a major, and he asked for a loaded pistol.

There was nothing else to do. Retreat had been called by fife and drum, but there was no retreat, only terror, cacophony, mutilation. Thomas Butler couldn't even walk. They found two loaded pistols, cocked them, and put them in Richard Butler's useless hands.

Or that's a pretty fair account of the last moments of Major General Richard Butler, as cobbled from the memories, and from other accounts based on the memories, of men who survived that victory of Indian fighters over the United States and men who heard about it later. A fair account, not the thing itself, of course. Butler died. How he died is a story, and what happened to the story is a story too.

As the losers would have it, the death of General Butler became a dramatic moment in the story of a horrifying defeat of troops led by General Arthur St. Clair in asserting legal claims of the United States in the region north and west of the Ohio River. Having become unsure of his whereabouts, St. Clair led about 1,500 officers and men, plus dozens of others—soldiers' wives, girlfriends, and children, the wagon and packhorse drivers—to a bivouac on the bend of the upper Wabash.

He failed to fortify his encampment. In the ensuing battle, about 650 American troops died, including nearly all of the officers, along with 50 civilians, including nearly all of the women and children—some claimed the total of the dead was more like 900—plus about 300 horribly wounded. Nearly a third of all of the nation's troops, that is, were killed in a few hours, and the survivors, in their panicked flight, took away unforgettable horror at the torture and mutilation to which the dying were exuberantly and ritually subjected, the rape and burning, the amputation and evisceration, the mouths stuffed with dirt.

General St. Clair himself survived. The scale of his loss, and the horror at how the dead met their ends, would become parts of a story whose title attached itself to his name: St. Clair's defeat.

Richard Butler, by contrast, became a hero. The Butlers had only recently come from Ireland—Richard was born there—and like other new American families they took themselves to be founders of a military, commercial, administrative, and courtly dynasty. Richard and his four brothers expected to take risks, over-deliver, and be flamboyantly rewarded. Four of the five were heroes of American independence, known as the fighting Butlers. "The Butlers and their five sons!" said General Washington, according to lore, glass in hand at Fraunces Tavern in New York at the Continental officers' farewell dinner. "When I wished a thing well done," said the Marquis de Lafayette, recalling his days in that war, "I ordered a Butler to do it."

> He leaned his back against a tree, and there resigned his
>   breath,
> And like a valiant soldier, sunk in the arms of death;
> When blessed angels did await, his spirit to convey,
> And unto the celestial fields, he quickly bent his way.

A topical ballad titled "Sinclair's Defeat" made the death of Richard Butler a household tale.

The victorious Indians had a different way of making the death of their old friend and enemy Richard Butler a narrative high point. One day not long after that battle at the Wabash, the famous Mohawk Joseph

Brant, a leader and diplomat of the Six Nations confederation of the Iroquois, took unsolicited and unexpected delivery of Richard Butler's dried scalp. He'd been served.

As the winners would have it, Richard Butler's death occurred not in St. Clair's miserable failure but in their confederation's great success. An alliance of western Indian nations, put together by the Miami, Shawnee, and Delaware people who lived, farmed, hunted, and did business north and west of the Ohio River, was successfully resisting an American incursion carried out in violation of normal diplomatic process and marked for decades by murder of noncombatants and wholesale burning of towns and food supplies. Joseph Brant's Mohawk, and the rest of the Six Nations, lived east of the Ohio River yet claimed all land to its west: they'd dominated the western Indians for generations. Now the western Indians led by Blue Jacket and Little Turtle had begun winning a fight they felt was just gearing up, and Brant and the Iroquois, having seemed at first to offer support, had lately seemed to waffle.

Hence the delivery to Joseph Brant of a piece of Richard Butler. Cut and yanked from the head, possibly while the heart still beat wildly for life, it traveled a long way to tell Brant the story of an overwhelming victory, a story that was also an indictment, an invitation, and a demand.

A fundamental shift was about to begin in North American life. With the losers' outrage and terror deepening, in response to St. Clair's awful defeat on the Wabash, and with the winners' excitement over their great victory mounting, a war would begin. The existence, purpose, and future of the United States of America was formed in that war.

And yet it would be forgotten. The first war the United States ever fought, in which the U.S. Army itself came into being, would never even be given a name.

So this all took place in present-day where?

You can walk a pleasant, quiet main street in what is now western Ohio to a plaque marking the site of Richard Butler's death, but that's the wrong answer. You can get the address in seconds. It won't help. Butler died in a deep woods, the trees widely spaced and so big around that it would take many men to circle some of them. It was late fall, the branches probably not yet completely bare, so if the smoke hadn't been so thick some sky might have been visible, but you'd have to tilt your head back to see it, and in summer that place was dim, full of birdsong and the sound of wind in leaves, the branches creaking far overhead.

But it's not just the shorn land and artificially exposed sky that make it impossible for us to go where this story took place. It's not even the astonishing rarity of descendants of the people who had lived there for so long. The story of the only indigenous alliance to win battles that might have defeated American expansion into the West, and the story of the founding of the U.S. Army, with all of its world-historical future coded in embryo, in the first war that the United States ever fought—the story, that is, of Americans' real emergence as a national people—is set in regions we don't recognize, map to our world, or have any bearings in.

2

THE TURNIP FIELD

George Washington was famous for controlling his emotions. In early December 1791, however, at the close of a wintry Philadelphia day, the president received news that caused him to give way to explosive feeling.

It was a Friday evening, and he was at dinner with other gentlemen in his rented mansion, a building officially known as the President's House. A uniformed officer rode up to the door, dismounted, handed his bridle to a servant, and knocked, arousing a porter. The porter told him the president was at dinner. The officer insisted he had important dispatches, so the porter sent a servant into the dining room.

Among the company at the table was Tobias Lear, Washington's personal secretary. Lear excused himself, went to the entry hall, and asked the officer to hand over the dispatches. The officer refused. He was an officer of the western army, he said, under orders to deliver these dispatches directly to the president, in person, and with no loss of time.

Lear went back to the dining room and whispered to the president. Washington left the room but returned quickly, apologized, and rejoined the conversation. The evening went on. The gentlemen joined the ladies in Mrs. Washington's drawing room, as usual, and as usual the president made sure to speak politely to each lady in the room. By ten, as usual, the guests had left. Only Lear and Mrs. Washington remained in the drawing room. Then, as usual, Mrs. Washington went to bed.

The president slowly paced the room in silence. Then he sat on a sofa by the fire. He told Lear to sit as well. At last he broke the silence.

"It's all over," Washington said. "St. Clair's defeated—routed. The officers nearly all killed, the men by wholesale, the rout complete—too shocking to think of, and a surprise into the bargain." He meant the Indians had managed to ambush St. Clair.

He rose. Lear rose. Washington resumed walking around the room, around and around and around. Near the door, he stopped short.

"Yes!" he shouted. "Here on this very spot I took leave of him! I wished him success and honor! 'You have your instructions,' I said, 'from the Secretary of War, I had a strict eye to them, and will add but one word: Beware of a surprise! I repeat it: Beware of a surprise! You know how the Indians fight us.' He went off, with that as my last solemn warning thrown into his ears, and yet!" Washington was shaking all over, throwing his arms up again and again in paroxysms. "To suffer that army to be cut to pieces, hacked, butchered, tomahawked—by a surprise! The very thing I guarded him against!

"Oh God, Oh God, he's worse than a murderer!" the president shouted. "How can he answer it to his country! The blood of the slain is upon him! The curse of widows and orphans! The curse of Heaven!"

He threw himself into a sitting position on the couch and fell silent. After a while, he spoke in normal tones.

"This must not go beyond this room," Washington told Lear.

That's what a man named Richard Rush said Lear told him. Rush had the story shortly before Lear's death; another version, told by George Washington Custis, the president's step-grandson and adopted son, circulated too, and Custis said he had it directly from Lear. There were only a few discrepancies in the two versions, and the point of the story, for both Rush and Custis, wasn't Washington's startling loss of control but the amazing self-possession that the great man always managed to maintain in the face of infuriating frustration. On hearing of the calamity, Washington got through dinner and the after-dinner hour without betraying even a hint of what overwhelmed him; half an hour after the outburst, he'd regained perfect calm. It was as if the moment in which he'd called down the curse of God on St. Clair's head never happened.

Mastery of emotion is one way to read the story. Loss of mastery is what made it worth telling. Washington could be brusque; he could be icy and even petulant. But the president had never before exposed such distress with anything like such violence. He never would again.

Beware a surprise. Calling down curses, Washington caused surprise, certainly to Tobias Lear, possibly more decisively to himself. The moment when Washington dropped his mask stayed with Lear until the end.

The United States was not at war. On the contrary, the United States was committed to avoiding war with the Indians of what it officially called its territory "North-West of the River Ohio," better known as the Northwest Territory. Avoiding war there was policy.

Instead of war, the Washington administration had been executing a series of diplomatic maneuvers for placing the Northwest Territory under U.S. control. The new nation had sovereignty there: all land between the Ohio and the Mississippi had been ceded by Britain to the Congress representing the former colonies in the Peace of Paris that ended the War of Independence in 1783. Still, in order to settle the Northwest Territory, the United States had to secure not just sovereignty but possession. Treaties had therefore been negotiated with Indians to draw new boundaries between land reserved for Indians and land now open, by Indian agreement, to American settlement.

That was the process. That was the policy. That's how the president had been planning and managing U.S. possession of the Northwest Territory and reporting it to the newly formed U.S. Congress.

So it wasn't a war, yet in violation of the treaties, certain Indian banditti, as the administration termed them, had been killing settler families living legally, per those treaties, in the Northwest. The killings, criminal on their face in administration terms, also involved what were called atrocities. Indians routinely caused not only death but terror by reveling in cruelty and extending enemy anguish.

And these banditti had remained surprisingly undaunted, for banditti. They'd effectively resisted even when, in 1790, a year before what became St. Clair's famous defeat, the administration had sent a smaller, targeted military expedition—a quick "flying strike," the cabinet had called it—to awe them and establish the security necessary to American settlement. That strike might be described as having avoided utter defeat, but it hadn't succeeded in establishing security, and some in Congress and the public had called it a failure for the United States and President Washington.

Washington knew better than anyone else that the flying strike had been a failure, and with mounting urgency he'd sent Arthur St. Clair, the governor of the Northwest Territory himself, on this latest operation, a more serious excursion to pacify the banditti for good and all and establish legal possession in fact. A more serious excursion, for pacification. Not a war.

That was policy, and when policy failed, and failed so finally and horribly, the geyser of emotion that broke from George Washington revealed the depths of its springs. This was a war. The United States was losing it, and losing this war would mean losing everything. To George Washington and the men who formed his circle and government, securing land across the Appalachian Mountains had formed a cause of taking up arms against Great Britain for American independence and a reason for forming a nation, more or less from scratch, out of a confederation of former colonies. There would never be any extricating the creation of the nation from the rise of the man. The defeat that brought Richard Butler and so many others to calamity in 1791, and made the president explode, had its origins in the distant time when George Washington had begun, against all odds, to come into himself.

Washington was seventeen, with nothing of his own and controlled by his mother. A boy.

The Ohio Company of Virginia: they were men. Every member was somebody, and every member was somebody to another member, by birth or marriage or both—that is, by women—in what amounted to a family business. When Lawrence Washington, his brother Augustine, and his father-in-law, Colonel William Fairfax, joined the founding member Thomas Lee in the Ohio Company, Lee was fifty-seven, one of the most prominent of Virginia planters, and there were four other Lees in the company, plus Gawin Corbin, who was a Lee cousin married to Lee's daughter, as well as John Tayloe, who had one daughter married to one of Lee's sons and another married to the company member Presley Thornton. There were Masons related to Scotts in the company, and Lomaxes related to Corbins and Tayloes both directly and through Wormeleys. There were Carters related not only to Lees but also to Corbins, Fairfaxes, and Tayloes. It went on.

Here were the ruling families of the Northern Neck, a peninsula jutting into Chesapeake Bay just north of the Rappahannock River. The Crown hadn't opened the neck to planting and settlement until the 1630s, and the business hadn't really ramped up until the late 1640s; older Virginia families, down along the James River, saw themselves as more truly Virginian than Northern Neck families. The Lees, however, took themselves for an ancient lineage, and their friends and relations in the Ohio Company saw themselves that way too: a cavalier aristocracy, training and riding the biggest and fastest mounts with grace and courage, foxhunting, breathing a free air.

George was related. He wasn't a member.

When he was seventeen, the Ohio Company of Virginia wrote a petition to the Crown asking for a grant of 500,000 acres west of the Allegheny Mountains. Blue Jacket and Little Turtle were small children when that petition was made. So was Richard Butler; he was still in Ireland. And yet events culminating that November morning, when Butler died and the confederation led by Little Turtle and Blue Jacket triumphed, began in the Ohio Company's petition, along with a host of related American efforts to develop land west of the Appalachians.

The idea the petition expressed was new. The Ohio Company wanted lands across the Alleghenies, it told the king, in order to serve him patriotically by settling the region with loyal English subjects in an orderly process. Authorized settlement would put an end to the disorganized, extralegal squatting that had been going on out there for some time and serve, the petitioners argued, two related purposes. One was to perpetuate the British fur trade with the Indians, bringing peltry in large volume more easily eastward on waterways that might, the petitioners dared to hope, flow ultimately into their own Potomac River. The company had already planned a new town for that purpose at the navigable head of the Potomac, possibly to be called Alexandria.

The other major rationale for allowing settlement in what the English and their colonists and traders called the Ohio Country was to block French fur traders and military personnel now operating there. Virginia petitioners alleged that the French trade had been encroaching illegally on the Ohio Country: French presence had recently been felt around the point where the Monongahela and the Allegheny Rivers converged to form the southwest-flowing Ohio River, roadway to the West. The British Crown had an incontestable claim to that land, the petition stated, and Virginia, under its charter from the Crown, did too. Indeed, Virginia's charter gave the province sea-to-sea rights to most of North America, from the Atlantic Seaboard all the way to the Pacific, however far that might turn out to be; nobody in Virginia knew. According to the Ohio Company petitioners, French violation both of Virginia's and of the king's rights west of the Alleghenies could be stopped only by the formation, under a British Crown grant, of a trading company supported by settlement there.

The Ohio Company was thus emphasizing, in seeking a massive land grant across the mountains, the benefits to the Crown of enabling British trade westward and blocking French incursion eastward. The way they spun it, allowing western settlement was a means to those ends.

But while it was true that the company began in large part as a trading effort, not solely as a land speculation, the Virginians were planters, and the size of the grants the company was asking for reflected aims having little to do with either furs or defense. The real attraction of the great forest across the Appalachians, north and south of the Ohio River, lay less in taking the beaver that lived there, or obstructing the French from doing so, than in the quality of that forest itself. The mightiness of the timber, never before cut, and the lushness of the bottomland vegetation had revealed to trappers and traders who ranged in that country the astonishing fertility of western soil.

Fertility, for these Virginians, was the ultimate resource. The most important crop they planted required new land, and then more new land, and then more, in perpetuity. They were tobacco men.

It was a tough business. Tobacco start-up was daunting: girdling gigantic trees, burning brush, planting amid acres obstructed by the stumps. Production was daunting too. Each year's crop demanded the same labor-intensive efforts, which had come to depend on importing, selling, and breeding mass numbers of enslaved Africans to carry out the hard annual process of transplanting each seedling to its own hill, keeping thousands of such one-plant hills weeded, topping each developing plant, and suckering it and removing pests until the harvest. Each leaf was then cut from its stalk by hand, staked to dry in barns dedicated to the purpose, and set to cure. Shipping required sorting, bundling, and packing for sail directly to consignment agents in England, in the case of the bigger, better-capitalized operations, which sometimes even owned their own ships, or to a local middleman, in the case of less wealthy producers. Then there were seemingly innumerable support systems—livestock, other crops, fencing, and more—also maintained by the ceaseless forced labor of the enslaved Africans.

And yet from the major players, systematically and hierarchically organized, like the Harrisons and Lightfoots on the James River and the Lees and Fairfaxes of the Northern Neck, to little-remembered small farmers who worked alongside a few enslaved, indentured, and tenanted laborers, Virginians grew tobacco. Along with other once-exotic products of the great powers' colonial adventuring—tea, coffee, opium—tobacco had been holding the millions of Europe in the grip of addiction since the mid-sixteenth century, and it was Virginians who had tweaked the delivery system for maximum market leverage. In 1617, 20,000 pounds of Virginia tobacco were shipped to England. The next year, 40,000 pounds. Soon 500,000 pounds went annually from America to England. Virginia's taxes and public salaries and household and business expenses depended on high tobacco prices in

England. Tobacco IOUs functioned in Virginia as a paper currency. Virginia's provincial government, with its royal lieutenant governor on the scene in Williamsburg and its legislature elected by the better-off planters, served as the industry's quality-control and regulatory agency. Everybody in government was in tobacco; everyone in tobacco who could get into government was in government. Tobacco profits brought together all phases of civil life. When the Ohio Company formed, the Virginia boom had been going on for more than a century.

But the soil died. Tobacco sapped nutrients, slowly at first, but inexorably and in the end precipitously. Extracting hard labor from enslaved Africans until they died was one key expedient of the business; extracting nutrients from good land until it became wasteland was another. For years tobacco planters had been playing out their land while constantly looking for new land to play out.

The search was always on. The goal, for those with capital to invest, was not only new planting but also financial speculation: an investment in land itself. Tobacco planters would always have to buy land, or rent it, or get hold of it somehow; whoever owned new land first was sitting on a bonanza possibly more profitable than tobacco. There were other crops to plant, too, and with so much of the good land east of the mountains already taken, and so much of that already exhausted, the second and third sons and new colonists and entrepreneurs seeking growth would need to plant west of the mountains. By the 1740s, it was past time to look beyond the Shenandoah Valley and start opening up that unknown western forest. The sheer scale of that untapped acreage, suggested incalculable value. The men of the Ohio Company had begun as tobacco planters. Soon their desire would be to own the American West.

The soil where George Washington was born in 1732 had been subjected to the rigors of tobacco production yet was considered fertile enough to take more. George's father, Augustine, known as Gus, had once had reason to hope he'd leave all of his seven surviving children wealthy. The house, built by Gus's father in 1718, modest by the standards of nearby families like the Lees, sat on the south bank of the Potomac, at the mouth of Popes Creek, well downstream from the rocky chutes where the Potomac made its long, crashing fall to a wild and swampy bug-infested floodplain, yet upstream from the wide, level waters where the river began its long entrance to Chesapeake Bay. Vistas were tranquil, but as elsewhere on the neck, and everywhere in Virginia, the purpose of the land wasn't contemplation of beauty but production of tobacco. When George was born, Gus Washington worked about twenty enslaved Africans as well as some indentured white laborers.

For all of that practicality, land did have emotional value too. At the Popes Creek plantation, George's great-grandfather and grandfather were buried, and Washingtons would always call that place their ancestral home. Mid-level planters like the Washingtons were hands-on, not so elegant. Children went barefoot; households and gardens and fields tumbled into each other, with livestock, the enslaved, the indentured, the tenanted, and the owners all over each other too. Yet middling and upper families alike, working this gritty business based on managing other people's labor in search of profit, liked to think of themselves as the kinds of people with ancestral homes.

Gus Washington's lesser status made him peripatetic. To be a force in Virginia, with respect and honor and a seat in the House of Burgesses— revered by its members as the first such house ever convened in America, more than a century old when George Washington was born—required constant acquisition. Gus was always developing new tobacco properties. He also owned an iron mine. For about three years the family lived in a small house farther up the Potomac from Popes Creek. Meanwhile, Gus was having a new house built, on a property across the narrowest part of the neck, on the north bank of the Rappahannock. Gus moved his family into the new place when George was six, and they began calling it, in distinction to their ancestral home and other purchases and plantations, the Home Farm. That's where George Washington grew up.

George had a right to high expectations. Things seemed to be booming. Gus's dedication to acquiring and developing land was such that it was when conducting a survey that he caught the bug that killed him. Virginians were forever conducting and documenting surveys: vigorously technical, mathematically detailed geographic studies. They took surveys of lands to which they sought grants, lands they were only considering buying, and lands they already owned. They were good not only with the compass, chain, and transit but also, in sketching and mapmaking, with the pencil. Any Virginia planter and speculator in fresh soil was also a sometime surveyor, and the province's official, professional surveyors were always in demand.

George was only eleven when his father caught the bug. Dying, in and of itself, shouldn't disrupt the progress of a Virginia planter's ambition. Dying was going on all the time. Everybody, gentry or poor, had a reasonable expectation of being subjected by death to acute, sometimes unbearable loss or avoiding that fate by dying sooner than others. In 1730, Gus had come home from installing his elder sons in school in England to find his wife had died. Mary Ball, Gus's second wife and George's mother, had lost her own mother at eleven, and of her children with Gus, George's sister had died in infancy. So the big thing for Virginia gentry was to found and sustain what amounted in Virginia to dynasties. The Hapsburgs wouldn't have called them dynasties, but Virginia's aristocratic style and culture were derived from impulses that fed the old dynasties too: cheating ever-present death by founding a people. Inheritance was everything. And land was inheritance.

That was Gus's problem. As he lay suffering, a lawyer was called in, and Gus made his will under pressure of imminent demise, confronting at the last minute certain issues that all Virginia planters had to face sooner or later. Some had greater resources than he for meeting them.

First sons were favored by law. Those rules had brought many second sons from England to Virginia; now they were sending many second sons over the Blue Ridge. Lawrence, the eldest son, was twenty-five when Gus died, and it was Lawrence who inherited the property at Little Hunting Creek, where the family had lived briefly while building the Home Farm. A sprawling twenty-five hundred acres with a water-powered mill, advantageously situated along the Potomac, it came with an adequate complement of enslaved Africans to make it potentially highly productive of both tobacco and cotton, at least for a while. When Lawrence took ownership, he remained enthralled by admiration for Vice Admiral Edward Vernon, the British naval officer he'd served in the fateful Battle of Cartagena, on the Caribbean Sea, in the most recent outbreak of hostilities among the great powers of Europe. Lawrence named the place Mount Vernon. There had been no house there, just a cabin, but Lawrence began building a fine house. He'd been educated in England and spent time with elegant British families and knew what the good life looked like. By now, he'd married advantageously: his wife, Anne, known as Nancy, was Colonel William Fairfax's eldest daughter, and Colonel Fairfax was cousin to Lord Thomas Fairfax, who owned millions of acres of the Northern Neck. Lawrence Washington the dashing war hero was already rising quickly in plantation society, and inheriting Mount Vernon gave him a big leg up.

The second son by Gus's first marriage, also named Augustine, inherited the house and farm at Popes Creek where George was born. There Gus now joined his own father, named Lawrence, and their fathers' fathers in the ancestral tombs of all Virginia Washingtons. So while the younger Augustine inherited something physically smaller and less potentially enriching than Mount Vernon, he inherited the family's source. Lawrence got the bustling future, Augustine the hallowed past.

George, first of a second hatch, got the comparatively stark present. His father left him the Home Farm. That bequest was both physically and emotionally less—smaller, with poor soil and no deep family history— but worse still, the Home Farm was to be overseen by George's mother, or, even worse, should she remarry, by her new husband, until George was twenty-one. His brothers were men. George was a boy, and a fatherless one at that, ruled by his mother and possibly one day by a strange man. In their teens, Lawrence and Augustine had crossed the ocean and seen the real ancestral home, England; they'd acquired learning and polish and connections in imperial officialdom. The same would have been George's portion, but income to George's mother and her five living children was drastically reduced by Gus's death. George would have to depend on the goodwill of Lawrence to bring him along, and dependence and lesserness looked lifelong.

In 1749, the governor of Virginia and the British Crown granted the Ohio Company of Virginia the 200,000 acres of woodland west of the Allegheny Mountains it wanted. Another 300,000 was to come if all went well. The company was to begin by establishing two hundred families on the ground, living free from quitrent, the customary up-front charge for new land, for ten years. And the company was to build a fort in the West, to be staffed by Virginia militia.

The grant seemed liberal. Yet making it reflected anything but a laissez-faire attitude on the part of the ministry. The British colonial secretary George Montagu-Dunk, second Earl of Halifax and president of the ministry's Board of Trade—he called himself simply Dunk Halifax— was asserting with new boldness the royal prerogative in the North American colonies. His granting the petition reflected the Crown's prior sovereign claim to that same land, on which all Virginia claims depended, in the Crown's view. By making such an unprecedented grant, the Crown was asserting its right to make the grant.

The assertion of that prerogative was new. For many years, the ministry had pursued what it called salutary neglect of the American colonies. Provincial assemblies of well-heeled colonists made laws; governorships of the seven royally governed colonies gave lucrative sinecures to highly placed noble courtiers in England, with governing mainly carried out by lieutenants; while lieutenant governors often came at odds with colonial legislatures, they also felt free to interpret their instructions loosely and negotiate freely with the legislatures to arrive at policy. Crown control over much of American political life had been loose.

Dunk Halifax was rising to power against the policy of salutary neglect. He wanted to impose on royal governors a strict observance of their royal instructions. He wanted to establish an Indian department as a wing of the British army to supervise white-Indian relations, in perpetuation of the fur trade. He wanted to finance these measures in part by collecting a stamp tax in America.

And by supporting new ventures like the Ohio Company, he wanted to promote American expansion westward and defeat French ambition to dominate trade. The big grant to the Ohio Company, along with an even bigger one to another Virginia organization, the Loyal Company, made explicit what Dunk Halifax took as given: the Crown held sovereignty over and had responsibility for managing the American West and, for that matter, of course, the American East.

As for the Ohio Company members, the grant excited them by abruptly enabling vast potential for development and wealth. But regarding that potential, the members took a view of their relationship with the Crown, the ministry, and Parliament notably different from that of Dunk

Halifax. To begin with, Virginia speculators believed, while the Crown might hold sovereignty over western land, managing purchases from western Indians was properly a matter for the Virginians themselves.

Related. Not a member. In his teens, George was already a strapping physical specimen of startling strength and energy, but his dependence on Lawrence's goodwill for advancement made him socially small and weak.

Fortunately, Lawrence liked George, and George admired his brother with an open intensity he would not bring to other relationships. The master of Mount Vernon and a Fairfax in-law, Lawrence had received appointment by the royal lieutenant governor as commander of the Virginia militia and was soon elected, with irresistible Fairfax support, to the House of Burgesses. With membership in the Ohio Company, he was well positioned to speculate and grow even richer. It looked as if George would never be so positioned. All he could look forward to, upon reaching twenty-one, was watching his small wealth steadily diminish as he tried to coax less and less tobacco out of the Home Farm's weakening soil.

The boy's first hope was therefore to get out. The Royal Navy beckoned: he might work his way up to an officer's commission. Lawrence encouraged the idea, and one day Lawrence's father-in-law, Colonel Fairfax, told George that a Fairfax-connected ship, now anchored in a Virginia harbor, would take George as midshipman if he jumped fast enough. Fairfax had joined up as a midshipman at fourteen, and look at him now.

Lawrence proposed the plan to George's mother. She kept them in suspense for weeks, then denied permission.

George couldn't get out. One day, he came across Gus's compass, chain, and transit. Lawrence let George use the turnip field at Mount Vernon to practice surveying.

Quick with math, punctilious in mapping and documentation, and breathless for a change in status, George Washington crossed the Blue

Ridge for the first time at the age of sixteen as a surveyor for the Fairfax family in its land investments in the Shenandoah Valley. Soon he was relied on by that most powerful family of the Northern Neck as a can-do dogsbody, a natural frontiersman always up for a job. With no real wealth of his own, George had hit on another time-honored way of getting ahead: making himself indispensable to the wealthy.

Far more than just a good surveyor, young Washington had an eye, it turned out, for fertility. He studied botany and geology and made close observations of timber, foliage, and water sources; he could identify the easiest places to clear forest and the best places to plant crops. He thus became adept at picking out the most valuable land for his principals and leaving the rest for others not so well advantaged. His surveying and appraising skills brought him income, and starting small, the youngster also picked out a few tracts of some of the better acreage for himself.

That changed everything. Before he was twenty, George Washington had bought and sold and parlayed himself into nearly three thousand acres of prime land. He still hadn't come fully into what he viewed as his relatively paltry inheritance when he began making his own way instead. His father hadn't left him much, but he was much like his father: always looking, always assessing, always seeking the advantage that others might have missed. If he could amass enough land this way, he might build plantations, grow tobacco, marry well, become a burgess, join the Ohio Company, maybe even buy an officer's commission in the British army.

George was becoming punctilious in transactions, too, with an attention to detail and a single-mindedness in the hunt for advantage that could verge on the maniacal. Now that he'd begun to gain, there wasn't much else on his mind. Prospects were lengthening, and the view lay westward.

Thus when George Washington first saw the Ohio River, he was doing what he'd become expert at doing: an errand. Twenty-one now, huge, fearless, and immensely strong, he'd already gone deeper into the West than many of the Northern Neck gentry who invested in the Ohio Company, and on this particular errand, George was officially in the service not of the Fairfaxes but of the new lieutenant governor of Virginia, Robert Dinwiddie. Yet Dinwiddie, a highly focused man, was in the service of the Ohio Company, and the company was in the service, in turn, of Dinwiddie. Land speculation and government were combining, in Virginia, in peculiar ways that would come to define George Washington's lifelong relationships to both.

Dinwiddie had seen a remarkable opportunity for personal gain in the great physical distance between him and those he reported to at home in the ministry. Though a royal official, he had become one of the Ohio Company's biggest investors, and he was able to use his reports to the ministry to advance the company's aims. Virginia burgesses who weren't members of the Ohio Company had western expansion schemes of their own, and they objected to this untoward alliance of royal clout and personal speculation, but along with his commercial allies among the burgesses Dinwiddie had stacked his council—it served as the Virginia legislature's upper house—with Ohio Company members too. He would be hard to stop.

The problem for Dinwiddie was that the company's investment scheme had stalled. Because Indians lived there, and because New France was increasing its activity there, the Ohio headwaters region remained too dangerous to attract American settlers. And it was settlers, not investors, who were expected to clear the land and add value. What the investors needed was a military force to police the region and provide security, and Dinwiddie had discerned a strategy for leveraging his governorship to that end.

Reporting to Dunk Halifax, the governor started painting pictures of French aggression across the Appalachians and reminding the secretary of the necessity of fending it off. In reality, with the end of the global conflict in which Lawrence Washington had served, perennial British-French hostility had hit a rare lull. The treaty ending that war had given both powers a right to trade in the Ohio Country, and it wasn't clear that the French had been especially active there, except in defensive reaction to the novelty of the Ohio Company grant; certainly the French weren't looking to clear and settle the region, as the Virginians were. And yet to advance the settlement project, Dinwiddie and the Ohio Company needed a military presence in the West, and in his reports to Dunk Halifax the governor invoked French aggression to make a case for providing that presence.

Dinwiddie also proposed sending diplomats to the Six Nations of the

Iroquois. That confederation, strung east to west across New York and Pennsylvania, claimed hegemony over Indians west of the Ohio and had long held a precarious balance of power between France and England in the North American fur trade: Iroquois diplomats were known at Whitehall and Versailles, and Dinwiddie wanted their support for England and Virginia against both France and French-allied Indians of the West. He wrote to other colonial governors too, asking them to raise provincial troops to lend Virginia military support for resisting supposed French aggression. Playing down the Ohio Company's plan of western settlement and his personal investment in it, he framed French movement in the Ohio valley as an unprovoked danger to Virginia, to the English colonies as a whole, and to British sovereignty in North America, requiring an assertive military response.

Meanwhile, he was making every effort to give New France and its Indian allies the impression that this burst of military activity came not from Ohio Company policy, not even from his own policy as Virginia governor, but at the command of the king of England himself. That reading could be expected to further rile the French, giving support to his story of their aggression. The time it took for information to travel between London and Virginia gave Dinwiddie a lot of room for sowing confusion, and his schemes were kept more or less secret from burgesses and council members who weren't Ohio Company members.

As for the majority of Virginians, they had no interest—financial, political, or emotional—in developing land west of the mountains. This was an upscale, inside affair, and Dinwiddie saw in the Fairfax-family connection George Washington a likely young fellow for executing the first step in his strategy.

Washington's errand for Dinwiddie, taking him farther west than ever before, was to order the French to stop making confrontational moves west of the mountains. New France's motives might have been largely defensive; still, the French had deployed an expedition on the Ohio River to document their claim to the Ohio Country. At the mouth of each Ohio tributary, the party had nailed to an especially big tree a copperplate imprinted with French royal arms and buried a lead plate below the tree stating a claim on the land. They'd started building new forts, also in reaction to American activity in the West: the French plan now was to string garrisons from the southern shore of Lake Erie down to the Ohio headwaters, blocking any aggression from the east. George Washington's task was to visit the commanders of those new French garrisons and order them, in the name of the royal governor of Virginia and His Royal Majesty the king of England, to cease and desist.

He took the long, hard trip guided by a frontiersman named Christopher Gist, who had bought a big chunk of western land from the Ohio Company and explored, surveyed, and did other jobs for the company out in the woods. Washington and Gist climbed with a party of men and horses to the crest of the Appalachians, and then, as they descended, Washington began encountering value like nothing he'd ever seen. This country was precipitous, but the narrow valleys, his practiced eye told him, were deep with the richest kinds of soils. At last, from a high, forested ridge he gazed over the point of land where the muddy Monongahela and the fast-running Allegheny flowed together.

Here was the origin of the broad Ohio. The river made a big turn northward before dropping straight into the heart of the West. In the setting sun, the bends were distant glints. This point at the headwaters was ideally strategic for commanding access to the West. And the French hadn't started a fort here yet. Washington quickly wrote as much to Dinwiddie.

His larger mission, though, was a failure. If Dinwiddie had expected the French fort commandants, dropped in on out of the woods by a big twenty-one-year-old, to tear down their forts, march their men up to Lake Erie, and sail up the St. Lawrence to Quebec, never to return, he wouldn't have been much of a strategist. The French officers were provoked, predictably enough, and sent the young emissary back with the defiant words that Dinwiddie had been counting on hearing.

Washington and Gist, alone now, without even the support of packhorses, were on their way back toward Williamsburg through the deep snows of December when they were halted by the Allegheny. That fast river, choked with big, swirling ice chunks, wasn't frozen enough to walk across. Though exhausted by hard travel, Washington was tough, Gist even tougher. Soon, standing on a raft of logs they'd cut from the forest—Gist had crossed many a river this way—the two men were gripping long, heavy poles, lifting and plunging them into the frigid water to maneuver around the moving ice.

They made it about halfway across when the raft was shoved by hard current against an ice pack. It jammed there. Washington was strong, but not stronger than Allegheny flow: pushing at the block, he lost his balance and toppled into the water.

He grabbed for the cut logs. With Gist's help the youth heaved himself, his clothing sodden with icy water, onto the raft. Gist realized his own fingers were frostbitten. They were in trouble.

They saw an island. Wading now, they made their miserable way to it. Somehow they got through that night without hypothermia. The river froze overnight; they crossed it the next morning and continued their journey to bring Dinwiddie the unsurprising news of French refusal to relinquish the Ohio Country.

Young George Washington, doing an errand. By now, he could handle pretty much anything. Yet even he had found this trip almost unbearably exhausting.

Still, he'd crossed the Appalachians. Most Ohio Company members knew the West as a portfolio position. Washington had been there, and he'd seen all that it was worth.

His next big move involved not just seeing the West but actually taking it. In the spring of 1754, Washington went back across the mountains, again on Dinwiddie's orders in pursuit of the Ohio Company's land interests. This time the mission wasn't to order the French away. It was to force them out.

The news of French intractability that Washington had brought back from the forts meant Dinwiddie was now officially empowered by Dunk Halifax to call up militia for the defense of Virginia. Because the French response had been predictable, Dinwiddie had started calling militia up well before getting the news, and he'd already sent men out to the forested point at the Ohio headwaters, on Washington's recommendation, with materials for building a fort under command of the Ohio Company's chief of construction. Dunk Halifax didn't know it, but when it came to

the West, the company and the royal executive were identical. Dinwiddie published and publicized Washington's reports from the scene, and
finally he scared the burgesses into funding some provincial troops; he
got the governor of North Carolina to send troops as well.

Then, in a move surprising many both at the time and later, he made
the twenty-two-year-old George Washington a lieutenant colonel and
placed him in effective command of what in the end turned out to be
about 160 men. Washington was to lead those men against the French
in the Ohio Country.

Receiving this commission and command was the biggest thing
that had happened to George Washington. Lawrence had died of tuber-
culosis the year before. George's grief was great. His ambition remained
undiminished; if anything, it was amplified, and with this military appointment he came close, if unofficially, to replacing his brother as
commander of the Virginia militia. He'd already begun gaining land
and status. Success in this operation might gain him not only further
reputation but also the British army commission he coveted. In his lonely,
uncompromising effort to gain manhood in terms dictated by the world
he came from, George was achieving what had once seemed impossible.
In some areas, he might actually surpass Lawrence.

His military objective was the strategic point at the Ohio headwaters
that he'd seen on the first trip. The French had interrupted Virginia's
fort building on the point, won a skirmish, taken the ground, and built
their own, far better fort. Neither Whitehall nor Versailles had been
spoiling for a fight—given imperial alliances, such conflicts spread too
easily now around the world—but the governor of New France, Marquis Duquesne, was as eager as his opposite number Dinwiddie not to
avoid war, and he had the same tools as Dinwiddie for manipulating the
bosses back home: distance, slow communication, and the ability to
exaggerate danger. The French fort at the point was now named Fort
Duquesne. Washington's mission was to coordinate with anti-French Indians in the region, attack Fort Duquesne with Indian support, and force
the French garrison to surrender.

Dinwiddie couldn't possibly have expected the mission to succeed.
There was no way a force of fewer than two hundred men could take a
decent French fort, and these men were inexperienced Virginia volunteers, poorly fed and armed, led by a gigantic youth with ambition and

enthusiasm to spare, and some reason for his increasingly high opinion of his own merits, but no knowledge of fighting or any sense of command. The operation didn't even carry enough ammunition for an assault
on a fort.

And yet exceeding what must have been Dinwiddie's expectations,
so spectacularly did Washington fail that not even Dinwiddie could
have predicted the fallout. Trouble began even before the unit arrived
in the vicinity of the headwaters. Washington was to make contact with
Virginia's ally Tanacharison, whose people, mostly Seneca transplanted
to the West, lived nearby. Washington and Tanacharison already
knew each other: Tanacharison had once enjoyed high status and commanded good fighters. Lately, however, claiming to represent all Indians
in the region, he'd personally granted both the Ohio Company operator
Christopher Gist and a Pennsylvania fur trader hundreds of thousands
of acres of land around the headwaters, so while the whites didn't know
it, Tanacharison's credibility with other Indians had fallen to nearly zero.
He had few fighters and no clout. What he did have was a plan for getting back on top.

In a message to Washington, Tanacharison rallied the Virginian to
continue toward Fort Duquesne no matter what and save Tanacharison's people from French menace. Washington, having climbed into
the Alleghenies, soon had his exhausted men camped at a spot known
as the Great Meadows, about sixty miles from the fort, a broad stretch
of flattish, open ground in the otherwise steep and twisty country.
There he received urgent word from Tanacharison that the French
were nearby, in force, with plans to ambush Tanacharison's people.
Thus the opportunity for George Washington's first battle presented
itself.

Washington sent an official report back to Dinwiddie, informing
him of his intention to find the French party, and while the scouts had
numbered the party's size at about sixty, Washington told Dinwiddie
they'd numbered it at seventy-five. Leaving most of his force at the Great
Meadows, on the morning of May 28 the Virginian and about forty of his
men, along with Tanacharison and a handful of his, climbed the steep
woodland toward the spot where Indian scouts had seen the French.
Just before first light, the party quietly approached a glen below a high,
rocky outcropping, a kind of shallow, one-sided ravine. Frenchmen were

obviously down in that glen, sheltering below the rock. Their firelight could be seen; their voices could be heard. Tanacharison's men snuck toward the glen on one side, Washington's on the other.

Nobody would ever know for sure what happened next. In the upshot, the French—there were really only thirty-five of them—had surrendered, with ten dead and many wounded. Who fired first was not agreed on. It was generally agreed, however, or at least implied, by everyone except Washington himself, that during the sudden series of events he was unable to exercise any effective command at all.

The leader of the French party turned out to be one Joseph Coulon de Villiers, Sieur de Jumonville. Under interrogation on the spot by Washington, Jumonville said he was traveling as a diplomat from Fort Duquesne, on his way to order the Virginians out of the region, just as Washington had ordered out the French a year earlier. Tanacharison told Washington that on the contrary Jumonville was leading a war party to ambush Tanacharison. But what Washington thought Jumonville was really doing there would come up only in the context of defending his reputation against a terrible charge. For while Washington was interrogating Jumonville, Tanacharison split Jumonville's head with a hatchet, killing him. Jumonville was a diplomat. Or if he wasn't really a diplomat, he was a prisoner of war, having surrendered. Anyway, there was no declared state of war. The execution was murder.

Or not. Others on the scene would say later that Jumonville died in the first musket fire. That story contradicted not only the murder story but also what others described as Tanacharison's removing Jumonville's brains and washing his hands in them, or eating some of them. He might have done that. Ritualized physical revelry in the body of a defeated enemy was common practice, and Tanacharison always claimed the French had boiled and eaten his father. Other reports would mention a French head impaled on a stick.

Washington denied all of it. In his descriptions of events, the first American shots came not from panicky Virginian tension, or by unfair Virginia ambush, but at his express order: the French had discovered the presence of the Virginians and Indians, ran for their guns, and fired; Washington ordered his men to fire in response; two volleys were exchanged; the French surrendered; Jumonville, already dead, was never a prisoner.

Such was Washington's report. It put forth an order of events that nobody else there remembered.

Whatever really happened to Jumonville, further problems quickly ensued for Washington. Tanacharison's next move was to send a secret message to the French commander at Fort Duquesne. The Virginians had surprise attacked Jumonville's party, Tanacharison told the French, and Jumonville had been executed by a musket shot to the head: the English had wanted to execute all the wounded Frenchmen, and would have done so, but for the Indians' rushing to interpose themselves and prevent the murder.

Tanacharison had his own plan. He'd roped Washington into it. Dinwiddie and Duquesne weren't the only ones trying to provoke a war between the British and the French in North America. Washington could now expect French reprisal.

Back at the Great Meadows, Washington meanwhile got busy in his tent writing versions of the story to reflect well on him and badly on Jumonville and the French. Reporting to Dinwiddie, he scoffed at length at the idea that the French party had been on a diplomatic mission. The young man's biggest takeaway from the scene of Jumonville's death would become one of the most quoted remarks of his youthful career. "I heard the bullets whistle and believe me, there is something charming in the sound," he wrote to his younger brother.

All of this writing to shore up his reputation—to relatives, to Dinwiddie, to his own journal—was spoiled by what happened next. Washington considered his action at the glen a victory, and he expected an attack in response. He therefore ordered a stockade built on the Great Meadows and wrote to Dinwiddie for reinforcements. Although he'd arrived at the site unopposed, Washington vowed to Dinwiddie that sooner than give up an inch of what he'd gained, he'd fight with unequal numbers if he had to.

He looked on his completed stockade with pride: a circle of seven-foot-high uprights in palisade, surrounding a peaked-roof hut. He named it Fort Necessity and imagined it holding off a force of five hundred with ease.

Tanacharison had seen French forts. Now he was looking at a low cylinder of raw timber in a broad, open field within easy firing range of thick woods on all sides. Still, he brought about a hundred women and children onto the meadow and made them dependents of this so-called fort, putting a strain on Washington's paltry resources.

Dinwiddie did meanwhile send reinforcements, but when they arrived at the Great Meadows, Washington saw they were just more of the untrained Virginians he was already saddled with. Then came some New Yorkers. They seemed even more down-at-the-heels, rowdy, and dissolute.

But the South Carolina provincial forces who joined Washington were, to him, the worst. These were crack troops. Their commander was only a captain, but he was commissioned directly by the Crown, and Washington's commission as a colonel came from a colonial governor; he was militia. A royal commission outranked a militia commission, in the mind of the South Carolina captain but not in Washington's. Neither man could get the other to report to him. The captain set up a separate camp and refused to use any of the Virginia colonel's signals and passwords. Washington just ignored him.

Worse news for Washington: Dinwiddie also sent word that he'd appointed a new commander for all colonial forces in this enterprise against the French. The commander was even now on his way to the Great Meadows to take charge, and he had both a royal commission and experience at the Battle of Cartagena. Dinwiddie ordered Washington to wait for the new commander before making any moves on Fort Duquesne.

That would rob Washington of the success he'd come all this way to achieve. He determined to move now, before the new commander arrived and without the South Carolina captain. By the time Dinwiddie received word of this adventure, Washington knew, it would be too late to stop it. On June 1, he moved out.

He never had a chance. On his way to attack Fort Duquesne, Washington hoped to recruit Indians for support. Nearly all declined: Washington's force presented itself as anything but confidence inspiring, but at least as important to the Indians—branches of Delaware, Iroquois, and Miami alike—was the young commander's manner. They found it intolerably dictatorial and superior.

Washington moved on, lacking significant Indian support, a condition that made taking Fort Duquesne, already wildly improbable, actually impossible, and he ran out of food while cutting trail over the steepest and roughest section of the Alleghenies. Men deserted hourly. When Washington got word that eight hundred Frenchmen and four hundred Indians, mostly Shawnee, were marching against him from Duquesne, there was nothing to do but turn back for the stockade in the Great Meadows, and turning back meant forcing the troops, starving now, to haul cannon and equipment over that steep and rocky trail with the enemy approaching fast. More men fled, and on July 1 Washington arrived at Fort Necessity with nothing accomplished, a depleted force, and the enemy on his heels.

It could have surprised nobody, even Washington, that in the ensuing Battle of the Great Meadows he was defeated. It didn't take long, and terms for English surrender seemed easy—surprisingly so. The victorious French commander, Louis Coulon de Villiers, was willing to allow the Virginians and the other colonial forces to march away, not in humiliation, but with drums beating, under a few simple conditions. The terms were written in French, so Washington had his regular interpreter translate them aloud in English. Both the captain of the South Carolina forces and Washington signed them.

One was an agreement that the Americans would eschew further military exploits over mountains: a tough term for Dinwiddie and the Ohio Company, yet diplomatically innocuous, because England and France had declared no war there; this didn't rise to the surrender of one power to another in the field. Another term: the French would keep the Americans' artillery. Again, no serious humiliation, given the stipulation that the Americans could beat drums during their exit.

But the document also referred twice to Jumonville's "assassination." Here Washington put his name to the confession of a crime. The French commander Coulon was the late Jumonville's brother. He wanted revenge on Washington: that's why the overall terms were so easy.

Triumphant, Coulon sent the signed document home, and copies were published in France, in England, in Virginia. Not victory, but defeat, coupled with confession of having murdered a diplomat, brought

George Washington his first fame. The only question, for many: Did the Virginian truly confess, or did he agree to sign a false confession to save his army and himself? Either way, poor show.

Later, Washington would say his translator, a Dutchman, hadn't given him an accurate translation. It was dark, the document hard to read. The exact meaning of the French word for assassination might be in question. If he'd known what the document really said, Washington insisted, he never would have signed it.

Twenty years later, in 1775, General Thomas Gage returned to England from America and gave testimony to Parliament regarding, among other things, causes of the war that had begun with George Washington's failed expedition and confession of murder. That conflict was called the Seven Years' War, also known as the Great War for Empire; Americans called it the French and Indian War. It had taken the trend set by previous wars among the great powers all the way to world war. Movements of millions of people occurred as far from Europe as Calcutta, Senegal, and Buenos Aires. The death toll was something over one million.

Thomas Gage had served in that war's scenes of carnage, including the famous defeat of General Edward Braddock by the French and Shawnee near the Ohio headwaters, in which Washington served too. Gage took part as well in key British successes against the French in Canada. After the Seven Years' War, he became commander of British North America and in that capacity was finally ordered to occupy Massachusetts, scene of so much growing American unrest. He tried to tell the War Office that what went on there amounted to outright revolutionary secessionism. He was ignored by his masters until what he'd predicted came true and a revolution broke out. Now he'd been recalled.

Under questioning from the friendly side of the aisle regarding causes of the Seven Years' War—by 1775, it was widely seen as the source of two painful decades of imperial dislocation and turmoil—Gage had a point to make. Looking back, it seemed as if nobody at the highest reaches of either French or British government had wanted to start the Seven Years' War: hence in part this House investigation. Gage was an Americanist, if a sour one, with a nose for developing trends in elite

American culture and psychology. Asked to give his opinion of the real cause of the Seven Years' War, he had a ready answer.

"The primary causes of the war of 1755," Gage asserted for the record, "which extended itself over the four parts of the world, are to be traced back to the banks of the Ohio." Then he made his point.

"Britain was then," he said, "as she always has been, duped by her colonies."

3

DRIVE THEM OUT

The Shawnee leader Blue Jacket had a war record beginning seven years later than George Washington's, and the difference wasn't a coincidence. Washington began his public career by starting the Seven Years' War. Blue Jacket began his by responding to disasters that descended on his people with that war's end. Acquiring western land formed Washington. Resisting incursion from the east formed Blue Jacket.

Each man would make a generation's ambitions at once public and personal, and it was Blue Jacket who, in 1791, with Little Turtle, would lead the western Indian confederation to a victory so total that George Washington, exploding with emotion, would start to bring about a decisive turning point in North American life.

For Blue Jacket, the struggle leading to that turning point began in the early 1760s. And it began with a simple idea: the enemy could be kept out of the West only by military confederation.

Confederation wasn't a novel idea in the early 1760s, but some of the nations living west of the Ohio River and around Lakes Ontario and Erie—Shawnee, Miami, Delaware, Ottawa, Wyandot, and others—had no tradition of coming together to form lasting integrated political and military units. The Six Nations of the Iroquois, by contrast, living east of the Ohio River, had built a powerful confederation of many generations' standing. Their unity was literal, in being geographic, and spiritual in that their geographic arrangement reflected in microcosm a higher reality. From east to west, the Iroquois were Mohawk, Oneida, Onondaga, Cayuga, and Seneca—plus Tuscarora from the south, recently admitted—and while each of those nations enjoyed political independence, the confederation thought of itself as a longhouse. Two bigger brothers guarded the openings at the longhouse's ends, Mohawk looking east, Seneca looking west. The Onondaga kept the central fire where all members traveled to meet on confederation business. The other two, Oneida and Cayuga, younger brothers, lived in between: the Oneida tucked between the Onondaga and the Mohawk, the Cayuga between the Onondaga and the Seneca. Peace was supposed to prevail within the longhouse, but the Six Nations were also supposed to foster peace—and when necessary, impose it by warfare—on other nations.

Nothing like that kind of unity existed among the nations in the Ohio valley. Indeed, the Six Nations were elder brothers to the western nations, having conquered many of them generations before, and the Iroquois had long viewed the entire region across the Ohio and around the Great Lakes as their own hunting ground, a place to move people they'd conquered in the interest of peace, and a bargaining chip in negotiations with the French and English. Not surprisingly, Indians living in the West sometimes resented their distant elder brothers' hegemony. But sustaining their own competing confederations had long faced obstacles.

For one thing, the Ohio Country was diverse, linguistically and in every other way. Truly multicultural living went on in towns shared by Miami, Shawnee, Delaware, Ottawa, and French- and English-speaking traders, where complicated long- and short-term leasing deals memorialized in complex beadwork documented terms for using land originally held by others. White people might call them all "Indian," but for generations before the Seven Years' War members of these nations generally hadn't thought of themselves as Indian first and foremost, in opposition to some singular form of whiteness. They defined themselves by membership in their families, extended families, regions, branches, and nations, in opposition to and cooperation with other western people, the Six Nations, and the French, English, and Spanish. Diversity of a kind the Six

Nations eschewed, even derided, had made the Ohio valley only inter-
mittently a scene of military and political unity.

Spiritual unity, however—that had long attracted particular members of all nations and branches. Now, in changed conditions arising
from the conclusion of the Seven Years' War, spiritual unity began combining with political and military ideas to make western Indian confederation more feasible. Blue Jacket, just coming to manhood, found these
new ideologies compelling.

Fundamentalist religious movements had surged perennially for years,
led by preachers warning converts of the corrupting effect of European
influences on their daily lives. Adherents of such movements swore off
the imported manufactured goods on which they'd come to depend.
They gave up their fiddle music, their reading, their couple dancing. They
moved out of their log houses and shed their tailored clothing. They tried
to revive and teach their children a host of nearly forgotten ways. Bever-
age alcohol was number one on lists of bad white influences: to feed a
devastating addiction to drunkenness, the preachers said, Indians had
overhunted the fur animals to scarcity, ruining commerce and starving
themselves in the service of degradation.

So as bad as whiteness was, the real enemy lay within. Indians themselves must be purified, the fundamentalists urged. Adherents not only
gave up white technologies but purged whiteness physically by ritual
vomiting. These nativist ascetic movements defined Indians as Indians
first and foremost, and defined the nations and branches as pan-Indian,
in opposition to white people and white ways. They called on all other
Indians to do the same.

When Blue Jacket was coming of age in the years before 1756, those
ideas began taking newly militant form. An Ohio valley Delaware named
Neolin had a dramatic story to tell the western people. In a trance, he'd
taken a long, hard journey to seek the master of life. On his way, he'd encountered a beautiful woman in gleaming white clothing, who had him
drop his things—he'd brought along an iron kettle, the classic European
convenience—as well as his clothing, and bathe himself in a river before
climbing a smooth, perpendicular mountain to which he was otherwise
barred by fire on every path.

Somehow using only one hand and his left foot, as instructed, he
found himself able to climb all the way to a beautiful town where a

young man escorted him, still naked, to the master himself. The master gave Neolin some news, which Neolin was to bring back to his people: not only the Delaware, but all Indians.

Or that's what Neolin told the Ottawa war leader Pontiac, according to a Frenchman from Detroit who said he'd heard Pontiac describe Neolin's story in detail. Neolin came back with a map of the universe, drawn up under the instructions of the master of life, with a pictograph prayer, also given by the master.

Here, then, was the news Neolin preached: In the beginning, the master had placed Indians where they ought to be and whites where they ought to be. Whites, tending naturally toward defiance of the good, had upset the balance by coming into the places meant for Indians. The command of the master of life was therefore for Indians to put things back in balance, whites where they ought to be, Indians where they ought to be, as it was in the beginning. Drive them out.

Neolin's story, while fundamentalist, was in certain ways novel, its details innovative. This single supreme being startled the Delaware visionary, for example, by informing him that the multiple spirits his people traditionally invoked by dancing before battle were delusions, manifestations of a single force of evil. Also, Indians should have only one wife. And while whites should have stayed where they belonged, and had rebelled against spiritual law by refusing to do so, really only the English speakers who wanted settlement in the West must be driven out. The French were by comparison more or less all right.

Neolin's prescriptions found eager listeners in Blue Jacket and other members of the generation now arriving at adulthood in the Ohio valley and around Lakes Ontario and Erie. The Seven Years' War had marked their childhoods in especially infuriating and saddening ways. The gruesomeness of the fighting had seemed to many on all sides to reach a new level of atrocity. Terrified by Indian raids carried out for maximum horror—babies killed in front of their mothers, mothers then killed too, children taken captive, torture reveled in—whites had abandoned homes and fled eastward all the way across the Blue Ridge, pulling back the American frontier. During the Seven Years' War, Indian unity had not prevailed: many Shawnee, a few branches of the Miami, and other western Indians allied with the French; the Six Nations Iroquois, along with most branches of the Miami, allied with the British. Hordes of every kind of English, Indian, American, French, and Canadian fighter killed and died trying to take and hold the point at the headwaters of the Ohio where the French had built Fort Duquesne, the strategic prize. In the most famous of those battles, Braddock's defeat on the south bank of the Monongahela, Braddock himself was killed, George Washington barely escaped with his life, and Shawnee fighters from the towns where Blue Jacket was growing up helped carry the day.

The young Blue Jacket heard those stories. Youngsters waited impatiently to take their places among the fighting men.

But in the end, the Shawnee's allies lost. Or worse, their allies gave up. After more than two hundred years, the king of France decided to abandon his North American empire, all of it, aside from a few islands, all at once. With that surrender, starkness and hunger came to the Ohio and Illinois Countries.

Neolin came preaching through a region devastated by warfare. Desiccated corpses from every belligerent nation still lay about its battlefields. Children played amid half-buried human bones. Neolin's vision had been formed in hopes that the French might remain or return, but for the first time the West had but one white presence, now newly dictatorial. As early as 1758, the British flag was flying above the fort on the point at the headwaters of the Ohio River: Fort Duquesne was now Fort Pitt. The British also soon enjoyed sole command of the great sweep of Lakes Erie and Ontario, occupying both the former French Fort Niagara at the eastern end, near where the Niagara River made its astonishing fall and glide into Lake Ontario, and the former French Fort Detroit, just beyond the western end of Lake Erie, and soon the long lakeshores between Niagara and Detroit were strung with British posts too, some taken from the French, others newly built. From Detroit, troops fanned out to penetrate northern and western territories formerly remote to England, where European presence had been almost exclusively French and sometimes minimal altogether. They occupied forts all the way up to Michilimackinac, the commanding connection of Lakes Huron and Michigan, and all the way out to the western bank of Lake Michigan. When peace was finally formalized in 1763, British troops went down the

Wabash and the Illinois all the way to the Mississippi, taking control, nominally anyway, over the many French settlers in towns abandoned by their king.

With British political and military monopoly came Indian privation. Such was the policy that Lord Jeffrey Amherst instituted upon taking military command of North America in his office in New York City. Back when competition had prevailed, making strong partnerships had required supplying Indians with European-made goods. Europeans liked to call such items "gifts," but while it pleased whites to see Indians as caught up in simpler forms of exchange, supplying the trading partners had really been a cost of cornering markets in a tough business. Ties between the interior Indians and France had been of longer standing, so British traders had taken special pains to lavish high-quality stuff on the Indian nations of the West.

All that was over, Amherst now announced. He needed to save the exchequer money after a bankrupting war, and there was no further need, he informed his subordinates, to induce Indian trade with supplies beyond the barest necessities. Buying friendship was poor policy, he said, involving moral hazard: austerity would keep Indians focused on their rightful work—hunting and trapping the fur supply—not distracted by diplomatic deals celebrated with gift giving, carousing, and war councils. Indians must bargain for the goods they needed, with traders licensed by the British and colonial governments; any supplies given must be considered part of the price of fur. In the absence of market competition, that price should be low anyway, Amherst noted.

Coupled with austerity came outright betrayal. One thing, at least, the western Indians had thought they might count on. They'd been assured that Britain's colonists would never be permitted to settle west of the Appalachians. That assurance was documented in the Treaty of Easton, signed in 1758 in Pennsylvania, where representatives of various western nations, under the nervous auspices of the Six Nations, had made a formal peace with the British, ushering in the very administration under which they now suffered. While the Treaty of Easton had also promised the Indians that the British wouldn't operate forts in the West except at Indian request, and was thus manifestly a dead letter, violation of the no-settlement clause posed Ohio valley dwellers with the worst problem they'd ever faced. Ohio Company and other speculators had wanted the French gone precisely in order to exploit their western land grants, and with the war now over, the investment companies were gearing up again to buy Indian land. Squatters were meanwhile moving in without any legal status at all. Loss of land would literally destroy the people who lived there. They wouldn't have had to hear Jeffrey Amherst speak openly, as he sometimes did to colleagues, of Indian extermination. Neolin's hearers had ample reason to respond to the theory of Indians as all good, once purified, and whites, especially English, as all bad.

With Neolin the Delaware preaching ultimate redemption, his Ottawa follower Pontiac began recruiting fighters for a holy war to bring about that redemption by driving out all whites. Pontiac said he would recruit the young and train them to fight using only bow and arrow. They would eat only dried meat and wear only skins. That much was familiar nativist fundamentalism, but Pontiac was going beyond the fad. Indian unity was now not only spiritual but also military. Freedom from white ways meant not separation but expulsion. The survival of all nations in the West depended on combining as one people.

Blue Jacket responded to that call. He didn't yet possess the wealth and power that would allow him, in maturity, to indulge sartorial flamboyance, hard drinking, and generally conspicuous consumption, but he was a highly confident and assertive personality, and it wouldn't be like him to readily renounce any pleasure or convenience. He enjoyed European goods. The asceticism part of the Neolin-Pontiac message wasn't for him.

Blue Jacket took something else from the call for pan-Indian unity. Though Shawnee, the young man readily followed an Ottawa war leader: Pontiac was putting together a force of multiple western nations and branches—Delaware, Shawnee, Ottawa, and others—newly unified in a commitment to reverse English incursion and dictatorial policy. Here was the beginning of the western confederation that Blue Jacket himself, in partnership especially with the Miami leader Little Turtle, would later build to such staggering size. At its height, it would force George Washington to contemplate, with explosive pain, the abject failure of his country's westward mission.

That all began for Blue Jacket in what British and American authorities called Pontiac's Rebellion. The term "rebellion" reflected whites' view of themselves as legal rulers of the Ohio valley, based on British victory over the French and their Indian allies, but Pontiac didn't intend rebellion. He was putting down a rebellion, by whites, against ultimate justice. To enforce sacred decrees, he was confederating Indian nations as essentially Indian. Pontiac's War was holy.

But not militarily decisive. The nascent Indian confederation did make impressive moves in 1763 and 1764, destroying eight western British forts and putting both Fort Pitt, at the Ohio headwaters, and the most strategic fort, Detroit itself, under siege. In coordinated events, the Shawnee leader Cornstalk—he was brother to Nonhelema, the female war leader and linguist—attacked settlements in western Virginia and western Pennsylvania, pushing back the whites' frontier. For months, it looked as if Britain's new western empire might really crumble. Jeffrey Amherst kept promising overwhelming retribution, but at first he was overwhelmed himself, short of troops: many colonial governments had refused to draft provincial forces in support. In that context, Amherst made the suggestion that would remain forever attached to his name. Couldn't the army, he asked his top officer, simply send smallpox to the Indians?

In the end, about five hundred British soldiers and hundreds of settlers died during Pontiac's War. Still, major fighting came to an end in 1764, in a combination of British military maneuvers and internal dissension among the Indian nations. Instead of driving out the whites as he'd promised, Pontiac sought a deal. Instead of the overwhelming retribution that Amherst had promised, British officials negotiated peace.

No chunk of the American West was lost or won in Pontiac's War. And yet in ways hard for white authority to discern, that effort had important effects on life in the West. Blue Jacket, for one, emerged committed, if not to spiritual asceticism, then to militancy and unity. Returning to the Shawnee towns where he lived, near the mouth of the Scioto River on the north bank of the Ohio, and taking up a career not only as a fighter but also as an ambitious businessman in the fur trade, Blue Jacket would soon find new chances to put what he'd learned to use.

As for settlers in western Virginia and Pennsylvania, as well as over the mountains around the Ohio headwaters, Pontiac's War amplified their racial hatred of Indians, already seething after the Seven Years' War. Many English-speaking settlers began defining all Indians, regardless of nation, branch, and traditional relationships with whites, as Indian, and as such inherently prone to savage violence. Indians needed rigid control, in the minds of some frontier whites. They needed extermination, in the minds of others.

As for the British army and the Crown ministry, Pontiac's War only enhanced their nervousness, frustration, and confusion about managing a new western empire in America. Actions the British government now took to address that problem began setting it at odds, less with militant Indians like Pontiac and Blue Jacket, than with certain ambitious citizens of its own colonies.

George Washington had come back astonishingly well from the humiliation at the Great Meadows in 1754. How he felt about starting a global conflagration wouldn't have been worth trying to guess. Denied by his mother a chance to sail away to imperial war, he'd brought imperial war to America. Denied a chance to see the big world across the ocean, he was opening, even making, what seemed a new world across the mountains. Certainly the outbreak of the Seven Years' War was the best thing that could have happened to his career.

In the fast pace of that conflict, Washington quickly put events at the Great Meadows behind him. He officially succeeded his late brother as commander of the Virginia militia and served as the British general Braddock's right hand, the local on the ground. Few had a better personal knowledge of the West, and Washington showed his natural fearlessness in encounters with the Shawnee, handling himself with particular aplomb in aiding the chaotic retreat of Braddock's routed forces from the Monongahela bank where Braddock himself was killed. Good fortune led to better fortune. During the war, he married the rich widow Martha Custis, adding mightily to his plantations.

And now he owned the turnip field where he'd begun his surveying. After Lawrence's death, Mount Vernon passed first to Lawrence's widow, but when she died, in 1761, it came to George. He'd already been managing it, and along with ceaseless buying and selling in western land speculation, improving and adding to Mount Vernon and trying to make it pay would provide Washington with constant, lifelong purpose.

He was elected to the House of Burgesses. By making his own investments in western land, he was superseding the Ohio Company that he'd served as strapping errand boy. By his early thirties, George had surpassed both Lawrence and their father as a man in planter society.

He still thought he might be a good candidate for a royal commission in the British army. He had the money now, and along with real bravery he looked good in uniform, and in civilian attire too. He'd become fastidious about every article of clothing, every accessory, every strand of hair or wig. He bought only the best, and the perfection of his ensembles, with his great height and might and seat as a rider—he was becoming famous as one of the great Virginia horsemen—gave people who met him a feeling of overpowering, well-contained intensity. No longer the long-limbed, hard-driving youth, he cast a grave charm now, a feeling of physical authority mixed with a remote kind of gorgeousness. He was gaining charisma.

He was adding cunning, too, to the single-mindedness he brought to commercial pursuits. Though overwhelmingly concerned, like others of his class and type, with honor and reputation, he was becoming adept at the sharp business practice and mingling of public and personal interest that marked the upscale endeavor of his world. At times those practices led to conflict. During the war, when General John Forbes, having taken over from the late Braddock, began planning a route of march from the western Allegheny slopes to retake Fort Duquesne at the Ohio headwaters, Washington urged the British commander not to cut road directly west to the headwaters. He advised instead clearing a road well southwest, then picking up General Braddock's old road north. That was the long way around, but Washington pooh-poohed all objections that fording an army across the Youghiogheny River in fall flooding, as his proposal required, would be dangerous, though it was, and he asserted that the more direct way couldn't be cut to make it fit for pack animals, all evidence to the contrary.

Forbes was skeptical. Pennsylvania and Virginia were competing to become the future destination for produce trucked out of a one-day developed West. Where Forbes's way would connect the Pennsylvania mountains to the Ohio River, Washington's way would keep the road in

Virginia. Too, one of Washington's own plantations lay in the direction he proposed, and it needed a road.

Outraged by the implication of economic self-interest, Washington wrote to everyone he could think of in power in Virginia. He accused Forbes of incompetence or, he hinted, worse, and he predicted inevitable failure to take Fort Duquesne. In response, the Virginia legislature voted to call its provincial forces back from the Forbes march. Washington had hog-tied Forbes's operation.

In the end, Forbes did follow his own route and take the fort. Even so, had some French prisoners, captured by Washington, not revealed the weakness of Duquesne's defenses, the prediction of mission failure might have been borne out, thanks to Washington's own actions. He was becoming somebody you didn't want to question or oppose. And while Forbes's success did contradict predictions of failure, that didn't bother Washington. He just turned it around, publicly exaggerating his own role in taking the fort.

Having established himself as a war hero, he resigned his commission in 1758, well before war's end. He wanted to give full-time effort to improving his many plantations and seeking further advantage in western land. He would bring ruthless creativity to overcoming all obstacles to that pursuit, many of them placed in his way by the imperial administration he'd risen by serving.

The ministry was hoping, with the resolution of Pontiac's War in 1764, to achieve calm military administration of the Crown's big, new North American empire west of the mountains. Instead, violence and chaos persisted. Indian movements to drive out whites terrorized squatters the British authority didn't want living there anyway. White militias, formed ad hoc, raided Indian towns, killing and scalping men, women, and children. Meanwhile, the big land-investment companies, Virginian and others, were applying for new and renewed grants that violated one another's earlier claims. With France gone, a bewildering multitude of players was rushing into the western land game now, with competing purposes and ambitions. All of that had to be sorted out by colonial governors, setting them at odds with one another while petitions and suits over claims and debts began choking the western counties' courts, the colonial legislatures' dockets, the governors' councils, and London lawyers' offices. It was becoming clear that neither the ministry at Whitehall nor the colonial governors in the East nor the British army in the West had any effective control over what went on at the margins of the American empire.

A signal example was the little town growing up, more or less by itself, behind Fort Pitt on the strategic point at the Ohio headwaters, gateway to the West. While the headwaters region was claimed by both Virginia and Pennsylvania, to the British it was part of no colony, and so Pittsburgh—pronounced "Pittsborough"—had no civil government, only the army in the fort. The town was tolerated, even encouraged, by a garrison far flung to one of the dark places of the earth and in need of services and supply. That protection, along with location, made it a natural and impromptu business hub, its rough shacks filled with bundles and stacks of smooth hides and silky furs, its mud streets bustling with commerce between whites and Indians of every kind, drinking, fighting: a model for the crudely booming American frontier town. Meanwhile, soldiers in the fort went on sorties to clear out other settlements popping up illegally around the headwaters. Pittsburgh's status was anomalous, and British policy everywhere in the West was anything but clear, anything but consistently enforceable.

And it was expensive. Supporting such a widely fanned-out military presence was gutting an exchequer already bleeding from the Seven Years' War. Dealing with squatters' illegal farms, big-time speculators' demands for grants and efforts to buy Indian land, and Indian attacks on settlers required high troop strength. Jeffrey Amherst had been recalled: his scabrous austerity, it was determined, had been a cause of Pontiac's War, and Dunk Halifax was out too. With Thomas Gage now in military command of North America, some in the ministry began thinking conservatively. They promoted a policy of slow but steady retraction of the forces, a withdrawal of British military presence in North America.

This policy of withdrawing the military over time signaled nothing like a return to benign neglect of the American colonists. On the contrary, the thinking went, only tighter control of Americans as a whole could justify the troop reductions. It was time, too, certain ministers

believed, for Americans to start footing some of their own bills: mild
taxation in the colonies looked like an effective way to pay for ongoing
expenses from the global war that General Gage, for one, saw Americans
themselves as having started in their own real-estate interests. New navigation acts involving these taxes—not to balance trade within the empire but to raise a revenue for the treasury, directly from American
colonists, for the first time—would become part and parcel of tightening Parliament and Crown control over American life and a cause of
colonial resistance to parliamentary and royal authority.

But the major tool for establishing peace in the West, which the
ministry believed would allow it to decommission many of its forts and
bring home many of its troops, involved the prevention of white expansion into Indian country. In 1763, reasserting the agreement made with
western nations in the Treaty of Easton, a royal proclamation froze
all settlement west of the Appalachians. This pause in expansion, the
Crown hoped, would allow it to consider ways of fostering orderly expansion under royal auspices and protecting Indian trade by protecting
Indian land. The proclamation's no-settlement rules hadn't been enforced
right away—the army had been distracted by Pontiac's War—but now,
with the speculation companies' reboots and the rising influx of squatters, the ministry was determined to enforce the proclamation's boundary line. It would enact its solution to white-Indian violence: segregation.

Soon to become infamous among certain ambitious Americans as
an exercise of tyranny, that line ran more or less along the crest of the
Appalachians, dividing the Ohio and Atlantic watersheds. East of the
line, colonial life as previously understood was to go on as usual, including observance of long-standing land deals made with all of the various
Indians living east of the mountains.

But everything to the west of the line, as far as the Mississippi River,
was now off-limits to white settlement. The entire British West was
officially reserved for Indians. Existing settlements west of the Alleghenies were to be removed by the British army, and that army was
to retain its presence in the West, in increasingly skeletal form, largely
to enforce this no-white-settlement rule. In the summer of 1764, two
thousand Indians of many nations and branches, eastern and western
alike, heard the proclamation's no-settlement provisions read aloud by
British officials at Fort Niagara on Lake Erie. The nations had a right

to their lands, the British announced. Only through official treaties with the Indian nations and sales certified by the Crown—not through deals with freelancing speculators or settlers—could those lands be transferred. The king would enforce Pax Britannica in America.

George Washington's rise as a speculator might thus have looked stymied. The original Ohio Company was in trouble: the new Virginia lieutenant governor, Francis Fauquier, had an attitude toward the company far different from that of his predecessor, Dinwiddie. Making gigantic grants to groups of speculators was a poor way to enable expansion, Fauquier argued; it inspired overweening ambition in investors and loosened Crown control over land. He proposed that the Board of Trade treat the old Ohio Company grants as subject to renewal and then not renew them. Company members, their investment now embattled, began seeking other ways of gaining the West, but enforcement of the 1763 proclamation line posed an enormous obstacle.

Washington kept at it. He founded the Mississippi Land Company with the young Virginia lawyers Thomas Jefferson and Patrick Henry, along with four Lees and some other Ohio Company members, seeking 2.5 million acres across the boundary line, but in the ministry's climate of restraint that plan got nowhere. He traveled to the Great Dismal Swamp, which flooded parts of coastal Virginia and North Carolina, and founded the Dismal Swamp Company in hopes of draining the area for settlement. Most important, he determined that he would not be prevented by a royal proclamation from laying claim to new land in the West. Instead of railing against the proclamation, as some of his contemporaries were beginning to do, Washington used the proclamation itself as a lever for gain.

He began by calming his fellow speculators: there were liberals as well as conservatives in British government; expansionist views had every chance of prevailing, in one form or another, in time. The proclamation line would have to be temporary, Washington advised, or at the very least, be shifted well westward soon. Others took the same view.

They were correct in sensing, at least, the incoherence of Crown policy regarding the West and the incoherence of both Indian and white responses to it. All of the many accounts that would, in the succeeding centuries, describe the positions of eighteenth-century British official-dom regarding American expansion westward, and analyze those posi-tions' causes and effects in America, would have no choice but to distort the subject simply by needing to be more or less lucid. Of course no series of events unfolds with the clarity that explaining them strives for, but in the case of British policy for the American West, clarity and reality come at odds to an extreme degree. Innumerable internal contradictions, sudden reversals, false starts, abandoned premises, do overs, baseless assumptions, side bets, and savage internecine politicking, along with their many unintended effects and non-effects on the ground in the American West, led to a condition of such mental and political chaos that simply by using the normal techniques for making sense out of confusion—chronology, logic, ranking of ideas, succession of tenses, grammar and syntax themselves—the very effort to explain obscures the nature of the reality under explanation.

Yes, elements in British government wanting westward expansion in America could be called liberal, those wanting to restrict expansion conservative, but most conservatives wanted expansion too—they just wanted it handled their way, or in mutually conflicting ways—and with nine prime ministers holding office between 1755 and 1775, each forming a government with its own secretaries and would-be secretar-ies knocking one another off and popping back up, error arises even in using the word "policy" to denote the clashing, overlapping relationships of each ministry plan—whether half-baked or brilliantly worked up—for restraining, or for enabling, or for both restraining and enabling Ameri-cans' westward ambitions. By the time any one of those many thoughts about managing the American West could be brought up or debated or abandoned or altered, many unaccountable things would already have happened, both in the American West and in England, to render the thought meaningless. A treaty might be negotiated in ignorance of or in redundancy to earlier ministry prescriptions. Colonial officers might misunderstand orders, deliberately or otherwise. A proclamation or directive might be issued many months before it could be received in America, in reaction to some situation either long since resolved or un-imaginably worsened by the time the communication crossed the Atlan-tic. Add to that the myriad influences, sometimes hidden and sometimes naked, of dozens of commercial lobbyists and high financiers and government cronies in London, in correspondence with dozens of agents and principals in Philadelphia and Williamsburg and Boston and adventurers and traders in the West . . . Because intellectual and communications disarray ruled all efforts of the king's ministers and their staffs when it came to the West, interplay between policy and action amounted only to a gaping vacuum, into which many a murky scheme might rush. Every account of the subject, from the deepest study to the crispest monograph, has no choice but to suffer from total inaccuracy just by being at all readable.

The ministry had a lot on its mind and was trying to do many things at once. America was far from the top of its list. George Washington, by contrast, enjoyed the luxury of total focus on a single pursuit, a list with but one item: gaining land. When it came to the royal proclamation line, Washington didn't just passively wait for it to be shifted westward, as he advised colleagues to do; he also actively ignored it. He went on investing in the West, and to the extent that others obeyed the proclamation, he gained the thing he was always seeking, advantage. Washington offered William Crawford, a land agent living near the Ohio headwaters, a percentage of any of the best lands in that region that Crawford could scope out and get surveyed and claimed for Washington, regardless of the prohibition, using any means necessary: putting up signs in the woods, slash-marking trees, writing down and keeping survey data, anything. Washington warned his agent to keep quiet about the project and to mark out many smaller lots rather than the few big ones that might draw attention. To further cover his tracks, Washington used aliases in making claims. By these and other means, by the end of 1770 he claimed, in one area alone, eighty square miles. His titles would have to be validated sooner or later, he told Crawford.

And things did seem to go pretty much as Washington hoped. General Gage and the ministry were waking up to the fact that enforcing a boundary at the crest of the Appalachians was impossible. Anyone can draw a line on mountains on a map, but Americans were crossing the real mountains to settle at will. Patrolling a border of great length through the highest rock in British America was no way to reduce military expense.

So in 1768, at Fort Stanwix in New York, Sir William Johnson, the British superintendent of Indian affairs, signed on behalf of the Crown a new treaty with the Six Nations Iroquois as claimants of all land west of the Appalachians. In order to create a more enforceable boundary, the treaty moved the royal proclamation line restricting white settlement from the crest of the mountains all the way west to the Ohio River. That shift abruptly placed claims like George Washington's, originally illegal, within the region of legitimate white settlement. For a long time, Washington's schemes seemed to be working out for him.

Blue Jacket was a Shawnee war leader now, and the deal the Six Nations made at Fort Stanwix in 1768 for shifting the line westward inspired him and his people to take direct action. The Fort Stanwix deal heightened tension between those who lived in the West and the Six Nations, who claimed it. From the Six Nations' point of view, the new Ohio River boundary seemed more readily enforceable. To get it, they were willing to deal away at Fort Stanwix the great tracts between the Appalachian crest and the Ohio headwaters, and to get the boundary fixed, with a promise of permanence, they also dealt away a big piece of the land they claimed south of the Ohio.

Part of that region was known as Kentucky. It was a hunting paradise, and that's because the Shawnee and other western Indians had maintained it as such for generations. Now, in one sweeping move at Fort Stanwix, the Six Nations permitted white settlement there. That wasn't a deal the Six Nations were empowered to make, in the view of the Shawnee and other western nations. As the westerners now moved to reverse it, Kentucky gained its reputation as a dark and bloody ground.

By 1770, white settlers were coming down the Ohio on flatboats to settle Kentucky in the first legal land rush in America. Because in white terms the region had been ceded by the Indians, Virginia asserted its sea-to-sea claim, determined that Kentucky was part of Virginia, sent explorers, and started writing land grants; North Carolina, in competition with Virginia, did the same. As far as Blue Jacket and other Shawnee living north of the Ohio were concerned, the region south of the river was still their hunting ground, not part of any colony, and in defiance of the

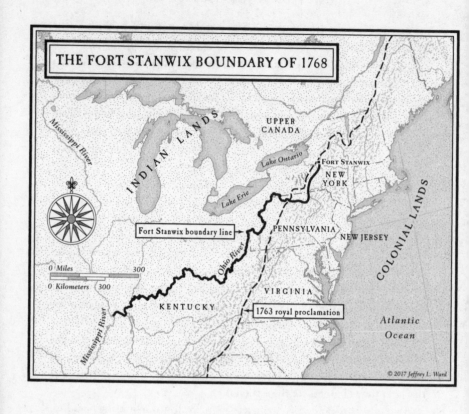

THE FORT STANWIX BOUNDARY OF 1768

Mississippi River

INDIAN LANDS

UPPER
CANADA

Lake Ontario

FORT STANWIX

Lake Erie

NEW
YORK

COLONIAL LANDS

Fort Stanwix boundary line

PENNSYLVANIA

NEW JERSEY

Ohio River

0 Miles   300

0 Kilometers   300

VIRGINIA

KENTUCKY

1763 royal proclamation

Atlantic
Ocean

Mississippi River

© 2017 Jeffrey L. Ward

Fort Stanwix Treaty, of the Six Nations' right to make the cession, and of white presumption of ownership, they began waylaying, terrorizing, and killing travelers on the river. They also crossed the river in raiding parties from the north side of the river to destroy new settlements on the southern banks.

Blue Jacket took the hard line: all Indians must now unify and resist this new white incursion, both in Kentucky south of the Ohio and west of the mountains north of the river. Indians not joining the resistance risked placing themselves at odds with their people.

And yet nothing about his lifestyle and manner suggested that Blue Jacket was nativist, fundamentalist, ascetic, or even racially antiwhite. He'd been moving along nicely in life since Pontiac's War. An especially adept and well-connected hunter and trader, enjoying relationships with the French operators still working out of Canada on English licenses, as well as with English speakers out of Virginia, Pennsylvania, and elsewhere, he participated in networks that were making him one of the richest of Shawnee businessmen in the region. He lived on a bank of the Scioto River, near its mouth on the north bank of the Ohio, about 350 long and bending miles southwest of Pittsburgh at the headwaters. Proprietor of a big household, Blue Jacket was becoming a clotheshorse, featuring tailored frock coats, sometimes scarlet with gold trim, and fancily decorated deerskin leggings. As his business grew, he came to own one of the big log houses in his town, built with European know-how. His sons were educated in English. His estate included enslaved Africans.

He married advantageously: one of his wives was a daughter of one of the biggest French traders, and through her Blue Jacket developed his ties with the Frenchmen working out of Montreal and Detroit. A leader in business, politics, and warfare, he had a reputation for swagger based on measurable success. The Scioto town where he lived would become known as Blue Jacket's Town.

For all of that easy intercourse with so many kinds of people, including the white traders who moved through the West, Blue Jacket passionately objected to white settlement. Yet asceticism, the total recoil from European goods, seemed counterproductive to preventing white incursion. Even Pontiac hadn't been able to demolish British forts by sticking with bow and arrow. Musket, ball, and shot were critical to driving whites out.

Certain other Shawnee leaders, by contrast, were urging restraint. It was becoming clear that the Crown of England and its officials sought, in perpetuation of the fur trade, some way of preserving Indian land and preventing white settlement. At one Shawnee meeting, the idea came up of sending an official delegation to the king in London. Six Nations Iroquois had at times done so, and the moderate Shawnee hoped they could obtain help from the British army in restraining colonists' settlement and speculation.

To the younger fighters and leaders of the Blue Jacket persuasion, however, the more practical idea was warfare. Pontiac had shown back in 1763 that British officials would improve policy only under pressure of war, and Indian unity was the key. In 1770, the Shawnee began sending diplomatic embassies not to London but to dozens of nations and branches living in all directions, including the Miami people around the upper Wabash, the Kickapoo near Lake Michigan, and the Cherokee and Creek in the South. They tried to get old enemies to make peace in the face of a common white enemy. They sent delegations to the Six Nations of the Iroquois too. While the Six Nations had signed the treaty that opened Kentucky to settlement and moved the proclamation line all the way to the Ohio headwaters, they were traditionally the western Indians' elder brothers. The Shawnee at once asked for and demanded Six Nations support for an all-Indian resistance to white encroachment in the West.

Gathered around the Scioto mouth where Blue Jacket lived, the Shawnee stocked up on guns and ammunition and hosted summit after summit to build a powerful confederation to drive whites out of the West. They were expecting a big war.

In the early 1770s, Thomas Jefferson was in his twenties, the son of a Virginia planter and land speculator and a planter and speculator himself; he was becoming an intellectual too, and a lawyer. At William & Mary, he'd studied mathematics, metaphysics, and philosophy. While reading law and clerking under the famed Virginia lawyer George Wythe, Jefferson found his Whiggism—the belief, grounded in certain strains of English thought, that property and liberty were intertwined in a natural right against sovereign intrusion and restraint—growing radical. Even as the ministry in London was looking for new ways of managing, regulating, and even preventing land investment in the American West, Jefferson began coming up with a broad philosophical and legal critique of Crown sovereignty in North America. In the end, his conclusions became dire.

A man of the Enlightenment and a proud rationalist, Jefferson looked to the future, not the past, yet he based his developing theory on a close reading not only of law, math, philosophy, and logic but also of history. As he began to see it, Americans enjoyed, by natural right, direct ownership of their land: not tenure granted by a sovereign but outright freehold, a right of utter, uncompromised possession. They also enjoyed a related right, critical to the former, to seek out new lands and possess them too. Americans' ancestors, according to Jefferson, were free Englishmen who had exercised just that right by coming to America. He followed that chain of history and logic all the way back to a happy condition that had prevailed in ancient England. The Anglo-Saxon ancestors of Englishmen had done first just what the Americans did later: leave home. From the northern European coastline, the Anglo-Saxons had come to England and there established this polity of rights. Freehold thus had its birth in the roving, freedom-loving Saxon personality.

All had been well, for many years, in the original Saxon England, an island of freemen holding lands in absolute dominion. No superior could claim or take property. Then the shadow fell. In the Norman Conquest of the eleventh century, an alien government, un-English, abridged the right of freehold. Norman rule exercised an abominable tyranny by invoking a supposed right of conquest to claim all land in England for the Crown. That crown might then grant some of that land, in feudal reciprocity, to vassals, who would hold it in tenure. So began the long, bad time.

But a right may be abridged, never killed. The Saxons did not give up possession, and out of that rugged insistence on freehold, not tenure, and the underlying right to seek new land and possess it, emerged the great modern British common law and Constitution. They gave property owners freedom to give or withhold consent to sovereign takings and intrusions. A parliament came to sit at court, representing the freeholders in obstructing or negotiating with the monarch. The long shadow of tyranny shortened in the rising sun of constitution and law and an electoral franchise based on property.

This story of the Norman Yoke, as it had become known, was hardly original with Jefferson. He'd gathered it from close reading of the English liberty authors like Edward Coke and John Milton, activists beloved by Americans, whose writings had played into the Parliament's struggle against the Crown in the 1660s. The novel thing that Jefferson did, partly under the influence of another of his mentors, the planter and speculator Richard Bland, was to apply elements of the Norman Yoke theory to the situation prevailing in America after the Seven Years' War. In Jefferson's reading, modern Americans were the last true Saxons, America itself the apotheosis of freeholding liberty, and the free life might go on here in perpetuity, if defended boldly enough. The key thing for America, now, was to push off Norman-style efforts of the modern Crown—German-born, anyway, not English—to crush English rights in America by asserting an illegal sovereignty.

There was a stumbling block, however. Americans had collaborated in their own oppression. The farmers who first settled Virginia were bamboozled by lawyers into believing that the Crown granted them their land. Americans had been duly paying the rents and fees and applying for grants. For generations they'd allowed the error to compound.

But if the British government now blocked their way west, Americans would be straitjacketed by a Norman tyranny. The thing that made men free, and in America exceptionally free—not only the happiness of freehold, but also, perhaps even more crucially, the right to *pursue* that happiness by movement into new land—would be stolen by a tyrant. The time had come to correct the original error.

The Crown, in Jefferson's developing view, had no right to allot western land. Only local legislatures elected by the freeholders or corporations formed by the freeholders could do that. Meanwhile, any individual could possess any land he wanted, as long as it was vacant.

Jefferson himself didn't pull all of these thoughts together in a cogent way until the mid-1770s, and while in the planter-speculator community his ideas had natural appeal, the radicalism of perfect freehold raised some eyebrows. The West wasn't vacant, and nobody thought it was. An especially horrible war had been fought there, sparked by American efforts to expand.

Still, ideas about freehold offered a new twist in justifying an assertion that some western land speculators, beginning with the Ohio Company, had been making for a long time: Crown and royal governors need not be involved to make purchase of Indian land legal. Maybe freehold extended to Indians too. If so, what was to prevent them from selling at will, to anyone they chose, regardless of proclamations and regulations? Taking this idea to the extreme, speculators might theoretically buy hundreds of thousands of acres of western land from any one or any group anytime, without interference from the British government. The whole cumbersome process of applying for royal grants—and, lately, of being turned down—would be rendered irrelevant.

In support of this exciting line of thought, American speculators began circulating a legal opinion said to go back to 1757. In it, the attorney general and the solicitor general of England stated baldly that buying Indian land required no royal permission. The opinion was known as Camden-Yorke, and for some speculators it took on qualities of an amulet. Armed with it, they might fend off British officials in the forts and make their own deals with Indians. George Washington carried a copy of Camden-Yorke in his diary.

The ministry, not surprisingly, condemned the whole idea of freehold in the colonies as a self-interested American fantasy. The Crown held sovereignty over its possessions: that was constitutional, and common law too. Only treaties negotiated by representatives of the sovereign power and the Indian nations themselves could make Indian land sales orderly and legitimate. Any other approach led only to violence, chaos, and disruption of trade.

And when it came to Camden-Yorke, the supposed legal opinion American speculators were relying on, that was nothing but a garbled misrepresentation of a real opinion. The giveaway was an odd turn of phrase the opinion employed: land could be purchased directly from those it referred to as "Indian princes." That's because the American version of Camden-Yorke tried to work around the word "moghul" in the original. The opinion really had to do only with actual Indians—the ones in India.

When Crown attorneys and officials learned of the spurious version

of Camden-Yorke circulating in America, they issued statements denying its legitimacy. They went on making every possible plan for obstructing what they could only see as upscale Americans' incorrigibility in
conjuring anarchic markets, stealing Indian land, and causing endless
imperial headache and expense. But a massive bet had been placed on
western land development. It was languishing, possibly dying now, thanks
to royal obstruction. In the developing thought of certain important
Americans, the freedom to make that bet might be fundamental to their
status as free Englishmen.

Heroes of the seventeenth-century liberty movement had been
willing to fight and die for such rights. Submission now, some of the
Virginians thought, might be tantamount to something they knew a lot
about: slavery.

In the fall of 1770, George Washington traveled westward, his first
western trip since the Seven Years' War. With his land agent William
Crawford, his plan was to float farther down the Ohio than he'd ever
been. He had yet another idea for gaining land there.

This latest scheme of Washington's was especially shrewd. It was
based on an old and nearly forgotten deal, made back in the early
1750s, when Governor Dinwiddie had been trying to enlist Virginia
troops for the Seven Years' War. Few had wanted to sign up, so Dinwiddie had offered bounty land: 200,000 acres on the south side of the
Ohio.

That offer was made only to soldiers, not officers. The land, once
conquered, was to be divided among the soldiers in lots with sizes to be
determined by officers' review of the soldiers' performance in the field.
Given all the restrictions on expansion, nothing had ever come of the deal.

But as soon as the Fort Stanwix Treaty opened those lands to settlement, Washington pounced. Framing the offer as if it had been made
not only to soldiers but also to officers, he mentioned the old bounty-
land deal to the new governor; then he wrote a class-action petition
on behalf of himself and all Virginia war veterans, both officers and
soldiers. The petition proposed that an initial survey be made at public
expense—the privates being too poor to afford it—in regions down

the Ohio where, though Washington didn't mention it, Crawford had already been secretly identifying the best land on his behalf. Virginia responded by allotting the petitioners the 200,000 acres, thus acquiescing passively in Washington's shoehorning the officer class into the original grant. All claimants were to file through Washington, Virginia ordered, and he was appointed, at his own suggestion, to hire a surveyor on behalf of Virginia. Not surprisingly, he chose Crawford.

So with his partner Dr. James Craik, Washington was now going west to meet up with Crawford and look over the grant. Following the old route toward the Ohio headwaters, they climbed into the Alleghenies and arrived at the Great Meadows, the scene of Washington's formative defeat after the death of Jumonville. Washington decided to buy the place. Arriving at Fort Pitt, they found the post on the point staffed only skeletally now, in keeping with the British hope for withdrawal. The party dined with the commander and a few Pittsburgh notables before setting off in canoes with Crawford and an escort of two Indians and an interpreter. Floating downstream, Washington closely observed the fine-looking, silt-rich bottomland on both banks of the river.

Back in Virginia, he met with the former officers of his old regiment. They voted to have Crawford make detailed surveys and proposed dividing the land by rank. The privates, with whom the original deal had been exclusively made, would get only four hundred acres each. Officers' portions were set by rank: corporals five hundred acres, sergeants six hundred, cadets twenty-five hundred, subalterns six thousand, and Washington and the other two field officers fifteen thousand each. At Mount Vernon, Crawford and Washington then spent days going over the surveys, and Washington presented the results to the governor and council, who approved the work in full, including what had now swelled to over twenty thousand acres in Washington's name: he'd bought up some of the others' claims.

Only later, when some of his fellow officers and their agents made their own trips down the river, and located the lands they'd been granted, did they see what had gone on. Crawford and Washington had laid out the lots so that Washington's holdings took almost all of the river frontage. Indeed, his tracts were almost all bottomland—flat, along the rivers, both fertile and easy to plant—what Washington called the cream of the country. The others got only a mile and a half of frontage. Their tracts then ran back from the river almost five miles into the woods. By Virginia law, no grant of Crown land could have frontage anywhere near as long as Washington's, but Crawford had neglected to take the standard surveyors' oath of office. He thus avoided committing perjury when submitting the work.

The other officers, furious, naturally hoped to have the surveys voided. Big events in global history conspired to defeat their expectations. As tensions between Americans and the Crown rose to a new pitch, George Washington would find indispensable roles to play, and in the aftermath of all that followed, Virginia would end up certifying all of his land claims and surveys, against all objections.

As the ministry in London now determined to do everything in its power to assert authority over colonial Americans and gain control over western expansion, certain Virginians who would become especially famous as patriots—Washington and Jefferson, but also Patrick Henry, Richard Henry Lee, George Mason, and others—began to identify their love of liberty with a complete break from all forms of English government.

Even most of those Americans at direct odds with British government had little or no expectation of American independence from England: that idea would rarely take public or official form until shortly before independence was actually declared. At first, as colonial legislatures up and down the seaboard began objecting to Parliament's actions—from the Stamp Act of 1765 to Thomas Gage's 1775 takeover of Massachusetts and more—their agendas only involved bringing Parliament to a sense of the wrongs it was committing against liberty and restoring the benign neglect that had prevailed before the Seven Years' War. For a long time, even among the most committed patriots, American independence just wasn't on the table.

But a minority coalition began forming as early as the first Congress in 1774, in favor of more extreme ends. To the surprise of many, the coalition's leadership was drawn mainly from Massachusetts and Virginia, colonies with seemingly the least in common.

The Yankees' move toward favoring independence was fairly easy to track. Boston, after all, was militarily occupied. Western Massachusetts farmers had strong traditions of self-government. Men around the Boston organizer Samuel Adams harbored reverence for what they saw as the natural rights of Englishmen, and Adams himself had suffered financially from colonial governors' interference in his family's business. Shippers like the magnate John Hancock had long been eluding imperial tax and tariff laws. Massachusetts elites had experience in traditions of backroom caucus, dedicating political machinery to opposing anything their royal lieutenant governors might try to do.

Virginia did have related traditions. The burgesses participated in the petitions and boycotts and other protests that defined the tense imperial relationships of the late 1760s and early 1770s. And yet the upscale speculators of Virginia who were becoming leading American patriots had a more complicated relationship with their royal governors than the Massachusetts patriots had with theirs. Back in the late 1750s, Governor Dinwiddie had allied himself with Virginia speculators' interests, and even as the ministry now began cracking down in earnest on westward expansion, the Washington cohort's chief aider and abettor in bringing the West into their portfolios was yet another royal lieutenant governor: John Murray, the Earl of Dunmore. In twists and turns of friendship and enmity with Lord Dunmore, the speculators around Washington would take a singular journey toward American independence.

Dunmore had arrived in Virginia in 1771, planning like George Washington's first gubernatorial sponsor, Dinwiddie, to use his office for profit. But Dunmore's ambition was huge. He thought he might defeat all land schemes, both in North America and at Whitehall, that competed with his own. He had no regard for the colonists' developing ideology of liberty, but high regard for the potential value of western land, and throughout the mounting imperial crisis Dunmore carried on close business partnerships with Washington and other speculators in a shared quest to dominate western development.

Washington moved easily in Dunmore's elegant social circle. It was Dunmore who first certified those shady patents worked up by Crawford. The governor used his position to bend to Washington's advantage yet another legal oddity. This was a provision of the royal proclamations of

1763 and 1768, ordering governors to set aside land west of the line for those Seven Years' War veterans who had served for the duration of the conflict. Colonels were to be granted five thousand acres, but Washington, though a colonel, hadn't served for the duration. In 1774 Governor Dunmore granted him the colonel's share anyway, and that gave Washington an idea. He urged his younger brother Charles to ask any veterans Charles knew—but only if they'd served for the duration—what they thought their grants might be worth. Charles was to ask casually, as if kidding around, then swoop in and buy, and he should keep George's name out of it. Added to gains made by his novel reading of the old Dinwiddie offer, these grants brought Washington another thirty-five thousand acres.

So even as Washington and his fellow burgesses, like other legislators throughout the colonies, began resisting acts of Parliament and the colonial executives who enforced them, Washington remained a business partner and beneficiary of a royal governor who was himself dodging imperial restrictions. Such were the intricacies of getting ahead in imperial, colonial, mercantile America. Washington was poling around the ice blocks, and while he couldn't see exactly what was coming, he wasn't going to fall off.

Patrick Henry, soon to become one of the most famous champions of American liberty, had a close connection with Governor Dunmore too. A passionate Whig from the western part of the province, Henry was a rising lawyer, largely self-taught, with a strong interest in possessing western land and in the liberty ideology of the seventeenth-century writers. He'd come to prominence in the Two Penny Case of 1763, arguing that the Crown's nullifying an act passed by Virginia burgesses, limiting the amount of tobacco paid to clergymen as part of their salaries, made the king a tyrant. By the mid-1770s, Henry was involved in multiple land ventures. Like Washington, he bought up veterans' bounty-land titles, and as Governor Dunmore's legal adviser in real-estate ventures he sought justification for the notion, popular with speculators, that individuals and companies had a right to buy land directly from Indians without Crown permission. After Henry reviewed the spurious Camden-Yorke opinion on Dunmore's behalf, a cousin of Dunmore's went all the way out to Kaskaskia, on the east bank of the Mississippi, to wave a copy in the face of the commander of the barely operating British fort there. The commander warned him off, but military government of the Mississippi region was weak. The Dunmore cousin held meetings with Indians and bought their land anyway, and when Dunmore and his cousin launched ventures to develop land purchased directly from Indians, Patrick Henry, George Washington, and others joined in.

Now in London a concept arose that might frustrate all of the Dunmore cohort's plans: the establishment of new royal colonies in trans-Appalachia. To get the American West under control, Lord Dartmouth, secretary of state, was willing to make that sweeping and controversial move. These proposed new colonies, outrageous to the speculators in Washington's circle, would force Virginia and North Carolina to relinquish their claims on western land, wiping out the speculators' investment, and, in the ministry's calculation, bringing the West under tight royal administration at last.

New companies were therefore quickly forming. In the chaotic atmosphere that marked all of the ministry's approaches to managing the West, Virginia speculators competing with the Washington and Dunmore cohort, serving as burgesses too, began pushing the house to support their investments in these new-colony projects encouraged by the Crown. It was in this climate that the patriot group began defining itself in total opposition to its Crown-connected business competitors in the Virginia legislature, and thus to the Crown itself.

One ambitious, royally encouraged plan especially drew the patriots' loathing: the Vandalia Colony. The idea was to carve out a colony south of the Ohio River and east of Kentucky, running from western North Carolina to western Pennsylvania and thus gobbling up by Crown and parliamentary fiat much of what had long been seen as western Virginia, where some of the highest-value investments had been made. And Dartmouth was piling on. Along with encouraging Vandalia, he planned to auction off, on behalf of the Crown, all of the other land that Virginia claimed south of the Ohio River, including Kentucky, which Virginia had determined belonged to Virginia and had begun to settle.

Dunmore's and Washington's circle in Virginia did more than vigorously oppose the Vandalia Colony. Their lobbyists fought the plan in

London, but more significantly for the developing imperial crisis, the patriots deployed their political machine to defeat the speculators supporting Vandalia in the House of Burgesses. As Richard Henry Lee, George Mason, and Thomas Jefferson worked on forming a majority to kill house approval for chartering the new colony, Governor Dunmore tried to block Vandalia in a sense physically, using executive power to hand his cronies big, new grants in the very areas slated for inclusion.

The ministry, for its part, kept up the fight. In June 1774, Parliament fired the most explosive round yet, the Quebec Act. Provisions of the Quebec Act went to extremes. Where the Vandalia project would exert control over much of the land south of the Ohio River east of Kentucky, and the related auction scheme would take Kentucky out of Virginians' hands, the Quebec Act drastically changed administration north of the river, transferring to the fourteenth British colony in North America the entire region north and west of the Ohio.

The Quebec Act outraged Americans well beyond Virginia. Quebec itself outraged them: unlike the original thirteen colonies, the fourteenth lacked any representative legislature, giving overwhelming power to the Crown, scandalizing many of the elite Americans who voted for and served as colonial legislators. Under the act, all of the old Ohio and Illinois Countries were now to be controlled by the royal governor of Quebec, placing traders under new controls, setting posts and tariffs, regulating alcohol sales, and permitting or denying land grants. The act also reasserted, on behalf of the province's overwhelming majority of French inhabitants, French civil law and French modes of land tenure, and it reestablished the Roman Catholic Church, anathema to many Americans.

No longer trying to draw and enforce lines, with the Quebec Act the British government had gone all the way. Between the Vandalia project and auction scheme, still in plan, and actual passage of the Quebec Act, a fait accompli, the home government was putting a final end to the effort that had begun with the Ohio Company in 1749, when George Washington was only seventeen, the effort into which he'd perhaps put more adventurous energy than anyone else. And the home government was achieving that end by means that not only Washington and his friends but also many others throughout the American colonies had come to associate with tyranny. A showdown had become inevitable.

Things were getting tricky for Lord Dunmore. He'd been telling his superiors that he was doing all he could to restrain the speculators and frontiersmen—they seemed, he said, to possess some inborn need to wander—but really he was among the most interested of those whose hopes the Quebec Act would ruin. So instead of enforcing the act, he tried to make it impossible to enforce.

To that end, he started a war. In 1774, even as the imperial crisis deepened, Dunmore moved on two fronts. He sent the Virginia militia against the Shawnee and other western Indians who had been raiding Kentucky settlements, and against the government of Pennsylvania, with the goal of taking Fort Pitt, finally abandoned by the British army. Who controlled Fort Pitt controlled the Ohio, entrance to the West. Dunmore wanted Pennsylvanians out of the headwaters region and Fort Pitt in the hands of his Virginia speculators. Brute possession, he figured, would at least slow down execution of the Quebec Act.

World-changing events would soon drive what became known as Dunmore's War down the list of important outbreaks of the mid-1770s. But nobody could see clearly what was coming. For some this conflict felt as if it might be decisive. The Shawnee down the Ohio, expecting white attack, had been stockpiling arms and ammunition and trying to build their confederation. They'd also been supporting the creation of the Vandalia Colony. While holding no brief for Great Britain, in any conflict between the English government and American speculators the Shawnee could see where their better hopes lay. Now Dunmore and the Virginia speculators were sending an army against them, and the Shawnee, no better at seeing the immediate future than anyone else, had reason to think this was the big one.

Their confederation remained inchoate, but in October 1774, Blue Jacket led men under the great Shawnee leader Cornstalk against western Virginia militiamen in the terribly hard-fought Battle of Point Pleasant. The Virginians were amazed by the Indians' skill: though outnumbered, Cornstalk's men killed seventy and wounded seventy more, fighting a superior Virginia force to a draw. Lacking an outright victory, the Shawnee couldn't solidify and grow their confederation, and under pressure of further attack they soon sent a truce flag to Dunmore's troops and agreed to refrain from crossing the river into Kentucky and from attacking boats bringing settlers downstream. By the spring and summer of 1775, new settlers were floating down the Ohio, and the frontiersman Daniel Boone led crews in felling gigantic trees for what would become the famous Wilderness Road. On the north bank of the river, Blue Jacket and the other Shawnee hard-liners looked for new opportunities for war with the Americans. Opportunities began coming on fast.

As for the Virginia speculators who were becoming fervent American patriots, they faced a contradiction. Dunmore was at once their partner in gaining the West and the representative of a hostile crown. In 1775, the governor outright prorogued the House of Burgesses in order to prevent its making a statement of support for Massachusetts, suffering under British occupation; in response, the Virginia Convention, an extralegal legislature formed in opposition to the governor's act of executive tyranny, sent delegates to two sessions of the Continental Congress, the intercolonial body meeting in Philadelphia, also extralegally, to assert American rights against Parliament. And yet the Virginia Convention also issued a statement of fulsome respect for Dunmore, praising the success of his war on behalf of Virginia's ambitions in the West.

Dunmore was beginning to see that he couldn't keep manipulating two masters. With his war on the Shawnee and Pennsylvania, he'd delayed and confused enforcement of the Quebec Act and other British plans, and he'd prorogued the burgesses partly in order to avoid having to read them Lord Dartmouth's orders regarding the West, but it couldn't go on. His bosses back home were unhappy about Dunmore's War. In the end, the royal governor had no choice but to enforce British rule.

And the moment Lord Dunmore ceased aiding the Virginia patriots' efforts to elude the law and gain land, he became not just no friend to his former partners but the foulest fiend they'd ever encountered. Rancor exploded with special intensity between Dunmore and Henry. In April 1775, responding to news of a shooting war between the British army and patriot militia outside Boston, Henry launched the first overt act of war in Virginia, leading militia to retake public gunpowder that Dunmore had seized. Dunmore was soon referring to his former associate as "a certain Patrick Henry," leader of "a number of deluded followers." It was clear that something personal had occurred between the governor and his real-estate lawyer. Neither man ever said what it was.

Later that year, Dunmore put the final touch on the list of crimes for which he would live, according to his former friends, in infamy. With the ad hoc Virginia Convention now in charge of the colony, and the governor executing office from a warship anchored off Norfolk, he made a startling proclamation. He offered freedom not only to any indentured servant but also to any enslaved African who would serve the Crown of England against the American partisans. He would form a black regiment.

That enormity went beyond anything the Virginia patriots could have imagined, even of the man they were now deriding as a traitor. As the formerly enslaved took huge risks, escaping both the patriots and the loyalists who had held them in bondage to enlist in what Dunmore called his Ethiopian regiment—one of the recruits had been held by George Washington—more than ever, Patrick Henry said, royal government had revealed itself as tyranny. Only war, Henry urged now, could keep Virginians and all other Americans from becoming slaves themselves. Dunmore, knowing his old cronies well, had hit them where they lived.

A spellbinding orator, tall and lean, with an aquiline nose, Richard Henry Lee had been working hard with Washington, Mason, Henry, and the others to pursue western land investment, avoid the British regulations that obstructed those investments, and disable their Virginia competitors, those Crown-supported burgesses invested in the Vandalia Colony. A son of the Thomas Lee who had founded the original Ohio Company, Lee addressed assemblages hypnotically and yet logically, weaving the air with a hand he kept wrapped in black silk to hide a wound: he'd lost fingers in a shooting accident. Now, representing the Virginia Convention in the Continental Congress in Philadelphia, he was turning his rhetorical and political skills to rallying other colonies behind the Virginia patriots' interests.

To that end, he formed a decisive alliance with Samuel Adams of Massachusetts. As the imperial rift deepened, and against the will of what appeared at first to be a majority, in Philadelphia Richard Henry Lee and Samuel Adams, aided by Samuel's younger second cousin John, accomplished a lot in a short time.

Lee and Samuel Adams made an odd couple. Abstemious, a deliberately shabby dresser, Adams wanted to make New England what he called a Christian Sparta. Lee, an elegant Anglican squire and a hard drinker, wanted to place Virginia's land policy in the hands of himself and the other speculators in George Washington's circle. One of Lee's first efforts in the Congress was thus to add the Quebec Act to the list of acts of Parliament that patriots called intolerable, including the closing of Boston's port, the takeover of Massachusetts's government, and the removal of defendants to England for trial. The Quebec Act, Lee argued, was the most intolerable act of all. While others disagreed, Samuel Adams abominated the Quebec Act too. Radical Bostonians viewed the pope as the Antichrist, and the Quebec Act's establishing Roman Catholicism revolted Adams. Together, Adams and Lee kept the act front and center as a signal example of British tyranny.

What they shared most deeply was the belief that if desire for American liberty was to be satisfied, America must become independent of Britain. Many in the Congress and among the public didn't see independence as the goal of the fighting that had broken out in Massachusetts. They still saw that fighting as a drastic way of bringing the mother country to the negotiating table and restoring rights lost after 1763. John Dickinson, the most powerful man in the Pennsylvania assembly, supported the war but opposed declaring independence, and without Pennsylvania's support, independence couldn't be achieved. Adams and Lee therefore collaborated with local Philadelphia radicals in a series of secret moves, both within Congress and out on the street, to bring down Dickinson's elected legislature. On June 7, 1776, having swung Pennsylvania, Lee placed before the Congress his famous resolution, written by Patrick Henry and Lee's other allies in the Virginia Convention, proposing American independence.

The Congress tabled debate on the resolution until July 1, but by then Lee had already hastened home. With American independence in the offing, the action for him was in Virginia: he had a coup de grâce to deliver. The Virginia Convention, dominated by the patriot circle, was busy writing its new state's constitution and setting new policies, and at the end of June the convention reviewed a petition by the Vandalia company, for land grants south of the Ohio, and denied it. Days later, on July 2, the convention's power to do so was confirmed when the

Congress up in Philadelphia adopted Lee's resolution for American independence. While Virginia's Vandalia speculators weren't likely to go gently, American independence drove a big nail into their plan's coffin, and other Crown projects for the West—the Quebec Act, the Kentucky auction—were finished. The speculators led by Washington, Mason, Henry, and Lee had prevailed, both at home and in the Congress. Virginia's land policy was now in their hands.

There was no going back. On July 3, Thomas Jefferson brought into the Congress the draft of the declaration he'd been assigned to write, seeking military alliances by explaining to the great powers the justice of having adopted independence. That same day, a British armada began landing troops in New York harbor, and the man in charge of readying the unskilled American army to resist invasion was George Washington. When his cohort in the Virginia Convention had sent him to the Congress, Washington had worn his old militia uniform, and cut his usual impressive figure, and with Samuel Adams's support he'd been assigned command of the Continental army. With British invasion, the Virginians had their man of action organizing American troops in the field and their man of thought organizing American ideas in the Congress.

Back in 1774, Jefferson had written a document titled "A Summary View of the Rights of British America," setting out his ideas about the relationship of tenure and freehold to tyranny and liberty. In 1774, those ideas had been too radical for the Congress. For one thing, Jefferson had attacked the Crown, when the official tactic had still been to attack Parliament and beg the king's succor. The Congress had declined to adopt Jefferson's "Summary View."

When drafting the Declaration of Independence, Jefferson didn't return explicitly to the right of landholding by freehold as the basis of liberty itself. He certainly didn't mention any natural right to buy Indian land directly from Indians. He didn't allude to a grimmer thought he sometimes flirted with. Western land was not of course uninhabited, and yet without the ability to possess it, fundamental American rights, as Jefferson had come to understand them, couldn't be enforced. It sometimes occurred to him that the kinds of people who had been living in the West for generations would have to be either removed or exterminated.

Later generations would come to think deeply, and with much

disagreement, about what Thomas Jefferson might have meant by the declaration's famous phrase "the pursuit of happiness." But Jefferson's colleagues in the Congress ought to have had a pretty good idea of what, at the very least in crucial part, he was talking about. Many were acquainted with the young Virginian's high regard, as expressed in "Summary View," for the happiness he believed arose from freehold, and especially from the freedom to pursue that happiness by unrestricted movement into new lands. His colleagues carved up his draft of the declaration, but they let that phrase stand.

Across the mountains and down the Ohio River, Blue Jacket and others in the western Indian confederation had no doubt about what was motivating Americans to drive the British out, and most of the Six Nations in the East were seeing things the same way. British government had become the Indians' only bulwark, though never a very strong one, against American speculators' ceaseless pursuit of happiness in possessing and settling new land. As the Continental Congress's military endeavor became a war for American independence, Indians prepared to defend their country from an onslaught by the former colonies now called the United States.

4

AN INQUIRY INTO
THE CAUSES OF THE LATE
UNFORTUNATE DEFEAT

In September and October 1783, thousands of delegates of more than thirty nations held a conference near the southwestern corner of Lake Erie. That more or less central location accommodated everybody from the Kickapoo living as far west as Lake Michigan to the Mohawk living south of the eastern end of Lake Ontario. As the fire burned on the banks of the Sandusky River, the conference confronted the immediate future of Indian unity.

Urgency had arisen from a surprising development. Since 1776, these Indians had been fighting, together and separately, against the United States, a phase of warfare that had lasted yet another seven years. Now England had surrendered to its former colonists. The delegates gathered at the Sandusky feared British surrender might signal withdrawal of long-standing British efforts on their behalf.

But no, Alexander McKee announced to the delegates: Great Britain would not abandon its allies. Of the British officials McKee had an especially deep Indian connection. This highly placed imperial administrator was, on his mother's side, Shawnee. Having fled Pennsylvania early in the war, he now served as the chief British Indian agent at Fort Detroit and remained committed to protecting Indian land from American incursion.

It was true, McKee admitted to the delegates assembled at the Sandusky, that per a treaty signed in Paris earlier that year, Britain was

relinquishing, in favor of the United States, all land in North America
south of the Great Lakes and the St. Lawrence River, excepting a slice
south of that river to give the British sole control of it. Britain would
retain only the land north of the lakes and the St. Lawrence.

But the British army still garrisoned its mighty lake posts, Niagara to
the east and Detroit to the west, as well as smaller posts between them
along the south banks of Lakes Erie and Ontario. Highly strategic, those
forts stood on what was now, per treaty, American soil and were therefore
supposed to be turned over to the United States. Negotiations were supposed to be going on for establishing a process for turning them over, but
negotiations had already bogged down, and fort commanders remained
on standing orders to defend the posts against any American effort to
take them by force. As a Shawnee and as a British official, Alexander
McKee told the gathered delegates that given British military presence
in the forts in support of Indian rights, and given a concerted show of
pan-Indian unity, he believed the United States might now be induced
to make a fair and reasonable peace with both the Six Nations and the
western Indians.

The nations gathered at the Sandusky were willing to consider good-
faith peace offers from the United States. They just didn't consider
themselves defeated by the states or in any way suppliant to them. The
British had been defeated. That was changing things, but the war
known to Americans as the War of Independence was to the gathered
nations yet another struggle to keep their land. The Americans had failed
to win it.

In the eastern theater, destined to become better remembered than
the western, General Washington had sent Major General John Sullivan
on a long campaign to demolish much of the Six Nations homeland.
Meanwhile, in an effort to seize and hold the West, Washington's general Daniel Brodhead had demolished not only Seneca towns in western Pennsylvania but also Delaware towns and other Indian sites well
into the Ohio Country, killing, rampaging through crops, taking prisoners, and burning buildings to the ground. Settler militias from Kentucky had meanwhile crossed the Ohio and attacked the Shawnee

towns on the north bank. American policy in both theaters was scorched earth. Indians reviewing the smoldering paths left by the Continental army had taken to calling General Washington the Town Destroyer.

Sometimes official tactics merged with atrocity. General Brodhead deployed western Pennsylvania militiamen to destroy Coshocton, a Delaware town north of the Ohio, but ordered the militiamen to refrain from attacking certain towns inhabited by Christian Delaware, fostered by Moravian missionaries: they remained neutral in the conflict and should be left alone, Brodhead ordered. His orders were disobeyed. Militiamen of the Ohio headwaters region were by no means fully under army command, and even Continental army regulars at Fort Pitt flirted with mutiny. In one series of attacks by western Indians into Pennsylvania, a white baby had been killed, spitted, and placed with its head facing west as a warning against white encroachment westward. In March 1782, more than 150 militiamen, under the leadership of one David Williamson, defied Brodhead's orders and entered a Moravian Delaware town, rounded up the people there, and accused them of participating in that raid.

The Moravian Delaware denied any involvement. The militia took a vote, and the majority voted to kill all the town's inhabitants. The Delaware spent that night in worship, preparing to die. The next day, the militia separated the men from the women and children, took the two groups into separate buildings, tied them up, beat their heads with mallets to knock them out, and scalped them all to death, around sixty adults and forty children. The militia piled the corpses in the mission house, burned the village to the ground, and left.

General Washington expressed revulsion at atrocities committed by both sides. To Indian combatants, however, no obvious distinction prevailed between local militias' impromptu massacres of noncombatants and Continental army expeditions to kill, burn towns, and deny food supply: the Indians themselves attacked towns and killed men, women, and children. Absence of distinction between atrocity and warfare seemed readily evident in what happened next. When General William Irvine took over at Fort Pitt, and raised volunteers for an official expedition against Delaware towns near Lake Erie, he gave a leading role in the expedition to that same David Williamson who had led the freelance Moravian massacre.

Now the atrocity tables turned yet again. Williamson was known to be volatile, so General Irvine asked William Crawford, the land agent with whom General Washington had once jiggered patents, to lend a steadying hand. In the ensuing expedition Crawford himself was captured. Indian policy regarding captives had changed after the killing of the Moravian Delaware. No more adoptions or enslavements. All Americans were to be killed.

William Crawford hadn't been at the Moravian massacre. He'd joined this unit only in hopes of providing order and preventing similar atrocities. And yet before he died, he was ritually tortured in many hours of beating, burning, shooting, and mutilation. The mass murderer David Williamson, for his part, came home unscathed. Such was the grim nature of the war that the Indians had been fighting—and in 1783, despite British surrender, were still fighting—with the Town Destroyer, the Continental army, and the American militias.

The war had fostered a new strategic alignment between the Shawnee Blue Jacket and the Miami Little Turtle. A well-regarded military leader now, Blue Jacket had been at constant war with Virginia militias from Kentucky. The Shawnee military objective remained to prevent white settlement in Kentucky and white conquest and settlement north and west of the Ohio, and in carrying out that objective the Shawnee had taken many losses, but they'd also achieved triumphs. In the famous Battle of Blue Licks in 1782, nearly a year after the famous surrender of Lord Cornwallis at Yorktown, Shawnee and other Indians, along with American loyalists and British troops, routed Kentucky militia led by Daniel Boone and others. Impromptu action went on constantly too: the Shawnee waylaid and killed settlers floating down the Ohio to Kentucky. Developing the knowledge he'd first gained in Pontiac's War, Blue Jacket learned that surprise attacks can overcome forces of greater size. He readily went on the offensive instead of digging in for defense.

He'd also changed his base of operations. As early as 1776, with the outbreak of organized American military aggression, he pulled out of the towns where he'd spent his life and led a hard-line Shawnee party farther into Indian country to towns on the Mad River, a more readily

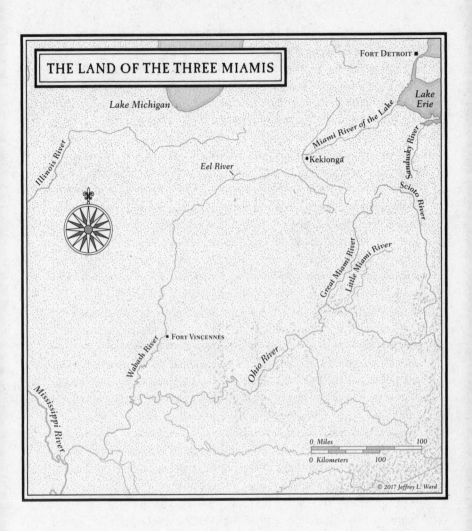

THE LAND OF THE THREE MIAMIS

Fort Detroit ■

Lake Erie

Lake Michigan

Miami River of the Lake

Illinois River

Eel River

•Kekionga

Sandusky River

Scioto River

Great Miami River

Little Miami River

Wabash River

■ Fort Vincennes

Ohio River

Mississippi River

0 Miles   100
0 Kilometers   100

© 2017 Jeffrey L. Ward

defensible position from which to raid. This strategic withdrawal brought
Blue Jacket geographically and politically near the man, so different in
style and manner, with whom he would collaborate successfully against
the United States: the enigmatic Miami war leader Little Turtle.

Little Turtle differed from Blue Jacket not only in personal style
but also in geographic frame of reference. The Miami leader's struggle
against white settlement began later than the Shawnee's in part because
Little Turtle's world focused itself well north of the Ohio River, looked
even farther north to the Great Lakes, and reached westward toward the
Mississippi. The Indians who lived there and the French- and English-
speaking traders they'd long dealt with thought of the region as the Land
of the Three Miami Rivers.

For there really were three different rivers called Miami in that
country, and the directions in which they flowed held Little Turtle's
world together and affected how his people viewed white threat. The
Great Miami's source lay 160 miles north of the Ohio River and ran
southward all the way into the bigger river. The Little Miami copied the
Great Miami, running southward to flow into the Ohio too. The third
Miami flowed in another direction, keeping Little Turtle's people connected not only to the Ohio and the Wabash and ultimately the Mississippi but also to the Great Lakes. Where the first two Miami Rivers were
Miamis of the Ohio, that big river's tributaries, the third was the Miami
of the Lake. From a headwaters well northwest of the Great Miami's, it
ran northeastward through a hundred miles of weird and tricky marsh,
prairie, and forest known as the Great Black Swamp, then fell as a white-
water rapids through a series of shallow rock ridges to enter the farthest
southwestern corner of Lake Erie.

At the headwaters of this northeast-flowing Miami of the Lake, the
Miami Indians had their heartland: Kekionga. Lying so far interior, well
north of the Ohio and south of the lakes, Kekionga had remained more
remote, to American officialdom, than the Shawnee towns. An idea prevailed among whites that Indian land remained, if not literally uninhabited, unimproved: Indians didn't clear timber and do agriculture except
in a desultory way, it was believed, so they couldn't be said to live anywhere in particular. They hadn't seen Kekionga. In late summer, high
green corn spread seemingly endlessly there, under a big sky. There were
rolling orchards and vegetable gardens and multiple towns of cabins and

tents. Prairies had been carved out of the woodland by controlled burning, hunting-park meadows with long-range views where animals came
in abundance to graze. Here was a combination plantation, trading center,
and civic complex, surrounded by a woodland shaped by trails and hunting grounds. Kekionga opened to the northeast on the Great Black Swamp
and Lake Erie, to the south on the Ohio River, and to the west on the
Wabash, the Illinois, and the Mississippi.

When Little Turtle was growing up, near Kekionga on the Eel River,
Miami attitudes about white incursion differed from those of the militant Shawnee. There were many Miami branches—some would say
that Little Turtle, who would become the most famous Miami leader,
wasn't Miami at all but an Eel River dweller—and the branches didn't
always act in concert: their country lay so far northerly and westerly that
aggressive ventures like the Ohio Company's hadn't reached their towns
so directly. In the Seven Years' War, some Miami branches had fought
in alliance with the French, others with the British. And because the
Miami had their own great hunting grounds to the west, and tended to
view the Ohio River as their far-southern boundary, loss of Kentucky
south of the Ohio didn't hold the meaning for them that it did for the
Shawnee.

In 1778, however, with the outbreak of the new war, things changed.
Exploits of a young Virginia explorer and speculator named George
Rogers Clark, shifting alignments and amplifying intensities in the
Land of the Three Miamis, drew Little Turtle into the action. Clark's
leadership, which would make him a hero of American Revolutionary
lore, began when he crossed the Ohio out of Kentucky on raids against
Shawnee who had been raiding southward. With the encouragement
of Patrick Henry, Virginia's new governor, Clark began a major campaign to conquer all of the old Illinois Country east of the Mississippi,
beginning by taking British garrisons near that river. Clark and Henry
hoped to exercise, by factual possession, the old charter claims that gave
Virginia the entire West, thus establishing the greater Virginia that
had made American independence so appealing to the land speculators
of that state. And because the long ministry policy of military withdrawal had left British forts pitifully understaffed, Clark did easily
take Kaskaskia and Vincennes on and near the Mississippi. Then he
looked northward. The ultimate goal was Fort Detroit, just northwest of

Lake Erie, the most strategic western position, commanding the entire region from above. Clark's idea was to subdue the western Indians, drive out the British army's somewhat more sizable western garrison at Detroit, and make a present of the fort to the Continental Congress on behalf of greater Virginia. Little Turtle first took up arms in opposition to that plan.

Some of the other Miami Indians at first allied themselves with the bold and dictatorial Clark. He was only twenty-five, almost unbelievably brash, and he did a good job of acting as if taking the barely defended Mississippi forts represented an astonishing victory. Elder and well-known Kentucky settlers like Daniel Boone and Simon Kenton were impressed enough to serve under him, and Clark was able to overawe some Miami people and solicit others, especially those living on the lower Wabash toward the Mississippi.

Little Turtle, living up on the Eel River near the heartland Kekionga, did not join Clark, and when Clark personally failed to take Detroit, the task of conquering that post reverted to an ally, the French cavalry officer Augustin Mottin La Balme. In the defense of the Land of the Three Miamis, Little Turtle prepared to meet La Balme in battle.

La Balme's men came up so fast on horseback from the Mississippi forts that they reached Kekionga before the Miami living there had much warning. If the Frenchman had thought things through, he might have successfully treated with the Kekionga people. He'd arrived in America with the Marquis de Lafayette, in alliance with the United States, yet he openly disdained Clark, his partner in taking the West, as an untutored backwoodsman. La Balme really seemed to be secretly hoping to retake all of Canada for France itself. Some among the Miami had happier memories of the French than of any of the English speakers; other Miami, seeking only neutrality, didn't want to fight either Clark or La Balme.

La Balme's behavior militarized them all. He seized the Miami towns at Kekionga and plundered the storehouses of two French traders, spending twelve days living high on the supplies. His men cooked and ate livestock and caroused on liquor, then, after two weeks of obnoxious partying, resumed their mission to take Detroit. Moving west of Kekionga, they went up the Eel River, and Kekionga's fighters, eager for revenge, shadowed them. La Balme stopped to camp just three miles south of where Little Turtle lived. The young man had been preparing. The Kekionga Miami gave Little Turtle permission to command an attack.

Just before dawn on November 5, 1780, Little Turtle led an action against La Balme's camp. The French recruits got off one volley. After that, it was all the Miami. La Balme was killed in the fighting, but some of his recruits made it back down the Wabash to Vincennes to tell the tale. Stopping La Balme, and thus obstructing George Rogers Clark's assault on the West, made Little Turtle's name.

Little Turtle became a war leader at Kekionga, bringing Miami branches together, in alliance with the British garrison at Detroit, against the Americans. The British fort at Detroit was never taken by Clark or by any other Americans or their allies during the war. Lacking Blue Jacket's commercial ambition and personal ostentation, Little Turtle was more philosophical yet at least as bluntly assertive, and by the time the nations met at the Sandusky in 1783, he'd become as militant as Blue Jacket for pan-Indian unity against American incursion. Blue Jacket's and Little Turtle's strategic sympathy in reviving a confederation of western Indian nations would soon have decisive effects on the future of the continent.

At the Sandusky conference, however, it was not any of the western Indian leaders but the famous Mohawk Joseph Brant who made the biggest pitch, both for solidifying Indian unity in the face of British withdrawal and for seeking a favorable peace with the United States. Brant's seeming all-importance in white-Indian relations made him a natural leader at this conference.

That importance was based in part on the Six Nations' traditional dominance in the West, still in force in 1783 despite some western resistance. Members of the great longhouse remained elder brothers to all western nations, and because Brant himself had long enjoyed a pivotal place in white-Indian diplomacy, his relationship with the British still holding the lake forts was perhaps stronger than any other Indian's. As a young man, he'd led Mohawk forces in alliance with the British against the French in the Seven Years' War. A fluent reader and speaker of English and an Anglican convert, he'd helped translate the Gospels into the Mohawk language. Slated to go to King's College in New York City, he'd instead had to fight on behalf of his British sponsors against Pontiac's confederation, but he remained at least as well educated in the European style as many of the white people he dealt with.

Brant had a family history, too, that made him a natural leader at this conference. He was nearly a brother to Alexander McKee's boss John Johnson, the British superintendent of Indian affairs. Brant's older sister Molly had been a girlfriend of Johnson's father, who had preceded his son as superintendent and fathered children with a multitude of women, English and Mohawk alike. Joseph Brant and the younger Johnson had more or less grown up together at Johnson Hall, the estate Molly Brant kept for the father on 400,000 acres near the Mohawk River in New York.

Brant was known even in London. In 1775, he'd sailed with a Johnson cousin to seek ministry funding for Mohawk operations against the Revolutionary Americans. An instant celebrity in the capital of empire, he was received at court by George III. Thanks in part to Brant's diplomacy, most members of the Mohawk nation did ally with England in the war; so did most members of the other Six Nations of the Iroquois. Many had now fled north of the lakes, and the Six Nations longhouse had been strained diplomatically by division over white alliances—the Oneida had fought on behalf of the United States—and hurt physically by Sullivan's and Brodhead's devastating campaigns against populations.

Brant was hoping to rebuild the longhouse, and as the fire burned on the Sandusky bank, he put forward a novel idea regarding the West and Indian confederation. All of this land, Brant asserted, belonged to all Indians equally, regardless of who was living on it. Indians of all nations should identify as Indians first and pledge to protect the West from American incursion.

Coming from Brant, that concept had multiple ramifications. The most obvious was the shoring up of pan-Indian unity in resisting American expansion. Some nations and branches attending this conference lived far to the west, others to the east; some had made only weak commitments to confederation. Brant was urging them all to unify to protect the West.

But his call for unity had another purpose, hardly likely to be lost on the delegates from the western nations. Brant was reasserting the tra-

ditional Six Nations stewardship of the Ohio valley. Some who actually lived in the Ohio valley had begun to take a dim view of the distant
Iroquois's influence. They'd seen the Six Nations deal away Kentucky.
They'd been building their own western confederation, led by the
Shawnee, the Miami, and the Delaware under leaders like Blue Jacket,
Little Turtle, and Buckongahelas. They'd kept Clark out of Detroit and
beaten Boone and the others at Blue Licks. Deference to the Six Nations as elder brothers had tradition going for it, but tradition was slip-
ping. At the Sandusky conference, Brant was trying to hold on to it.

Despite all that tension, at the Sandusky conference Indian unity did
prevail, and Six Nations leadership remained in force. With Alexander
McKee presiding for the British, and Joseph Brant for the Iroquois, the
gathered Indians made a pledge.

None would ever sell or make any other land cessions to the Americans without the permission of all. Any private deals or treaties made
with individual Americans or the American government would be illegitimate on their faces.

McKee made a further proposal. Having pledged the support of
British officials still in the lake forts, he asked the militants to take a
pause in the fighting and explore the possibility of a just peace with the
United States, a peace acknowledging Indian rights to Indian land.
Given pan-Indian unity, as asserted by Brant and agreed to by all, the
militants agreed. They would suspend all significant fighting and see if
the United States would agree, in turn, to cease invading.

To the American Congress, the place where the Indians' Sandusky meeting took place lay in the Territory of the United States North-West of
the River Ohio, the Northwest Territory for short. That vast region, only
becoming organized on paper as 1783 was coming to an end, spread
north and west of the Ohio River all the way up to the southern shores
of the Great Lakes, embracing the whole eastern side of the great
Michigan peninsula and running all the way out and down to the Ohio's

mouth at the Mississippi border with Spanish America. The territory thus included all of the old Ohio Country and the part of the old French Illinois Country lying east of the Mississippi: all, that is, of the rich bottomland, hill country, and grassland that the American investing class had been barred so long from developing, via British schemes that Americans condemned as tyrannical. With victory over the Crown, the American Congress held sovereignty there at last.

Questions were asked, and would go on being asked, as to why Lord Shelburne, in charge of the team negotiating in Paris, gave away so much. Ceding the vast and valuable West as a spoil of American victory assaulted the honor of many British military men, especially those on the ground working with Indians. Making the colonies independent didn't seem to call for ceding them all that land to their west. For generations to come, writers would call Shelburne's cessions surprisingly generous.

Shelburne's team, in negotiations with the American team in Paris headed by Benjamin Franklin, did float some alternatives to wholesale cession. At one point, the British suggested that exact terms of independence, including western borders, be resolved between England and each state separately. The Franklin team rejected that idea out of hand: terms must be negotiated with the states as a whole, via the Congress through which they'd confederated in order to fight the war they'd won.

And in the end, Shelburne and everybody else involved had to know what the war had been fought for. America was already in the Ohio and Illinois Countries. It had been there for decades. England had been fighting with itself for just as long over how to manage that fact. And American desire to possess the West had only intensified during the struggle for independence. The Congress had recruited sufficient troops by offering bounty land as additional payment: much of that land would have to be located across the Ohio. Plus there was the war debt. The Congress had borrowed some money from foreign allies, and a great deal more money from rich American investors; the foreign debt had to be paid and the domestic creditors reliably supported with interest payments or, in one developing scheme, with interest payments combined with western tracts.

American independence without the American West wouldn't be American independence at all. Ceding the great region that Britain had long been struggling to reserve for Indians wasn't generous but a sine qua non of peace.

The region represented a political anomaly that would affect all concerned in unpredictable ways. The negotiators in Paris drew not just a new boundary line but a new kind of boundary line, unprecedented by all of the drawing and redrawing that had gone on, for so long, in Paris and Whitehall and Madrid to alter maps of an imagined North America. This line didn't divide something called the United States from something called Great Britain, making a frontier between two nations, as between France and Spain or France and Germany. Such national frontiers, though often contested, had the purpose of separating sovereign states and helping define the concept of statehood itself.

The line that the ministry and the Congress arrived at in Paris in 1783 lay between two entities radically other than that. On the south side of the line: thirteen sovereign, confederated states, legally represented by a meeting called the Congress, physically bordering one another down the Eastern Seaboard in reasonably neat succession. Their eastern boundaries were defined naturally by the Atlantic coastline, but their northern and southern boundaries divided them politically along lines created originally via charters issued by the very Crown that was now giving them up. Those boundaries were to remain in place, yet their imperial meanings had been transformed. That was strange.

The states' western borders took the strangeness all the way. The West that the Congress was now supposed to control amounted to a gigantic mishmash: old claims, old and new dreams, crisscrossing map lines. Because not all of the colonies had sea-to-sea claims like Virginia's and others', drastic inequalities of land wealth prevailed among the confederated entities. Paying soldiers bounty land, for one thing, was far easier for states that claimed great tracts stretching westward. States that did assert such claims were in conflict with one another, too: Connecticut, for example, more or less acknowledged that its extension westward was interrupted by the existence of New York yet claimed its sovereignty resumed west of that state, exactly where Virginia claimed uninterrupted sovereignty. All of these claims, too, derived from royal charters: With the colonies set free from royalty, how enforceable were the claims? Virginia, Pennsylvania, Maryland, New York, and others were struggling for dominance as projected eastern entrepôts for all future western bounty; investors in canal- and road-building projects were betting against one another in bringing the potential fruits of a potentially settled West to preferred destinations. Meanwhile, the contention between Virginia and Pennsylvania still went on over the all-important Ohio headwaters region, gateway to the West.

And yet in Paris the entire American West was ceded, as a single entity, to the American Congress. There was no American nation, and yet the West, not simply an acquisition but a political and economic dynamo, was shaping rapidly emerging new ideas about the future of an independent America that many Americans had never before considered. The territory was at once a kind of colony of the Congress and an American nation in embryo.

If the newly independent states and their Congress represented diplomatic anomalies, so did the new region north of the line. Not a sovereign nation either, that region was still a British colony, recently the fourteenth.

Quebec was strange in part because of the presence there of so many Americans. They'd fled propertyless as refugees from the former colonies. A vast region, to be run on the ground by British governors and military officers, was now populated to the east by many remaining French speakers still operating under French law and religion, and to the west by few white people at all, and those mainly refugees from the newly independent states just across the line. That whole thing was to be overseen from a difficult distance by Whitehall.

To reduce confusion, Franklin floated an idea of his own during the negotiations. Maybe England had better cede all of its North American possessions to the United States. Why not just hand over Quebec, Nova Scotia, and Newfoundland, and abandon the continent altogether, as the French had once done?

That was a nonstarter. Instead, the ministry began looking for ways

to manage Quebec, and the Congress began figuring out how to organize its huge acquisition south of the lakes and west to the Mississippi.

In that context, the Congress passed an ordinance. As a delegated meeting of sovereign states, the body couldn't pass laws: it didn't govern anyone
living in the states, but just as it had taken responsibility for managing
the war, the Congress now took responsibility for managing the West the
war had won. It could and must govern Americans living, trading, speculating, and even thinking about the region north and west of the Ohio,
and to make that possible, Virginia, for one, was induced at least to renounce its old sea-to-sea claims. In exchange for ceding its western land
to the Congress, Virginia received a reserve within the territory, bounty
land for its veterans: George Rogers Clark would soon become one of
the territory's biggest landowners. Connecticut too made a deal: for a
dedicated strip of Erie lakefront at the Cuyahoga River's mouth, the
state relinquished all claims on the West. Other states with western
claims joined in the creation of this first public domain of the collective
United States, and the 1784 ordinance, first of three, made preliminary
rules for procedures that would one day, it was hoped, form new American states out of the Northwest Territory.

Meanwhile, and crucially for its ensuing relationship with the western Indians, the Congress established a military presence to provide
the new territory with some sort of order. This wasn't an extension of
the Continental army. That victorious force, demobilized throughout
1783, was officially disbanded in June 1784. It was during the formal farewell to his officers at Fraunces Tavern in New York City that George
Washington made his toast "to the Butlers and their five sons." Only
about eighty men remained; they were stationed mainly at West Point.

To manage the West, the Congress created a new force and placed
it under command of Colonel Josiah Harmar. He was thirty-one,
American-born, militarily schooled only in the recent revolution, having
served for the duration and seeing action in famous campaigns led by
General Washington in New Jersey. For one year afterward, Harmar had
been private secretary to the Pennsylvania politician Thomas Mifflin,
when Mifflin was serving as president of the Congress. It was Harmar

who carried the 1783 treaty, now ratified by the Congress, back to Benjamin Franklin in Paris.

Before and after that year, however, Josiah Harmar had known no adult life other than that of a full-time officer. He was a career army man, and in the United States in the 1780s that was a strange thing to be, because the victorious Congress didn't create any real, regular army to replace the Continental army. In forming its new military entity, the Congress allowed for raising a total of only seven hundred men, "from the militia": paid volunteers, divided into eight infantry companies, plus two of artillery. Most of the men were to come from Pennsylvania, so a Pennsylvania commander was needed; hence Harmar's appointment, on Mifflin's recommendation. In 1784, Harmar marched his small group of recruits from Philadelphia out to Fort Pitt and began training them. Reporting directly to the Congress's secretary of war—first Benjamin Lincoln and then, beginning in 1785, Henry Knox—Harmar commanded what passed not only for military administration of the Northwest Territory but also for the whole armed might of the United States anywhere.

Although he served as the highest-ranking American military officer, Lieutenant Colonel Josiah Harmar had few officers under him. From West Point, Major John Doughty brought out to the Ohio headwaters a part of his famous artillery company, originally raised under Alexander Hamilton, the sole vestige of the disbanded Continental army. Doughty took command of Fort Pitt, and there were a few other officers, but Harmar had nothing in the Northwest that a military man would call an army, and maybe in compensation he became something of a stickler, a model officer modeling officerhood. He always carried Baron von Steuben's drill manual, on which all American military training remained based, and he made himself busy deploying his far-flung, skeletal force in support of the Congress's first efforts to manage its West.

Harmar's first big move was to take troops all the way out to Vincennes and Kaskaskia, the old French Wabash and Mississippi forts and settlements. George Rogers Clark's operation had made those forts technically Virginian for a time, but for years American profiteers and speculators had been running the towns like independent, even criminal city-states. Now that the Congress technically held the region, the inhabitants left over from New France, long at the mercy of freebooters, had been begging for some kind of government. Harmar flew the

U.S. flag at old Fort Vincennes for the first time and voided land grants self-conferred by the American gangsters. He installed Colonel Jean-François Hamtramck, born in Quebec and a decorated Revolutionary officer, to put the hammer down on Vincennes and Kaskaskia and try to persuade the French inhabitants not to emigrate to the Spanish side of the Mississippi. Just before heading back up the Ohio, Harmar himself did cross the Mississippi to pay an official visit to the Spanish commandant on the west bank at St. Louis.

Back at the Ohio headwaters, Harmar's men got busy searching out illegal farms in the woods and evicting squatters. And in a related move, despite many competing calls on his attention—he was building forts down the north bank of the Ohio from Fort Pitt—Harmar was happy to assign a detachment of sixty men to escort a surveying team led by Thomas Hutchins, the Congress's geographer.

Hutchins's mission was another critical element in the Congress's plans for managing the Northwest Territory. In early 1785, Hutchins and his team descended from hills about forty miles northwest of Pittsburgh, forded the Ohio, entered the territory with chains, compasses, transits, and levels, and with Harmar's military protection began what became the famous Seven Ranges Survey. With patents and lots laid out on paper, and squatters evicted, the Northwest Territory might be turned into real estate, an asset ready for well-managed development.

Crucial to developing that asset, of course, was management of western Indians. In 1784, not long after the Indians at Sandusky pledged unity in seeking a just peace with the United States, the Congress appointed three commissioners to meet with as many Indian nations as possible and arrive as quickly as possible at a new treaty. Reflecting realities that Congress believed had emerged from U.S. victory over the British, this treaty was to establish new rules for white-Indian relations and set out new locations for Indian habitation, not only in the Northwest Territory, but also in the Six Nations regions to the east.

One of the commissioners was Richard Butler of Pennsylvania, the sometime Shawnee friend and translator, a well-regarded expert on Indian affairs. He was joined by Arthur Lee, youngest son of the original Ohio Company founder, and Oliver Wolcott of Connecticut, a signer of the Declaration of Independence. The commissioners sent messages far and wide, calling for a meeting with all of the western Indians and their

Six Nations elder brothers, to begin in September 1784, at Fort Stanwix, on the Mohawk River in New York.

It was there that in 1768 the Six Nations had dealt away Kentucky
and agreed to move the proclamation line west to the Ohio River. Now
Richard Butler and the other commissioners expected the Indians to
concede far more than that.

The Mohawk diplomat Joseph Brant, considering strategy for the upcoming treaty negotiations with American commissioners at Fort Stanwix, believed the best Indian tactic would be to show the united front
he'd called for at the Sandusky conference. But many of the militant
western Indians of the Blue Jacket–Little Turtle party expressed skepticism about gaining any fair outcome from a meeting with the United
States. They had promises of British support from the unevacuated
forts on the lakes, and the British superintendent of Indian affairs, John
Johnson, had even issued Blue Jacket a commission: it named him an
official war leader and instructed other Indians to follow him. Johnson's
seal and signature were on the document, and Blue Jacket took care of
it. He and the other hard-liners felt they had the backing to ignore the
American invitation.

Brant wheedled and pressured them, and he achieved significant
support for the peace effort when many western delegates, including
some of the serious hard-liners, did arrive at Fort Stanwix in the fall of
1784, mistrustful yet ready to negotiate. But Richard Butler and the
other commissioners were late. Exact timing was never a feature of convening a meeting this big. Still, after a few weeks, most of the western
Indians left Fort Stanwix in disgust: winter was coming, and they had
long distances to travel. When Butler and the other commissioners did
at last arrive, they found mainly only the Six Nations delegates in attendance, and while the commissioners had hoped to treat with as many
nations as possible and get this job done all at once, they went ahead
anyway. After the usual days of partying and solemnities, they opened
the proceedings, in buildings newly constructed for the purpose.

The commissioners began by reading aloud the treaty signed by the
Americans and the British in Paris. All land south of the new boundary
with Quebec, the commissioners informed the delegates, had been

ceded by the British to the United States, which now held sole sovereignty there. The Indians were thus a defeated and subject people, and the Americans had come to let them know the terms of surrender to the United States.

Brant and the other Six Nations delegates sat stunned. This wasn't a treaty negotiation among sovereign entities at war. This was a proceeding for the unconditional surrender of the Indians.

A key article of this surrender, the commissioners went on, would be renunciation by the Six Nations Iroquois, and by all other Indian nations and branches, of their claims on western land formerly reserved for Indians by the old Fort Stanwix Treaty of 1768, hereby superseded. The western Indians not present at this meeting must henceforth live peacefully within new, smaller regions, behind a boundary to be dictated by the United States and drawn much farther west and north than the old royal proclamation line at the Ohio River.

The Six Nations must also make amends for allying with the British during the war. They were to renounce claims not only to the West but also to their own living space in the East. All of the Iroquois were now to be confined to set-aside regions in New York and Pennsylvania, with the exact extent of the regions to be negotiated separately with those states. The great longhouse would be broken up.

Finally, given the absence at this meeting of western delegates, the Six Nations must stipulate to being the sole entity empowered to negotiate and conclude a peace on behalf of all Indians, those in the West and even some from the South. Agreement to these conditions must be made by the Iroquois on behalf of the Ottawa, Chippewa, Huron, Potawatomie, Miami, Delaware, Cherokee, Chickasaw, and Creek. Indian submission was universal, and it was up to the Six Nations to let the others know.

Butler and the other commissioners did take a moment to explain the urgency behind these dictates. The great growth of the American people, and the need to settle war veterans, meant the United States needed to use the land.

Joseph Brant walked out, taking some of the delegates with him. Those who remained at the meeting, shell-shocked, did sign the new treaty.

A rift in the Indian position thus opened, with fateful consequences. The Seneca Cornplanter was perhaps the best-known signer of the new Fort Stanwix Treaty, and the western hard-liners, hearing of his compliance, expressed outrage. At the Sandusky meeting only months before, all of the western nations and all of the Six Nations had agreed to act together—nobody could sign away territory without confederation approval—and the westerners hadn't even been present at the Fort Stanwix event: to them, the new treaty was illegitimate on its face. Having fought perhaps the hardest against the United States during the war, Cornplanter received special treatment. The Americans gave him a nice grant beside the Allegheny River in Pennsylvania. And while Joseph Brant had walked out and refused to sign, his inability to prevent Cornplanter's signing exposed, in westerners' eyes, the limits of Brant's and the Six Nations' power.

Two years later, Six Nations leaders would refuse to ratify the treaty that Cornplanter and the others signed at Fort Stanwix. Refuse as they might after the fact, to the western hard-liners the Six Nations simply looked defeated. The growing western confederation led by militants like Blue Jacket and Little Turtle was less and less inclined to trust the Iroquois, more assertive about defeating moderation among their own people, and increasingly eager to continue the long war against incursion by the United States.

To Richard Butler and the other commissioners, however, the Fort Stanwix Treaty looked like a job well done. They had signatures from delegates of some of the most powerful Iroquois nations—overlords, in white terms, of the western Indians—and while the commissioners hadn't wanted to make treaties with nations separately, now they thought the approach might be strategic: divide and conquer.

So in 1785, at Fort McIntosh, a new fort on the Ohio near Pittsburgh, U.S. commissioners imposed similar terms, this time on certain western Indians. These were cowed delegates of some branches of the Delaware and Wyandot, and again they acted in the absence of confederation attendance. For this meeting, the American commissioners even declined to travel up to the mouth of the Cuyahoga at Lake Erie, where most of these Indians lived, but insisted the Indians travel to Fort

McIntosh, and at the meeting the commissioners cited not only the Peace of Paris but also the new Fort Stanwix Treaty, as signed by Cornplanter and others: to the Americans, that treaty now served as precedent. They granted the Delaware and Wyandot a small reserve near the lake.

Again the few attendees signed. Again the signers thereby isolated themselves from the main body of the confederation. Again the commissioners scored their own efforts a success.

They scheduled one more meeting, the last they'd ever need, Richard Butler thought. This time the meeting was to be with the Shawnee and Miami. Those two nations, Butler knew, were at the core of the western confederation, its most militant members, and remained on a serious war footing with the United States.

So for this one, the commissioners did travel. In the fall of 1785, they came far down the Ohio to a point just past the mouth of the Great Miami. They had Josiah Harmar's troops do some quick blockhouse building there, including a dedicated meetinghouse, and that became Fort Finney. The commissioners had to wait in that spartan outpost for months. A few Indian delegates slowly came in, and it wasn't until late January 1786 that the commissioners finally had their say. Only a small group was there to listen, mainly a branch of somewhat moderate Shawnee, bucking the confederation's wishes even by showing up.

These Shawnee moderates were conflicted. Resisting hard-liners like Blue Jacket, they hoped for a fair deal with the United States, yet they knew what had happened in the earlier meetings. The two most important leaders here were Captain Johnny, seven feet tall and in the eyes of some Americans as ugly as he was huge, and until now a militant—he'd lambasted signers of earlier treaties—and Moluntha, a true moderate, elderly friend of Americans and husband of Nonhelema, "the Chieftess." Butler, again serving as an American commissioner, was reputedly another of Nonhelema's husbands, and that might bode well for gaining some understanding, but George Rogers Clark, the Kentucky raider, was serving as a commissioner too. He was perhaps the Shawnee's worst enemy, and not one they were inclined to respect.

So even the American commissioners had to admit that this meeting didn't go as smoothly as they thought the others had. They took the same position as in earlier meetings, announcing a new reserve for the Shawnee and Miami: lands well north of the Ohio, west of the headwaters of the Cuyahoga and Muskingum Rivers and east of Fort Detroit. That would remove the Indians' access to the Ohio and the lakes and, should the United States ever take over Detroit, put them under American guns.

The gigantic Captain Johnny pointed out angrily that the land was actually all Indian. Butler could tell the younger leaders were especially ready to fight. One of them ended an impassioned speech of defiance by placing a string of beads on the table. The beads were black. That meant war.

Butler rose, picked up the string of beads, and dashed it against the table. He walked out. Clark leaped up and used his cane to push the string off the table. Deliberately stepping on it, he followed Butler out of the meetinghouse.

The display seemed effective. Two days later, the Indian delegates signed the treaty. Moluntha, the aged moderate, feared American reprisal; Captain Johnny's motives would remain forever mysterious. In any event, the moment those men signed the treaty, any status they might have enjoyed among their confederation peers evaporated. Richard Butler, at times a Shawnee friend, had in the process exposed himself in the eyes of the western Indian confederation as an enemy on the order of George Rogers Clark.

To Butler and Clark, the western Indians had now been pacified, the Northwest Territory secured. Their work here was done.

The misconception quickly became obvious. The pause in fighting that the militants had grudgingly agreed to at Sandusky in 1783 ended abruptly with the Fort Finney Treaty. To the dismay of the Congress and states that had sent the commissioners to dictate peace, the woodland now exploded with violence. Parties of confederation militants raided Kentucky settlements, slaughtered travelers on Ohio flatboats, and threatened the American forts near the Mississippi. Soon George Rogers Clark was back in business, crossing the Ohio with militias from Kentucky to raid Shawnee towns. Amid fallout from the treaties, both sides' rhetoric now invoked total extermination.

The Mad River towns where Blue Jacket had moved came under attack in October 1786, when a massive Kentucky militia, with leaders including the well-known frontiersmen Boone and Kenton, crossed the Ohio under the militia commander Benjamin Logan and moved north-ward, traveling upstream along the Great Miami. Seeing mounted Ken-tuckians galloping across a prairie toward their town, inhabitants began fleeing, but the riders fell on them, killing and taking prisoners.

Moluntha lived here too. Too old to run, he surrendered to the ma-rauding Kentuckians with his wives and children, walking toward them carrying a large peace pipe and pointing to his house. Though discred-ited with the Blue Jacket party for signing the Fort Finney Treaty, he was respected for his age and openly flew the American flag there. His wife Nonhelema was captured too, and the Kentuckians formed a deep circle around the prisoners.

Moluntha was passing tobacco around when one of the captains pushed his way through the crowd and confronted him. The man de-manded to know whether Moluntha had fought at Blue Licks, that great Shawnee victory over the Kentuckians four years before. Moluntha, not understanding and trying to placate the man, nodded affirmatively in a friendly way. The captain drew a small ax, knocked the Shawnee to the ground with its butt, then hacked into Moluntha's head and took his scalp.

It was against orders. The captain would be convicted of murder. That didn't matter. The killing of a moderate Shawnee, an old man who had rejected militancy in the interest of peace and signed a bad deal with the Americans: that tale served as inducement to militant recruitment.

Logan's men also systematically demolished the Mad River towns, and Blue Jacket withdrew yet again. It was plain that he needed to get his operation even farther into the interior. Moving northward from the Mad River, he went all the way up to Kekionga, the Miami heartland, where his fellow hard-liner Little Turtle now served as war leader. The militant Shawnee branches quickly built new towns near the rolling fruit trees and spreading cornfields around the headwaters of the Miami of the Lake. The Americans' treaty process had brought about utter coales-cence of the western militants, under the two most effective war lead-ers, Blue Jacket and Little Turtle. Miami, Shawnee, and Delaware were now living and planning for war together at the breadbasket and head-quarters Kekionga.

In 1786, the Kekionga militants gave both their own moderates and the United States an ultimatum. In the biggest conference since the Sandusky meeting, many nations convened at Fort Detroit, in collaboration with the British troops still holding that fort. Alexander McKee was again in attendance, and the mere fact of British sponsorship gave a strong hint of British army support for the hard-line Indian position. The militants told the moderates that none of the treaties made since 1783 were valid. The boundary between white and Indian land must forever be the Ohio River, as per the old Fort Stanwix Treaty of 1768.

Though made in uncompromising terms, even that ultimatum involved a big concession. The Shawnee were at last resigned to the fact that Kentucky had been lost for good and could not feasibly be retaken. Too, the confederation was stipulating now to the boundary line's having moved westward from the crest of the Appalachians, where George III had originally placed it, to the Ohio. A return to the terms of the old Fort Stanwix Treaty, in 1768 so seemingly onerous that it had inspired the Shawnee to make war, was all that even the most militant hard-liners were demanding now.

With those compromises in mind, the confederation sent the Congress an official letter, signed by many leaders of many nations. Denying the validity of all of the treaties signed without confederation permission, the unified nations asked the United States for a new meeting to set, for the first time with due process, the real, agreed-upon boundaries of Indian country and arrive at a peaceful conclusion of the war. That letter arrived in Philadelphia in the spring of 1787.

That letter was received and reviewed by Arthur St. Clair, just appointed by Congress to a new office, Governor of the Northwest Territory. St. Clair's appointment coincided with the opening of proceedings that would become famous as the Constitutional Convention, with General Washington presiding. The coinciding events weren't coincidences. St. Clair exemplified the ethos favored by Washington and the most focused delegates to the Constitutional Convention: ending the confederation of American states and creating an American nation.

Others dissented. Some of the nationalists' oldest friends in the

Revolution, Patrick Henry for one, remained antinationalist, partisans of state sovereignty. Henry was still committed to Virginia first and foremost. Accusing the nationalists of betraying hard-won liberties of the states, he boycotted the convention.

But men like Washington, other Virginians like James Madison and Edmund Randolph, the New Yorker Alexander Hamilton, the Pennsylvanians Robert Morris and Arthur St. Clair, and many others envisioned immense new opportunities arising from an interstate economy that might operate in partnership with a government empowered to make laws obligating and benefiting citizens throughout all states. The nationalists remained state partisans too—Washington invested in canal and other projects he hoped would favor him and Virginia—but in the military union for independence, and in American financiers' investment in that effort, they'd identified a potential for dynamic growth: high finance wedded to ambitious public projects. Key to that vision was well-organized continental expansion. Combining big investment with development of that rich, untapped western land, and ultimately creating new western states there, the nationalists hoped to establish a growing commercial empire to rival those of the great powers.

The old desire for the West had thus changed form. It was no longer purely individual, or even purely corporate. The early investors who became American revolutionaries had hoped to possess land beyond the settled regions of the colonies in order to gain wealth through buying and selling it for settlement and planting. Thinking on a grander scale now, they wanted to push the union originally formed for war beyond its original borders and into the West, achieving for the United States a physical and economic greatness never before imagined, firing new engines of growth, gaining greater and more lasting forms of wealth, surpassing their European forebears.

This national amplification of some of the investors' original goals regarding western land involved some unexpected shifts. The institution of slavery, for example, was prohibited in the Northwest Territory by ordinance. Southern tobacco growers viewed the states one day to be founded in the territory as future competitors. The South would therefore support territorial ordinances only on the condition that big-scale tobacco cultivation be made prohibitively difficult there. Banning slavery did that, and nothing better showed the morphing of western land investors from tobacco men into real-estate men than their ready toleration of that ban. Washington himself had been out of the tobacco business since 1766: the crop diversification on which he was basing his hopes for profit at Mount Vernon offered far greater sustainability, and he hoped one day to end his plantations' dependence on slave labor. The great natural resource north of the Ohio, land itself, might expand the country through similarly multifarious enterprise.

Nor did slaveholders have any reason to fear that the ban in the territory augured some federal effort to end slavery altogether. Only five of thirteen states had yet ended the institution; it persisted as well in new public domains south of the Ohio River, Kentucky and Tennessee. Neither the Articles of Confederation nor the Constitution soon to supersede them empowered anybody to outlaw slavery. To underscore that fact, a new ordinance provided for the capture and return of enslaved Africans who might cross the Ohio seeking freedom.

What all nationalists, slaveholders and otherwise, did object to, regarding the territory, was some disorganized flood of settlement. Washington and other veteran western land investors had taken to disparaging late-coming hopefuls as "speculators," "land-jobbers," just what the British had called the Washington cohort. And indeed, Washington's own western buying was by now more or less complete. Among the Revolutionary veterans were thousands of potential buyers and tenants, and Washington was hoping for sales. That plan required clear title, demonstrable security, legal and orderly processes, and the right conditions on the ground. Public land in the Northwest must go to companies capable of establishing major settlements, creating stability, and attracting the millions of buyers and settlers, both American and foreign, whose labor would clear the forests and gain the investors hefty returns by advancing the United States westward.

Some believed the westward advance might one day embrace the entire continent. With the approval of the Congress's secretary of war Henry Knox, Josiah Harmar carried out a covert American operation to explore beyond the legal boundaries of the United States, sending Lieutenant John Armstrong across the Mississippi into Spanish territory. While Armstrong's secret mission didn't get very far, nationalists would persist in their old habit of taking boundary lines for temporary inconveniences.

So when Arthur St. Clair reviewed the Indian confederation's letter calling all treaties invalid and asking for a meeting to set a real boundary, he'd
already begun overseeing and securing government-certified investment
and development north of the Ohio, vanguard of the national project. As
a man of the headwaters and a committed nationalist, he was perhaps
uniquely qualified to carry out his mission.

Born in Scotland in the 1730s, St. Clair had served as an officer under
Jeffrey Amherst against the French in Nova Scotia and risen to lieutenant
in the British capture of Quebec. Notably thin and good-looking as a
young man, with long chestnut hair, he'd resigned his commission at the
end of the Seven Years' War and gained lucrative appointments from Philadelphia to carry the province's administration westward. With money
from his father-in-law, he bought four hundred acres west of the Alleghenies, just east of Fort Pitt, and soon became the largest Pennsylvania
landholder around the Ohio headwaters. St. Clair operated plantations
and commercial mills, invested in the fur trade, and served as the chief
provincial official for bringing Pennsylvania's government, in competition with Virginia's, to the disputed and disorganized headwaters scene.

Like young Washington the dedicated Virginian, the young St. Clair
mingled personal and provincial ambition. The running of the royal
proclamation line, and then the passage of the Quebec Act, impinged
painfully on St. Clair's and Pennsylvania's efforts to establish themselves
at the headwaters. Virginia impinged painfully on those efforts too.
Hostility prevailed between St. Clair and the Virginians who occupied
Fort Pitt during Lord Dunmore's War in 1774.

And yet in 1776 St. Clair accepted a colonel's commission under
Dunmore's former Virginia colleague Washington in the Continental
army. Commanding the Third Pennsylvania Regiment, St. Clair took part
in the failed American invasion of Quebec, received promotion to the
rank of major general after the Battle of Princeton, and was at Yorktown
in 1781 for the British surrender. In that military context, he became an
American, with a western vision no longer parochial but national, even
imperial. After the war, he served as a Pennsylvania delegate to the
Congress, then became its president, and now he'd accepted its lucrative
appointment as governor of the territory.

Now, having reviewed the confederation's letter, St. Clair determined to lead a final round of discussions. He would not rely on claims of American conquest. Instead, on orders from a committee of the Congress, consistent with General Washington's advice—soon to become President Washington's policy—to avoid western Indian war, St. Clair planned to buy the land from the Indians. With purchase now in mind, the governor invited members of the western Indian confederation to a meeting scheduled for the fall of 1788 to address any issues that had arisen during the treaty process. The extremes of confidence that St. Clair brought to this meeting would lead directly, if unpredictably, to his disastrous defeat at the Wabash in 1791.

In scheduling this meeting to end all meetings, St. Clair chose a location that the Indians considered in itself an outright attack: a fort that Josiah Harmar had built and named for himself on the north bank of the Ohio, thus establishing American military presence within the disputed region. Here at the mouth of a south-flowing Ohio tributary called the Muskingum, the American flag flew high over a broad swath of ground opening on vistas of flowing water. Across the Ohio from Fort Harmar lay far-western Virginia and then, farther downstream, Kentucky, and from the fort one could observe the land rush on a more or less hourly basis: maybe ten thousand people per month, legal and illegal, steering flatboats, barges, and canoes crammed with families, luggage, livestock, and boatmen. And Fort Harmar gave protection to another aggressive project, both cause and effect of St. Clair's appointment as governor, his major purpose in governing: the first real-estate development certified by the Congress for the Northwest Territory.

This was Marietta. Also on the north bank of the Ohio, directly across the Muskingum from Fort Harmar, a new Ohio Company—not Virginians this time, but New Englanders, under the veteran Revolutionary officer Rufus Putnam, among others—had cleared ground and built a town. Putnam was a close associate of George Washington's. The company's partners had accompanied Thomas Hutchins in making his surveys, helped write the Congress's new ordinance for the territory, and backed the appointment of Arthur St. Clair as governor. They signed contracts with the United States granting them 1.5 million acres north of the Ohio for $1 million in federal war-debt instruments, when the worth of those certificates had fallen to only about 12 percent of face value. The original idea had been to sell western land for $1 per acre. That would have brought the Congress significant public revenue. In the Marietta sale, however, the Congress's willingness to accept its own paper instead of gold, that paper's deep depreciation, and a one-third discount thrown in to cover any losses to the buyers arising from bad land pushed the real public revenue down to about nine cents per acre, a sweet deal for the company, which also received in the transaction an exclusive option to buy, on similar terms, everything west of its Muskingum tract down to the mouth of the Scioto, in the end a total of about 5 million acres. The company's support for St. Clair's appointment was rewarded as well when, as governor, he appointed two of the company's directors to the lucrative civil positions of territorial judge and territorial secretary.

"The greatest private contract ever made in America," Putnam's partner Manasseh Cutler called the deal. St. Clair himself owned more than a thousand acres of the company's grant. Colonel Harmar became a shareholder too. In the new public domain the Northwest Territory, now under proto-national management, American government and American enterprise were one.

The partners named the settlement on the Muskingum after Marie Antoinette, queen of France. Though protected by Fort Harmar, Marietta had its own militia: the settlers drilled on ground the founders named Campus Martius, after the Field of Mars in ancient Rome. On July 4, 1787, the fort gave a salute, and soldiers at Fort Harmar crossed the Muskingum to join families and single men from New England under big trees on the riverbank. After a feast, they drank toasts to the United States—the new Constitution was even then being debated—and to all mankind. American expansion, in advance of and inspiring American nationhood, was under way at last.

The western Indians observed this flagrant incursion north of the Ohio River with a growing certainty that they had no alternative but to continue the war. For there was worse news yet. Another north-bank American post, Fort Washington, had just been completed, even farther into Indian country, a good hundred miles down the Ohio River from Fort Harmar. Near the mouths of the Great and Little Miami tributaries, Fort Washington stood on high, cleared ground overlooking the Ohio, and it was even bigger and stronger than Fort Harmar, the best post ever built on the river, Harmar boasted, with buildings two stories high and two-story blockhouses on the corners.

And Fort Washington too was dedicated to the protection of a north-bank settlement. This enterprise had a grant from Congress smaller than Marietta's but still, at one million acres, significant, and St. Clair enhanced its significance: the new settlement's position, effectively half-way between the Pittsburgh headwaters and the Ohio's mouth at the Mississippi, made it the ideal spot for his gubernatorial headquarters. St. Clair named the settlement Cincinnati, after the hereditary organi-zation of the Revolutionary officer class, with reference both to the re-publican virtue of Cincinnatus of ancient Rome—the general who declined power, retiring to his farm after leading troops to victory—and to the man known as the American Cincinnatus, George Washington. The United States had now projected itself farther into the woodland than the great man himself had ever gone.

To the western Indians invited to meet at Fort Harmar, in full view of the building of Marietta, and painfully conscious of Fort Washington and Cincinnati downstream, all of this fortification and development amounted to naked military aggression in the very territory whose future they were supposedly being invited to discuss. And yet at a pre-meeting for the Fort Harmar gathering, Joseph Brant, still hoping to maintain himself and the Six Nations as go-betweens, suggested the western Indians make one last compromise in favor of the United States. Brant proposed setting a new boundary, at the mouth of the Muskingum where Marietta now lay. That would shift Indian country westward, opening a great swath of the Ohio Country to further Ameri-can settlement, and making Marietta legal, and it was the kind of idea that made the militants wonder if Brant had finally become truly use-less. Some Wyandot of the Sandusky Bay region, however, favored the Brant compromise. There were still moderates in the confederation, hop-ing further accommodation might lead to a decent deal for a permanent boundary against white encroachment.

Between the moderates and the Blue Jacket–Little Turtle hard-liners,

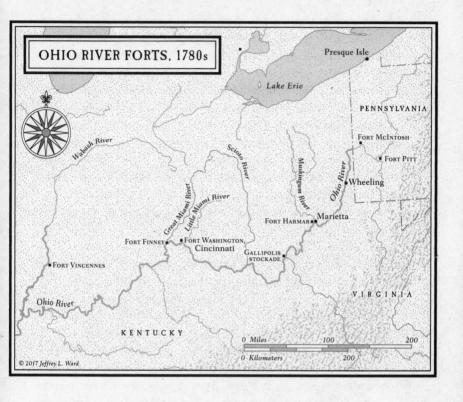

OHIO RIVER FORTS, 1780s

Presque Isle

Lake Erie

PENNSYLVANIA

FORT McINTOSH

FORT PITT

Wabash River

Scioto River

Muskingum River

Ohio River

Wheeling

FORT HARMAR   Marietta

FORT FINNEY   FORT WASHINGTON,
Cincinnati

GALLIPOLIS
STOCKADE

FORT VINCENNES

Great Miami River

Little Miami River

VIRGINIA

Ohio River

KENTUCKY

0 Miles   100   200

0 Kilometers   200

© 2017 Jeffrey L. Ward

conflict was worsening. At this pre-meeting, a group of Wyandot held out a long bead belt to the Miami delegation. They asked the Miami to take the other end as a sign of unity in seeking compromise with the United States at Fort Harmar. The Miami refused. A Wyandot delegate took the belt and placed it on Little Turtle's shoulder. Little Turtle shrugged it off. The belt fell to the ground. The Wyandot moderates walked out of the meeting.

Still Brant pushed for compromise, and somehow he managed to drag out of the militants an agreement to cede, at the very most, those chunks of land already settled around Marietta—if, that is, the Americans would negotiate the rest of the West in good faith. Given the extremity of that compromise, the Indians wanted a compromise in return: a change of location for the meeting. They proposed to meet not at Fort Harmar, that heavily fortified U.S. position built illegally on their land, but in the forest some ways up the Muskingum. Agreeing to that change would show American good faith.

Getting these concessions from the militants had cost Brant a lot of effort and risk to his status, but now he had reason to hope that in the face of U.S. recklessness in building and fortifying the north bank, and in the face of understandably stiff resistance by western hard-liners, he might be wresting peace from a faulty diplomatic process. So via his son, he sent a letter to St. Clair at Fort Harmar, asking the governor to consider, as an advance concession, the Indian offer to allow some white settlement in the Marietta region. And he asked for the change of venue for the discussions.

St. Clair sent word right back to Brant. The whole proposition was altogether inadmissible, St. Clair stated, and he indignantly accused the Indian confederation of acting under British control. He rejected out of hand both the compromise boundary and the change of location. The meeting would take place at Fort Harmar, St. Clair declared, where the United States would, once and for all, purchase all of the land over which it had sovereignty and designate a reasonable reserve for the Indians.

That was it for Joseph Brant. He determined to boycott the Fort Harmar meeting. He'd been talking with British officials in Fort Niagara about a new plan anyway. He might bring some of the Mohawk, and maybe others of the Six Nations, into British-held territory north of the new border. Many Iroquois were living there already, refugees from the American

campaigns that had destroyed their towns. Making such a move permanent would divide the Six Nations' centuries-old confederation; still,
St. Clair's rigidity amplified Brant's desire to get his people onto British soil.

Brant advised the western Indians to boycott the Fort Harmar meeting too. Already uneasy with his attempted compromises, they needed
no advice from Brant to stay away, and it might have come as no surprise
when only about two hundred Indians showed up at Fort Harmar in
the December chill for St. Clair's be-all-end-all treaty-and-purchase
process. They were mainly Seneca—American aligned already—along
with the moderate Wyandot and some Delaware with weakening ties
to the militant confederation.

St. Clair moved briskly forward, greeting the few Indian attendees
with the usual solemnities. The commissioners this time were himself,
Butler, and Harmar. They began by announcing to the few Indian delegates that the American effort to conquer Indian land was over. The
United States instead now formally recognized the Indians' right to sell
the land. Because the United States was sovereign, however, the Indians
must sell to the United States, and sell now, and for that purpose St. Clair
had brought $23,000. Upon sale, certain lands would be reserved for
the Indians west of the headwaters of the Cuyahoga and Muskingum
Rivers and east of Fort Detroit.

That reserve was identical to the one in the Fort Finney Treaty that
had restarted the war. It would push the Miami and Shawnee well north
of the Ohio, squeezing them into less than half the living space they'd
accepted when moving the boundary line from the crest of the Appalachians to the river. It flew in the face of every confederation demand. But
the hard-line western Indians weren't here to argue about it, and when
the few Indians at the meeting did sign the Fort Harmar accords, St. Clair
was able to report to the Congress that the rebellious confederation was
broken, the land legally bought and secured.

The first full-scale military collaboration of Blue Jacket and Little Turtle had a somewhat hasty and impromptu quality. It came in 1790, in
response to a march of fifteen hundred American troops, under Josiah
Harmar, from Fort Washington on the Ohio River all the way up to

Kekionga to destroy it. The United States was newly a nation, and this military effort, though not large, was its first.

St. Clair, Harmar, and Henry Knox had been planning an operation like this even before the Fort Harmar meeting. One purpose of that meeting had been to isolate what they saw as the few remaining banditti holding out at Kekionga and then awe them with a punitive raid, burning and looting their towns and crops in the old manner of the Revolution. As St. Clair and Knox eagerly pitched this idea to their new boss, George Washington—he'd been inaugurated as president in April 1789 even as they were making their plans—the expedition would amount to a low-risk "flying strike," a mop-up. The main body of the western Indians, they reported to the president, had been brought into agreement with the United States via the Fort Harmar Treaty. A flying strike would demolish a weak resistance with little expense, enforcing the treaty's accords and demonstrating the security of the settlements. Harmar was simply to destroy the banditti center of operations at the headwaters of the Miami of the Lake and come back to Fort Washington, having tamped down any potential for flare-up, thus preventing war.

On that basis, the president authorized the expedition, and the new U.S. Congress funded it. But getting the operation together sounded easier than it was, and thanks to some chaotic planning Harmar couldn't advance until October. Miami and Shawnee leaders at Kekionga faced problems too. Viewing the Fort Harmar Treaty as the last straw, an outright act of war in itself, they'd been waiting for an invasion and expecting a fight, but fall hunting season gave them little time to gather the massed force of the confederation to resist Harmar's invasion. Runners went out, but while response was enthusiastic, it was slow.

The Kekionga towns were quickly and efficiently evacuated. Women and children and the elderly were sent northward; traders carted away their supplies. Then the fighters burned their main Miami town to give the invading army no shelter there, a common tactic. They disappeared into the woods to observe and consider Harmar's maneuvers.

When the American advance force arrived, it found the biggest town empty and smoldering. Meanwhile, Indian reinforcements began quietly arriving and tracking Harmar's moves as the Americans looted the entire Kekionga complex. The troops were given free rein to destroy. They burned the remaining towns, seemingly heedless of Indian presence nearby. Corn, buildings, and fruit trees were demolished. Years of records in the form of bead belts were destroyed in the process. Little Turtle and Blue Jacket and their forces kept watching. They noted that Harmar had little control over his men and let his units get spread out. In pursuit of greater destruction, he kept dividing his army, some going down to the Shawnee towns at Chillicothe, others heading west to the Eel River. Patiently, over days, the Indians silently and invisibly surrounded the whole strung-out operation.

At last a Shawnee party surprise-attacked a Kentucky mounted unit and forced it to retreat. The Kentuckians launched a retaliatory operation, and the Indians killed dozens of them and sent the rest fleeing. Meanwhile, American detachments moving on the Eel River towns met Little Turtle's fighters. The few American regulars had been heavily filled in by hastily recruited militia, and facing Little Turtle's forces, the militiamen bolted, running back into the regulars who were trying to hold a line. The American advance had become a rout.

Harmar understood what was happening. These weren't banditti. This was a large and highly organized force. With 183 men dead and missing, he withdrew down the Great Miami toward Fort Washington on the Ohio. That was the end of the flying strike. Harmar had accomplished his mission: he'd burned and plundered the towns.

Accomplishing the mission meant nothing. The effort was seen as a national embarrassment, and Washington, choosing to blame Harmar, suggested without any basis that the officer had a drinking problem. Harmar, the lifetime army man, stickler for procedure, would bitterly resign his commission in 1791 and demand a court of inquiry into his conduct. He'd be cleared, but the damage to his reputation was done. History would not be kind to Josiah Harmar.

The follow-up mission, a much larger and more serious operation, was expected to relieve the national embarrassment caused by Harmar's supposed incompetence and put the matter to rest for good and all. To that end, Arthur St. Clair himself assumed direct command. Before St. Clair left, President Washington had him over to the President's House, took him into the parlor, and gave him a single warning. Beware a surprise.

The youngest Butler brother, Edward, and three soldiers were taking turns in teams hauling the wounded Thomas Butler over frozen, deeply rutted mud when Edward realized something else was wrong with Thomas. It was November 5, 1791, and having left their elder brother Richard with two pistols under a great oak, they'd been moving away as quickly as possible, in this difficult fashion, from the horrifying scene of Indian victory over St. Clair.

Edward took a moment now to stop and assess his brother's condition. Blood was gushing from the other leg. Mangled too, it had been wounded by a shot. Thomas seemed on the verge of passing out.

Edward whipped off his coat and then his shirt and used the shirt to apply pressure to Thomas's leg. There was no time to lose, and their halting progress soon resumed, but every step caused the wounded man to cry out, and soon he was begging his carriers to leave him on the ground to die. Edward, too young to have served in the War of Independence, had become perhaps the toughest of the Butler men, and he had his orders from the doomed Richard: save our brother. The party kept moving.

Around them, in pain, fear, shock, and exhaustion, a long line of beaten men was moving south in chaos on the rough forest road their expedition had so recently cut, felling big trees parallel to the course of the Great Miami on the march northward only days before. They'd advanced in four columns, spread out through the woods, pack animals and baggage trains and artillery on this cut track in the middle. Now they were fleeing down the track, without shoes, on wet ice, their feet numb and bloody. They'd left comrades at the scene of battle with chopped-off limbs, hacked scalps, one man with his head on fire, a woman impaled.

In the retreat, the sole surviving woman could no longer carry her baby. She set the child down on the trail and stumbled forward, weeping. Some men veered wildly, heads caked with drying blood: they'd been scalped yet remained alive. Some crawled. The few remaining horses strained under two and three men each. Almost all were unarmed: men sprinting headlong out of the carnage had thrown down their heavy muskets. Those who could move faster were doing so still, running and pushing the others in hopes of ensuring a getaway. Nobody knew whether the victors were following in order to finish the job.

Suddenly out of the woods and onto the road crashed a group of men, also bewildered. This was a unit that St. Clair had assigned, in the last desperate moments of defeat, to serve as a rear guard for protecting the withdrawal. The officer in charge had become separated from his men, and they'd scattered into the woods, lost, and had only found the road by chance. So there was no rear guard. The whole train was defense-less. Should even a small party of the enemy force come alongside them, there might be literally no survivors of the failed advance. The United States, so recently formed, had achieved no effective military advances, and this was its first great retreat.

But it wasn't a retreat in the military sense, General St. Clair saw, not a maneuver, but outright flight. He had nothing to ride but an old, plodding packhorse. No longer for years now the lithe, chestnut-haired striver, St. Clair was obese; he'd been plagued by gout during this mis-sion. Gray hair hanging, coat shredded, aged body near collapse, the general felt anguish with each jounce. He'd been under no illusions about the fitness of the army that he and Henry Knox had hastily re-cruited for this operation, really just a hodgepodge of militia and volun-teers on short-term enlistments, with some new regulars and a remnant of Harmar's small regular force. St. Clair was an old soldier, and he knew this kind of army added up to a mess, yet he'd been sure that even a force as mangy as this one could defeat the Indians of Kekionga and build a fort there. Now all he could do was try to get his few surviving men out of here without further disaster.

Southward the army's remnant stumbled and limped and crawled and ran, and finally that afternoon those up front began arriving at the forward post they'd built only a month before. This small, bare log struc-ture had little to offer. A regiment of fresh troops was here: they'd never made it to the battle scene and could provide some fallback defense. Yet there was no medical staff or equipment, and the barely completed pick-eted enclosure was only ten feet by ten. Still eighty miles north of the Fort Washington headquarters on the Ohio's bank, St. Clair's men fell through the gate of this small and spartan fort, some passing out on its postage-stamp enclosure, others moaning and shouting in pain.

American woodland forts were named for heroes of American inde-pendence and national government. Honoring the theorist of American liberty founded on roving in pursuit of happiness, this was Fort Jefferson.

The retreat paused here. There was nothing else to do.

All afternoon and into the evening the dazed and wounded men kept coming in. St. Clair knew they couldn't stay here. This wasn't a strong fort, just an impromptu post, thrown up during the failed advance. Small outposts like Fort Jefferson depended, literally for life, on heavy, steady supply from behind. In the march forward, big herds of cattle and wagonloads of flour had accompanied the men, but now the fort had only three hundred pounds of flour—one day's ration—and no meat, and the men hadn't been fed for twenty-four hours. Provisions were on the way north from Fort Hamilton, the next post back, but the enemy might soon follow up its victory by surrounding Fort Jefferson and attacking the supply convoy. Then the soldiers would starve, die of their wounds, or be slaughtered in place.

St. Clair had to keep what had once been his army moving toward the Ohio. Even with stragglers still coming in, at ten that night he placed the fresh regiment at the front of a new line and started pushing his troops back through the fort's gate and onto the track. Their only chance now was to go all night, pass Fort Hamilton, and somehow gain Fort Washington. That structure would offer a measure of security: it was large and well built, readily defended and better supplied, with an unwounded garrison left behind for defense, communications upriver all the way to Fort Pitt, and supply from the Cincinnati settlement. The survivors found themselves trudging yet again, in the dark, through cold swamps filled with fallen logs and thick roots. Frigid first light revealed a line strung out for a full five miles, a commander's nightmare, open to easy attack. There was no formation now, no plan beyond keeping moving, resting only as dictated by necessity, and living long enough to get out.

It was slow, and by the time the men arrived at Fort Washington, on November 8 in a cold rain, any sense that this was an army was long gone. Having gained the relative safety of the fort, the men took up drunken anarchy and what under normal circumstances would be called desertion. There was no room here anyway for the number of men who needed shelter. Those who could walk left the fort to carouse in rough and rowdy Cincinnati. The first major military effort of the United States was over. The new nation had no army left.

St. Clair succumbed to exhaustion and pain both physical and emotional. He'd lost 700 people, maybe more, including about 650 officers and men, with most of the officers killed—both Edward and Thomas Butler survived—plus hundreds of wounded. Now, in its flight, he had no army at all. In seclusion, he effectively relinquished command.

He did, however, fulfill his duty by filing a report. On November 9, he wrote Secretary Knox a detailed and straightforward account of the horrible defeat that the United States had just suffered.

So great was St. Clair's anxiety and depression that he couldn't sleep and hardly ate or drank, and as he wrote, he lived on bread and sips of tea. Harmar's failed flying strike had been an embarrassment, but St. Clair's overwhelming defeat, with the total destruction of the American force, was about to become subject to the first congressional investigation ever carried out by the U.S. House of Representatives: what the North Carolina congressman John Steele would call, in February 1792, an inquiry into the causes of the late unfortunate defeat.

As St. Clair sipped tea and wrote in physical and emotional distress, causes eluded him. It wasn't that he couldn't take responsibility. In plain language, he described the failures of his own command. He knew that he and his officers had failed to bring discipline to the troops. The most disgraceful thing, St. Clair reported to Knox, was the craven behavior of the men: because they fled, officers died in droves. He and Knox knew responsibility for that failure lay with the commander.

But St. Clair also insisted he'd been defeated by superior numbers. He admitted to Knox that he couldn't prove that the Indians had fielded more troops than he; still, he was sure they had. Indians could never, he and Knox believed, defeat a European-style army, properly disciplined. While St. Clair knew he lacked that kind of disciplined army, he remained sure that the Indian victory could not, by definition, have come from any superiority other than numerical.

It was not for Arthur St. Clair to uncover the causes of the defeat of the United States in its first big national effort. To do that, he would have had to look back half a century, when the Ohio Company of Virginia made a petition for a grant west of the Alleghenies and George Washington wasn't a member. St. Clair would have had to observe everything in the long, perennially frustrated desire to possess the West through eyes other than his own. He was hardly alone in being incapable of doing that.

He concluded his report and sent it to Knox in Philadelphia. The report arrived late in November, and late in the day, and Knox, though knowing Washington was at dinner, sent the bad news straight over to the President's House.

PART II

WAR DANCING

5

STANDING ARMIES

When he received St. Clair's report, George Washington was the greatest man in the world, if the term meant what George III would mean by it when calling him "the greatest character of the age." Such terms denoted the rare personage who abruptly alters the European sphere beyond all recognition by the creative use of force, thus writing his name on an epoch. That's how they looked at it. There had been Alexander and Julius Caesar and Charlemagne. Soon there would be Napoleon. Unexpectedly, to say the least, now there was Washington.

Greatness had always meant conquest. Because achieving American independence didn't perfectly fulfill that requirement, the achievement was all the greater. Commanding an army not to reconfigure Europe but to develop a new empire on another continent, Washington drove off a superior army and liberated a king's holdings. He presided over the making of a nation on principles of republican liberty beloved by English Whigs, yet heretofore more literary, in European thought, than political. He hadn't only changed the world as they knew it. He'd changed the terms of greatness itself.

Napoleon would reject the whole idea. After failing to take over the world, he would supposedly explain, "They wanted me to be another Washington." He and George III and others were referring to the peculiar thing that gave Washington his greatness: declining to retain power.

It began with giving up army command after the victory over England. Washington didn't keep his army in the field, a move that the enlightened crowned heads found nearly impossible to believe. This was how power should change history, not how power really changed history. The man "returned to his farm," as people liked to say, not a founder of empire like Caesar but a defender of simple republican virtue, like Cincinnatus, who was called twice from his fields to the defense of Rome, instantly relinquishing command after securing victory.

The story got better. In 1789, inaugurated on the balcony of City Hall in New York, unanimous choice of a college of electors for solo executive of the newly founded United States, Washington seemed coaxed by duty back from a bucolic postwar retirement. Always a dresser, he wore the laurel and drapery of civil virtue with conviction. He seemed made for statuary.

Given his lifelong ambitions, however, the reality of the situation he faced with St. Clair's defeat had to feel like a ludicrous disfigurement. Where the nose should be, the dry gash. A regally raised forearm lacking a hand. During the years between resigning his commission and ascending to the presidency, he'd actually been taking constant political and commercial action—for him the two were always intertwined—to gain, develop, and profit by land and to restructure the United States as a nation. He hadn't had to return to his farm, because in a sense he'd never left it: farms were commercial endeavors, and the farm of Washington's imagination and ambition was so big that it embraced the American West. He'd become the greatest man in the world not by trying to become great but in single-minded pursuit of expanding and securing the farm. In that process, the needs of the new republic and the needs of its American Cincinnatus had become one. The country could not do without him.

So as the retired commander in chief, he'd lent savvy and prestige to the presidency of the Potomac Company well before there was anything like a presidency of the United States, hoping to use locks and dredging to get that twisty, resistant river to serve as a placid highway for produce from the West. Informally, he'd advised members of the Congress on Indian policy and evaluated details of the relevant Northwest Ordinances, and given his immense prestige and expertise, informally usually meant decisively. The effect of his influence in retirement had been

noticeable far from Mount Vernon. Even as men under his associate
Rufus Putnam had felled timber and built Marietta on the north side of
the Ohio River, Washington had lent support to the nationalist effort to
dispense with the Articles of Confederation and bring about an American nationhood in part enabled by, in part enabling, westward expansion like the Marietta partners'. Now the United States was a nation,
and he was the president of the United States, his own and his nation's
ambitions identical.

And yet despite the tireless efforts to possess the West in which
he'd come into his own—from poling across the ice-choked Allegheny
to trying to take Fort Duquesne from the French, extending through
ferocious campaigns against the Indians in the War of Independence,
even to presiding over the creation of a United States led by a solo
executive—it had now emerged from St. Clair's report that George
Washington, and the United States in whose survival his own life had
become so fully bound up, had failed in those efforts once again.

This forty-year failure, now abject, even possibly final, had a potential
solution, and Washington had long known what it was. But when it
came to the sole realistic means of achieving success in the West, his
advice, which in other areas equated with his determination, had met
concerted resistance.

The potential solution was to form a real army. While the Constitution made the president the commander in chief of the army, the U.S.
Congress had chosen to make George Washington commander in chief
of pretty much nothing. The United States had no real army, and giving
it one wasn't something the president could do by fiat. On receiving word
of St. Clair's defeat, however, Washington began making a plan. The result would alter the country and the world.

Lack of an army was something he'd inherited. When he took office,
there had still been only the single small regiment in the Northwest Territory under Josiah Harmar, plus those few men at West Point. Harmar's regiment had been temporarily augmented to take Kekionga in the
failed "flying strike," and the force had been augmented again, to take
Kekionga under St. Clair, but only by one more regiment: six hundred

regulars in total. Because no effective operation could be carried out that way, Washington and Knox had been forced to supplement. They'd recruited six hundred militiamen, serving not under federal command but under the men's state governments, and they'd implemented a half measure, permitted only grudgingly by Congress: eight hundred "levies," recruits subject to federal authority yet enlisted only on short terms.

That hodgepodge exemplified the way many Americans believed all national military efforts should forever be staffed: a regular force, if any, kept skeletal and made dependent on short-term recruitment from militias under the various states' commands; plus short-term enlistment of volunteers under the management of Congress, if absolutely necessary, not too many of them at that, and dedicated only to the individual mission. Any military organization bigger and more regular than that, anything standardized under national executive authority, anything persisting in times of peace, revolted the majority in Congress and many American citizens. That would be a standing army.

A standing army. That's what the United States lacked when Washington took office; that's what Congress had still declined to give him. In the Whig rhetoric that had inspired, attended, and justified the War of Independence, the term referred to a tool of tyranny: the professional, full-time soldiery maintained by a monarch at public expense in both war and peace. The British army was a standing army, and its occupation of Boston served as a prime example of how such armies might be used to terrorize citizenry. Recruited, in the standard American view, from the dregs of society and paid as professional soldiers, such troops were hirelings of kings, compelled to go anywhere and do anything a tyrant might demand.

Americans had always relied instead on what they called the militia. Many Americans believed they had, anyway. Technically, the militia was the entire able-bodied, free, white, male citizenry, sixteen to sixty years of age, obligated to serve in the defense of a province. Often self-armed, though also armed and provided with ammunition from public armories, and trained on a regular basis by officers elected, up to a point, by the men, each member of the militia stood ready to serve without pay as a soldier when needed, then return to ordinary activities when a threat was repelled. The virtue of such a system, many had long believed, lay in keeping military activity focused solely on the immediate defense of the citizenry itself. Nobody stood to gain from perpetuating war; service was an obligation of citizenship, not a paid job; thus no colonial governor could impel a soldier to overthrow or threaten representative systems. The militia had become the American idea of how to have an army.

Idea, not reality. By as early as the middle of the eighteenth century, the militia system had fallen into decline. Many provincial militias were prohibited from serving beyond their borders, and because that made it hard to garrison men in forts, scout enemy operations, and stay away from home for extended periods, the colonies adopted a second approach: they began recruiting, drafting, and paying short-term forces—they called it recruiting and drafting from the militia—for the intermittent imperial wars. That's how Lawrence Washington had served under Admiral Vernon, how George Washington had served under General Braddock. In the long offensive maneuvers necessary to making war for empire, paid American forces served as far from home as Cartagena and Quebec.

The enrolled, ordinary militia therefore rarely served in war. It gained little experience in real fighting. British commanders referred to the paid provincial forces as militia only because they'd been drawn from the obligated, supposedly trained force of citizens: the men weren't in that sense full-time regulars but part-time semi-regulars, deployed in a particular action. Often they were draftees, and anyone with money could hire a substitute to fulfill his obligation; even when no formal draft prevailed, there was always the backdoor version, just like the soldiers despised in Whig ideology as hireling dregs. Regular British officers forced to rely on this form of army made "American militia" a term of opprobrium.

And yet as the independent colonies geared up to drive the British out, the freedoms they were fighting for seemed, to many Americans, embodied most nobly in the state-oriented militia system. Just as individual provincial legislatures had sanctioned and commanded their own militias, when the Revolution came, even Continental regulars were raised by the states, per proportion. Early in the war, Virginia, for example, had fifteen infantry regiments ready to serve in the Continental army: they formed the basis of what was called the army's Virginia Line. Virginians assigned to other Continental regiments, reshuffled and moved about throughout the war, remained always Virginian. Then there was the Virginia State Line, which saw action within the state and sometimes adventured outside it. Military power is sovereign power, and the states had declared themselves, in concert, sovereign. Americans who located their freedoms in the representative legislatures that the British had been hampering saw the legislatures' power to recruit from the militia as critical to the freedom they were fighting for.

The inexperienced commander in chief of the Continental army, however, had a different experience of the state-oriented military. George Washington had to cope every day with the miserable effects of the states' failure to pay their apportioned requisitions and the Congress's inability to force them to. He had to deal with the short-term enlistments caused by the states' recruiting systems and the Congress's accommodations to them. Because all troops were fielded both by the federal government and by the states, officers held commissions from two entities. Militiamen expected to elect their own officers and to walk away from conflict, or run, if they didn't like it. Short-term enlistments ended abruptly with major operations under way. Calling the militia into service slowed down farming, curtailing army supply. The soldiers were prone to desertion, drunk, insubordinate, and motivated at times solely by vicious flogging. Command was sometimes impossible to achieve.

In opposition to long-standing American military traditions considered sacred to liberty by many Americans, General Washington condemned the militia system as a mere reed, pernicious in its unreliability. Like his predecessors in the British officer class, he was referring less to the old American idea of local defense, on which he only sometimes had to rely, than to the motley force of poorly motivated, irregular, and semi-regular citizen soldiers, recruited via the states, on which he had to rely all too often. It was the militia, Washington said, that put him in retreat across the Delaware in 1776 to cower at Valley Forge all winter basically undefended. If it weren't for the unmanageability of the militia, he believed, Philadelphia wouldn't have fallen to the British. A permanent force of regulars, uniformly trained, would have ended the war years earlier, Washington was sure, and depending on militia had nearly lost it.

Many other Americans believed the militia system had won the war while avoiding dangers inherent in standing armies, thus making the

Revolution's success exceptionally American. In imagination, the hired soldiery that had really served under Washington mingled with a beloved image of unpaid family-man farmers poised to grab their muskets and go blasting away at grubby, low-life hirelings of necrotic empire. That confusion would prove stubborn.

After the Revolution, those who defended a state-sponsored militia as the best military organization for a free people came at odds with Washington and his political allies on a host of related matters. The group that had become nationalists during the war—Washington, St. Clair, Robert Morris, and the young members of the Congress Alexander Hamilton and James Madison—naturally wanted federal control of the army: to them, economic growth, the military, and nationhood went together. But many of George Washington's Virginia colleagues and competitors in western land speculation had remained antinationalists, state sovereigntists. Patrick Henry, for one, and Richard Henry Lee, for another, were powerful thinkers and speakers and highly organized politicians, crucial to declaring independence, and they too had an interstate lobby, making common cause with fervent state sovereigntists like Elbridge Gerry in Massachusetts and William Maclay in Pennsylvania. For all of their own desire to invest westward, state sovereigntists saw the nationalists' efforts as potentially tyrannical. The Congress must be the states' instrument, as these men saw it, not the other way round, and during the war they'd resisted anything that looked like the federal body's presuming on its war powers to dictate to the states. With victory in the war, they expected the Congress's power to diminish, not grow, leaving the states and their citizens free to enjoy independence as they pleased.

For the nationalists, only warfare thus held the country together, and peace became the problem. The nationalists' worst fears of what peace might bring came true in April 1783, when the New York delegation to the Congress made a signal request. New York wanted to deploy part of its Continental army forces to the British forts in New York, supposedly now to be abandoned by the British army, to keep those forts out of Iroquois hands, under the command of New York.

The nationalists recoiled. States weren't supposed to have their own armies and military goals. All defense was supposed to be mutual, overseen by the Congress. But because nationalists and state sovereigntists alike saw military authority as a sovereign power, why wouldn't New

York, now independent of England, expect to take control of its own military? Why wouldn't any state? Alexander Hamilton, a New Yorker, managed to make that particular application go away, but the scare to the nationalist project was real.

Young Hamilton was even then coming into his own as the most energetic and brilliant of the nationalists, with a strong interest in the connections between national finance and national military power. Anything but the planter type whose goals had informed the young Washington's ambitions, Hamilton was an up-and-coming New York City lawyer, having arrived from the Caribbean only in 1773, with few connections and soaring ambition. He had insights unique in the American governing class regarding the interrelationships of the military and financial spheres in the booming commercial American empire that he, Washington, and others now hoped to promote. In Hamilton's view, a concentration of wealth in public credit, necessary to national growth because it yokes financial power to state power, and a concentration of military power in a federal army, necessary to national defense and adventure, might reinforce each other, enabling the pursuit of a commercial empire to rival that of Great Britain. Nationalism, that is, needed a national army.

With peace finally formalized in the Peace of Paris in 1783, Hamilton took the bustling lead, under Washington's aegis, in trying to shore up nationalism by establishing just such a military force. He got the Congress to appoint a committee—chaired by him, naturally—to address issues facing the American military in a postwar world, whipped up a set of committee recommendations, and sent them to Washington. Hamilton had served as the general's de facto chief of staff during the war, and already fully agreed on the thrust of these recommendations, the two were now operating as a kind of cabinet without portfolio, the august executive tasking his eager subordinate for a memo. They wanted a nationally run, professional, regular American military, deployed at key frontier points and operating solely under federal control, with uniform supply, soldier recruitment dictated from above, and an academy for officer training. They wanted to dismantle the militia system. They wanted that widely hated thing, a standing army.

Knowing his political opposition, however, Washington cloaked desire in politeness. On receiving Hamilton's list of recommendations, the general softened them and incorporated them in a document titled "Sentiments on a Peace Establishment," ostensibly offering some friendly advice from an important military man now stepping into retirement. Washington submitted "Sentiments," at Hamilton's formal request, to Hamilton's committee.

Washington's "Sentiments" was adroitly politic. It didn't express the general's real views of the militia's egregious failings during the war, and it didn't say he hoped to disable the militia as a national force. Washington made the usual Whiggish remarks about the best defense of freedom resting with militia, and he tried to coax the Congress to create a regular army only as a sort of adjunct to militia, existing in peacetime, yes, but only as a small force, really nothing to be afraid of. Privately, Washington confided to his old Revolution comrade in arms Baron von Steuben—a standing-army specialist—that he was asking for the bare minimum, what he thought he could get: really he wanted a far bigger army than that. And what he proposed was actually large. It would have 2,361 officers in peacetime and be quickly expansible in wartime. But Washington tagged it for the Congress with the reassuring word "small."

Washington would forever try to school him, but Hamilton could not learn to hide controversial plans in soothing language. He incorporated Washington's "Sentiments" in his own findings and presented the whole thing to the Congress as "Report on a Military Peace Establishment," a document whose title alone, blunter than Washington's, was guaranteed to shock and outrage his opponents. Unlike Washington, Hamilton failed to make de rigueur mention of the virtues of militia. Why should he, when local defense was irrelevant to the real purpose of an army? He proposed creating a regular, professional, peacetime army even larger than what Washington had suggested, and the federal government, Hamilton said, should recruit all men and appoint all officers, as well as command them, pay them, and supply them. Militias being worse than useless, Hamilton proposed that local defense be carried out by an elite corps of volunteers, also overseen by the federal government and serving during wartime as the reserve. The plan centralized everything military in America in the federal government and took everything away from the states.

Here was the nationalist vision unabashed. Every fear of tyranny harbored by people from Patrick Henry of Virginia to Elbridge Gerry of Massachusetts seemed borne out in Hamilton's proposals. Hamilton's report was really calling for a quasi-national government founded largely on military power. In related efforts, Hamilton had been trying to get the Congress a direct taxing power over citizens throughout the states, earmarked for paying interest to wealthy investors in the Congress's war bonds. Like war-making power, taxing power was a hallmark of sovereignty: the states guarded their taxing power just as jealously and resisted a federal tax as they resisted a federal army. All nationalists wanted these things, but Hamilton kept admitting it.

Four days after he submitted his military report, soldiers stationed in barracks in Philadelphia sent a letter to the Congress meeting in the statehouse there to demand payment owed for their service. The Congress didn't respond until sixty soldiers marched on their own hook from Lancaster to join the city troops. Four hundred armed men then surrounded the statehouse. Hamilton persuaded them to give the Congress a reprieve, then tried to get Pennsylvania's government to call out the militia against them. On learning the militia couldn't be relied on not to side with the troops, Hamilton made no effort to conceal his disgust. With the Congress in flight to Princeton, New Jersey, this rebellion of a Continental line only seemed to Hamilton to confirm his critique of the existing system.

Yet the Congress, reconvened in Princeton, put off dealing with his report. Washington himself came to Princeton to add new recommendations and further gravitas; still, when debate on the report began, in late October, there was barely a quorum. With peace in the offing, the Congress itself was eroding and American unity with it; the antinationalists were strong. David Howell, a delegate from Rhode Island who had long fought Hamilton's programs, railed in the faltering body against the ineluctable Hamiltonian connection between the countrywide tax Hamilton wanted the Congress to levy, earmarked for paying interest to holders of federal war bonds, and the establishment of a topdown army. Because the entire Revolutionary officer class had been made federal bondholders in lieu of back pay, Howell, Gerry, and other antinationalists condemned Hamilton's plans as tax collection at gunpoint for the benefit of the gunmen.

The nationalists had no choice but to back off on forming a standing army. They focused instead on trying to get the militia under federal control. They tried to get uniform militia training and inspection, tougher fines, and arsenals and magazines supplied by the Congress. They didn't get much. As the 1783 session ended, forming a regular American army might have seemed a faded dream.

Everything changed in 1787 when the nationalists won. They gained not military and taxing power for the Confederation Congress but something far greater: the Confederation Congress's total demise. They persuaded many who remained deeply skeptical of national authority to end the confederation and replace it with a true national government under a constitution.

That the new government would have the power to concentrate American military power at the federal level made it controversial. And yet military strength was part of what sold the Constitution. By 1787, even state sovereigntists had gotten scared. Ad hoc populist militias, not state sanctioned, had been forming in rebellion against states' plans to pay off public bondholders and tax ordinary people for the purpose. Nationalists and state sovereigntists alike were fretting over the confiscatory social leveling they believed these freelance militias espoused. An emerging populist movement hoped to force government to restrain the power of wealth and operate on behalf of the mass of ordinary people. To elites, property itself was now facing a jeopardy just as great, though from another direction, as when Crown and Parliament were exercising tyranny.

Some populist radicals really did want to socialize wealth; others only wanted to obstruct wide income disparities, but it was true in any event that state militias, drawn from the mass of the public, couldn't always be relied on to counter the uprisings. Militia privates were more often in sympathy with rioters and rebels than with the legislatures that called militias out. The most famous populist uprising occurred in western Massachusetts. Called Shays's Rebellion after one of its leaders, Daniel Shays, a veteran of the War of Independence, that effort went so far as to try seizing federal matériel stored in an armory at Springfield. The militia did beat the Shaysites, but it was a near thing, and there was no power the Congress could bring to bear, at least openly: it had no legitimate way to use federal force on citizens within a state. Henry Knox sent some troops, but he had to pretend they were going to fight Indians. Samuel Adams called for the death penalty for the Shaysite rebels.

Shays's Rebellion came out of the Berkshires, in the western part of the state, and the whole Appalachian and trans-Appalachian West fostered these populist movements: self-created western militias, far from the seaboard power centers, turning on their distant state governments. Knox anxiously reported to Washington that the goal of poor westerners like the Shaysites was demolition of investment, confiscation of wealth, and enforced social equality. Hamilton described Daniel Shays himself as a demagogue and desperado. Populism was at its most intense even farther west, across the mountains, and especially around the all-important headwaters of the Ohio, where small farmers, squatters, and landless laborers were making common cause with those in Kentucky and western Virginia and western Maryland to resist eastern authority and deny eastern investment in the West. There was talk of western secession, self-formed states, local alliances with foreign powers. As veterans of the Revolution, these ordinary westerners were armed and organized, and if left unchecked, their movement would mean no bounty land for officers, no interest payments for investors in war bonds, no payoff for speculators with titles to vast acreages of western land. The West would be taken by Indians and poor whites, eternally at war with each other, and the elite East would be cut off from the payoffs it had worked so hard to realize.

State sovereigntists were creditors and land speculators too. They recognized the need to block the armed populist movement. The state governments had tried, but they were weak: rioters shut down courthouses during debt cases and demanded laws for debt relief. More concentrated power over the populists was needed, yet state sovereigntists hoped somehow to gain that power without giving up the key governing powers enjoyed by the states.

As debate developed in the summer of 1787, delegates to the meeting that became the Constitutional Convention fought about nothing more intensely than about where military authority, a sovereign power, should lie. What the nationalists wanted had been clear for years: a standing army and national control of militias. The antinationalists were sure that placing militia training and command under what they still insisted on calling a central, rather than a national, government would rob the states of their liberty, turning the states, as Elbridge Gerry argued with heat, into mere drill sergeants passing on orders from above, departments of the nation, no longer sovereign entities. Because that's exactly what the nationalists did want, James Madison took the lead in soothing such objections, and by the time summer ended, the convention delegates, with George Washington presiding, had done some amazing things.

To begin with, they created a new representative body. Because state sovereigntists were hair-trigger sensitive to anything that tended to elevate national sovereignty, the delegates named the new body the Congress, but it wasn't a congress: that term referred to a representative gathering of sovereigns. It was the opposite: a national legislature, with a lower house to be elected directly by the qualified voters throughout the states, thus wielding sovereign power over all of the citizens throughout all of the states.

They created an executive power. This would be neither a committee nor a creature of the representative Congress but solo and chosen independently of Congress by a college of electors, selected by voting processes within the states. Because the Confederation Congress had been presided over, as had the convention itself, by an officer called the president, the new Congress called this new executive by that innocuous name, but there was no presiding involved: the executive wasn't to chair a body but to enforce Congress's laws throughout all the states. Some framers proposed titles for this role adapted from the English Crown's executive functions: "His Electoral Highness," for example. To others, that sounded absurd, but such a title might have been more accurate than the one actually arrived at.

The old Congress, as a meeting of a confederation of sovereigns, had actually been federal. What the convention instituted was the opposite, but as if to smooth the transition, they called the whole national government the federal government anyway.

When it came to military matters, the Constitution of the United States, as signed that summer, gave the U.S. Congress among other things the power to create an army, with funding expiring every two years to keep it subject to representative approval. The Constitution made the president the army's commander in chief. It placed the states' militias under national control. Thus was the vision realized, which Washington, Hamilton, Morris, Madison, Jefferson, Franklin, John Jay, John Adams, and other famous proponents of American nationhood had long been working for.

The whole thing made Patrick Henry, for one, sick. Anything but a populist social leveler—one of the many things he didn't like about the Constitution was its failure to mention the sanctity of property—Henry wanted to suppress popular attacks on elites, but without resorting to what he perceived as the structural tyranny of the Constitution, robbing state governments of autonomy. Yet he and his allies lacked a significantly workable plan, and men like Washington, once Henry's partner in land speculation and American independence, had the bigger frame now. A national government might gather up the great wealth of the nation and bend it in appropriate directions. If the Potomac canal and other schemes worked out, for example, Washington thought Virginians would see far greater benefits under national government than under any other regime. Along with Henry, George Mason and others among Washington's old allies disagreed, and in the Virginia debates on ratifying the Constitution, they fought hard to prevent ratification. Other state sovereigntists, now known by the counterintuitive name anti-federalists, fought ratification in other states. Promises that once it was ratified, the document could be amended struck Henry as absurd. He was a lawyer. Who signs a binding agreement on the strength of a nonbinding promise of improvements later? And how could only nine of thirteen states' agreeing to ratify make the Constitution binding on all?

But it did, and the electors unanimously chose George Washington as the first president of the United States. The nationalists knew their success in creating this government was thanks to him. As tireless as ever, he'd brought his worldwide prestige as a Cincinnatus to the creation of American nationhood.

The painful irony was that they'd gotten everything except the one thing critical to nationhood, the basis for everything else: an army. The

Constitution didn't create an army. Article I, Section 8, gave the newly formed Congress the power to create one, with the two-year appropriation limit. To do so, Congress would have to pass unpopular laws. The national military power was a new thing, and the old thing stubbornly persisted: widespread objections to a standing army.

So when it came to military matters, the U.S. Congress followed the model established by the Confederation Congress. The former body had never funded the skeletal Josiah Harmar regiment in any meaningful way. Basic budgetary expenses had simply gone unpaid, and even as white-Indian violence raged in the West and squatters took over land, Henry Knox's requests to the Congress for funds to enable security had gone unheeded. That mentality persisted in the U.S. Congress. After ratification, New England had fallen into a fever of antimilitarism, and Elbridge Gerry, for one, now representing Massachusetts in Congress, kept trying to re-debate the fait accompli Constitution. The frontiers had their militias, Gerry argued: Why should Congress deploy any top-down army? Gerry supported using western land sales to fund or pay off the war debt, and that scheme required possession of and security in the West, but the contradiction didn't register. Gerry was expressing the majority opinion: passionate opposition to forming a regular army.

Hence the hodgepodge approach that had proved so disastrous to the St. Clair expedition. Knox hadn't even dared ask for the full-scale regular army that everybody knew the administration had always wanted anyway: such a request might have killed the whole expedition in Congress. Instead, the administration had trumpeted its plan to recruit the short-term levies, and it had persisted in the notion that the Indians at Kekionga, despite having turned back Harmar's flying strike, amounted only to undisciplined banditti. The levies would prove, Knox had promised, at once militarily effective and monetarily efficient.

Now virtually all of the officers, plus much of the whole force, levies, militia, and regulars alike, were wiped out.

Facing up to the horror of St. Clair's defeat, Washington knew what had to be done. He'd always known. Without western investment: no nation. Without a standing army: no nation.

The youth heaved his gigantic frame, soaked and streaming, from the frigid Allegheny . . . Washington had the skills, hard won by the administrative aspects of military command. He'd started out tough; over the years, he'd redefined the very concept of toughness, and yet he was losing the forty-year war in which he'd first come into manhood. This quagmire the nation had fallen into, potentially fatal, must gain him the army he'd always known was essential to national existence. Conquest had become the only choice.

From the bank of the Wabash where they'd left so many hundreds of mutilated bodies scattered below gigantic trees, the fighters led by Little Turtle and Blue Jacket headed for their headquarters and heartland, Kekionga, at the headwaters of the Miami of the Lake. They were filled with satisfaction in a victory they knew was decisive. The women had arrived at the site, once victory was secure. Now men and women alike walked loaded down with scalps, clothing, food, and munitions, leading and driving a few captives and herds of captured animals. Winter was falling fast, and in woodland life every winter was hard: the supplies were welcome.

The leaders of the western Indian confederation now had what they needed. The Fort Harmar Treaty was a dead letter, not only in rhetoric, but also in the hundreds of bodies littered for miles under the big trees. Recruitment to the confederation could be expected to amplify quickly, and there wouldn't be any quick U.S. response: the fighters had killed almost all of the American officers. No longer could anybody dismiss western Indian unity as a chimera with no chance of preventing American expansion.

Yet despite great satisfaction, the confederation's core members at Kekionga faced significant challenges as they settled in for the winter and considered their next moves. Obviously, their towns were no longer safe. Twice the United States had come after this big, polyglot community with its strategic location at the headwaters of the river that flowed northeastward, in tight bends, toward Lake Erie and Fort Detroit. Harmar's earlier campaign had damaged their breadbasket, the spreading cornfields and rolling orchards, and they'd burned their own towns to throw him off. While they'd destroyed St. Clair's follow-up force before it could get anywhere near Kekionga, paperwork captured at the victory site revealed that the American objective had been to take the heartland of the Land of the Three Miamis and build a fort here.

So even as they relished the impossibility of any quick regrouping on the part of the enemy they'd so thoroughly devastated, with winter falling fast the Indians began making new plans for the spring. They would need to build the confederation further and develop their strategy. And they would need the help that the British army in Fort Detroit had promised them.

When Alexander McKee first heard news of the Indian confederation's victory over St. Clair, he couldn't believe it. Was it really possible that the Miami, Shawnee, Delaware, and others hadn't merely repelled American attack—they'd done that before—but routed, beyond any chance for quick recovery, the best military force that the United States had to offer?

It seemed too good to be true. When he began to believe it, McKee was filled with new excitement.

As the man the Indian confederation went to for British support, few men were more feared, loathed, and disdained than Alexander McKee by the Americans involved in trying to take possession of the Northwest. To his machinations they ascribed all Indian military success. Behind-the-scenes scheming, American officials said, by the man routinely referred to, then and for generations to come, as McKee the traitor and McKee the notorious Tory accounted in their minds for long-standing frustration of American attempts to possess the Northwest.

And it's true that Alexander McKee had been important to the western Indian confederation's planning and supply. From his bustling storehouses and trading post at the foot of the long, beautiful rapids of the Miami of the Lake he'd helped organize many of the raids most notorious among Americans during the War of Independence. He'd urged and fostered Indian unity in preventing American incursion across the Ohio. He'd been present during the slow, awful death by torture of William Crawford after the Moravian Indians' massacre. Before St. Clair's recent failed effort against Kekionga, it was Alexander McKee who had brought wagonloads of ammunition and guns down from Fort Detroit and advised on organization. A final Indian success of the kind Blue Jacket and Little Turtle now contemplated, holding the United States back behind the Ohio for good, would depend on his continued commitment to their cause.

That commitment had sources perhaps unique among his contemporaries. McKee was at once a high-up British colonial administrator living the gentleman's life in Detroit, a well-connected land speculator benefiting from Crown grants in Canada, a fur trader with a going concern at the Miami rapids, and an experienced, hands-on frontiersman with one of the most peripatetic weekly calendars of the era. He was also American, and he was what the British were now calling loyalist.

And he was Shawnee. Born in the 1730s in the Susquehanna valley of Pennsylvania, McKee was the child of an Irish fur trader and a woman captured in infancy from a white family in North Carolina and adopted as Shawnee; she grew up in a Shawnee-Delaware-Iroquois town on the banks of the Susquehanna. There she met the elder McKee, then licensed by Pennsylvania to trade across the mountains, and when she left home with him, she became known as Mary McKee, but she never spoke much English, and she retained Shawnee ways all her life. Alexander was raised in both worlds.

That was complicated enough, and even his maternal lineage was in question. Alexander's parents weren't married when he was born, a younger McKee brother would later assert in court when trying to gain Alexander's property. In the end, it wouldn't be clear to anyone—except to Mary McKee, and she wasn't talking—whether she was Alexander's biological mother and simply unmarried to his father at the time of the birth or had adopted the son of another Indian woman with whom Thomas McKee had been involved. Anyway, to Alexander, Mary McKee was his mother. He lived both Shawnee and white.

Growing up multilingual in many Indian languages, he received a strong education in English. He was verbally gifted, and the refinement and clarity of his written prose exceeded that of most of the best-educated elites of his day, let alone the average frontiersmen. He began his business life working at his father's store in the Pennsylvania backcountry and his military life in an action related to General Forbes's retaking the fort at the headwaters from the French during the Seven

Years' War. In that violently contested boundary land around the head-waters of the Ohio, Alexander McKee learned that his natural ability to navigate conflicting cultures made him extraordinarily useful to well-funded and powerful people on all sides of all the lines.

As those lines began shifting with such dramatic effect in the late 1750s and early 1760s, McKee became, like many other ambitious Americans, a busy agent of the embattled British presence in the West. Traveling overland from Pittsburgh on errands of negotiation up to Detroit, and down the Ohio to Blue Jacket's region around the mouth of the Scioto, he tried to get his own fur trading going while mediating deals among English soldiers, traders from Pennsylvania and elsewhere, the Pennsylvania government, and Shawnee and other Indians. Deal making across racial boundaries became McKee's business. He knew Shawnee and other Indian formalities from childhood, and he quickly picked up the arcana of imperial administration. By the early 1760s, he was a Crown official, deputized to take temporary charge of the British Indian agency centered on Fort Pitt. McKee communicated with Indians regarding developments in fur-trading regulations, convening meetings with hundreds of attendees of multiple nations and branches. His main effort was to push back against the tendency toward white-Indian violence that was coming to mark the period. His mixed background could not admit such a division. In order to manage and forestall conflict, he placed his own Shawnee agents in the Shawnee villages down the Ohio, listening in.

So some might have called McKee's best talent double-dealing. Yet despite the spying, McKee retained credibility with Shawnee relatives, friends, and business associates throughout the region. What would have been, for almost anyone else, a set of divided loyalties—nobody was less a "pure" Indian than McKee—presented him with opportunities. By the late 1760s, he was splitting his time between Pittsburgh and the Shawnee towns down the Ohio. He could explain one group to the other, but he also kept listening, selecting details, and communicating intelligence privately—warning British soldiers of impending Indian attack, for example—whenever he thought doing so might defuse violence.

McKee sought a fair deal for Indians. British enforcement of the 1763 proclamation line, for example, would keep out squatters and speculators. That reconciled his ambitions for getting ahead as a British official with his desire to protect the world he came from. Yet McKee never saw any conflict of interest in his own speculating, and the moment the 1768 Fort Stanwix Treaty moved the line westward, he was buying. Both a private fur trader and a British official, he built a big house on the Ohio River, just north and downstream from Pittsburgh, a place that became known as McKees Rocks. He served as a justice of the peace for the new Pennsylvania county of Bedford, in competition with the overlapping Virginia counties. His multitude of provincial, imperial, and Indian offices and roles were overlapping too.

The emerging imperial crisis was no more visible to McKee than to anyone else. In 1770, when George Washington took his trip down the Ohio with William Crawford to scout good land, the party stayed with McKee at McKees Rocks before embarking downstream. None of them could have had any intimation that twelve years later McKee would be present at the horrible killing of Crawford. They talked during dinner about land and speculation, and McKee accompanied the party downstream for a day or two. For him, the cordiality of that relationship didn't yet conflict with loyalty to the Shawnee. He'd married a Shawnee woman, and in the year he met Washington, McKee and his wife had a child. McKee lived in the river-view house near Pittsburgh. His wife and child lived in a town down the Ohio around the Scioto mouth, where Blue Jacket and other Shawnee were even then beginning their raids on white settlements in Kentucky. Some even said McKee's wife was Blue Jacket's sister. McKee commuted between Pittsburgh and the Shawnee towns and made it all work.

Then it didn't work. During the series of political and cultural breakdowns and shooting wars around the Ohio headwaters, McKee finally found himself with no choice but to run.

That was in 1778, when he'd become so generally relied on in western Pennsylvania and the Ohio Country that his flight from the Americans he'd known and worked with rocked multiple social worlds throughout the West. McKee had continued to believe the Shawnee would do better with the British than with an independent America. He'd already been working with the British to ally Six Nations and Shawnee branches against the Americans and attack settlements, and yet his American connections remained strong. When Arthur St. Clair, operating at the headwaters on behalf of Revolutionary Pennsylvania, learned that McKee had been commissioned a lieutenant colonel in the British army, he only put McKee under mild house arrest in Pittsburgh. When Richard Butler, now a Continental colonel, got word that McKee had been invited to Fort Niagara, to give the British intelligence on Fort Pitt, Butler's regard for McKee remained so high that at first he refused to arrest him.

Others didn't feel that way, however. Patriotic fervor at the headwaters quickly became so explosive that McKee was eventually taken into protective custody in Fort Pitt. When, in March 1778, a rumor spread that he was planning to murder headwaters patriots, he bolted into the Indian country he knew so well, heading north this time, for the British garrison at Fort Detroit.

In making that move, McKee abruptly came to combine every type that American partisans around the headwaters hated: loyalist, traitor, fugitive, renegade Indian. They feared he would rally the western Indians and attack Pittsburgh. Other loyalists in the region kept their heads down, weighed the odds, and considered whatever they might learn from McKee's example. Should they stay or should they run? What McKee knew was that the Americans at Fort Pitt were in no way ready to mount an operation against Fort Detroit. He communicated that information to British officers there. He was never going back.

Among the headwaters patriots, McKee's legend grew as the war went on. So did his circle's. When leaving on the run, he'd formed up a party: another fur trader, Matthew Elliott, Elliott's Shawnee wife, and their children; and they all brought along their African slaves. Also joining the defection were the Girty brothers James and Simon, captured as children and raised Seneca. Even more than McKee, it was the Girtys, especially Simon, who gave Americans the willies. Flamboyantly violent, relishing his fame as a "white savage," Simon played up the image that would make him, in American lore, a kind of anti-Boone, the frontiersman gone demonically wrong. It wasn't all made up. With McKee, Girty did attend the death of Crawford, yet something about Girty inspired Americans to place him beyond the pale of horrific violence that marked all of the back-and-forth of the boundary-land life. Not just a line crosser, worse than an enemy, Girty had gone over, people thought, to the Indian side, but his whiteness made him worse than Indian, perverted, a monster so evil and otherworldly, it was once said, that it could only be he who goaded Indians to excesses of violence. It was rumored that Girty, as agent provocateur, incited the Pennsylvania militiamen to massacre the Moravian Indians. His violence was at once as real as everybody else's on the scene and totally unreal.

The way Alexander McKee looked at the situation, he hadn't changed: the others had. He was a loyal Shawnee and a loyal British administrator, as concerned for his honor as he'd ever been. It had always been tricky to manage being both, but he'd had some success in bringing peace and promoting the steady flow of commerce until the day when some Americans, by no means all, largely out of a desire to take Indian land, had made it impossible for him to be a good Shawnee and Englishman while also remaining a good Pennsylvanian and American. It was the Revolutionary Americans, not he, who had turned their coats. In remaining what he'd always been, McKee had sacrificed his land and home.

So he organized Indian attacks on Kentucky and against George Rogers Clark on the lower Wabash. That job was made for him. He was uniquely able to rally Indians on behalf of what the British saw as British interests, which McKee wholeheartedly supported, and of what the Indians saw as Indian interests, which he supported just as strongly. Where conflicts occurred in that relationship, McKee mediated them by his very presence. His mode was solely binary now: the old fluidity was no longer possible. The War of Independence, which had turned his life upside down and lost him his property not only in Pittsburgh but also in Lancaster and in Kentucky, hardened him. He and the United States had gone to war with each other, and he'd attended the torture and killing of Crawford. Some lines could no longer be crossed.

After the Peace of Paris of 1783, Alexander McKee's every effort was bent on aiding the Kekionga confederation in enforcing the Ohio boundary line. Addressing the big Sandusky conference, he promised continued British support in hopes that a show of Indian unity would bring the Americans to their senses. That hope was dashed as he watched the Americans try to dictate terms at treaty meetings, watched as they built forts on the north bank of the Ohio and broke ground at Marietta and Cincinnati. He'd been living in Detroit for fifteen years by then, on what was now unsurrendered American soil near the British-held fort that commanded access to the western interior. He was still in the fur business, with his storehouses at the rapids of the Miami of the Lake, and as a crucial Indian agent he'd risen so high in British administration that the Indian Department had bought him a house in Detroit staffed with white servants and enslaved Africans. He'd joined the Church of England. As a refugee from the War of Independence, hence a leader of what the British were coming to call United Empire Loyalists, he'd received investment land across the Detroit River on the legitimately British bank, and he engaged in finagling worthy of a Washington to get more land there illegally. The British civil servant and the Shawnee leader had merged in concerted obstruction of American possession of the West.

British support had become more critical than ever, McKee believed, to Indian survival. That belief accorded with the two things he wanted most: perpetuation of Indian life in North America and perpetuation of his own life as an English gentleman in Detroit.

Filled with optimism by the victory over St. Clair, McKee traveled southwest from Detroit, up the Miami of the Lake, to its headwaters at Kekionga to meet with the Indian confederation leadership. The totality of the confederation's defeat of St. Clair, he hoped, would awaken the United States to the need for equity in their relations with the western Indians and inspire his British superiors to get serious about providing the Indians with outright military support, maybe even commit troops, maybe even build a new fort, for Indian protection, forward on American soil on a bank of the Miami of the Lake. Those had become McKee's goals.

The Indians were meanwhile facing up to their towns' exposure. The Harmar and St. Clair expeditions showed them that Kekionga lay too far for comfort from McKee's operation downstream at the rapids of the Miami of the Lake, with its speedy direct communications with the British troops at Detroit. The confederation needed greater proximity to

McKee and the fort and greater distance between their families and American aggression.

McKee agreed. He was concerned about the coming of winter, always Indians' hungriest time, about the departure of the farther-western allies to their own towns, and about a hope, evident among some of the civic leaders, to use the victory as an opportunity to sue for a favorable peace with the United States. McKee and the hard-liners stood in firm opposition to that idea. A safer location would help them keep their line hard.

So with McKee's support, Little Turtle, Blue Jacket, and the other leaders determined to move nearly all of their towns' inhabitants—men, women, and children—out of Kekionga and resettle northeast, at least temporarily, down many bends of the Miami of the Lake, about forty miles from Kekionga as the crow flies. At a fertile, pleasant spot known generally as "the Glaize," the confluence of the Miami of the Lake and its tributary the Auglaize River formed a broad, level point of land, ideal for building new towns. Captain Johnny, the fearsome, seven-foot hard-line Shawnee who had mysteriously signed the Fort Finney Treaty with Moluntha, was already established at the Glaize: he was back in the hard-line camp. The confederation Indians weren't abandoning Kekionga's fields for good. But they made a major migration.

Moving a whole set of towns was challenging but feasible. People living around the southern shores of Lakes Erie and Michigan and the banks of the three Miamis had moved many times in their long histories. Relocating meant clearing new ground, dividing it up for spring planting, building houses and putting up tents, and situating families in the dwellings. Trying to beat the worst of winter, this exodus—in the end, it involved about two thousand people—was heading up the Miami of the Lake to the Glaize by early December. Here the former residents of Kekionga would resettle, organize themselves in new towns, and await spring planting and military maneuvers.

Not only geographic considerations inspired Little Turtle, Blue Jacket, and the others to join Captain Johnny at the Glaize. They were facing privation. Organizing the operation against St. Clair had kept the men from hunting, and summer flooding had destroyed much of the corn at Kekionga; what they'd saved had been used to feed the allies gathered from distant western towns. Nor had the fields at Kekionga fully recovered from Harmar's campaign. Resettling at the Glaize would put the whole core of the confederation closer to McKee's stores and operations on the banks of the long rapids, and closer as well, only a day or two by quick feet, to the British fort at Detroit, well stocked with food and arms. The only problem, as far as some confederation leaders were concerned, was that reliance on those food sources increased Indian dependence on both the British army and the Shawnee Indian agent McKee.

Blue Jacket, as a fellow Shawnee, had McKee's ear, and McKee had Blue Jacket's confidence. But the Miami leader Little Turtle had some pointed questions about the real nature of British support for the western confederation.

Those questions reflected Little Turtle's idiosyncratic approach to Indian unity. Where Blue Jacket made a splash, Little Turtle was enigmatic; where Blue Jacket drew charisma from brash confidence, Little Turtle's charisma came from an unusual mix of calm delivery and startling bluntness. He said what he thought, and what he thought was often unexpectedly skeptical, for a leader. His idea of life had melancholic features: nothing works forever, the wheel is always turning, relying on past military success causes military failure. That somewhat mystical, even tragic idea of power fostered an ambivalence absent from the nativist purism that had marked movements like Neolin's and Pontiac's. Blue Jacket, though by no means an exemplar of racial purity, was drawn to the Shawnee dream of return to an ancient homeland, but Little Turtle's tragic sense was less eschatological, more practical. Forcing the United States to respect a boundary at the Ohio was more on his mind than the ultimates.

So in assessing what it would take to follow up the victory, Little Turtle saw problems. Still, he believed that if they were faced, they could be solved. His main concern had to do with what the confederation might realistically expect, for all of McKee's protestations, from the British army occupying Fort Detroit. While the United States had been seriously set back, Little Turtle knew that a defeat like the one he and Blue Jacket had just handed the United States always inspires an enemy to amplified aggression. Only if the British too amplified their help, Little Turtle believed, could the Indians withstand the next military assault, make American settlement north and west of the Ohio impossible to sustain, and keep Americans out of Indian country for the foreseeable future. If things went wrong now—and he knew they could—the victory over St. Clair, the greatest the Indians had achieved so far against the United States, might become the greatest victory that Indians would ever achieve. That wasn't inevitable, but it was possible.

Little Turtle knew what a truly final victory would require. The Indians needed, he believed, big guns. He wanted British artillery.

6

METROPOTAMIA

It is with great concern that I communicate to you the information received from Major General St. Clair of the misfortune which has befallen the troops under his command.

Although the national loss is considerable according to the scale of the event, yet it may be repaired without great difficulty, excepting as to the brave men who have fallen on the occasion, and who are a subject of public as well as private regret.

A further communication will shortly be made of all such matters as shall be necessary to enable the Legislature to judge of the future measures which it may be proper to pursue.

On December 12, 1791, President Washington began maneuvers to alter for all time the long-standing role of the military in American life. In a message at once terse and urgent, he officially informed both houses of Congress of the defeat of St. Clair's forces. He appended St. Clair's November 9 report describing the rout.

As brief as it was, the message put Congress on notice. The loss might be repaired without great difficulty, the president said. Certain congressmen would know right away what he meant: a regular army. They were prepared to obstruct him.

Washington, for his part, had promised further communication to

help the congressmen decide on a proper course. He meant he would
try to make it impossible for them not to do what he wanted.

His weapon was paperwork. Washington's cabinet got busy building
a file to present to Congress, a file so huge, so overwhelmingly unan-
swerable, that it would put the legislators in a position in which they
would find further refusal to form a standing army politically infeasible.

Meanwhile, reports of sheer terror among white dwellers throughout
the West began to flood toward the eastern public. These reports weren't
exaggerated. Amid the continuing chaos at Fort Washington, Arthur
St. Clair was able to provide no real security, either for the wounded,
rowdy horde in and around that Ohio River fort or for the few soldiers
left hungry and exposed in the forward forts Hamilton and Jefferson, so
hastily built during the stymied northward march. Nor could St. Clair
calm settlers in the Cincinnati settlement. He had a bad relationship
with them anyway. Far from behaving in the orderly manner that he,
Washington, and others had envisioned for the proper settling of the
West under certified government partnerships, the ordinary Cincinnati settler had long struck St. Clair as obstreperous, demanding, and
what he called licentious: before it had much else, the town had taverns, and the investors and developers were part of the problem too.
Living in the biggest houses and on the largest tracts, they'd been ignoring federal surveys, causing fights over boundaries. They sold land
lying well beyond the scope of the grant, forcing some who had paid for
land, now classified squatters, to rebuy from other owners. Cincinnati
had never had any evident civil government, and before his expedition
against the Indians St. Clair had repeatedly placed the settlement under
martial law. The settlers, though uncowed, resented it.

Now, with St. Clair's abject defeat at the Wabash, they were not only
resentful but also panicked. Nobody in Cincinnati or anywhere else in
the West knew what the Indians planned to do next. Having sent his
report to President Washington, St. Clair found himself presiding help-
lessly over general fear and paralysis.

So he placed Fort Washington, along with any control that might
be someday gained over Forts Hamilton and Jefferson, in the hands of

James Wilkinson, lieutenant colonel commander of a force of Kentucky volunteers, an able and well-liked leader, and left Fort Washington, bound for the capital. St. Clair would face Washington in person in hopes of being absolved and saving his job as governor.

He didn't know it, but he had reason to hope. Tobias Lear had listened to the president calling down the curses of widows and orphans and even of the deity itself on his general's head, but right after warning Lear never to let those curses leave the room, Washington had again fallen silent. Then he'd told Lear, "General St. Clair shall have justice. I looked hastily through the dispatches, saw the whole disaster but not all the particulars. I will receive him without displeasure; I will hear him without prejudice; he shall have full justice." St. Clair, however, took the long trip to Philadelphia in a state of miserable suspense.

With St. Clair heading east, Colonel Wilkinson took over Fort Washington and did begin restoring some order. Misery still reigned in the battered remnant of the army. To relieve it, Wilkinson began trying to establish regular communications with the forward forts to his north. Fort Hamilton, closer to Cincinnati, was mainly a supply way station, but farther up at Fort Jefferson three hundred or so wounded men still somehow existed in privation and terror, unable to leave the fort for fear of attack. The trip between Hamilton and Jefferson took two days, and supply convoys could easily be waylaid. Wilkinson planned to build a new station between them. He would name it Fort St. Clair.

Rumors of an imminent Indian follow-up attack meanwhile traveled quickly from Cincinnati over the river to Kentucky, through the Virginia frontier, up the river to Pittsburgh, and throughout western Pennsylvania. Alarm was intense not only on the Ohio River at Cincinnati, Marietta, Louisville, and Pittsburgh, but all the way to the mountains and even east of the mountains. Militias mustered and found themselves low on arms and ammunition. Muskets left unattended had rusted, with broken stocks and missing hammers and locks. Some militiamen refused in any case to leave families undefended to go on patrol. People were crowding with their livestock into forts, blockhouses, stockades. Some felt military expeditions against the Indians only aggravated the danger; others were ready to march on Kekionga on their own. Some communities hired freelance scouts claiming to offer protection as great Indian fighters.

The eastern public, reading and hearing these accounts, felt first shock, then depression. It wasn't just the fact of the defeat that made the mood especially grim, or even the magnitude of it, but the particularly violent horrors the few survivors of the battle had witnessed in the aftermath. Stories of breasts torn from women's bodies, butchery of people still alive, the merciless delight of the victors in the ingenious torture of the victims: it made gripping, chilling reading and incited an urgent desire to do something about it.

The Washington administration found itself on the receiving end of much bitter complaint. From Pittsburgh came an official memorial angrily begging the federal government for immediate military help. Should the Indians follow up their victory at the Wabash, Pittsburgh's political leaders said, the village would collapse, the surrounding country would be overrun, the grisly deaths of countless men, women, and children would ensue. The Indian victory would make it easy for the western confederation to recruit young men of the Six Nations, the Pittsburghers pointed out, leaving western Pennsylvania vulnerable to attack not only from its western frontier but also from the east. The town had no garrison, no arms, no ammunition, and why not? the memorial asked rhetorically. During the Revolution, Pittsburgh had been garrisoned, and things were worse now.

The Pittsburghers' implication was that the federal government had failed western Americans not only in settlements down the Ohio but even east of the river. Rubbing it in, that memorial didn't come directly to the president from the Pittsburgh civic leaders but had been forwarded, without overt comment, by Pennsylvania's gregarious, contentious governor, Thomas Mifflin, from the statehouse in Philadelphia, only a block from Washington's house. During the War of Independence, Mifflin had been among those officers questioning Washington's competence and seeking to have the commander replaced. Their relations had long been tense at best. Mifflin intended his forwarding of the letter as a rebuke.

Mifflin's action coincided with an alarming back-and-forth that Secretary of War Henry Knox was having, not with Pittsburgh's city fathers but with state militia lieutenants in the four western counties of Pennsylvania. This tense discussion bore directly on the unresolved question of where American military authority might lie. Yes, the federal government would send troops to Fort Pitt, Knox assured those militia leaders, and yes, he further assured them, when it was demanded of him, the federal government would pay for recruiting local scouts and woodsmen to guard the frontier. Responsibility for protection would not lie with state and local budgets, Knox assured them: it would lie with the nation.

And yet from across town Governor Mifflin responded with only guarded enthusiasm to Knox's offer of federal support for frontier militia recruitment and supply throughout western Pennsylvania. While the governor did want, he said, to put such measures into effect, he noted a problem: he'd already spent money from his own state budget on defense for the western counties. So along with federal money for further recruitment, could he get a reimbursement out of Knox's budget for the money he'd already spent?

Yes, said Knox. If he hadn't, Mifflin would have turned up his nose at federal funding, some disaster would have struck western Pennsylvania, and the president, not the governor, would have been blamed. Naturally, as soon as Knox made the commitment of federal funds, Mifflin's enthusiasm for the plan became unqualified: he agreed to get military efforts on the frontier going right way, yet such military efforts would be entirely under his own direction, Mifflin reminded Knox. Despite federal funding, long militia traditions gave the state governor, not Knox, control of operations on the ground. Though held up for federal cash, Knox had no say in how it would be spent, what supplies would be purchased, how the men would be trained and deployed. Disaster still seemed likely to strike western Pennsylvania, and the War Department was helpless. Military authority lay in other hands.

All this terror-laced communication and wild alarm, arising from a gruesome military defeat on his watch, might have looked disastrous for George Washington. As usual, he stayed focused. During the closing weeks of 1791, the president organized an all-out executive-branch effort to leverage these complaints, demands, and expressions of fear to bring about what he wanted.

This effort represented a major cabinet project, and most of the work was done, under Washington's close supervision, by three key cabinet members. The expertise of Attorney General Edmund Randolph was little needed in this phase, and while the number of tie-breaking votes John Adams cast in the Senate would never be exceeded, the vice president never had any cabinet role. It was Secretary of War Henry Knox, Secretary of the Treasury Alexander Hamilton, and Secretary of State Thomas Jefferson who now went into high gear.

For all of the intensity of Jefferson's and Hamilton's rivalry, already becoming painfully obvious to Washington and destined to fascinate Americans for generations, both men were strong partisans of the national West. They never would have been selected for Washington's cabinet if they weren't, and each had long applied a lot of thought to American expansion. Neither had significant personal investments on the line. Each was after something bigger than financial self-interest: authorship of the American future.

Jefferson had backed off speculating in land-investment schemes, and he'd never traveled west of the Blue Ridge. While he was as acquisitive as a person can be—objects from all over the world crammed the rooms and hallways of his famous home, Monticello—his urge to explore strange new worlds on his own was weak. Less and less did he seem to want to leave Monticello. When he did, his travel was eastward, to wherever the Congress was sitting at the moment, and to Paris, answering the call and possibly the lure of duty.

On paper, however, Jefferson was already expanding America westward on an imperial scale. He'd come around in the early 1780s on Virginia's sea-to-sea claims, breaking with Patrick Henry on the issue and supporting the cession of western land to the Congress. Serving then as governor of Virginia, Jefferson had ordered George Rogers Clark out of the Ohio Country forts and back to Kentucky in favor of the United States. Like the other Virginia nationalists led by Washington, Jefferson saw bigger opportunities in the national context.

The great British land cession of 1783 gave life to his ideas about what Virginia and America might become together. When the old Congress wanted to write its first ordinance for managing the Northwest, Jefferson, the inveterate amateur of invention, architecture, and design, took to his desk, and drawing on techniques of cartography, surveying, civil administration, drafting, property law, math, and republican government, he created a rational society. On the map of the Northwest, he neatly drew new states, as rectangular as the irregularity of nature would allow: Sylvania, Michigania, Cheronesus, Assenisippis, Metropotamia, Illinoia, Saratoga, Polypotamia, and Pelipsia, five to the west of a line drawn north-south through the Ohio River's falls at Louisville, Kentucky, and four to the east. There was one special irregularity, caused by the oddball resolution of Virginia's and Pennsylvania's western borders. To resolve it, Jefferson created a special slice and called it Washington. Within each region he then drew rectangular townships, forty-nine square miles each, and he divided each into rectangular lots. There was to be nothing oddball about Jefferson's West: in this plan, the ten regions were to become, one day, under an orderly process, new states of the Union. Each would have schools and flourishing arts and sciences. America would grow by degrees into what he called an empire for liberty.

This design made him something other than Virginian. The rectilinear plotting had antecedents not in Virginia but in colonial New England. Nor was there to be slavery in Jefferson's Northwest Territory—although in Jefferson's version, soon superseded, the ban was to begin only after 1800. While in life he would never give up forcing hard labor from enslaved Africans in support of his ostentatious lifestyle, the empire of liberty gave Jefferson a fresh start on paper, where the stay-at-home slave master might become at once a New England abolitionist and a roving Saxon exploring the unknown future. Jefferson got in touch with George Rogers Clark to propose an expedition. It was rumored that the British were considering exploring west of the Mississippi, despite Spanish claims there. Jefferson asked Clark whether the Kentuckian would want to lead a party in exploring the continent all the way to the Pacific.

Jefferson called the land on which he drew his rectangles uninhabited. He knew it wasn't. He laid Metropotamia, for example, over the Land of the Three Miamis. He'd already told Clark, in 1779, that when making moves against the Shawnee the goal should be "their extermination, or their removal beyond the lakes or Illinois river." Unless the Indians changed utterly, Jefferson was coming to believe, Indians and Americans could not together inhabit the western world he was creating.

Jefferson's plans for the West were superseded by the ordinance of 1787. It threw out his regional nomenclature, changed the townships' forty-nine square miles to thirty-six, and sent the geographer Thomas Hutchins to do a real survey, escorted by Harmar's troops. The ordinance also prohibited slavery in the territory immediately, not in 1800, when the institution might have taken such firm root that it might never be pulled out. Jefferson spent nearly five years in Paris as minister to France before returning in 1789 to take up his cabinet appointment under Washington. Yet his commitment to the Northwest Territory and the empire of liberty persisted.

Now, in Washington's quickly developing cabinet project for forcing Congress to create a standing army, Jefferson's work was informed by pro-French enthusiasm. He hated the British. Their presence in forts on American soil revolted him, and he was always up for war to stymie British interests. Where Jefferson dissented from Washington's army project had to do with the critique of the militia system. He hadn't commanded in the Revolution and remained a full-fledged participant in the militia school of American military thought, philosophically opposed to standing armies. To Jefferson, as to many other Americans, St. Clair's defeat showed the inefficacy of regulars, not militiamen. That made him odd man out in the cabinet when it came to forming a regular force for the United States. He kept that dissent to himself, for now.

Hamilton loved the British and hated the French. He too was no obsessive land speculator. His friends and mentors were speculators, often wild ones, in both land and public securities, but Hamilton's ambitions soared above personal gain: he was building an American commercial and military empire to rival that of England. Because his plans involved concentrating the wealth of the nation via a national debt, thus linking private gain to public benefit, he was a committed supporter of the interstate American investing class that speculated in both federal bonds and western land. He wanted to calm the markets' wildness and make public finance and the public domain sites of rational speculation. Official grants and orderly settlement of the West, in private-public partnerships under strict national supervision, were among the tools for achieving his goals.

As he'd long made clear, another key tool for Hamilton was the standing army. Nearly every other member of his generation's governing class, even Washington, expressed the concern that unless very carefully managed, professional armies might be turned against the citizenry. That meant nothing to Hamilton; if anything, such uses of military power inspired him. When it came to carrying out his national finance programs, for example, white settlers west of the mountains had been proving at least as obstructive as Indian nations. Hamilton's allies out in Pittsburgh, big-scale farmers and distillers, were nervous about populist threats to their operations there.

"There is a western country," Hamilton had assured St. Clair, by letter. "It *will* be settled." The emphasis was his. He wasn't talking only about Indians.

Henry Knox was the only cabinet member who had succeeded himself as secretary of war, having served in that capacity in the defunct Confederation Congress, with no executive to report to then. Where Jefferson and Hamilton were trying to bend the policies of the Washington administration to big, competing ends, Knox was first and foremost loyal to Washington. Early in the Revolution, he'd harbored the same doubts about the commander as Mifflin and others, but for years Knox had been identifying his personal ambition and his ideas about proper American government with Washington's career.

For a character seen by some colleagues as one-dimensional—to Hamilton, Knox was a plodder who, annoyingly enough, outranked him militarily; to Jefferson, Knox was a Hamiltonian tool—his view of the West was unusually nuanced. A Bostonian, Knox held few land investments in the West. In the vast Massachusetts backland to the north, Maine, he owned millions of acres. He saw western settlers as fatally unruly, never to be tamed, wilder than Indians, and compared with Jefferson's, Knox's ideas about Indian land and sovereignty were uncomplicated. It seemed to him that the Indians had sovereignty. It would therefore be inconsistent with national honor to deprive them of it by force. Only by victory in a just war, or by Indian consent, could land be taken, and a just war couldn't be a war of choice.

But as a practical matter, Knox didn't sort the matter further than that. He believed Indian consent had been achieved, via the Fort Harmar

Treaty and the purchase of the land. He'd defined the defiant Indian confederation as disgruntled banditti, and even after Harmar's discouraging failure he'd insisted that the banditti could never defeat a disciplined white army. Discouraged yet again by the awful defeat of St. Clair, Knox had become deeply skeptical of American success west of the mountains. Yet he would carry out Washington's western policy with dogged, unflagging commitment.

And when it came to creating an army, nobody had less confidence than Henry Knox in the militia system. The failure of the militia enlistments and levies in the rout at the Wabash further proved the system's fatal weakness, and Knox wholeheartedly believed in the necessity to American nationhood of regular, professional troops.

The cabinet was up against passionate opposition to forming a regular army. That opposition was surprisingly broad based: an omni-partisan coalition orchestrating strong popular support. The anti-army coalition brought together politicians as divided on other issues as westerners who believed local militias should be empowered to exterminate all Indians and easterners who deemed any expansion into Indian country immoral.

Then there were the old antinationalists of the 1780s. They'd become the anti-federalists during the constitutional ratification controversy, and now they were in Congress. Washington's supporters called them simply "anti's": a party of "no," opposing anything the president proposed. But even some of Washington's strongest supporters looked askance, with the failure of Harmar and the gruesome defeat of St. Clair, at continuing a disastrous military effort in the West.

Many members of Congress simply wanted to cut the Gordian knot. They favored unilateral withdrawal from the West. Not every American citizen, putting it mildly, had a financial stake in national expansion westward; not every representative of those citizens saw the nation's future in terms of such expansion. Some in Congress had been reluctant to form the Northwest Territory at all. Some had actually hoped for a smaller land cession in the Peace of Paris. It was a feature of republican thought that a representative government can't survive in a nation too widespread.

And some were involved in an idea influenced by certain English poets. The Native way of life struck many easterners as admirably lean and tough, in keeping with republican virtue. An Indian was believed to enjoy, in the supposedly natural state, an especially virtuous relationship to nature, uncontaminated by the greediness represented by white land and money speculators. Indians seemed instinctually egalitarians. "Lo!" demanded Alexander Pope in 1734,

> the poor Indian, whose untutored mind
> Sees God in clouds, or hears him in the wind . . .
> To be, contents his natural desire,
> He asks no angel's wing, no seraph's fire;
> But thinks, admitted to that equal sky,
> His faithful dog shall bear him company.

Samuel Taylor Coleridge would soon be devouring accounts of the New World. In descriptions of Native life, the poet would find inspiration to imagine a better society than that of imperialist, industrialized England. Coleridge and his friend Robert Southey planned to emigrate, with their families, and establish an egalitarian intellectual commune in the wilds of western Pennsylvania: they would talk metaphysics while felling trees, they said, criticize poetry while hunting, and write sonnets while plowing. Luckily for all involved, the project fell through.

One of the most ardent proponents of the virtuous Indian was Benjamin Franklin Bache, the more famous Franklin's grandson. He published a Philadelphia paper called the *Aurora*, dissenting from Washington administration policies, including what he considered the appropriation of public funds for Indian war in the West in service of private investments. Bache saw the Indians as a better class of human being, carrying on in fact what republicans only aspired to.

Others, lacking any admiration for what was taken to be a Native way of life, nevertheless had another idea for avoiding conquest and wholesale killing: assimilating the Indian people into what they saw as the American way of life. People from Henry Knox to the Pittsburgh lawyer Hugh Henry Brackenridge to the North Carolina senator Benjamin Hawkins believed that Indians must, to survive, ultimately give up their own nationhood and join the people of the United States, with whom sovereignty was now deemed to lie. They didn't suggest that Indians would vote or otherwise take part in the political process: few free blacks, or women, or white men without property were qualified to vote, yet they were citizens and thus, it was said, represented in American politics. What the Indians needed, assimilationists believed, were lessons. The savages, they wrongly thought, moved about and didn't settle, hunting but not farming, or if they did farm, it was crudely, and mostly done by women, and thus they didn't improve their land. Because legitimate ownership equated with improvement, Indians must be taught to farm using white implements, live in white-style towns, wear white-style clothing, and worship in Christian churches. Many Indians already did all of those things yet remained committed to driving off American incursion. Still, the notion of teaching Indians white ways persisted, among many moderates as the humane solution, and it came to devolve on a hope for switching traditional roles. Indian men must cease hunting and fighting and raise crops and herd animals. Indian women must cease farming and learn housewifery. Removing hunting grounds, some white assimilationists believed, might actually be a boon to that process. Just not by conquest.

Principled nonviolence was in the air too. On December 16, while Washington and his cabinet were working on the documents for Congress, a group of Quakers sent the president a letter begging him to end what they saw as unjustified aggression on the part of the United States against western Indians.

The petitioning Quakers were pacifist. The American nation, like every other nation, by definition was not.

Washington began his assault on Congress's resistance to forming a regular army by moving quickly but deliberately to tell Congress a powerful story with an unavoidable conclusion. This wouldn't be some timorous explanation, submitted defensively and at the behest of Congress, of presidential failure. This was possibly the only chance the Washington administration would ever get to put Congress in a position where it would have little choice but to do what Washington and his closest allies had long wanted it to do: create a regular army. They intended to control the narrative.

They built it from the ground up. The story began with a hefty collection of War Department records. These documents showed the president and Jefferson meeting, a full year earlier in Philadelphia, with the Seneca leaders led by Cornplanter who had signed the new Fort Stanwix Treaty and were now aligned with the United States. There were letters showing the administration's many efforts to employ friendlier Six Nations Indians, including Joseph Brant, as go-betweens to prevail on the western Indians to attend the treaty meetings. Then came a flurry of documents detailing exhaustive preparations for St. Clair's mission in the face of Congress's stubbornness about spending money and creating a regular army. The story came to its climax with the statement of a returned captive, reporting firsthand on the activities of Alexander McKee and Simon Girty in supporting the Indian confederation from British Detroit, the Indians' imperviousness to negotiations for peace, and their arming for war against St. Clair.

The story broke off there. Congress knew what came next. Hundreds of American bodies, tortured to death and desecrated on snowy ground.

The story this growing file told, on page after page, was not of executive failure but of congressional irresponsibility. The document was becoming gigantic with what it presented as ceaseless executive efforts, unaided by any adequate military appropriations from Congress, to defend American settlements in the Northwest Territory even while doing Congress's bidding in trying to make peace. Because Congress would create no regular army, the executive had been forced to supplement its two tiny regiments of regulars with the militiamen and the levies. St. Clair's report, which had already been submitted to Congress, made it clear that while the regulars had performed poorly, both the militia and the levies had been unmanageable and, in the end, nonfunctioning under fire. Now hundreds of them were dead, as were the regulars and the officers. While the administration had sold the levy plan hard when asking Congress for money for the St. Clair operation, the story told in this raft of documentation was that relying on any short-term enlistments must prove fatal and that given Congress's moods and policies, the slaughter at the Wabash might have been nearly inevitable.

Once Knox had that huge box of paper ready to dump on both houses of Congress, he wrote a document to precede it: a narrative and argumentative overview of the situation. This document was addressed officially to Washington, as if in response to a request for a report, but it was really written, with Washington's input, for Congress, just in case the body tried to miss the point of all the documentation submitted. The narrative played up and piled on examples of the thoroughness with which the administration had sought peace and had then worked within the under-serviced recruitment system. The administration labeled that whole record—both the documentation and the introductory narrative overview—"A."

For there was more. After the gigantic "A" came the briefer "B." Titled "Statement Relative to the Frontiers Northwest of the Ohio," "B" drew blunt conclusions from fact-based "A." Having achieved, "B" said, an amazing degree of peace with Indians from the Iroquois to the Choctaw and more, yet faced with nothing but violence from the western Indians, the administration nevertheless at the bidding of Congress had tried to come to terms, at Fort Harmar, with those recalcitrant tribes. Colonel Harmar's effort to awe them had then failed, and General St. Clair's effort to establish an American post at the most strategic point in the Northwest had failed too, for three reasons, which Knox argued from sources in "A": deficient numbers of troops (he didn't need to underscore that was thanks to Congress's limits on recruitment); those troops' *want of sufficient discipline* (he did underline that); and the lateness of the season (which he didn't need to point out had occurred because of delays in passing laws for funding). And where once the confederation really had been nothing more than a small band of disgruntled banditti, Knox added, now large numbers of Indians would be joining the confederation, precisely thanks to the United States' failure. There was a danger of young fighters joining the confederation even from the South and even from among the Six Nations Iroquois.

Hence a stark reality. "An Indian war of great extent has been excited," Knox wrote, "not only contrary to the interests and intention of the general government but by means altogether without its control."

What to do now? The answer was painfully straightforward, utterly unavoidable. Prepare for major warfare. There was no option. Anything less than doing whatever it took to achieve victory would be criminally irresponsible. Knox pointed out that defensive measures along the frontier—the kind of thing Congress found easy to approve, because traditionally carried out by militia—were entirely inadequate to the nature of the threat. Ending the war, he said, must be accomplished as quickly as possible before things spun further out of control. The only way to do that was to bring the western Indians to an ample conviction of the military superiority of United States.

But the United States didn't have military superiority, as St. Clair's defeat had proven. So following the argument in "B," the cabinet therefore worked up what it called simply "The Plan." Here was everything the nationalists had been trying for since 1783: a regular, uniform, national American army.

Knox addressed the overarching issue first. This force was to exist, he said, not on a situational basis, not only while conflict prevailed, but "during the pleasure of Congress." The army would continue automatically—that is, funded via the budget every two years, unless a law was passed to end it.

Now here it came, this time with no softening of the ambition. To begin the standing force, Knox proposed 5,168 noncommissioned officers, privates, and musicians, enlisted for three years and paid between $3.00 and $6.00 per month. He broke that total down, for now, into a four-unit cavalry squadron, four companies of artillery, and five infantry regiments, each composed of three four-company battalions, with one regiment of all riflemen. Basic annual expense for pay, clothing, forage, and so on would be $782,197.42. Add $244,279.63 for the special expenses of the proposed new campaign against the Indian confederation. That brought the total to over $1 million annually, but subtract for this year the money already appropriated by Congress, and the balance required now was only $675,950.08. The president should also have general authorization, at his discretion regarding pay, to hire mounted volunteer militias and Indians of allied tribes. Taken together, provisions in "The Plan" came close to doubling the total annual federal budget.

They'd gotten it all together pretty fast. By December 26, 1791, Knox had the new American army wrapped up in the great physical and political weight of "A," "B," and "The Plan." On January 11, 1792, both houses received the package, forwarded by the president, along with a brief cover letter that Jefferson, Hamilton, and Knox had worked to death through many drafts and Washington had signed.

The matter was to be taken up first by the House of Representatives. The House tabled the executive-branch paperwork—literally put it on the table, so the members could peruse it at leisure—and scheduled debate on the proposed army bill for January 16.

So the fight could begin. It would demand of Washington not only all of his inveterate toughness but also all of the political adroitness he'd acquired in maturity, and would now bring to a high point.

At Alexander McKee's post on the riverbank, the rapids still moved, drawing wading herons and thousands of ducks and gulls, but other rivers slowed, then paused. Swamps frozen thick offered easy crossing through scrub, and beaver had gone under their pyramids of gnawed, tilted branches. Below high, swaying branches, snow lay feet deep. Prairies were platters of high drift, and a fine whiteness swooped about revealing wind patterns, skies blazing blue, then dull gray.

All winter at the Glaize, the Indian confederation's new base of operations, hard work went on. The hope was that by late spring, cornfields would stretch for ten miles along the southeasterly bank of the Miami of the Lake. On the opposite Miami bank and on both banks of the Auglaize, new towns already stood.

The winter, however, was even harder than usual. The men tried to track game, but they'd started late, thanks to military operations; then the deep snow fell early. Their farther-western allies the Kickapoo and Potawatomie and Wabash and others were back in their own towns, facing their own winter problems, and soon hunger began to stalk the confederation's new headquarters. Having moved closer to McKee and Detroit, the Indians found themselves with no choice but to appeal to the British for help, and not in this case for military support but for the basic means of survival: food, blankets, and seed. Little Turtle wanted British artillery. The immediate want had become British food and warmth.

Alexander McKee found himself working hard on two fronts: at the

Glaize, he tried to keep the confederation together; up at Detroit, he tried to solidify British support. He built a small stockade of his own at the Glaize, right on the point of the rivers' confluence, and Simon Girty, the fabled terror of the American frontier, moved there to serve as agent on the ground. Soon the point had a French baker and an English silversmith.

What McKee and his Indian allies were creating at the Glaize, even as winter set them back, was a multicultural domestic and military complex, blending Indian and European ways, armed against white expansion into the Land of the Three Miamis. Along with Little Turtle's new Miami town, which went up a few miles west of the Auglaize confluence near the mouth of a still-smaller tributary, there were three Shawnee towns: Blue Jacket's, Snake's, and the oldest on the site, Captain Johnny's. More than a mile up the Auglaize sat Big Cat's Town, a Delaware settlement where Buckongahelas lived. A highly varied assortment of people thus inhabited riverbank towns within about ten miles of the stockade and the other services at the central confluence: not only Miami, Shawnee, and Delaware, but also Mohawk emissaries from the East, Cherokee emissaries from the South, French and British traders and artisans, the western Iroquois whom whites called Mingo, and a multitude of mixed-race children and adults. Here was a new expression of, or a reversion to or a revival of, a notion of the old American West, when expansion for white settlement hadn't yet become a reality, when European forts had often been built at Indian behest.

This revivalist community was well fortified against a common enemy. Blue Jacket was spending the winter organizing recruitment far and wide. If that process went well, the Glaize would soon serve as the military gathering point for everyone from Ottawa living nearby on the Miami of the Lake, to Ojibwa and Potawatomie from as far away as Lake Michigan, in preparation for a final springtime offensive against the United States.

What bothered McKee was that a combination of winter and hunger was preventing the confederation from immediately following up its victory over St. Clair. Fighters had returned to the scene of the battle to better hide artillery and disable weapons left behind, and they'd harassed the forward American post, Fort Jefferson. Yet the core at the Glaize was letting down the other nations, in McKee's opinion, by not pressing its military advantage against the United States. What if the confederation's core had followed the routed troops under St. Clair on their retreat toward Fort Jefferson and Fort Washington? The Americans would have had no chance. Almost all would have been killed. What if the Indians had demolished the forward forts Jefferson and Hamilton and then gone all the way, attacking the barely defended settlers at Cincinnati, then at Marietta, then moving upstream and overland and threatening the American nation with organized military force as far east as Pittsburgh? What if Pittsburghers had been forced to witness Indians celebrating victory by desecrating corpses right outside town? American dreams of expansion westward might suffer setbacks so disastrous they couldn't be overcome for generations, and by then much else might have changed too. Who could say what might happen?

But concerted aggression of that kind wasn't the confederation's way. While the Indians centered on Kekionga and the Glaize were well practiced in raiding south to the Ohio and across it, killing and terrorizing families in homes and soldiers outside forts, the kind of action that Europeans defined as major military operations—pitched battles and maneuvers—were for these Indians always defensive. The United States was trying to invade Indian country; the Indians weren't trying to invade the United States. The confederation would fiercely attack any attempted incursion and would decline to sue for peace. That was the plan for forcing Americans to withdraw eastward and respect the Ohio boundary. That's all they wanted. McKee might imagine a relentless, terrifying offense, made when the enemy was still weakened by rout—to him, that was the only true defense—but most of the Indians didn't see things that way. Their traditional military mode was to fall back, regroup, and make plans for a later sortie.

Anyway, any successful Indian offensive against the entire U.S. frontier would have to involve British troops. McKee knew that, and that's what he wanted most. He tried to impress on his colleagues in Detroit, and on those back at Montreal and Quebec and in Whitehall, the strategic advantages of maintaining well-fed, well-armed, uncompromising Indians to face down the Americans. All of the confederation leaders saw the rum trade as deleterious to the Indian will to fight, and in January McKee wrote with urgency to Sir John Johnson in Montreal, noting his intention to requisition five hundred bushels of army corn for the Glaize Indians' immediate sustenance, along with seed corn for spring planting, and begging Johnson and others to find new ways to block the selling of rum out of Detroit to the Indians. Mckee even pushed his superiors to build a British fort near the rapids of the Miami of the Lake, on uncontested American soil, but his bosses wouldn't hear of it. They tasked McKee only with feeding and arming the confederation up to a point, deploying his friend Girty as military adviser, and giving the Indians whatever might legitimately be construed as protection. Troops and heavy armaments and fortifications he could not get. Guy Carleton, Lord Dorchester, governor of the Province of Quebec, was firm in that policy. When Dorchester himself came to Detroit, and addressed the confederation Indians, he promised British support in terms so bureaucratically vacuous that he only amplified Indian mistrust and left McKee stewing in frustration.

Hence McKee's double challenge, reflecting his own dual nature. He had to keep his British bosses as fully committed to Indian efforts as possible, and he had to maintain the Indians' attachment to the British. This winter, some of the confederation Indians living farther to the west, near the Illinois River, had started talking to the Spanish across the Mississippi about allying with Spain instead of England. Such a move would set some elements of the confederation against others and against the British. The fur trade might dry up overnight. McKee could only hope that once British higher-ups received the news of Indian victory over St. Clair, he could inspire them to more serious support. But while information traveled quickly on the ground, it traveled slowly over oceans, and by early 1792 Whitehall still had no knowledge of the St. Clair defeat.

Before that, however, McKee received some information that gave him new hope. Only a week after the confederation's victory at the upper Wabash, John Graves Simcoe stepped from the gangplank of the *Triton* onto a dock in British America. Simcoe harbored a famous disdain for the United States, and he was McKee's new boss. This arrival was the best news McKee could have heard.

As the House of Representatives took up discussion of forming a regular army, debate was expected to be fierce and controversial, leaving members vulnerable to criticism. The body met on the ground floor of its recently acquired quarters beside the Pennsylvania State House, and whenever it was time to put other matters aside and debate the army bill, officers cleared the public galleries and closed the doors. With privacy secured, the Speaker of the House would leave his chair, and the House would form itself as a "committee of the whole": all members of the House acting as a committee, for the purposes of debating a recommendation for the House, when it would reconvene as the House; during such a session a committee head took over the chair. This mechanism allowed for free debate without pledging anyone to anything before he could see who else was saying what.

Because no record of debate was kept, nobody would ever know exactly what went on, in the representative branch of the United States government, to overturn the longest-standing traditions in America having to do with the military. And yet while Congress was able to block history's view of its proceedings, the executive branch was able to subject the debate to day-by-day scrutiny, thanks to the president's allies in the House. Washington's cabinet thus began maneuvering as cleverly as possible through a difficult process.

On January 19, the House asked Hamilton for a report on funding the army Knox had proposed in "The Plan." Hamilton instantly presented a detailed report. So far so good. Then James Madison, now serving as a congressman from Virginia, was appointed chair of a select committee to present a bill for forming an army.

Heading this committee was emblematic of the tight spot Madison occupied in Congress. A Virginia planter, lawyer, and intellectual like Jefferson, but more exhaustively and systematically learned in government, less mercurially creative, politically cagier, Madison had teamed with Hamilton in the Confederation Congress to push the nationalist project. The two young members had pored over law books in search of ways of reading the Articles of Confederation to give the Congress more power. A rigorous theoretician, Madison had played perhaps the leading role in bringing nationhood into existence during the Constitutional Convention and the ratification debates, again in concert with Hamilton, and his stature was high enough to have made him a U.S. senator. Yet he served in the lower house because state legislatures appointed senators, and Patrick Henry had used his political machine to punish Madison for what Henry saw as a betrayal of Virginia in bringing nationhood about.

By now, coping with so much anti-federalist sentiment at home had begun to affect Madison's commitment to federalism. He'd also become violently opposed to the direction he saw his old partner Hamilton taking the country. While the Virginian had gone along, though throwing up some obstacles, with parts of Hamilton's finance programs, he'd balked at the creation of a national bank. Now Madison in Congress and Jefferson in the cabinet were aligned against nearly everything Hamilton was trying to do.

Still, like everyone else, Madison valued his relationship with Washington above all. His main role in Congress in 1792 was still to help Washington get things passed. On January 25, Madison's committee presented a full-fledged military bill, based largely on Knox's recommendations for creating and funding a regular army. The administration might have thought it was out of the woods.

But it was only upon presentation of that bill that it became evident what the administration really had to fear. The anti-army faction in the House introduced a motion to strike out of Madison's proposed army bill not its heart—the formation of a regular, permanent force—but the language that would get that heart beating: the bill's proposal to augment troop strength to around five thousand men.

That was a neat trick. No alternative number was advanced in the proposed amendment. Knocking out the call for five thousand would open a debate that would allow congressmen to tut-tut about the proposed army's untoward size and expense, making them look Whiggish and republican, undermining the bill's entire purpose while enabling them to seem to support the bill as a whole, thus eluding charges of irresponsibility. The fate of Washington's effort to create an army—in Washington's terms, the fate of the American West and of the United States itself—had come to rest on whether the House motion to strike out the augmentation of troop strength would pass. Debate now focused on that.

The cabinet had some weapons it had been holding in reserve. Knox had been working with Jefferson and Hamilton on yet another document, not for Congress this time, but for the general public via the press. Over Knox's name, this op-ed explicitly framed the St. Clair defeat as a legislative failure to create and maintain a regular army, and it pitched the public directly on the plan for creating the army that was now before the House. Jefferson drafted an introduction to the article to go over Washington's name; Washington had Hamilton tweak that intro and sent it back to Jefferson for a final revision; then they backdated it to January 16, when the debate in Congress had first begun. That made the letter look innocent of what was now occurring in debate while nevertheless answering criticisms raised there. With the article and the backdated letter complete, they were waiting to learn from allies in Congress the optimal time to release.

That time had come. The House, having debated for weeks in secret, threw open its doors on Thursday, January 26, and allowed reporting on proceedings regarding the army bill. The idea was to let the members engage in two big days of public oratory, specifically on the motion to strike augmentation of troop strength out of the bill. Getting on the record via the committee of the whole, they would present their rationales and misgivings and position themselves to gain credit for any military success and to avoid blame for any military failure. After seeing how all of that played with the public, they would reconvene as the House and hold the real vote.

So the administration, tipped off by allies in Congress to the public display in the House, sent the press Knox's pitch for the national army, with its rebuttal of charges that the proposed army was unnecessarily big, along with Washington's cover letter. The public's reading about and debating the issue put the congressmen under pressure. Administration allies in the House also requested new paperwork from the president. Right after the St. Clair defeat, when the administration had engaged in those direct exchanges with angry western Pennsylvania militia leaders, Knox had written to Washington, for the record, to note that the militiamen's letters only demonstrated the crying need for a federal law placing state militias, in a uniform manner, under control of the federal War Department. Further exchanges with Governor Mifflin and the militiamen had dragged on well into January, so neither the letters nor Knox's comment on them had been included in the big package the administration had sent to Congress. But now, as House business opened on Monday, January 30, with Knox's article appealing directly to the public and public debate having concluded just the Friday before, Knox sent those letters to Congress.

The House had scheduled this same Monday for its real vote on striking troop augmentation out of the bill. For Knox and Washington, the timing was perfect. The letters from western Pennsylvania dramatized better than oratory ever could the inadequacy of the militia in coping with potential attack. The House held the vote. The motion to strike out language calling for augmentation of the army was defeated. The five thousand regulars remained in the bill.

The administration could breathe. The division was 34–18, a significant show of support for the army bill as a whole. And indeed, in the follow-up vote on the whole bill, the House did vote 29–19 to give the president and his allies what they'd wanted for so long, a national standing army.

The administration had taken a big step toward victory. But now the bill had to go upstairs to the Senate. There the president would face opposition not from political enemies but from some of his allies. Efforts to resolve that opposition were to have, in the forests far from Philadelphia, a series of unsettling effects.

Standing beside John Simcoe on the dock of the south bank of the frigid St. Lawrence River were his wife, Elizabeth, a renowned London socialite, and the youngest two of their five children. Above them, as they stood bundled up at the water's edge, soared that walled, gated citadel of a city Quebec. The return of John Simcoe: here was a potentially decisive event, Simcoe himself hoped, in the history of the New World.

He was returning to scenes of exploits that had made him famous in the lost war against the rebelling former colonies. Now he was lieutenant governor of something recently named Upper Canada: in the quick and efficient way of great powers, yet another set of lines had been drawn on a map in a room thousands of miles from the scene, with attendant rules and hierarchies for administering the resulting new place. Gone forever, just like that, was the British Province of Quebec, whose formation had caused so much trouble in the Ohio and Illinois Countries in the 1770s and helped start the War of Independence.

The new map of Canada, and the new jurisdictions there, flowed directly from that war. The overwhelming majority of inhabitants of Canada were still French-speaking people, under British rule since the departure of France in 1763, but new people had recently come north. Some of them, like McKee, Simon Girty, and Matthew Elliott, had left the rebelling colonies during the Revolution, but after the treaty was signed in Paris, many more had fled, and in the end about fifty thousand people relocated north of the border. Many loyalists settled in Nova Scotia, but in the West, around Lakes Erie and Ontario, about ten thousand English-speaking newcomers now needed help. Though a distinct minority, these settlers came trailing clouds of glory. They had special importance to the Home Office and to British imperial policy in general.

For they were at once English and American. They had fully British orientation, with origins in Pennsylvania, New York, New England, and the American South, and they'd shown loyalty to Parliament and the Crown in the face of threat and danger. They'd left on the run, in chaos and fear, giving up money, land, personal possessions. Many came from cities and long-developed farmland; now they were pioneer families, trying to start over in the great forests around the lakes and the St. Lawrence. The prime minister, William Pitt, dubbed them United Empire Loyalists because they linked British North America with the rest of the British globe. Their monarch was eager to settle, reward, and empower them.

So Parliament created a vast region for the convenience and prosperity of the United Empire Loyalists. On the new maps, "Upper Canada" now referred to a region south and west of what was now called "Lower Canada": because the axis of the new division was the St. Lawrence River, "upper" meant not northerly but upstream, near the river's sources in the Great Lakes and the Ottawa River; "lower" meant downstream, approaching the sea. The old colonial governing and trading cities, Montreal and Quebec, were thus in Lower Canada. That section retained its French law and the established Roman Catholic Church, per the old Quebec Act, but Upper Canada, with its special purposes, was to be given a new kind of government, with long-range plans for establishing military and urban centers to develop it. The region would be ruled by English law, as American refugees would naturally want, and Anglicanism would be the established religion. Representative legislatures were now to be created in both sections of Canada for the first time.

It was in that context that John Graves Simcoe was appointed governor of Upper Canada. That made him only a lieutenant governor; Lord

Dorchester remained governor proper of all of this vast, newly structured place called Canada. To his frustration, Simcoe was to carry out, in Upper Canada, Lord Dorchester's orders, not to govern there himself.

Still, Simcoe might find ways to get a pretty free hand. He and Dorchester were already at odds. As far as Dorchester was concerned, his home base in Lower Canada remained the heart of the province, the real Canada; Upper Canada was nothing much but a source of anxiety. And after giving his bland speech of supposed support to the Indians, Dorchester had left Quebec City for London, arriving there when Simcoe hadn't yet been appointed. Dorchester put forth his own candidate for governor of Upper Canada: not John Simcoe, but John Johnson, head of the Indian Bureau at Fort Detroit, an able administrator in getting loyalist refugees settled. When that nomination was rejected by the home secretary in favor of Simcoe, Dorchester took offense.

So Simcoe had known even before sailing from England to start his new job that he had no friend in his absentee boss. They saw everything differently. Dorchester had enjoyed success as a commander against the Continental army in its failed invasion of Quebec in 1776, but in his late sixties he seemed a grumpy pragmatist, without ambition or inspiration, reflexively tossing wet blankets over every new idea. Regarding British military presence around the lakes, Dorchester remained committed to the hard-to-define defensive policy of the Home Office: don't let the United States seize the disputed posts; keep the Indian confederation fed and loyal; don't commit British troops to any action against Americans unless the forts are attacked; be prepared to defend, in every way, the status quo. Dorchester didn't enjoy thinking about the contest over the United States' Northwest Territory and the strategic lake forts. He saw no new opportunities there, just headaches. And he was still in London.

That's where Simcoe was different. And that's why Simcoe's arrival in Canada gave heart to Alexander McKee as he shuttled among his house in Detroit, his storehouse at the rapids of the Miami of the Lake, and his stockade at the Glaize, always hoping for renewed British support for the Indian confederation. Simcoe and McKee shared a point of view on the North American future.

❖

The Marquis de Lafayette's military capabilities? "Distinguished in every American gazette by name," Simcoe said, "and nowhere by action." General Nathanael Greene, who pushed General Cornwallis around the South? Brave, Simcoe admitted, that's all: "He flew from defeat to defeat."

Simcoe had worked his way through every battle of the War of Independence, mentally refighting it. Thirty-nine now, he was a veteran commander of the loyalist company known as the Queen's Rangers, having distinguished himself at the Battle of Monmouth Court House in New Jersey, and by firm and daring command in many other actions in that war, and he took personally both the loss of the war and Lord Shelburne's wholesale cessions of western territory.

Upper Canada, Simcoe now thought, might reverse or at least ameliorate that painful, humiliating loss. The new nation to the south remained inchoate, unstable, and unsure, its northern boundary set only on paper, not in fact. Its foreign policy might be especially easily undermined by the executive's need for the support of legislators.

As for any military prowess the United States might have, Simcoe held that as nothing. American incompetence in the field was the great subject with him. For Monmouth to be scored an American victory, for example, was an absurd affront to history. Goaded by the rise in hero worship, especially in France, for the republican Americans led by the greatest man in the world, Simcoe had published a counter-history of the entire war. Despite the American victory, on every page his book demonstrated to his own evident satisfaction the Continental army's failings.

He saved his deepest disdain for General Washington. A medium-level Virginia land hustler and opportunist, Washington was "not to be dreaded" in the field, Simcoe reported. The American victory over Lord Cornwallis at Yorktown, for example, was due to French artillery, and Washington's enemies Charles Lee and Thomas Mifflin had often saved the army by telling Washington what to do. There was no reason to praise Washington's grace, either, in declining to become a tyrant after the war: Washington could never have pulled that off anyway. Simcoe wrote his book in 1787, while the United States was forming itself as a nation, and it mattered little to him, he noted, whether Washington became the president or went back to being a Virginia land jobber.

Given Simcoe's certainty of American incompetence, the little-populated region of Upper Canada in which Lord Dorchester took only a fretful and worried interest, so small compared with Lower Canada, so remote and uncivilized and low in everything but name, might rise, the new lieutenant governor thought, and flex a strong arm of unexpected imperial might. Such was Simcoe's vision. Refreshed culturally by the United Empire Loyalists, operating under codes of law long beloved by Englishmen, protected by the dug-in British army, and occupying an overlooked strategic position, Upper Canada might outclass old French Lower Canada and pose a particular kind of challenge to the United States, right where the new nation was at its weakest.

For below the new boundary line, Simcoe knew, much was in flux. There were loyalists to the Crown still living in the state of New York. Vermont was an independent republic, run with paramilitary flair by a self-created gang of insurgent land speculators from Connecticut; they were looking to join the American union as a state or make a deal with England. The Six Nations had split: the Mohawk leader Brant and his people had indeed made their move north of the border and were living on the Grand River in what had become Simcoe's Upper Canada, and Six Nations people still around Fort Niagara had connections with the British army there. On arrival in Quebec Simcoe didn't yet have the good news of victory over St. Clair, but he did know the western Indians were unifying in resistance to American possession of the old Ohio and Illinois Countries.

So Home Office diplomatic policy might remain purely defensive, and Simcoe might be subject to Dorchester's orders to maintain, at all costs, the status quo. But the volatility of the situation in and around Upper Canada led him to believe that chances might emerge to redress losses that the British Empire should never have taken in the first place. Sometimes Simcoe imagined responding to U.S. aggression on the Upper Canada border by leading British troops all the way to George Washington's lair at Philadelphia.

Meanwhile, what the Washington administration had warned Congress about began to occur. Despite privation and even famine, caused by one of the harder winters the western Indians had known, Shawnee diplomacy was showing its characteristic organization and intensity. Blue Jacket was meeting with great success in his winter recruiting efforts. Thanks to its victory over St. Clair, the confederation was growing fast.

Blue Jacket sent runners far and wide. They carried the dried scalps of the fallen enemy, war pipes, and the wide belts of beads that called other nations to war. They spread the news of victory and pressured those who had been hanging back to join the fight. As nearby as the bank of the Detroit River across from the fort, Moravian Indians settled by a Christian mission listened as Blue Jacket's people demanded they cease neutrality. As far away as the lower Tennessee River, a war pipe was carried to rally the Cherokee. One mission went up to Joseph Brant on the Grand River west of Lake Ontario. Another mission crossed the Mississippi to meet with Shawnee living in far-off towns on the Missouri River.

Blue Jacket himself traveled. Locally, he met with Alexander McKee and the British officers at Fort Detroit, but he also went all the way to the banks of the upper Mississippi and the Illinois River.

The idea was to get all nations to send both fighters and diplomats to a spring conference at the Glaize, the biggest yet. There the diplomats would confer and the fighters would prepare for an even greater victory, should the United States try again to conquer Indian country. The way Alexander McKee looked at it, the sheer size of that conference might be enough to make clear to the Americans that Indian resistance was insurmountably unified, that peace could come only from Americans' staying east of the Ohio. The conference should also help get a more serious commitment of British military support. With John Simcoe having landed in Quebec, and soon to come west, and with Blue Jacket's widespread recruiting getting such strong results, McKee took heart for the spring.

Even as the Washington administration's army bill, as passed by the House, went to the Senate, in the House the pro-militia faction tried some rearguard moves. This new flare-up came from an attempt to reform the old militia system.

The Constitution had placed the militia under federal authority. Yet it would take legislation to administer that rule, and some in Washington's party were pushing for a militia-reform act, in hopes of getting federal, constitutional control of what had always been the state-run system. Hamilton, Washington, and Knox had always wanted to end that system, and this might be their chance. The old anti-federalist opposition, inveterately pro-militia, could of course be expected to obstruct any attempt at reforming the old system.

But now there was a twist. Certain leaders in the anti-army coalition—the Jefferson protégé James Monroe was one—had a counterintuitive tactical inspiration. It occurred to them that getting some kind of uniform militia bill passed might obviate the need to form the big regular army after all. So in February, with the army bill in the Senate, the House did agree to take up militia reform, as a tactic for stymieing creation of the army. As debate began, some of Washington's supporters, sniffing out the opposition's tactics, came to think, in turn, that failure to get a good militia bill might make the need for a real standing army overwhelmingly obvious to the Senate. So even some administration allies in the House became less than fully committed to achieving control over the militia. Some radical republicans, meanwhile, flat out denied federal authority over the militia, despite express constitutional language: they were still trying to unratify the Constitution.

Some congressmen just didn't care. The session was ending. They wanted to go home and would vote just to end discussion.

So while a militia-reform bill did emerge from the House in February 1792, it didn't reform the militia. Congress ended its session and the members went home with no command structure reporting upward to national government, no provision for uniform training or equipment overseen by federal authority, no fines for noncompliance—really, not much to comply with. The bill looked back, not forward. It relegated militia to an impromptu, ad hoc role in local defense and kept militia out of national defense and adventure. Unlike the army bill, the militia bill was so meaningless that the Senate would be able to pass it with virtually no debate, and Washington signed it. He was presumed to have done so with distaste. Reforms that he'd long been calling for remained absent from law.

And yet failure to genuinely nationalize the system had killed the system. The militia had become as irrelevant to national strength as Alexander Hamilton had always said it was. Given that irrelevance, and given the horrible defeat of St. Clair, there seemed no practical alternative now to forming the standing army that the Senate was now starting to debate. Washington often seemed to view with distaste things that actually worked out for him. Maybe in this case he really felt the distaste. Nobody would ever know.

When the Senate took up the army bill passed by the House, Senator Benjamin Hawkins of North Carolina began playing an important role. A member of his state's planter elite and a frequent crosser of lines between the administration's allies and the emergent opposition, where his sympathies more naturally lay, Hawkins had credibility with President Washington and served at times as his political ally.

They'd worked together. In the Continental army, Hawkins had served on Washington's staff as an interpreter of French. He was no anti-federalist: a long-standing nationalist, he'd served in the North Carolina House and the Confederation Congress; as a county representative in North Carolina, he promoted ceding the state's western lands to the federal government and the call for the Constitutional Convention; he lobbied hard for ratification. In the U.S. Senate, Hawkins was by no means among the great speakers, but he was a well-respected politician, thinker, and committee worker with a reputation for being tough but fair. He sided with James Madison in opposing Hamilton's establishment of a national bank; as tension developed in the cabinet between Jefferson and Hamilton, Hawkins leaned naturally toward his fellow planter Jefferson, but he sided with the pro-Hamilton faction and voted in favor of an excise tax on whiskey, through which Hamilton would fund interest payments to the federal bondholders; most senators did, in the end. And while at times Hawkins served as an administration critic, he was among those who took notes on Senate debates and sent them to the cabinet for the president's information. He dined often at Washington's table.

In the Senate debate over the army bill, Hawkins came to the fore because he had specific expertise in Indian matters. Appointed by the late Confederation Congress to negotiate with the southern Indians, he'd learned and written up Cherokee and Choctaw vocabularies and was known by the administration to possess a sophisticated understanding of Indian politics south of the Ohio River. Hawkins's opinion would be influential.

He harbored grave reservations both about implementing the army bill passed by the House and about making war in the Northwest Territory. Neither a gung ho expansionist nor a romancer of noble savagery, Hawkins hoped and expected that the United States would gain sovereignty and effective control over all the land in the Northwest that had been ceded by England, yet he also hoped and expected that national goals might be achieved ethically. That meant eschewing conquest. He was among those hoping to persuade the Indians to adapt to European-style farming practices to assimilate Indians into the whole people of the United States, where national sovereignty was now generally believed to lie.

And when it came to military policy, Hawkins understood the opposition party's concerns. President Washington might easily be seen as capitalizing on grisly defeats to gain the standing army that the administration had been pursuing since the early 1780s, before there was an administration, or even a nation to administer. In Whig thinking, tyranny always seeks warfare to bulk up military force and shore up executive power.

Those concerns led Hawkins to suspect that the administration's efforts to get peace by diplomatic means, via the process culminating in the explosive Fort Harmar Treaty, had been halfhearted. The suspicion was far from unreasonable. Would an Alexander Hamilton—so fully on the record with regard to the importance of a national army, so generally filled with martial enthusiasm—really have been working to prevent war and bring about peace? Benjamin Hawkins, in considering the army bill, arrived at the position that until diplomatic means of achieving peace with the western Indians were sincerely tried, no full-scale invasion of Indian country by the United States could be morally justified. The military buildup called for in the army bill passed by the House should be passed by the Senate only if the Washington administration began sincere negotiations for peace.

As the Senate debated the bill, Hawkins could see that the body was nearly evenly divided on passing it and that his views placed him in the center of the divide. He could see both sides and had reservations about both; he might therefore swing the final vote one way or the other. That position gave him unusual power to gain an agreement from President Washington to approach the crisis in the Northwest in ways that would satisfy Hawkins's and others' moral and political qualms while still allowing them to support the bill.

So in debate and early voting, Hawkins began by opposing it. His grounds were those expressed by the anti-army faction: building a regular army was an inducement to use such an army, and regular armies are conducive to tyranny. If the administration were serious about peace in the West, it would be pursuing negotiations for peace, not preparing for war.

The administration was naturally watching the Senate debate with intense anticipation. Early committee-of-the-whole voting suggested that the army bill faced defeat, 15–12, and two New York senators—Aaron Burr and Rufus King—had been absent during preliminary committee voting; Burr, at least, shared Hawkins's reservations. But if Hawkins and two others would switch sides, the margin would reverse in the president's favor—there was also John Adams's tie-breaking vote—and America would have its army. Burr, at least, seemed likely to switch if the right concessions were made.

Senator Hawkins now sent a passionate letter to President Washington. It set out Hawkins's reservations about the army bill and the Indian war and positioned Hawkins as the voice of loyal, reasoned opposition. He wanted no offensive operations, no invasion, only defensive capability, and he wanted a military buildup only if serious pursuit of a negotiated peace went on too.

That position was the moderate position, one might have said, and its moderation let Washington discern a sliver of wiggle room, possibly put there by Hawkins for him to see. On some issues, a middle ground doesn't exist. Washington believed he could show Hawkins that this army-and-Indian issue was one of them.

For the centrist idea that Hawkins espoused contained a logical fallacy. It was a priori now that the United States was involved in an actual war. What Hawkins seemed to be trying to have both ways was the question of whether the war was just or unjust. Hawkins couldn't fully believe it was unjust, or he wouldn't favor providing for the military buildup under any conditions. If one took the war to be not unjust—that is, as Washington saw it, just—the question of offensive versus defensive operations was strategic, not moral, and Washington had enough experience in the field, and believed Hawkins did too, to know that making solely defensive operations against Indians was always a losing strategy. Offensive measures must therefore be taken, and that obviously meant troops would have to advance into the enemy country. Once you cut through all the hand-wringing, Hawkins really was in favor of an invasion of Indian country and knew that only a real army could carry it out.

Washington and Hawkins kept much of their exchange private. Later onlookers would deduce the deal they arrived at only via one letter and some fragments of Washington's anxious notes to himself, along with behaviors on both sides not satisfactorily explainable any other way. The result was Hawkins's seeing his way to supporting the bill and bringing others with him, under the condition that Washington make some key concessions. Those concessions, soon to have strange effects on the action ensuing hundreds of miles away in the Ohio Country, would ultimately cause a crisis.

The most important administration promise was this: even as the new, national military force was created, and even as it went into heavy buildup for war, the executive branch would engage, with seriousness and energy never seen before, in peace-making diplomacy with the Indians. Hawkins and others expected to see undisguised emissaries, traveling into enemy territory, not as spies but as diplomats making the Indian confederation genuine offers of peace. If those offers were properly made, and properly negotiated, the army could stay put, war be avoided. Any other approach to gaining Indian land would be immoral.

Given those concessions, the Senate passed the army bill 15–12. It could hardly have been closer, and Senate-House conferences would amend certain portions of the law. Still, there was now no doubt of the president's success. The final bill would pass on March 5.

Washington and Knox had to find a new commander, begin creating

a new kind of American army, and get it ready to conquer the Northwest. They also had to begin a new kind of diplomacy, at cross-purposes
with conquest.

Hawkins had also demanded that Arthur St. Clair never again command
troops against Indians. That demand Washington found easy to meet.
Shortly after the House debate had begun, St. Clair had arrived in Philadelphia from Fort Washington. He was hoping for a full-scale military
inquiry into his conduct at the Wabash. He hoped for vindication.

Washington wanted St. Clair cleared. As he'd told Tobias Lear, he
wanted justice for his general, but to Washington that meant civil justice: a House inquiry, the president hoped, would conclude that St. Clair
had acted appropriately enough under the circumstances, based on the
raft of paperwork Knox had submitted to Congress, in part for the purpose
of eliciting just that conclusion. After Harmar's failure, Washington had
hung Harmar out to dry, but in this case he wanted public blame for
St. Clair's defeat directed solely at Congress, not at St. Clair.

Military justice for St. Clair, however: no. A court-martial or other
army inquiry would only open a can of worms. Washington was willing
to support St. Clair by easing him out of command and retaining him
as governor of the Northwest Territory, but he knew that the full military investigation St. Clair was hoping for could only embarrass the administration at this touchiest of moments. With the House and Senate
having passed the army bill, Washington could expect the House to
exonerate St. Clair.

In that process, however, at the end of March George Washington received a note from Knox that disturbed him. The secretary had been ordered by the committee investigating St. Clair to supply certain documents
that hadn't been included in the earlier raft of paperwork. The committee was looking into possible irregularities of supply and wanted to review
some correspondence on the matter sent to Knox by the late Richard
Butler, as well as some official correspondence of the quartermaster.

This was the first-ever House investigation of the executive branch
and the first-ever demand by Congress for executive documents. Compliance or refusal would set a precedent. Knox wasn't comfortable

submitting executive-branch papers at the demand of Congress without Washington's permission.

Now Washington did need Attorney General Edmund Randolph. The president met with Randolph, Knox, Jefferson, and Hamilton and presented his position: he neither acknowledged nor denied the propriety of what the House was asking, Washington said, but there might be executive papers so secret that they shouldn't be handed over to Congress. The department heads agreed that the executive should hand over only those papers whose disclosure, in the president's judgment, would not harm the public good. Also, they said, the House had no right to pressure a cabinet member directly. It must address such inquiries only to the president.

Washington and the cabinet agreed to speak to the members of the committee and persuade them that the privilege was the president's. In this particular case, Washington could see his way to handing over everything demanded, but he wanted it understood that in doing so he set no precedent giving Congress a right to anything it wanted. Two years later, Washington would stand on the precedent for executive privilege he'd established in the St. Clair investigation by refusing to give certain treaty documents to Congress.

Meanwhile, St. Clair had been repeating his request for a military inquiry. With the usual displays of blank politeness, Washington kept giving him nothing but a firm no. At the end of March, St. Clair sent Washington a note saying he'd like to wait for the results of the House inquiry before resigning but was willing to resign now, if Washington thought it necessary. Washington wrote back to say that it was necessary. On April 7, St. Clair did at last tender his resignation, along with an outpouring of complaint and aggrievement. Washington didn't respond. The St. Clair matter was thus resolved.

All this time, Washington and the members of his cabinet had been mulling over what they saw as a poor set of choices for St. Clair's replacement as commander. "Replacement" was really a misnomer: the army to be led by this new commander would be fundamentally different, not only in its composition and internal structure, but also in its existential source and ultimate purpose. In total contrast to the short-term levies, few regulars, state-run militias, and elite volunteers that St. Clair had commanded, the army that the administration had finally persuaded

Congress to create was based on regulars to be enlisted by federal authority for long periods and kept entirely under the uniform command of the president, not of state and county militia officers and legislators.

Yet it existed only on paper. Anyone selected to lead this uniform national force must create, train, and supply it, develop its strategy, execute its tactics. Then he must defeat the western Indian confederation and conquer the Northwest Territory. The cabinet met a number of times on the matter without getting anywhere.

Then, on April 12, 1792, Washington made a surprise appointment. His choice of new commander would revolt many in a Congress that had been induced, more or less kicking and screaming, to give the president the opportunity to make it. But Washington was the commander in chief. The Senate was only to advise and consent, and Senator Hawkins, for one, made it a rule to approve all military appointments without inquiry. The Senate confirmed the appointment with only some dark muttering.

The president chose Anthony Wayne. There was reason to wonder whether this would turn out to be the worst decision Washington ever made.

Only nine years earlier, when Anthony Wayne mustered out of the Continental army with the brevet rank of major general, few would have called him a poor choice for commander. As a brigadier general for much of the war, Wayne had long deserved promotion, everyone agreed, to the rank he achieved only on leaving the army: he was an established hero of independence, with victories in New York, Virginia, South Carolina, and Georgia. If he'd wanted the job his friend Josiah Harmar sought, commanding a remnant of the old army and recruiting a small new regiment for duty in the Northwest, Wayne could have had it.

But like most of the other high officers of the Continental army, Anthony Wayne had no evident desire to continue in military life. With the war won, there was no army to speak of anyway. Harmar was nine years younger, with a lower rank and a relatively uneventful record. Wayne was a repeatedly wounded veteran of major combat command, at thirty-eight already a rough old-soldier type. He was ready to pluck the fruits of independence he'd fought so hard to achieve.

He hoped to find fortune in civilian life. Officers as a class had been made gentlemen by the commutation of their back pay to federal bonds; they'd also been paid in debt instruments issued by their states. In the absence of a national government, however, payoffs were at risk, and Wayne wanted to leave his wife and children rich.

In the summer of 1783, he assisted his friend and superior officer General Nathanael Greene in the logistics of demobilizing the Continental army in the South and arranged to send home the men and officers of the Pennsylvania Continental Line he'd led to victory in Georgia and South Carolina. In August, having sailed from Charleston, he arrived in Philadelphia to weeks of riotous acclamation. Among Washington's officers, Wayne ranked in fame only below Greene, Knox, and Lafayette. As Pennsylvania's conquering son, he was feted at balls and soirees in the mansions of people like his friend the financier Robert Morris, the richest man in America, and at casually celebratory meetings in taverns and coffeehouses over rum, rye whiskey, wine, coffee, and tobacco.

Men would do almost anything now for a flash of Washington's attention. They stepped in front of one another to get in his way; they bragged about drawing a distant nod. In the fall of 1783, Washington was passing through Philadelphia on his way home to Virginia from New York and invited Wayne to visit him at Mount Vernon. Wayne was ill at home in Chester County when the invitation came: like many of the toughest men of his class and generation, he suffered from random fevers, and now he had gout. Too much fun at his own long party had sent him to bed.

Yet he seemed to live among a chosen few. The great general had paid Wayne the compliment of an invitation to the magnificent farm that Washington was even then making himself great by returning to. In 1783, the future couldn't have looked better for Anthony Wayne. Seven years later, he'd blown it.

Wayne might have seemed well set up for success in his new pursuits. He held property now in two far-flung places. In Pennsylvania he owned Waynesborough, the ancestral Chester County home built by his grandfather and namesake. The younger Anthony had received its proprietorship from his aging father in 1774; the father had died not long afterward. A symmetrical stone house in classic eastern Pennsylvania style, it stood three stories high. Brick chimneys served eleven fireplaces in big rooms. The farms ranged over more than a hundred acres

of mixed planting. During Wayne's long wartime absences, the operation had thrived under the auspices of his wife, Mary, and it was thanks
to her that it thrived during his brief and distracted visits home too.

Wayne was emotionally attached to that family seat, but his big
opportunity now lay southward, in coastal Georgia, scene of his victories. The Georgia legislature had honored him with an official gift of an
850-acre rice plantation called Richmond, confiscated from a son of the
former royal governor. Lying about twelve miles up the Savannah River
from the tidewater capital, the estate was supposed to come complete
with an imposing plantation home and all outbuildings and accoutrements necessary to raising and shipping rice on the large scale that made
low-country fortunes. The state even added to that reward a nearby
smaller property called Kew.

Best of all, Wayne's former commander General Greene received a
slightly larger Georgia plantation not far from Wayne's. Greene had begun the war as a private and had become the Revolution's most effective general, and Wayne respected him more than any man other than
Washington. So the two northern comrades in arms—Greene was
from Rhode Island—were to become neighbors as southern planters. A
new, interstate America, unrestrained by British imperial priorities, was
bringing high finance together with speculation in big land, big agriculture, big development, big production, and big markets both local
and global. Americans of Anthony Wayne's class and background were
standing on the threshold of an era that would dwarf their fathers'
successes and give their children seemingly unlimited prosperity. Such
were the rewards of the war they'd risked and sacrificed so much
to win.

It was in winning that war that Anthony Wayne had come into his own.
His inner life was defined by a special relationship to combat. Too young
to serve in any of the wars that had marked the British imperium in
America, he'd spent his boyhood fascinated by all things martial—both
grand strategy and the techniques of hands-on, day-to-day leadership—
even as militia shape-up and actual fighting with Indians went on around
him. His father could see that his son had little knack for the upscale

farming life that made the Wayne family living, so he sent Anthony to school with an uncle, and Anthony took over the place, dressing the boys in a makeshift motley of military and Indian-looking attire and staging drills and battles in the school yard.

There were black eyes and cracked heads. Anthony's father threatened to remove him from school and give him hard labor at home, at the nastiest farm jobs, unless the boy stopped playing army and started studying.

The father knew his son. The prospect of hard farmwork did the trick. Anthony mended his ways, became a strong student, entered the Philadelphia Academy at sixteen, excelled in mathematics, left at eighteen, and by the late 1760s had become a surveyor, farmer, and husband. He lived at Waynesborough with his wife; he was the father of a girl and a boy; he was building modest wealth at a reasonable pace. He took one trip to Nova Scotia to survey and invest in land, but mostly he stayed home. He'd flirted with buying a commission in the British army, but when it came down to reality, he spent his twenties with the martial romance stifled.

Then came American tensions with England. In 1774, at twenty-nine, Anthony Wayne became a Chester County representative in Pennsylvania's patriot Provincial Convention. Then he served in both the Pennsylvania assembly and the province's ad hoc Committee of Safety. He sought what to him was the plum assignment: recruiting and training a province-wide militia, and when he got that job, the romance rekindled, this time with a real object: preparations for defending Pennsylvania against British incursions. Men followed Wayne readily. He was handsome and intense, and he made fiery speeches, throwing his whole heart and growing prosperity into the cause of American liberty. In the spring of 1775, the intercolonial body calling itself the Continental Congress was reconvening in the ground-floor room borrowed from the Pennsylvania assembly in the statehouse in Philadelphia, when news arrived from Massachusetts that fire had been exchanged by British soldiers and local militia in Lexington and Concord. Anthony Wayne was soon a colonel in the Continental army, commissioned both by that army and by the Pennsylvania Committee of Safety, and he took command of the Fourth Battalion of the Pennsylvania Line. Almost everybody in that battalion had volunteered to serve expressly under Wayne.

A life in regular army, building a competent force nearly from scratch, pursuing glory in the field: all of that had come about at last. Emotionally, after 1776, Wayne never really went home. It was in the army and in command that he had much to learn.

Learning was painful. Between 1776, when he took command as a colonel untested by any battle, and 1783, when he was breveted out of the army a seasoned major general and war hero, Wayne was forced on a daily basis to master feelings of angry urgency, even flirtations with insubordination. He had to learn how to be led.

Wayne wasn't alone among the Revolutionary officers in beginning the war with a combination of high excitement and zero experience. Henry Knox, for one, had been a bookseller in Boston with a special interest in cannon large and small. Bookselling was no effete enterprise: a first-generation urbanite of northern Irish stock, Knox was a sometime street brawler and gang fighter; he had a sense of tactics, but his military knowledge came from years of nosing about in books on artillery and fussing over the ins and outs of deployment. When the time came to use big guns against the British army in Boston, it was a mark of Continental army weakness that no American was better informed on the subject than Henry Knox.

That worked out pretty well. Knox became the Continental army's artillery commander; later in the war, he became Washington's right hand. Still, the lack of field experience on the part of so many top officers limited Washington's choices in the early fighting. The commander himself had never done anything like what he was doing now: commanding a poor excuse for a full-scale regular army, supplemented by the militia recruits he found so impossible, fighting a more or less European-style war against one of Europe's greatest imperial armies. With no idea what might happen in the pitched, open-country battles typical of that kind of warfare, the general couldn't afford to engage. The Congress's diplomatic goals involved getting him military help from France. Washington's strategic goals involved little more than keeping an army in the field while avoiding major conflicts.

For Anthony Wayne, military glory had long been a gleaming dream.

He found real-world command of an American army another thing. By no means was every man who happened to be commissioned a colonel in the Continental army in the ideal emotional and mental position to learn what had to be learned. Learning wasn't fun for Wayne either. But it turned out that he could do it.

It began with his first battle. This was during the American attempt to take the city of Quebec, in June 1776. Wayne had marched his Pennsylvania battalion from Philadelphia all the way up to Fort Ticonderoga, the formerly French fort commanding the strategic point where the top of Lake George nearly met the bottom of Lake Champlain. From Ticonderoga, Wayne put his men on sailing barges onto the lake, northward toward the St. Lawrence River into Canada. The trek from Philadelphia had taken more than a month, and Wayne had tried to spruce up his men along the way. In Albany, where the battalion took a few days' break from marching, he ordered his men to shave, wash, and powder their hair and turned them out to drill. He was pleased by the effect. He already believed appearance affects performance. Watching the two hundred barges entering Champlain, he thought his armada resembled the Greek fleet on its way to Troy.

Other American troops had preceded Wayne's all the way to the very walls of Quebec, but to the disgust of Wayne and others they'd since withdrawn. The new American commander in the north, General John Sullivan, wanted to reverse the retreat, or at least make British troops pay a price. The idea was to test British resolve: Why retreat unless forced to? Why not find out whether Quebec might actually be taken? Those questions accorded with the green Wayne's mood too. By early June, Wayne had his troops bivouacked on the south side of the St. Lawrence River, at Sorel, about eighty miles upstream of Quebec.

They'd been joined by other Pennsylvania regiments. One was under the command of Arthur St. Clair, forty then and far more experienced than Wayne, having served in the French and Indian War and not in an American provincial force but in the regular British army. Wayne instantly resented St. Clair. The older man was a colonel like Wayne, but senior, because he'd been given command of a battalion formed earlier than Wayne's. Nothing about St. Clair's experience in battle could justify to Wayne the seniority of St. Clair. The younger man would spend years complaining about it.

These Pennsylvania colonels gathered on the St. Lawrence. Serving directly under General William Thompson, they had orders to attack a force of British regulars reported by intelligence to be stationed on the opposite bank of the river, at the town of Trois-Rivières, twenty-five miles downstream on the way to Quebec. The number at Trois-Rivières, anywhere from 300 to 800, it was reported, seemed vulnerable to surprise attack by the combined forces of the five Pennsylvania divisions: 1,450 men led by Wayne, St. Clair, and three others. They began advancing downstream in boats to Nicolet, on the south bank across from Trois-Rivières. There, just after midnight on June 8, Thompson gave his colonels the order of battle for the late night and early morning of June 9. Wayne was keenly aware that this would be his first real test.

The ensuing Battle of Trois-Rivières, as it came to be known, was a disaster for American strategy. But not for Anthony Wayne.

Crossing the river and landing on the north bank at about 2:00 in the morning, Thompson left a guard with the boats to preserve a line of retreat back across to Nicolet and down to the base camp at Sorel. The bulk of the force began marching eastward on a road along the river, through dark woods toward Trois-Rivières, with French-speaking locals as their guides.

The guides had chosen the wrong road. As light dawned, soldiers in British ships guarding the riverbank spotted hundreds of Americans approaching Trois-Rivières. Cannon aboard the ships began bombarding them, and the Americans were forced to move away from the river and into the woods. They found themselves foundering in a huge expanse of thicket, sunk in mud sometimes as high as their waists. Hours went by as the men and their commanders struggled for dry ground.

Wayne found a way out of the swamp. He'd managed to keep his few hundred men together; now he brought them exhausted and covered with mud onto an open plain.

He tried to draw the men up in battle formation. From the river to his right, the ships' artillery kept throwing shells, but Wayne shouted orders, his ensigns relayed them, and his men responded by forming a line to move on Trois-Rivières. Before the men could fully form, however, Wayne was faced with a big detachment of crack British regulars appearing seemingly out of nowhere, firing on his not-yet-formed line.

Wayne ordered his light infantry to skirmish with the British, hoping to hold them off long enough for his heavy line to form. His men responded under fire just as they'd been trained: at Wayne's command, the light infantry withdrew and the main line emerged, firing repeatedly in perfect formation. As they advanced against the British attackers, Wayne found himself waving his hat and shouting orders as loudly as any bugle. He ordered both his left and his right to wheel. Wheel they did, smartly. Wayne was flanking the British line on each side. His muskets' lead was slamming the British soldiers on the middle, the left, and the right. The attackers had become retreaters, and they tried to retreat in good order, but Wayne, his forehead seeming to gleam in the late-morning light, his body seeming to expand beyond its real size, never let up. Soon the British soldiers broke formation. They ran from Colonel Wayne's army.

A small and brief exchange, yet something of a technical gem, for a neophyte. Pitched battle on open ground employing classic maneuvering: everything Washington rightly felt leery of letting his green officers pursue. Wayne had begun disadvantaged by mud, surprise, and inferior numbers, but he had the rules of combat, and it turned out he could think on his feet and had no fear. He had the knack, by no means natural to every field commander, of seeing a situation instantly as a whole, sensing enemy vulnerability, and without needing time to puzzle the matter out, imagining how to take advantage of it. He'd trained his men, and they'd done as he ordered and set a British army detachment to rout. Wayne had been imagining this moment ever since the blackened eyes and broken heads of his play sorties in grade school.

In the field that day, however, with a swamp at his back and Trois-Rivières to his front, he had no time to savor the moment. There were not, as intelligence had reported, somewhere between three and eight hundred British troops in Trois-Rivières; there were two or three thousand, under command of the dashing, ruthless general John Burgoyne. Before

Wayne's startled eyes, Burgoyne's troops now appeared between Trois-Rivières and Wayne's line, an overwhelming force entrenched behind breastwork with field artillery. The men Wayne had sent packing, it turned out, were only an advance force.

Just as Wayne realized the trouble he was in, his fellow colonels brought their own troops out of the muddy swamp, greeted with furious lead and shells from the British forces at their front; meanwhile, artillery continued to harry them from the ships to their right. So Wayne made another quick decision. He moved his troops forward into the flying lead. So did St. Clair and the others. Soon the Americans had advanced into the midst of a hellish firefight. In the thick smoke, they were only about eighty feet from the enemy's front line.

The troops showed bravery, but what could they accomplish, outnumbered in this heat of deadly fire? It couldn't go on. Rethinking quickly, the American colonels called a retreat, and their men managed, under pressure of enemy fire, to retreat while holding formation.

Wayne's force was the last to leave. He and his two hundred men stood their ground, facing fire. Once the other battalions were safely away, Wayne called a retreat too, and his men stepped carefully backward toward the woods, still firing. Then, turning to flee westward, they avoided the swamp by taking a road inland, away from the river. Wayne could only hope to get far enough from the line of British fire to track back toward the river, locate the boats left there for retreat, get across to Nicolet, then march back to the base camp at Sorel.

But Burgoyne saw what was happening. He dispatched fifteen hundred men to cut off the Americans' move to the river. Wayne felt a ball graze his right leg as, hurrying now, he and his men overtook eight or nine hundred soldiers fallen behind the other American commanders. There was nothing to do, Wayne realized, but round up this big, disorganized, frightened force and try to keep it moving away through the woods.

They ran right into the British cutoff troops. Denied access to the river, Wayne knew his men were too exhausted and confused to stand and fight. He changed direction. He turned the huge retreat farther inland, then turned again, marching back toward the river, effectively circling the British force. It kept firing at the Americans from fixed positions in the woods throughout this entire enervating maneuver, and the Americans returned covering fire, desperately seeking the bank where they'd landed. Luckily for Wayne, the British didn't advance.

So Wayne did arrive at the escape spot. But the boats were gone. The guard assigned to assure the line of retreat had been forced to take them downriver, all the way to Sorel, or have them seized by the enemy.

The river now cut off escape. Wayne had one move left. With about eleven hundred men—his own troops and all the stragglers—and assisted mainly by a Lieutenant Colonel Allen separated from St. Clair's battalion, Wayne kept moving westward on the wrong side of the river, trying to put as much distance as possible between his men and the British forces forward of Trois-Rivières. For two full days, with food running low and near exhaustion, Wayne and Allen pushed the men through those woods. Along with Wayne's leadership, now an accomplished fact, they had some luck. Burgoyne would have preferred to follow quickly: if he had, Wayne's troops would have succumbed. But Guy Carleton, the governor of the Province of Quebec, and Burgoyne's superior—he would one day be made Lord Dorchester—had a longer plan to trap and destroy American forces in Canada. Carleton held Burgoyne back.

Wayne and Allen finally managed to get their spent troops to a spot across the river from Sorel. Boats sent from the American side ferried them back to camp. The failed American attack on Trois-Rivières and Quebec was over.

In the American encampment at Crown Point, at the bottom of Lake Champlain, Wayne had some justification for the certainty he expressed to anyone who would listen that he and Allen had saved the American army in the north. Wayne reported the assertion by letter to the Pennsylvania assembly and praised his troops' bravery and discipline in battle against overwhelming British numbers. His superiors concurred, calling Wayne brave in command under fire. He'd sustained a minor injury: that ball grazing his right leg.

Arthur St. Clair, by contrast, had given up command during the retreat because he'd stubbed his toe. That's the story, anyway, that Wayne told people.

By the time General Washington sent him south, in the summer of 1781, to serve under the Marquis de Lafayette in Virginia, and then under General Greene in South Carolina and Georgia, Wayne had become more than a brave, talented, and skilled commander. Unhappy whenever yanked back, he'd taken part at first in a string of American failures and then in some provisional American successes. Some of the successes could have been accomplished only via the finely tuned mix of Wayne's furious desire to drive forward and the restraints imposed on him by George Washington.

Other officers complained that Wayne was impetuous and irresponsible, seeking personal glory instead of collaborating in feasible tactics. They had reason. In his early days in Washington's army, Wayne seemed to itch for combat regardless of likely outcomes. After the withdrawal from Quebec, he'd spent a long winter doing nearly nothing as commander of Ticonderoga in the cold woodland at Crown Point. Released at last from that duty, and arriving in Washington's camp in New Jersey, then on the move throughout Pennsylvania, Wayne wanted to get right into things. In the meantime, he'd been promoted to brigadier general, and given his success during the American failure at Trois-Rivières, he had good reason to think he'd do well in major campaigns.

In his Pennsylvania expeditions under Washington, Wayne showed personal courage and sometimes adept command. But the results were unhappy. Begging Washington by letter to come up with the main army and engage General William Howe as he advanced on Philadelphia—"For God's sake," Wayne wrote, "push on as fast as possible"—he described Howe's army as vulnerable, and he couldn't understand Washington's caution. With no response from the commander, Wayne moved forward anyway. Near Paoli he stumbled into a surprise bayonet attack. In the end, Wayne had to retreat under circumstances that led his critics to wonder why he hadn't done so earlier. This time the retreat was anything but orderly, and nearly two hundred of Wayne's fifteen hundred soldiers died on British bayonet points; a hundred were wounded. The British took maybe twelve casualties.

Some weeks later, at Germantown, Wayne sought revenge and redemption for Paoli. For a moment, he and other American officers thought they might have it. But again Wayne was forced to retreat, and again the retreat was chaotic. His men, blundering in fog, mistook friendly troops for the enemy, panicked, and ran.

Like the other American commanders—like Washington himself—Wayne was in over his head. Howe meanwhile marched into Philadelphia and occupied it, the Continental Congress fled to Baltimore, and Washington withdrew his army to the broad hill country known as Valley Forge, above the Schuylkill River west of Philadelphia. The units spread out over the steeply tilted ground, built hut barracks, and dug in for a rough winter.

Wayne considered desire for forward movement anything but irresponsible. The winter of 1778 daily confronted him with the plight of his men and other troops stuck at Valley Forge. As he went from hut to hut, he saw not only cold and disease beating down brave men but also mental and emotional depression. Wayne always identified inaction as the source of depression. He felt called upon to relieve it.

When the time finally came to attack, Wayne got his chance. It was summer now, and hot. France had at last entered the war on the American side, and General Henry Clinton, having taken command of British forces, was ordered to evacuate Philadelphia, march north through New Jersey to Sandy Hook—the southern boundary of New York City's lower harbor—take boats up to the city, and concentrate British efforts there.

Wayne was not alone in urging Washington that now was the time to pounce. The major generals Marquis de Lafayette and Nathanael Greene agreed. Clinton's columns would be strung out along the road across New Jersey: the Continental army must seize this rare opportunity for a heavy attack to stop British movement.

Charles Lee, Henry Knox, and others disagreed. They argued that it would be suicidal to commit the main body of American forces. They advised only light, harassing maneuvers against the British columns.

Washington was ready, at last, to side with the activists. On June 28, 1778, the American effort began when Washington sent four thousand men in an advance party to attack the British rear guard as it left Monmouth Court House on its trip northward. The idea was to use this harassment to slow the whole British line, requiring the main force to turn back to aid its rear, thus buying time to bring up the main Continental force and mount a serious assault on the main British force, on ground of Washington's choosing.

Washington assigned Charles Lee command of this advance attack. Lee demurred: he still called the whole idea infeasible. Washington offered Lafayette command instead. At that, Lee changed his mind and accepted command. An eager Anthony Wayne was placed under the wavering Lee. Lafayette now shared command with Lee while also serving under Lee's command, and Wayne and Lafayette were under direct orders from Washington himself, thus not fully subordinated to Lee. Poor communication prevailed. When Lee, Wayne, and Lafayette met in Englishtown to plan their advance attack on the British rear, Lee's interpretation of Washington's orders was that he should use his own tactical judgment in the field and advance or retreat accordingly. Wayne's interpretation was to attack and to keep attacking, no matter what the troops encountered.

The next day, General Washington, advancing with his main force along the Monmouth Road, was shocked to encounter Lee's force in full retreat with British troops in close pursuit. Lee himself soon appeared on the scene and hurriedly offered the commander explanations. As other officers watched in amazement, and British forces drew ever nearer, the commander dressed Lee down, and Lee actually shouted back at the commander.

That was unaccountable. Washington relieved Lee of command and sent him in disgrace to the rear.

So far, things had not gone according to plan, and the British were approaching. Only now did Wayne arrive in haste, having resisted joining Lee's retreat, holding his ground against a British force growing bigger by the moment. Lee had even pulled support from Wayne's flanks and failed to respond when Wayne sent him urgent messages for help. To Lee, Wayne was being unrealistic, self-interested, insubordinate, continuing what Lee believed must soon become a losing battle. To Wayne, only Lee's reluctance to fight made the battle a losing one.

Washington was thinking quickly. The fearless Wayne was before him in a sweat. This moment would set the course for Wayne's future.

Washington, drawing up his army under the unexpected pressure of attack, gave Wayne charge of the disgraced Lee's remaining forces, ordering him to make a stand with those men and delay British onslaught while Washington arranged his main force about a thousand yards to the rear.

Wayne now made himself indispensable. The heat had reached 104 degrees. Men were dropping; a hundred would die of heatstroke. The British, arriving in pursuit of the retreating Lee, began a powerful assault with cavalry, infantry, and cannon. Wayne did as ordered. He held them off just long enough for Washington to make a strong line, with Greene's men as the right wing and those of Lord Stirling, the New Jersey earl who had sided with the Americans, on the left. When Wayne could no longer hold the British off, he withdrew, prudently and in good order, to the main army, which then advanced with force.

John Simcoe was there, leading the loyalist Queen's Rangers and, like Wayne, distinguishing himself, and Simcoe would later make the characteristic point that Monmouth couldn't really be counted an American victory. But it wasn't an American loss either. After hours of heavy fighting, with each side repeatedly advancing and withdrawing, the British withdrew and night fell, ending the action. Washington's plan to attack in the morning evaporated with the dawn: the British had moved out under cover of darkness. Howe continued to Sandy Hook and into New York. He thus achieved his objective.

Still, for the first time in pitched battle, under Washington's command, the Continental army had not yielded ground. Anthony Wayne's performance was crucial to Washington's first success in war.

Always restless for action, always frustrated by delay and restraint, never understanding why the commander kept him on such a short leash, Wayne nevertheless became one of Washington's most important officers. He always chafed hardest against Arthur St. Clair. His fellow Pennsylvanian struck Wayne as passive and only semi-competent. St. Clair not only outranked him but indeed, as the war went on, commanded him: in 1779, a reorganization of the Pennsylvania Line placed St. Clair in charge of the whole thing.

Wayne protested violently. He didn't mind remaining only a brigadier general himself, he said—really, he did mind—but he hated to take orders from St. Clair, of all people. St. Clair had continued to criticize him for conduct at Paoli. Wayne accused St. Clair of having failed, like Lee, to send troops when Wayne had requested them at Monmouth. In a letter to the Congress, Wayne threatened to resign his commission.

He never sent the letter. Instead, even as he repeatedly urged the Pennsylvania assembly unsuccessfully to promote him to major general, he began looking for a new assignment. What he really wanted was a special, independent command of his own. He wanted that command to come directly under General Washington.

In 1779, he got his wish. Washington was forming an elite light-infantry corps. Wayne asked Washington if he could lead it, and Washington quickly agreed. Pulled temporarily from the Pennsylvania Line, and thus from the aegis of St. Clair, Wayne was delighted to command two thousand veterans handpicked from across all regiments of the Continental army. He reported now to only one man: Washington.

It was in command of his own light infantry that Wayne achieved the signal victory of his Continental army career. The battle for which he would be best remembered—regardless of later, more important exploits—came on the Hudson River in New York.

The British were still in possession of New York City, but thanks to American victory at the Battle of Saratoga the Continental army controlled traffic on the river north of its Fort Clinton at West Point. In May 1779, however, a British fleet sailed up from New York and managed to seize a particularly strategic formation not far downriver from West Point, a narrowing of the waterway formed by high, rocky outcroppings on both sides. The British now occupied Verplanck on the east bank and Stony Point on the west. That was part of General Clinton's strategy for drawing Washington's forces out of the highlands and out of New Jersey to fight a pitched battle.

Washington didn't bite. But he did want Verplanck and Stony Point back.

Peering through telescopes positioned in the mountains to the north, Washington and Wayne observed the British garrison at Stony Point.

The formation was really a high, wooded rock, rising almost straight out of the river on a point of land, at once a natural citadel and a highly improved fortification. The fort's main gate opened westward, looking away from the Hudson. The high ground had been made even higher and harder to climb by major earthmoving. Man-made hills swooped upward to vertiginous heights overlooking the river. Down below, beginning along the river's edge and continuing uphill, carefully constructed thickets of huge, sawed logs with sharpened points climbed steeply and then ran around the area to make it seem impenetrable from any direction.

This was no place, Wayne advised Washington, for frontal assault. Wayne proposed instead to attack by surprise, at night, his men ambushing and overcoming sentries posted at the pointed logs down at the river, then scaling the rock in silence. Because any sound from the river would alert the British garrison to the attack, Wayne's light infantry would carry unloaded muskets. This was a bayonet operation, to be achieved by close-up stabbing and slashing.

Washington agreed. He also informed Wayne that during the operation the younger man was officially empowered to alter tactics as he saw fit.

Armed with both a good plan and the confidence of his chief, Wayne left West Point on July 15 with only two hundred men and first traveled west, hoping to avoid British detection. Then he turned south and east toward the river and the bottom of Stony Point. The surprise was timed to begin exactly at midnight. To divert the garrison's attention, Washington had authorized a frontal assault, fake, with ostentatiously loud musket fire at the fort's main entrance away from the river. Exactly at midnight that tactic went into effect. It startled the British sentries and roused the garrison to defend its gates.

In the darkness down by the river, Wayne's advance men were waiting in silence. They heard the exchange of fire above. Wielding bayonets, the advance team attacked sentries posted in the obstructing tangle of sharpened logs and overcame them, and then the team worked hard and fast, and yet as quietly as possible, to cut a way through the mess of sharp log and brush fortifications. With that barrier reduced, Wayne's main force proceeded up the steep slope toward the garrison.

Silence prevailed. The troops had been told that any man who fired a musket would be instantly executed by an officer.

For a change, everything went as planned. At the top of the slope, the surprise bayonet attack came off perfectly. Even when Wayne took a musket ball to the head and went down, the charge went forward. He got up and kept moving, and his light infantry took Stony Point without difficulty. They captured more than five hundred British prisoners and turned Stony Point's cannon on Verplanck across the river.

The victory became instantly famous, for reasons more of morale than of strategy. Congress struck a gold medal for Wayne. Letters of congratulations came from delegates to Congress, from other officers, from friends. Washington hadn't intended to hold the position, and with American evacuation the British would soon retake Stony Point, yet victory there boosted both Wayne's reputation and the American mood. An important officer in whom Washington placed trust, Anthony Wayne was now a certified war hero.

From there, Wayne's army career rose to the glory of 1783, during actions in the southern campaigns under Lafayette and Greene that were anticlimactic, compared to the derring-do at Stony Point, if strategically far more decisive. Wayne's light infantry had been disbanded; he'd been returned to the line. But his importance to the Continental army's growing success against the British army was both a fact and a story now. His skill and his reputation were assured. Along the way, he got a name.

Mad Anthony. Some of Wayne's fellow officers criticized him as a rash commander, and the nickname might have seemed to refer to hot-headedness, but the man who gave it to Wayne meant something else. Or he probably did. The story had versions. A private in Wayne's command known as Jimmy the Drover, or Jemmy the Rover, who for some reason liked to call himself "the Commodore," was arrested by civil authorities for some misdemeanor and placed in jail. The Commodore was a serial deserter; nevertheless, he told the jailers that he was a good friend of Wayne's—there was some truth to the commander's affection for Jemmy—and sent a request to his commander to get him out of jail. When word came back that Wayne had refused to intercede, and indeed would have the Commodore flogged if he didn't mend his ways, the Commodore appeared stung. "Anthony is *mad!*" he said, and with bitter sarcasm he added, "Farewell to you; clear the coast for the Commodore, Mad Anthony's friend."

Nobody knew exactly what he meant, but the name stuck, and as used by his men, it seemed to have less to do with reckless, impulsive motion than with those qualities' very opposite: a growing obsession with military discipline. Wayne had come to prize and enforce sharpness on parade, immediacy of response in battle, dress as a mode of self-esteem, and obedience to orders. He had access to patience now, but his brand of patience, anything but serene, involved ceaseless vigilance.

Mad discipline didn't conflict with characteristic bravado. Lafayette, who commanded him in Virginia, thought Wayne went off on his own too easily. Under Greene, whom he so admired, in South Carolina and Georgia, Wayne expressed hurt and aggrievement at any perceived slight from his chief: Greene was forever couching Wayne's orders in reassurance of the high regard in which the subordinate was held. When Wayne's feelings were hurt, even General Washington heard about it. When the commander ordered Wayne to leave Lafayette in Virginia and travel farther south to report to Greene and help expel British forces from Wilmington, Charleston, and Savannah, Wayne bucked. It looked at first as if he'd be serving not directly under Greene but yet again under St. Clair, so Wayne wrote to Washington asking for a winter leave. Or, Wayne suggested, maybe he could just travel very slowly toward South Carolina, take his time.

Washington responded by noting that Wayne could of course make his own plans for the winter but that traveling south to meet Greene, even if slowly, would be more in keeping with military propriety than going on leave. In response, Wayne took a tone. He'd now been placed by Washington, he huffed, in a position where he couldn't in good faith accept a leave: he would start south immediately. Washington dealt with Wayne the way he dealt with everybody else. Ignoring both the tone and the hurt feelings it revealed, the general simply noted in the most businesslike terms his acceptance of that plan. Anthony Wayne did go to South Carolina. He helped mop up the War of Independence, and he accepted, with his plantations there, the gift of a grateful state.

So why, in 1783 and the years following, when Wayne returned to civilian relationships domestic, romantic, political, and economic, should he encounter difficulties so great that by 1792, when Washington appointed him the first real general of the first regular American army, he seemed so washed up, so terminally devoid of judgment, that for some the appointment called the president's judgment too into question? When he embarked on new enterprises after the War of Independence, this beat-up hero, socially considered somewhat vulgar, though undeniably charming, experienced a steep decline in what mattered most of all, to him and to his contemporaries: reputation.

Some of his problems began at home. Wayne was a gregarious man. With other men he enjoyed both warm friendships and intense contests, sensitivity to slight, efforts at dominance. But he was a natural gallant too, in the crusty, old-soldier mode popular in the day, and during the war he'd flirted happily with the pretty and accomplished daughters of families with grand homes where he billeted himself. He'd also courted and been courted by a rich and beautiful young woman from Delaware, the toast of Philadelphia society, named Mary Vining.

Readily excited, Wayne was sometimes deeply stirred. He became emotionally attached to Miss Vining. More painfully, he harbored an ache for his sometime confidante Catharine Greene, wife of Nathanael Greene, his superior during the war and his good friend. In these problematic ways, he could get close to women, and women could get close to him.

But he couldn't even pretend to be reliable at home. He just wouldn't stay there, and he couldn't manage to give his wife what many other men of Wayne's type considered a wife's most elementary due: public respect. It's not that he actively tried to disrespect Mary Wayne. He liked her. He called her Polly. During the war, he wrote as often as he could, addressing her as "dear girl" and complaining when she didn't write to him.

Mary's feelings for him, however, got worn down. The entire Pennsylvania campaign had taken place in Wayne's own neighborhood—the Paoli debacle occurred almost on his own doorstep at Waynesborough—but his visits home were rare, and even when he did visit, he was distracted. Early in the war, Mary felt a passionate longing for his presence, and while her letters bravely assured him, in nearly unpunctuated torrents, that she was keeping up the farm as best she could—in fact she made it pay better than he ever did—most recipients could not have failed to sense her battling with despair and terror. She reflected on the innocence of their baby boy, all unknowing of the danger his daddy was in, and she expressed stark, lonely dread at the thought of British occupation of the farm. Having learned he'd been in battle, Mary reported, she'd hardly been able to master her anxiety.

Wayne responded with rote apology, brushed off her concerns, jollied her along, and instructed her firmly, from a distance, on how and how not to raise his children, especially his son. He paid them little attention either.

Now that the excuse of military duty was over, Wayne's fun in town with Miss Vining only escalated. He made no effort to hide it. Mary Wayne had meanwhile become a saddened realist.

In the summer of 1784, Wayne sent a characteristic note from Philadelphia, alerting her to the fact two veteran officers would be calling on her and she should keep them to dinner and by all means give them Madeira, claret, and porter, if she had it; the Waynes' daughter, Peggy, was to go to one of the veterans' wives in York; Wayne himself was unavoidably detained in town and would be going to Wilmington before coming home. He hoped for a loan that would help him benefit at last from his valuable estate in Georgia.

His shift of attention to Georgia ushered in a painful chapter. Wayne had begun his civilian career, not unwisely, by leasing out the Georgia plantation and pursuing political ambitions in Pennsylvania. Radically democratic and populist, the state's 1776 constitution had removed normal property qualifications for voting and holding office. Pennsylvania had thus become the scene of a throw down between high financiers and land speculators, led by Washington's friend and Hamilton's mentor Robert Morris of Philadelphia and the representatives of a coalition of small farmers, small artisans, tenants, and laborers. The radicals were trying to devalue bondholders' and land speculators' investments. They were using state government to distribute credit and opportunity in egalitarian ways. To the upscale, the Pennsylvania legislature represented everything that was going wrong in an independent America.

As an officer and an aspiring gentleman, Wayne joined in an elite movement to remove populist measures of 1776 from his state's constitution and restore some semblance of the relations formerly prevailing between the investing class and ordinary people. Nominated in 1783 to serve on the council of censors, constitutionally empowered to assess the document and recommend changes every seven years, he took an approach to electoral politics that presaged the troubles he was about to encounter in other areas. On Election Day, Wayne raised militia troops and Revolutionary veterans, formed them up, and marched them over to the statehouse to vote for him. When poll watchers objected, he yelled, "My men will vote!" and the poll watchers, intimidated, admitted his claque. The men even got to cut the line. That strong-arm method triggered an assembly investigation.

But what Wayne most wanted was to make a killing, the kind of fortune a man could leave his children and know that they and their progeny would never have to work for a living or worry about money. Others were doing it. Wayne's best friends, the Greenes, were living down in Georgia on their magnificent plantation, and they seemed to be piling up a fortune. He wanted to join them in the rice business.

Rice production represented a new kind of farming for Wayne. Southern plantations were at once bigger and more tightly focused than farms in Chester County. Dazzling profits in rice came via the forced labor of African men, women, and children in the miserable, dangerous, highly skilled work of ditching and diking wetlands full of snakes and alligators, then weeding the crop and fending off rodents in standing water breeding disease-bearing mosquitoes. That process occurred within the institutionalized logistics, mechanics, and transactions of the grand-scale slavery economy. Chester County had slavery too, but agriculture there had long depended more on indentured whites. By the end of the 1770s, enslaved blacks in Pennsylvania numbered only one in thirty; in 1780, under the radically egalitarian constitution, the assembly passed a law requiring gradual abolition of the institution.

So while Wayne had experience as a farmer, it was a frustrating fact for him that without enough of what he wasn't alone in calling "the curly heads," bought at a low enough price, the Georgia estate given to him as a potential gold mine couldn't become a paying proposition. He would have to be on the scene to get things happening, he felt, and in order to buy the labor power he needed, he would have to borrow money.

He sent an application for a loan of 50,000 guineas to the well-regarded Amsterdam banking house of the brothers Wilhelm and Jan Willink. The Willinks had given the United States a loan for financing the War of Independence and were now investing in American land. Wayne enclosed the deed to Waynesborough as collateral and mentioned his friend Robert Morris as a reference, as well as Peter John van Berkel, the Dutch minister to the United States.

Application in the mail, Wayne started spending. He wrote to agents in Georgia, instructing them to acquire sufficient Negroes and everything else he might need to raise a mighty rice crop. Those agents bought the slave laborers from a dealer in Charleston with a mixture of up-front cash and obligations to pay the balance over time at reasonable interest. As usual in such transactions, an invoice was presented on a standard ledger sheet, light red rules going one way and fine double and single lines going the other, with "List of Negroes" neatly written at the top. The first page gave the names of men and boys—Match, Mingo, George, Virgil, for example—with ages and skills such as blacksmith, hostler, and general labor. The next page listed the women and girls: Clarissa, Fanny, Nancy, and so on. The eldest among Wayne's first purchase was sixty-two; the youngest was two. They were all to be delivered to Richmond, the estate.

Wayne had meanwhile arrived in Charleston. He stocked up on food, drink, and other things he'd need for living at Richmond while getting a crop raised. Having arranged for delivery of those supplies, he took the packet to Savannah and arrived there to a grand welcome and a series of parties: the conquering hero again returned. Arriving upriver at Richmond at last, he found things in disastrous shape. The forty-seven slaves weren't enough to raise rice; they were already bogged down in making the neglected property arable at all. There were acres of ditches to dig. Getting a crop planted and tended, then selling the harvest for the revenue needed to recoup the outlay: that looked unrealistic, this year anyway.

❧•❧

In elegant, light-filled rooms above a canal in perhaps the oldest financial center in the Western world, the brothers Willink were reviewing Wayne's loan application with the skepticism that was part and parcel of their trade. The applicant had used Morris's name, so the brothers wrote to Morris, letting him know with reasonable frankness, just between professional lenders, that this was a particularly difficult time to lend to those they didn't know.

They wrote the same day to Wayne himself. With the requisite elaborate politeness of their trade, they assured him he would never have needed even to mention Morris or Minister van Berkel in order to induce them to exert their best efforts in favor of a man who was entitled to their just esteem, et cetera, and yet they were sorry to say that in the current climate—for politeness, they threw in concern about an impending Dutch war with the Holy Roman Empire—they found themselves in too precarious a position to allow themselves to impose on him by instructing him to draw on them at this time. They closed by assuring General Wayne that if at some future time they had the smallest likelihood of success in finding themselves able to lend, they would of course be honored, et cetera, et cetera, and getting that note out the door, the brothers had reason to think they'd brushed off the Wayne application in no uncertain terms without giving the applicant any cause for offense. They did this kind of thing all the time.

Wayne took no offense at the Willinks' letter. Far from it. To begin with, the letter took a long time to reach him, and in March, having not heard anything, he'd already sent them another letter alerting them to the fact that he would indeed be drawing on them soon, per his application, for a cargo of Negroes. They hadn't yet received that note when they wrote their rejection. Wayne's blithe presumption of approval wouldn't arrive in Amsterdam until months after they'd sent what they took to be a polite yet plain refusal, and when Wayne did receive their letter, in late May, he was delighted. He took the brothers to be saying they'd be approving his application any day now—just as soon as this Dutch war with the empire was revealed to be a chimera—and he wrote gratefully back to say that the eventuality he'd meanwhile alerted them to in March was now a reality: on the strength of their assurances of soon being in a position to extend him credit, he'd bought the Negroes. The brothers could expect his agents to be presenting a note for redemption. And he went about buying tools and other things and telling his agents to bill the Willinks, with whom, he said, he had an account of 50,000 guineas.

In September 1785, Wayne learned from one of his agents, Edward Penman, that his first note drawn on the Willinks had been denied. The Willinks said Wayne had no account with them. Penman now wanted his money from Wayne, and so would Roger Saunders, Samuel Potts, and Adam Tunno, men who had sold and brokered the sale of the slaves and now expected the ongoing payments. Penman could only flatter himself, he told Wayne, that his trust hadn't been misplaced.

That was as close to fighting words as you could get and still hope to maintain a relationship. The other creditors started writing to Wayne as well, demanding payment in similar terms.

Wayne's first response to these demands was to ignore them. His credit was good. He had an account with the Willinks of Amsterdam; people hounding him for small amounts of cash were petty and grasping. He was overwhelmed with repairing and ditching Richmond and getting it ready to plant, and once that was done, profits would be so huge that none of these matters would seem meaningful at all.

He did write to his supposed lenders. He reminded the Willinks that they'd said all his documents were duly authenticated, his file in order, the only impediment to lending had been some issue between the Holy Roman emperor and the Netherlands. That issue having been resolved, "I had fondly flattered myself (most agreeably to your declaration)," Wayne wrote, "the favorable turn of circumstances would have enabled you to prove by *fact* your desire of serving me." In a tone of wounded feeling, he demanded the return of his papers and the deed to Waynesborough. As long as those documents weren't yet in his possession, he reasoned, he was empowered to keep drawing on the Dutch firm. So he did. Given the distance involved, it could take six months for a note to bounce.

For the Willinks, the Atlantic mail-packet time started giving the debacle a slow-motion, catch-up quality of nightmare. They had to cope with delayed sensations of financial shocks they'd actually sustained, without knowing it, months earlier in far-off Georgia. Only after respond-

"They were tobacco men": In this typical English ad, slave labor and a glorified planter lifestyle are meant to enhance the product's appeal. (George Arents Collection, the New York Public Library. *Tobacco Dealer's Trade Cards.* The New York Public Library Digital Collections. http://digitalcollections.nypl.org/items /b3af248f-3cc5-7070-e040-e00a180638c0)

Young George Washington in the 1750s, excited by western land speculation and about to fall into the icy Allegheny. (Woodcut book illustration by K. Bobbett)

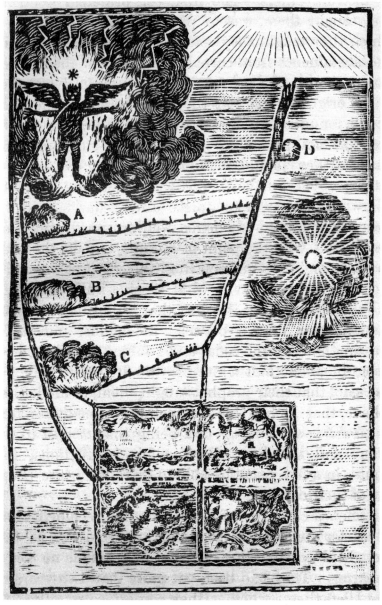

"Drive them out": the prophecy of Neolin, the Delaware visionary who inspired Pontiac's War, depicted in a woodcut, as poorly recalled and explained by a white captive.
(From "A Narrative of the Captivity of John M'Cullough, Esq.," in Archibald Loudon, *A Selection of Some of the Most Interesting Narratives of Outrages Committed by the Indians in Their Wars with the White People*, Vol. 1. 1888 reprint of 1808 edition)

A wagon leaves Ipswich, Massachusetts, bound for the New Englander Rufus Putnam's Marietta settlement on the Ohio River. (Art and Picture Collection, the New York Public Library. *Dr. Cutler's Church and Parsonage at Ipswich Hamlet, 1787. The Place from Which the First Company Started for the Ohio, December 3, 1787.* The New York Public Library Digital Collections. 1902. http://digital collections.nypl.org/items/510d47e1-3191-a3d9-e040-e00a18064a99)

Fort Washington was the strongest of the U.S. posts on the contested north bank of the Ohio River. It protected Cincinnati, the first settlement in a vast real-estate speculation. (Library of Congress)

While some say this portrait is of the Shawnee British official Alexander McKee's son, family history has it that this is the elder McKee himself. (Museum Windsor, 1976.4.1)

A rare likeness of Little Turtle, said to have been copied from a painting made by the famous portraitist Gilbert Stuart and destroyed when the British burned Washington in 1812. (BAE GN 00794 06185300, National Anthropological Archives, Smithsonian Institution)

Portrait of John Graves Simcoe on the eve of his triumphant return to North America in 1792. (Toronto Public Library)

Paucane. a Meamis Chief

by Mrs Simcoe 1794

Elizabeth Simcoe, wife of the governor of Upper Canada and an accomplished watercolorist, made this sketch of a Miami leader in profile. (Library and Archives Canada, Acc. No. 1938-223-42)

Anthony Wayne, captured in woodcut in his Continental army days. (Library of Congress)

The mature Wayne— possibly hoping to look more genial than his reputation as "Mad Anthony" would suggest. (Library of Congress)

Known to Spain as its spy number 13, James Wilkinson, shown here in the 1820s, served as second-in-command to Anthony Wayne and undermined him at every turn. (Filson Historical Society)

President Washington reviews a wing of the gigantic militia he raised in response to the Whiskey Rebellion in western Pennsylvania. (Kemmelmeyer, Frederick [ca. 1755–1821]. [Attributed to] *Washington Reviewing the Western Army at Fort Cumberland, Maryland*. After 1795. Oil on canvas, 22 3/4 x 37 1/4 in. [57.8 x 94.6 cm]. Gift of Edgar William and Bernice Chrysler Garbisch, 1963. [63.201.2]. The Metropolitan Museum of Art. Image © The Metropolitan Museum of Art. Image Source: Art Resources, NY)

A mural depicting Anthony Wayne, by Alfred D. Crimi, in the Wayne, Pennsylvania, post office. For many years, Wayne's conquest was glorified and memorialized in American public spaces.

ing to Wayne's initial demonstration of outrage—"we cannot see that such a letter ought to be an inducement to draw on us"—did they receive the further notes he'd drawn on them. The normally sober Dutchmen expressed their growing panic, letting Wayne know they were seeing that he'd "pushed your drafts so far as 19,588." Because they'd already made it perfectly clear that they couldn't pay those amounts for him, "this gives us a great deal of concern," they said. Most people would have read that remark as a howl of pain and rage.

The Willinks were trying to explain to Wayne what to them was horribly plain. Various reputable agents were beginning to tell people that the Willinks' firm was turning down bills. In the lending business, such stories were the kiss of death.

Betrayed by imaginary lenders, Wayne began referring to his real creditors as persecutors. He hadn't yet received his paperwork back from Holland, he assured the persecutors, so there couldn't be any real problem with the Willinks' honoring his notes. He complained to the slave broker Penman, whom he'd begun to hate as he'd never hated anyone before, that the Willinks' keeping his papers was as unaccountable as their refusing his bills, but Penman didn't care about any of that: he was demanding money from Wayne that he, in turn, owed creditors on whose deaf ears no doubt fell his own bitter complaints about Wayne's faithlessness. Wayne's idea of reassurance was to send Penman news like this: "At all events, the next crop will be adequate to the purpose unless something very extraordinary should intervene." That didn't reassure Penman. It couldn't really have reassured Wayne.

At last he wrote to Robert Morris's partner Thomas Willing of Philadelphia, complaining about the Willinks and blaming them for his now being so "embarrassingly circumstanced" as to need a loan from Willing—3,000 pounds sterling. He mentioned in passing the gout in his knee, which he reminded Willing came from a wound sustained while serving the cause of liberty. Still, Willing didn't lend, and Wayne's letter meant that now everybody in high-finance circles in Philadelphia— Wayne's favored circles, which he was trying to join by making his pile—could see what was happening to their war hero down in Georgia.

Not that Wayne was alone in trouble. Throughout the country, the entire land, bank, and development speculation in which his Philadelphia friends like Morris and Willing were so deeply involved had become a classic bubble always threatening to burst. The busy western land market was becoming saturated in a peculiarly dangerous way: everybody was in it, to the maximum of their credit and beyond, so there was nobody left to sell titles to; meanwhile, investors responded in zigzag fashion to rumors suggesting the land would become valueless and to rumors suggesting it would skyrocket. Massive loans were out for investment, made by rich men to other rich men, some made by merchant houses, others involving Robert Morris's bank, all secured only by titles to millions of acres far away. Because any show of financial weakness would mean disaster, Morris and his friends bought fancier and fancier carriages, dressed their families in nicer and nicer clothes, drank better wine and whiskey, and entertained competitively. Debtors' prison loomed.

In 1787, Anthony Wayne's creditors began bringing lawsuits. That's when things really got bad.

It felt to Wayne like a conspiracy. Georgia had granted him an estate in no shape to plant. Pennsylvania had failed to reward him adequately in cash for his war service. He suffered from gout, related in part to the multiple wounds he'd received in the service. Nathanael Greene died, and Wayne was distraught by the loss.

At the same time his feelings for Catharine Greene intensified. There was something more than codified gallantry in his letters to her. Wayne made his feelings clear, and Catharine took them seriously, and yet, caught up in the frustrations of business, he ignored her letters back. With what he now thought might be his dying efforts, he was trying to build a sufficiency for his children. Other men of his class and background seemed able to do so, but somehow he'd become embroiled in a monstrous unfairness. The situation kept boggling his mind.

The only way out seemed to be to keep fighting. In responding to demands and lawsuits, Wayne's proud and wounded tone wasn't appreciably different from the tone he'd sometimes adopted with superiors during the war—once even with Washington himself—and these men were not his superiors. His ceaseless demand for his creditors' respect—meaning special treatment based on his extraordinary merit and the unique challenges he faced—could only convince them they'd never collect. He routinely put off responding to their demands; when he finally did respond, he would blame his gouty war wounds, make a florid general case for his own supposedly well-known uprightness, and blame his victims. To Penman he complained that he'd never experienced the torture of a debtor until making contract with Penman, and he wished he'd never done so.

To wipe out the debt, he offered Penman his smaller estate, Kew, worth so much more, in Wayne's eyes, than what was owed: Penman could pay the balance of the value back to Wayne in prime Negroes, 50 guineas a head. Penman's rejection of that offer only revealed, Wayne believed, the real purpose of the persecution. The creditor sought not justice but the personal ruination of Anthony Wayne. So it was war, and all was fair.

This whole time, he'd been moving back and forth between the ports of Savannah and Philadelphia. The trips could be harrowing: on one, everybody almost drowned, and Wayne's best horse was washed overboard. In Pennsylvania, he was occasionally at Waynesborough but far more often in Philadelphia, squiring Miss Vining at events thrown by hostesses like Barbara McLaine; he had a gallantly flirtatious relationship with her too.

Where Wayne was failing in Georgia rice, Mary Wayne was making a real go of Chester County wheat. When Wayne wrote to her from Richmond, he complained with evident sincerity of receiving too few letters from her, but he wrote rarely himself, and when he did, it was with a bluff "pardon me, my dear girl, for so long silence occasioned by a variety of disagreeable circumstances." In one letter, he told her he would be home sometime in June; in May came this: "I have just time to request you not to expect me until you see me." That was typical.

His daughter, Peggy, now entering her teens, longed for her father's presence at home and tried at times to get his attention. Her letters came in a conspicuously neat and tiny hand, submissive, expressing forgiveness for her lifetime of separation from him. Those letters mainly went unanswered, but when Wayne was briefly at Waynesborough, he enjoyed Peggy. She was beginning to take on all the female qualities her father admired: pretty, amiable, and accomplished, she treated him with the utmost respect. Wayne expected his son, Isaac, to achieve big things in a world of temptation and had no sympathy for what he saw as Isaac's tendency for waywardness and laziness.

Meanwhile, Wayne was considering bolting Georgia for Pennsylvania for good, imagining he might thus escape the lawsuits. Such a measure would be fully justified, in his opinion, by the unfair treatment he'd received, especially from the persecutor he could sometimes only bring himself to refer to now, with disdain, as "the man Penman." Sometimes when writing the name, he underlined it like a curse.

But he found even that option blocked. He did at last have the deed to Waynesborough back from the Dutchmen, but Waynesborough itself came under threat. His creditors brought suit to seize it in lieu of payment. Not only Wayne's wife and children but also his mother and mother-in-law lived there, and the lien seemed to Wayne but one more outrageous illegitimacy heaped on his suffering spirit. He'd long since given up believing that Pennsylvania had any regard for his sacrifices on its behalf, but with the property under threat of seizure it occurred to Wayne that he might actually face arrest for debt if he came home.

He owed Robert Morris's bank money too. He wrote instructions to a friend in Philadelphia to stuff the bank's hungry maw, as he put it, with the state and federal bonds he'd received in lieu of officer pay. That paper had fallen vertiginously, but it was 1787 now, and Alexander Hamilton had begun making his efforts to get the bonds funded by a new, national government at full 6 percent interest on face value. That's why Morris's bank, unlike Wayne's other creditors, would readily accept federal certificates, at the prevailing deflated values, and in high volume, for debts. Many people had no confidence in the bonds—hence their depressed face values in the market—but with Hamilton in office the finance insiders around Morris had good reason to hope for federal taxes earmarked to fund the bonds at face value. A great bailout on both bond and land investment seemed in the offing, and Wayne wanted to keep his western land certificates for his children.

Thus, as 1787 came to an end, Wayne risked another visit to Pennsylvania to serve in his state's convention to ratify the Constitution of the United States. Wayne's nationalism was natural. His allies in the ratifying convention were his old allies who had pushed back the radical democracy of the state constitution. Even if the potential funding of federal bonds that made the national project exciting to so many financiers and officers should fail—the war-bond and western land markets were fluctuating wildly now with investors' hopes and fears—American nationhood might ameliorate some of Wayne's problems. He hoped for federal appointment.

He was in some fear of arrest in Pennsylvania for debt, but he and his lawyer had come up with a scheme for sheltering Waynesborough from seizure. Through intermediaries, Wayne asked his mother and his mother-in-law to sue him for dower rights to the estate. As the widow of Wayne's father, Wayne's mother had a one-third interest in the property for her lifetime. Because his mother's right had vested at the death of her husband, her claim could be said to have priority, thus obstructing claims of Wayne's creditors. Wayne's idea was that once he'd extricated himself from his financial problems, the women would withdraw their suit. It wasn't clear why his mother-in-law too should enjoy dower rights, but piling on was never anathema to Wayne, and he hoped the suit would cause a court to stay any foreclosure sale, frustrating his creditors and giving him an edge, at least, in negotiating the debt down.

But his mother refused to cooperate. He'd barely communicated with her for years. On inheriting Waynesborough, he'd become legally bound to pay her an annuity, but he'd stopped paying after two years, and she, Mary, and Mary's mother now viewed Anthony as incorrigibly irresponsible.

So Wayne could now add his own mother and the other women in his family to the list of his persecutors. Meanwhile, he made the man Penman an offer that, he informed Penman, was so good it simply couldn't be refused: Penman could take all of the Georgia property. Wayne just wanted out. While many of the Negroes were no longer just superannuated, he admitted, but dead, he would make up that number in what he advertised as young, healthy, seasoned working slaves, plus the proceeds of the previous two years' crops. That was the deal.

Penman asked how much rice had been harvested in the past two

years. Wayne wouldn't tell him. Penman, near despair, could only say
that the offer was obviously unacceptable.

Back at Richmond at the close of the 1780s, Wayne faced the fact that
he'd failed. He stopped even paying taxes on the estate. With his creditors, he continued to accept no responsibility, but he wrote to Mary
Wayne and confessed, for the first time, his drastic money problems. He
would, he vowed, find a way to settle something on both Mary and
her mother, and unlike most of his letters to her, tossed off at best, he
worked hard on this one.

He wrote as well to his mother. He let her know he'd been trying to
hide from her how badly things had gone. He'd been drawn into a hope
of making money and leaving his children something big, but now he
couldn't extricate himself, he told her, and he might never be able to
come home. He'd given her money to be used on behalf of his children,
and he made that money over to her now, as the best he could do. His
tone in both letters was that of a dying man making final statements.

And yet Wayne now saw new hope. The national government had
formed. He believed he might save his reputation and at least begin to
repair his finances by finding a role in it. He would stand for office.

So it might have seemed the last event in the strange decline and fall of
Anthony Wayne when, in March 1792, he was tried in the House of
Representatives for election fraud.

He'd come back to Philadelphia protected, as he saw it, by his new
status as a congressman from Georgia. Even during the end of the states'
confederation period, he'd had his eye on federal appointments. He'd
written to Washington with fulsome congratulations on the presidency;
he'd proposed himself to Knox as military commander for the southern
region; he'd tried to get Catharine Greene to intercede for him for that
position. None of it had come to anything, but taking his seat in the
House of Representatives in 1791—he'd leveraged the corrupt political
machinery of his friend Thomas Gibbons, a Georgia lawyer, to win the

election—gave Wayne a chance to come home and put himself in full view of the president and others who made federal appointments.

And he was finding ways out of the worst of his financial disasters. His mother had finally come around and agreed to the scheme whereby her suit for dower rights would block the creditors' seizure of Waynesborough. Thus stymied, one of those creditors now agreed to take the Georgia properties: there was no other way of realizing anything. Soon Penman and the others got into a room with lawyers and divided up their losses. Wayne reveled in what he took to be the vindication of having forced his persecutors to accept nearly useless properties in lieu of the money he owed them. In the end, after haggling over the value of Negroes, one of the creditors actually owed Wayne 800 pounds.

Wayne thought Waynesborough was now safe. But a new persecution arose: the old ladies, as he called them, had seen an opportunity to gain some control over him. They refused to withdraw the suit. Wayne exploded, threatening to let the county foreclose the property for his debts; that would leave the women homeless. Any man of honor and feeling would see this approach as fully justified and reasonable, he asserted. The women capitulated.

So Wayne got Waynesborough back. The farm was a going thing, thanks to Mary, and he had fifteen hundred speculative acres in southern Georgia, rental properties in Philadelphia and Harrisburg, a thousand acres in Nova Scotia, fifteen hundred acres of bounty land on the Ohio River, plus war bonds. In the aftermath of financial disaster, Anthony Wayne found himself far from broke. In both politics and private life, he seemed to be flourishing at long last. He was serving in the House of Representatives on December 12, 1791, when President Washington's terse note came in reporting the defeat of St. Clair. Wayne would have expected little else from his old nemesis. He took part in the secret debates on the army bill held in January 1792, and while in the public committee of the whole he spoke, somewhat surprisingly, against augmenting troop strength, he changed his vote at the end and went with Washington.

He spent some time at Waynesborough with Mary. And he considered the situations of his children, worrying about Isaac but not about Peggy. Peggy was married now. When she'd fallen in love, her intended had sent a six-page letter to Wayne at Richmond asking permission for the marriage. Wayne didn't respond. Hearing nothing for months, the young people fretted; finally, Wayne's friend Sharp Delany wrote to Wayne to ask directly if he opposed the marriage. Wayne wrote to Delany that he approved. He didn't write to Peggy or her fiancé, and he didn't go to the wedding.

Isaac, for his part, had spent six years in college; now he was clerking for a lawyer. Wayne had doubts about Isaac's work ethic and made efforts through his intermediary Delany to pass on criticisms and keep the youth on as tight a financial leash as possible.

Back in Philadelphia, Wayne hung around with Mary Vining and Barbara McLaine. Catharine Greene had written him a letter of hurt feelings for his emotional retreat; she'd also begged, in terms intended to engender obligation, his help in getting Congress to make good on money long owed General Greene's estate. In the House, Wayne supported a bill to do so.

He seemed to have beaten all opponents. He'd survived.

Then it all came crashing down. In March of 1791, he found himself forced to sit in the House and listen to a speech denouncing his chicanery in gaining his seat. His accuser, James Jackson, was the former congressman whose seat Wayne had, according to Jackson, stolen. They'd been friends in Georgia, but now Jackson had brought suit, and as Jackson presented the House with what would turn out to be hour after hour of shouted, voluminous, and irrefutable evidence against the legitimacy of Wayne's office, Wayne sat surprisingly quietly. On the rare occasion when there was anything to say, he let his lawyer speak for him. Mainly the lawyer begged for delay, on no real grounds, only hoping to postpone the inevitable. Wayne could see how this would go. Nobody was directly accusing him of a crime, but nobody could harbor any doubt of what his political supporters had been up to when trying to best the incumbent the year before, and the implication was that Wayne could not have been ignorant of his operatives' shenanigans.

In one of the counties Wayne had carried, Jackson was saying, nine more people voted than were registered. In another, returns favoring Jackson had been conveyed, by a Wayne crony, not to the governor but to Wayne himself: what happened next Jackson said he would leave to his hearers' imaginations. In another county, Wayne's supporters, unhappy with the majority for Jackson, destroyed the returns and held a second election after the polls had closed, awarding thirty-nine fabricated votes to Wayne. Jackson, thundering that the election fraud authored by Wayne and his crony Gibbons was worse than British corruption, was working himself into a frenzy of indignation. He characterized Gibbons as one "whose soul is faction, and whose life has been a scene of political corruption, who never could be easy under government—!" Breaking off only when called to order by the Speaker, Jackson apologized to the House. Then he went on and on and on.

On March 16, the House voted unanimously that Anthony Wayne was not entitled to his seat. Weeks later, Wayne received news from Secretary Knox that President Washington had appointed him commander of the army for the conquest of the Northwest Territory.

8

THE PEACEFUL INTENTIONS
OF THE UNITED STATES

Shortly after arriving in Quebec, John Simcoe learned with pleasure of the Indian confederation's victory over St. Clair. He wanted to go west and inspect the situation for himself, but there was ice on the St. Lawrence and interior headway by water was impossible until the thaw.

So the Simcoes rented a house and moved furniture they'd brought from London into it, and Elizabeth Simcoe began making the best of being stuck in Quebec for the winter. Not all wives of officials would have looked forward to living at Fort Niagara, but Elizabeth Simcoe did. Adventurous, an accomplished watercolorist, she was interested in nature and in seeing new sights, and for all of the Niagara post's remoteness the British army lived as high as possible in its forts. There would be officers' wives and balls and teas. For now, however, Quebec would have to do.

Simcoe meanwhile took a trip overland to Montreal to make nice with John Johnson, who had been passed over in favor of Simcoe and reduced to handling only Indian affairs. Soon back in Quebec, the governor began assessing the many administrative, civil, and judicial problems facing his new province. He had to create a government—really, a society—largely from scratch. And while he couldn't yet get out there, he was always considering his larger goal of pushing back America's new sovereignty in the West.

THE PEACEFUL INTENTIONS OF THE UNITED STATES

George Beckwith, a British agent in Philadelphia, sent Simcoe some American newspapers with juicy details of the battle at the Wabash. Beckwith's agency wasn't so secret: the Englishman cultivated a relationship with Alexander Hamilton, who favored him with any information from Washington's cabinet that in Hamilton's judgment might, when passed on to Beckwith's superiors, further American interests with regard to England. Thanks to Beckwith, and thanks in part to Hamilton, Simcoe could expect to get an inside view of the Washington administration's plans.

He needed more. In December, therefore, Simcoe sent Captain Charles Stevenson from Montreal to Philadelphia to meet with both Beckwith and the new British minister to the United States, George Hammond, recently arrived in the temporary capital. Stevenson was Simcoe's close friend and right-hand man; the governor had brought him to Canada.

Stevenson traveled southwesterly toward Philadelphia through Vermont and upstate New York. It was the worst time of year, and the Englishman considered the roads disgracefully bad, but the idea was to gain a sense of how inhabitants of those American regions so near Canada felt about the president's war on the western Indians, and felt generally about the governments of the United States and Great Britain. Simcoe's vision of the American future involved, along with regaining as much control as possible over what was now the Northwest Territory, heavily influencing, at the very least, a slice of U.S. territory in upstate New York and northern New England, as well as the self-created, independent republic of Vermont. Many people in the mountainous areas remained disaffected from the United States, and the region gave access to Lake Champlain, even to the Hudson River. If the British army could stay in the forts at Detroit and Niagara, Canadians might regain not only the Northwest but also access to the main rivers of New York and New England, shifting the whole effective boundary of Canada well southward of Lakes Erie and Ontario. Simcoe sometimes even imagined regaining New York City.

So as Stevenson traveled south, he carried on conversations. Vermont seemed to be in play. Under the Connecticut strongman and land speculator Ethan Allen and his brothers, the region had declared its own independence of England in 1776, had given itself a constitution, and was now in negotiations with Congress for admission as the fourteenth state, but it had also begun negotiations with Lord Dorchester to become part of Canada. Stevenson came to think that not only Vermonters but also many New Englanders and New Yorkers opposed the American war for the West. Some saw the war as unjust; others found the Indians' victory terrorizing. One damned, canting Yankee, Stevenson reported to Simcoe, described St. Clair's defeat at the Wabash as God's punishment for American wickedness.

Arriving in New York City, Stevenson learned that the Philadelphia packet was delayed for repairs. Then, in the capital at last and exhausted by his trip, he began meeting behind closed doors with Minister Hammond.

One of Simcoe's schemes involved gaining a British role as mediator in the conflict between the western Indians and the United States. In Philadelphia, Stevenson presented this mediation idea to Hammond. American public sentiment was against continuing an Indian war, Simcoe's theory ran, and the United States faced the possibility of yet another defeat in the field. If America hoped to end the war by treaty, as it said it did, and if British officials in the lake forts might serve as mediators, an opportunity would arise to negotiate a new Canadian-U.S. boundary, more favorable to England.

Minister Hammond approved of the idea. Like Simcoe, he wanted Britain to keep the forts for good, and Hammond and Secretary of State Jefferson had arrived at a stalemate on the issue of handing them over. Hammond's official position was that while the British were indeed required, per the Peace of Paris, to evacuate the forts, the United States was required, per the same treaty, to enable the collection of debts of American citizens to English merchants and lenders. Furthermore, loyalists' property must be restored before the British would even hear demands for evacuating the forts, or for giving U.S. ships access to British ports, or for any of the other treaty obligations that Jefferson was insisting on Britain's fulfilling. Hence the talks' stalemate.

If the Americans would agree to British mediation with the western Indians, Hammond now privately agreed with Stevenson, the British might wangle a big buffer zone between Canada and the United States: an Indian country north and west of the Ohio River, enforced by the British army and connecting western Indians to British commercial and diplomatic interests. The region wouldn't technically be given back to

England. But the Indians would ask for the forts to remain in British possession, as security. The United States would be cut off from the lakes, from ease in the fur trade, from western settlement.

Hammond took a moment to remind Stevenson that as minister he was guided by instructions from home: he couldn't simply demand the forts in perpetuity. But because he was supposedly negotiating with Jefferson for British evacuation, he did have it in his power to procrastinate. The problem, in Hammond's view, was this: if the United States were to make peace with the Indians now, the British would be left out, the Indians turned against them, and the forts possibly seized by the United States. It was urgent, Stevenson and Hammond therefore agreed, not only to insist on a mediation role in the dispute but also to obstruct any American peace efforts not involving British mediation.

The Indians must be sustained on a war footing. That plan would soon excite Alexander McKee.

Stevenson reported his meetings with Hammond in a series of letters to Simcoe. This was in January and February, when the regular-army bill was still in debate in Congress; meanwhile, discussions were developing for Vermont to join the Union, and both processes threatened Simcoe's and Hammond's plans. It was all the more important, Stevenson urged Simcoe by letter, to keep the Indians well supplied and fully anti-American. In these dispatches, Stevenson acknowledged that Simcoe, like Hammond, was bound by official policy: the governor wasn't of course authorized to fight a full-scale proxy war from Upper Canada. And yet, Stevenson reminded his friend and boss, optimistic speculations about British support could easily be circulated among the Indians. That would keep them focused on war against the Americans, hold off any surprise peace agreements, and enable a British mediation role, all the while retaining plausible deniability of British involvement.

Stevenson didn't get back to Canada until spring. Alexander McKee, in Detroit planning for the biggest Indian confederation conference yet, had in the meantime scheduled a trip east to meet John Simcoe.

President Washington now began acting on the deal he'd struck with Senator Hawkins for passage of the army bill. Even as he began creating the United States' first regular army—considering Anthony Wayne as commander, making lists of appointed officers for review by the Senate, and planning widespread recruiting operations to fill ranks on a scale the nation had never known—Washington convened the cabinet at the President's House on March 9, 1792. The agenda was to review ways and means of bringing about the diplomatic effort that, in the minds of war-averse senators like Hawkins and Burr, but not in the minds of Washington and his cabinet, might secure the Northwest without fighting and thus make the ongoing army buildup unnecessary.

The cabinet's immediate order of business that day was to assess intelligence received in a report from a pair of spies the administration had sent up to the lakes back in early January. That was when spying, not the open diplomacy now demanded by Hawkins, had been policy. The administration had sent orders to James Wilkinson, still in command at Fort Washington, to send spies into Indian country from there, and Knox himself had employed Peter Pond and William Steedman, experienced traders with Indians and fairly typical of the type, to travel under plausible cover as traders on private business to the British at Fort Niagara. Pond and Steedman were to mix with any western Indians who might be there, gather intentions, sound them out. The spies were to learn everything they could about the Indians who had defeated St. Clair, their numbers, their losses, the state of their prisoners and plunder, to get a sense of the total arms in Indian hands, and to suss out any intentions they might have for a spring campaign.

Pond and Steedman set out for Niagara on January 10. Arriving at Fort Niagara in late February, they introduced themselves to Colonel Andrew Gordon, British commander of all forces in North America, as traders on private business. Their secret hope was to get access to Indians around the fort and, along with gaining intelligence, insinuate, as Knox had put it, the humaneness of the United States and the nation's willingness to forgive even the horror of the St. Clair defeat, while also reminding the Indians that because they'd been the aggressors, they must beg a peace from the United States, not the other way around, and that the United States could conquer and even exterminate them anytime it wanted to. What they told Colonel Gordon they wanted was permission to move fur-trading supplies westward through British territory.

The colonel instantly sniffed their real agenda, but he played along. In the friendliest of terms, he declined to allow them to travel farther west or to arrange transport for moving supplies through British-controlled territory. Instead, Gordon took this opportunity to send his own offer and threat, stated only implicitly, back to Philadelphia.

He mentioned casually to Pond and Steedman that he'd heard the Indian confederation had lost only 50 men in victory over St. Clair, with only 150 wounded. He played into the spies' prejudices by giving credit for that victory not to Little Turtle and Blue Jacket but to McKee's man Simon Girty, whose fearsome mystique Gordon now helped advance: he described Girty as a renegade white man from Virginia or Pennsylvania, Gordon wasn't sure, who led the Indians. In that context, Gordon offered his visitors some friendly advice. With leaders like the ruthless Girty, the Indians were only improving as fighters, he noted. In the St. Clair victory, they'd rallied three times, an unusual move in Native tactics, and the United States would find them a tough opponent in any further conflict.

Accordingly, Gordon floated Governor Simcoe's and Minister Hammond's plan for running a new boundary line. The only way the United States could ever have peace, Gordon said, was via British mediation. What if the United States, England, and the Indian confederation appointed one commissioner each, and the three sat down to discuss new borders for Indian country, to be enforced on Indian behalf by British troops?

In fact, Gordon further intimated, this new line was already being drawn, by Simcoe and other high-up British officials in Canada. It was to run from the Genesee River, a Lake Ontario tributary, whose mouth was about sixty miles east of the fort at Niagara in New York, to the head of the Allegheny River, also in New York, then down to Pittsburgh, then down the Ohio all the way to its mouth at the Mississippi. Everything north and west of that new boundary would be Indian country.

Pond and Steedman were startled. What Gordon was describing would impinge on two states and remove the gigantic forests of the old Ohio and Illinois Countries from effective American control. It would restore many of the effects of the Quebec Act that had pushed America into rebellion in the first place. It would cut Americans off from waterways crucial to the fur trade. It would give the British, not the Americans, sole access to Lake Michigan and thus to the farthest West.

It would drastically limit American expansion for settlement. And it would make the contested forts now on U.S. soil forever British.

For that, the Indians would give peace, with Great Britain the honest broker. Having outlined the proposition, Colonel Gordon sent Pond and Steedman home. They immediately sent Knox a report on the startling proposal.

Reviewing the Pond-Steedman report, while considering the round of new diplomacy they were required to enact, the cabinet was habitually tense. The mutual hatred of Hamilton and Jefferson had been rising to a pitch nearly unbearable to Washington, and in this discussion Jefferson was odd man out. Torn between his love of militia and his suspicion of regulars, on the one hand, and his empire of liberty and his hatred of the British, on the other, he was in favor of the war yet against the standing army policy in which Hamilton, Knox, and Washington concurred.

Yet he never openly objected to creating a standing army. The bitterest of differences were expressed obliquely. Today, for example, Jefferson and Hamilton disagreed on the mere veracity of the Pond-Steedman report. Hamilton, giving England the benefit of any doubt, said Pond, not known for reliability anyway, must be exaggerating Colonel Gordon's statements about a new boundary. In his own conversations with Minister Hammond, Hamilton confided, the new line proposed was really far less onerous than what the spies were reporting.

Jefferson, forever galled by the knowledge that Hamilton had conversations with the British minister, and possibly also with the agent Beckwith, outside Jefferson's auspices as secretary of state, suspected England—and privately the Treasury secretary—of treachery. He pointed out that whether Pond was personally reliable didn't matter: Gordon wouldn't have communicated these ideas if they didn't reflect policy. Had the new boundary come up only in the Pond-Steedman report, it might be ascribed to an overambitious colonel running his mouth on no authority, but the administration had a letter from Samuel Kirkland, a missionary to the America-oriented Iroquois in New York, confirming it. Kirkland's letter reported talk going around Fort Canandaigua that because the United States was unable to refund fortunes lost by loyalists transplanted to Upper Canada, a new line would have to be drawn for those loyalists' benefit, and the British would hold the lake forts to protect both loyalists and Indians from American encroachment. John Simcoe, it was further rumored, had sent an official from Canada to Minister Hammond in Philadelphia to begin drawing the changes on the map of North America. The Pond-Steedman report had independently identified that man as Stevenson, and Jefferson reminded his fellow cabinet members that they'd all known Stevenson was in town and closeted with Hammond. There was no reason to doubt that a new boundary line was the British goal.

So hot was Jefferson to punish England for this scheme that he proposed building a small fort at Presque Isle, on the bank of Lake Erie between Niagara and Detroit. That would, he said, cut troops at Niagara off from their comrades at Detroit and the western Indians.

Hamilton, deeming Jefferson's knowledge of warfare nonexistent, countered by noting that such a move would, obviously, incite England to an outright war that the United States wasn't ready to fight. Knox agreed with Hamilton—"as usual," Jefferson jotted sourly in his notes—and the president went with the more experienced majority. No new fort at Presque Isle.

But they all agreed without compunction—"una voce," as Jefferson put it—that there would never be any British mediation of the United States' conflict with the Indian confederation. When John Simcoe got word of that decision, he began considering ways of overcoming it.

It was in the March 9 cabinet meeting too that Washington decided to send a new emissary west to the Indians. Not another spy: this mission would be an undisguised embassy of peace, a party traveling through the forest not in secret but as a "flag," as diplomats were called. That's what Senator Hawkins and the antiwar faction in Congress were demanding.

For this errand, Knox recommended Captain Alexander Trueman, a Maryland veteran of the War of Independence. The destination the president proposed for Trueman was Fort Vincennes, all the way out on the lower Wabash near the Mississippi. That fort was well under

U.S. control now, and Jean-François Hamtramck, still its commander, had been making inroads with some of the Indian confederation's allies living that far west. Ties to the Kekionga-Glaize headquarters were weakest there, and Hamtramck believed he might achieve a separate peace with lower Wabash Indians. That would not only fray the confederation along its western edge but might also gain the United States some valuable Indian fighters for attacking the confederation.

But shortly after the March 9 meeting, Washington changed his mind about Trueman's destination. A new approach began shaping the administration's policy, with new complications for the West.

This new approach emerged from meetings with members of the Six Nations of the Iroquois. Even before the defeat of St. Clair, Six Nations delegations had been invited to Philadelphia for a conference: the hope then had been to court their neutrality in the western conflict. Now the idea was to employ them as go-betweens in the administration's newly assertive efforts for peace talks with the western Indians. American authorities still constructed the Six Nations as both the dominant and the most civilized of Indians, still credited them with their old claim, demonstrably tired, that they were in white terms overlords of Indians in the West. While certain Iroquois leaders had already been invited, the administration had recently lengthened the list.

As they arrived in Philadelphia in March for the conference, the more influential Six Nations leaders were facing tough political and social challenges. Some branches—called "tamed" by their western confederation detractors—had accepted the onerous terms of the Fort Stanwix Treaty of 1784. Led by the Seneca Red Jacket, they now lived on land reserved for them by that treaty, on the banks of Buffalo Creek, near the mouths of the Buffalo River and the Niagara River at Lake Erie. Effective British control of Fort Niagara still placed even those Iroquois beyond effective control of the United States; British agents had advised the group not to travel to the conference at Philadelphia, but many did so anyway. The other major Seneca leader, Cornplanter, who had also signed that treaty, was now one of the United States' most important Indian allies, and he lived on his Allegheny River grant in Pennsylvania. The Six Nations had always been a confederation, never operating under a single policy, but the abruptness of these geographic migrations and political divisions had divided the once-mighty empire to a degree never known before.

As for the famous Six Nations diplomat Joseph Brant, his credibility with hard-liners like Blue Jacket and Little Turtle had been dented nearly as badly as Cornplanter's. Before the Fort Harmar negotiations, Brant had tried to bring about a compromise, damaging enough in the eyes of western hard-liners, and then St. Clair had disrespected him. In frustration, Brant had led many of the Mohawk in a migration to the Grand River, west of Lake Ontario. On a bend of that river, the British had built an Anglican chapel of frame and clapboard, officially called St. Paul's but known as the Mohawk Church, with a convenient canoe landing and room for settlement. The biggest town was Brant's Town, where Brant lived in a two-story house. He'd always been a British ally. Now he lived on British soil. The loss of face he'd suffered with the western Indians had been brought to the Washington administration's attention a year earlier by its Niagara contact Samuel Kirkland.

And yet in the emerging administration narrative regarding the sincerity and energy of its new peace efforts, Joseph Brant remained the key intermediary with the Western Indians. So crucial indeed was his role supposed to be that he hadn't received the same invitation as everyone else: in February, Knox had written Brant a personal invitation, telling him the United States considered him too important to be ganged in with all the other chiefs in a big crowd. And still the Mohawk leader was hanging back, considering his options. He hadn't arrived in Philadelphia.

The conference in the capital thus proceeded in the absence of its supposedly most important attendee. To the sound of fife and drum, fifty Six Nations leaders rode into the city, and the usual blend of solemnity and entertainment ensued, at great federal expense. For six weeks, tobacco was smoked, toasts drunk, beads exchanged, and long speeches were read aloud at crowded gatherings in the statehouse and elsewhere.

It was during this conference that the administration's new idea arose regarding negotiating peace in the West. Discussions with Six Nations diplomats, the administration would soon report to Congress, had revealed that the hard-line western Indians were laboring under a terrible misconception. Evidently, they believed the United States had been fighting a war to take their land.

It was all a big misunderstanding, and the misunderstanding must be corrected as quickly as possible. For the United States had no designs on any land not already formally ceded by the Indians, per agreements summed up in the Fort Harmar Treaty. For $23,000, the Indians signing the Fort Harmar Treaty had agreed to shift the boundary of Indian land west of the headwaters of the Cuyahoga and Muskingum Rivers and east of Fort Detroit, placing the Miami and Shawnee well north of the Ohio. If, as the United States now surmised, some Indian groups felt they hadn't been fully represented at the Fort Harmar meeting, that situation could easily be corrected, and all groups embraced in the accords, with appropriate payments made. The whole thing could be quickly wrapped up in one final meeting, to be held at the Indians' convenience.

This became the administration's line. Denying, with protestations of embarrassment and apology, any U.S. desire to take Indian land, the administration defined "Indian land" as any land not ceded in the Fort Harmar Treaty.

That definition had already been rejected in full by the western Indian confederation, both in words and by the destruction of the American force led by St. Clair to enforce the treaty. Even bringing up the Fort Harmar Treaty was tantamount, from the western Indians' point of view, to an act of aggression. Nevertheless the cabinet, telling Congress that it could see light at the end of the tunnel, began pursuing the peacemaking diplomacy it had promised Senator Hawkins by bombarding the confederation's core at the Glaize with a message all the more inflammatory for being framed, in flowery diplomatic language, as a major concession made by the United States in the interest of avoiding the unfortunate necessity of launching a follow-up attack that would inevitably wipe the Indians out. The new diplomatic message was to invite, with open arms, everyone into the terms agreed upon at Fort Harmar.

In pursuing this new line, at the Six Nations Conference the cabinet urged Cornplanter, Red Jacket, and an American-aligned Stockbridge Mahican named Hendrick Aupaumut, known to many whites only as "Captain Hendrick," to travel west to the confederation with protestations of the United States' absence of designs on even one foot of Indian land. Not only were the intermediaries to carry the message; they must try and persuade the western Indians to comply.

As Captain Trueman, too, set out on his peace mission, his message incorporated this new line, and so did his destination. Instead of going all the way out to Vincennes, as originally planned, he was now to take the new message right into the heart of the confederation at the Glaize. And the cabinet added John Hardin to the mission. A Kentuckian, Hardin was well known and roundly disliked by western Indians for having served with George Rogers Clark in demolishing Miami and Shawnee towns during the War of Independence. Then, during Harmar's "flying strike," Hardin had led the mounted Kentucky troops that Little Turtle defeated so badly near Kekionga. Now, in conjunction with Trueman's errand, Hardin was to go to the Wyandot, in the Sandusky Bay towns at the western end of Lake Erie, and communicate the same message: an apology for any misunderstanding, and a confirmation of the Fort Harmar Treaty, with payments to be made to any nations and branches feeling they'd been left out, all framed as a concession made by the United States to obviate the need for a final, fatal attack on the Indians.

So it was that in the spring of 1792, the Washington administration sent two American peace emissaries, as demanded by moderates in Congress, not in disguise as spies but openly—given their entourages, even ostentatiously—deep into a forbidding region controlled by a victorious enemy who would view any unsolicited overture as an act of war. Though carefully phrased in what might have sounded like the pacific terms required by congressional moderates, the message with which the administration entrusted these emissaries made no mention of the Ohio River boundary demanded by the confederation. It simply reasserted the legitimacy of the treaties that had inspired the confederation to make war in the first place, offered more money for compliance, and made compliance the sole condition under which the United States would refrain from attacking again.

Alexander Trueman, having been promoted to major for the purpose of this embassy, traveled from Philadelphia to Pittsburgh, then down the Ohio to Fort Washington. There, under the aegis of the fort's commander James Wilkinson, he met John Hardin, who was to carry the administration's new message to the Sandusky. Trueman left the fort on May 20 in the direction of the Glaize, wearing military uniform, along with a servant and an interpreter. Hardin's party, similarly accoutered, left the same day.

By May 29, Trueman was still about sixty miles from the Glaize when an Indian and his son, on a hunting trip, joined his party. As Trueman was making camp that evening, the Indians said they were leaving, for fear that the whites would attack them in the night: it was three against two.

Trueman offered to have his servant, William Lynch, tied up to even the numbers. When Lynch was tied, the Indians shot Trueman and hatcheted Lynch to death. The interpreter fled, but the Indians coaxed him out of hiding on the assurance that they wouldn't kill him. Taking the interpreter captive, they scalped Trueman and put his body in the river. Taking the captive and the paperwork containing the administration's message, they went to the Glaize.

Hardin didn't get anywhere near his destination. A Shawnee party offered to escort him to their town, and while he was sleeping, they killed both him and his servant. The guide accompanying Hardin had been captured as a child and raised in Indian towns; he survived the attack. Again, documents with American protestations for peace on the Fort Harmar terms were taken to the Glaize.

As George Washington knew from early experience, most people deemed assassinating diplomats a violation of basic rules of conflict among legitimate nations. When the administration in Philadelphia began receiving accounts of the deaths of its emissaries in the distant forest, it put those accounts on the record.

The cabinet was building another file. It was to be submitted, when the time was right, to the Congress that had demanded the president exhaust peace negotiations before resuming warfare.

On June 14, 1792, General Anthony Wayne arrived in Pittsburgh. Only weeks after the appointment reversed his situation in life, Wayne confronted a place unknown to him, with plans to whip an army into shape for invading a place even more profoundly unknown to him.

Along with a cadre of dragoons who had escorted him from Philadelphia, Wayne found at the Ohio headwaters only about forty men under a captain. They were left behind from Harmar's and St. Clair's failed mobilizations, having never descended the Ohio to Fort Washington. Wayne also discovered that while army contractors had six flatboats' worth of supplies ready to go down to Fort Washington, the rivers were so low this summer that the boats couldn't be loaded even to half capacity and still float. Wayne wrote to Henry Knox to report that situation, and he described himself as a fish out of water: a general without an army.

The whole setup at the headwaters, from town to population to fort, looked unpromising. The fort Wayne's few men garrisoned was new. Fort Pitt, once the most fought-over prize of American empire, had subsided to ruin. On Knox's instructions by letter from Philadelphia, a new fort had been built, under the supervision of local contractors and a local quartermaster, with a degree of slowness, waste, and flat-out rip-off that tested Knox's patience to the extreme. The fort stood just up the Allegheny River from Pittsburgh, and the day Wayne arrived, it was officially named Fayette, after the Marquis de Lafayette, in a ceremony involving firing two twelve-pound cannon and hoisting the U.S. flag until it fluttered high over the fresh timbers on the riverbank.

The fort was a concern for Wayne at first glance, on closer inspection a disaster. It looked across the Allegheny at land to the north and west, less rolling than marked by abruptly rising hills. That's where the disputed territory began. And yet the fort was not designed, to Wayne's eye, for effective defense. Knox had meant it for a jumping-off place and rear supply for Wayne's expedition, once a real army had been raised and trained, to seize Kekionga and the Glaize. Fayette was thus smaller than Pitt, its design less comprehensive, and Wayne judged it vulnerable to attack. Pittsburgh, with its mud streets, small houses, trading stores, and a few fine homes, lay only barely behind the lines, and Fayette faced down Indian country without taking a strong attitude. A party crossing the river armed with torches could set the whole thing ablaze anytime, raze the stockade, explode the magazine. The soldiers would never know what hit them.

So among the skeleton crew he commanded on arrival, Wayne established a twenty-four-hour watch. Poor staffing made true vigilance impossible, and that would be true of the downstream forts too, now under his command, though Wayne had never seen them, most notably Fort Harmar at Marietta, and Fort Washington at Cincinnati, where James Wilkinson was still in command. Only about five hundred of the men St. Clair had led up the Miami were left alive, and most of the regulars, many incapacitated by injury anyway, had left the army when their enlistments were up; the militiamen had gone home too. As for the smaller forts built up the Great Miami on St. Clair's march toward the heart of Indian country—Fort Hamilton, Fort Jefferson, and soon the new Fort St. Clair that Wilkinson built between them—they were understaffed, lacking in provisions, vulnerable. Wayne knew too that the western Indian confederation would be meeting at the Glaize, after its tough winter, to regroup and follow up its victory.

Nothing looked at all encouraging to the general. Yet for every imaginable reason, personal and national, he had to succeed.

Soon Fort Fayette was bustling. Wayne's and Secretary Knox's daily lives had become a flurry of reading and writing and sending each other page after page of lists and schedules of companies on the march to Pittsburgh, complicated data on arms, uniforms, horses and livestock, civilian support systems, food, and, critically important, exact funds allocated for each. As the companies converged on Fort Fayette from points in New York, Georgia, Pennsylvania, Virginia, New England, and elsewhere, great wagonloads of arms, clothing, supplies, and the coin assigned for upkeep were moving from other points, and Knox had to keep Wayne apprised, on the record, of every movement of every one of these many component parts of the developing army. The secretary's management style became minute, even granular, and aside from those moments when he became overstressed, he kept it dry.

In return, Wayne kept Knox under steady pressure. It remained Wayne's belief that clothing was as crucial to military performance as food, money, and arms and that giving subordinate officers what they felt they needed kept them focused on more important matters. Before troops had even arrived, Wayne was telling Knox that word from the forts downstream was that the men there were almost destitute of clothing; indeed, commanding officers at those posts called the situation a disgrace to the service. "For God's sake, send it forward (if not already done)," Wayne wrote, "that I may have it in my power to shut their clamorous mouths." Smallpox and sexually transmitted diseases came into Fayette with the men, Wayne reported, and there was only one doctor; Wayne told Knox he needed a dozen. Eight howitzers had arrived, but without wheels or carriages. The dragoons' coats were already coming out in the elbows and under the arms: remnants of blue cloth and needles and thread must be ordered and sent on. It was indispensably necessary that some effectual mode of transportation of stores be adopted, because a Captain Porter of the artillery was saying he'd seen quantities of public stores left at several taverns along the road in open sheds. And on and on.

Knox sometimes pushed back. In response to Wayne's complaining about a lack of arms, he noted that General Edward Hand had recently forwarded 548 rifles to Pittsburgh and that number was exclusive of the 50 that had been forwarded in March. He was funny, too, once. "Major Rudolph," Knox wrote to Wayne, "has inspected the horses and men who were at Elizabeth Town and highly approves the former."

Desertion was Wayne's most immediate problem. Signing up for war was easy. Captains were charged with personally recruiting their companies by establishing offices in their locales, often in taverns, and publishing the recruitment proposition: a signing bonus, good clothes, free travel, adventure in service of national honor. Once an infantry captain, say, had commissioned a lieutenant and an ensign and signed up just over a hundred privates, he would promote twelve noncommissioned officers from among the men—he'd be looking ideally for six sergeants, six corporals, and between eighty and ninety privates—and start marching them westward while communicating with the War Office in Philadelphia, which coordinated with Wayne in Pittsburgh. Very soon, for the men and officers alike, things became no fun. Marching really meant endless slogging and hauling, in rain, heat, and cold, loaded down with equipment. These men were regulars, by the terms of their enlistments, but they weren't yet regulars in any other sense: they struggled along hard roads and faltered quickly with irritation, regret, blisters. There was heavy drinking and a lot of mouthing off.

Arriving at last in Pittsburgh, eastern soldiers and officers alike, from city and country alike, free and formerly imprisoned alike, found the place creepily primitive and wild, surrounded by the steep mountains they'd barely survived crossing. And yet their imaginations might have made Pittsburgh, compared with where they were going, as familiar as the family hearth. They had no control over their fates. They couldn't know how many days they would spend floating downstream. They did know that after hundreds of miles of twists and turns on the

Ohio stood the headquarters where they were bound: Fort Washington, at the Cincinnati settlement, deep in the contested country. They knew that the river, the forts along the way, and even headquarters itself were subject to Indian attack. As bad as the march had been, reality began to hit hard once the march was over and training began. Running away looked to many like the only reasonable choice.

Discipline is what Wayne was famously mad for, and he knew what to do. Flogging was carried out by company musicians, the fifers and drummers and sometimes buglers. Both in battle and at camp, music had to be constant: communicating orders, dividing the day's routine, setting the pace of march. Musicians were busy no matter what was going on, achieving perfect synchronization at exact moments. Often they were boys, and other than the women employed in laundry and sewing, they were the lowest-ranked people in the army, just a human clock and megaphone, unarmed noncombatants. Their music made things run, so they were assigned to punish the infractions that kept things from running well.

Sometimes a fifer, more often a drummer, would wield the classic nine thongs knotted at the ends in lashing the bare back—the bare ass, for especially egregious offenses—of an offender tied to a tree or post. Blood would soon pour from the lacerations. Fifty lashes, given with a drummer's command of tempo, would turn the back into an open, quivering mass of agony. Some soldiers received their punishment in staggered form, given time to recover just enough to be flogged again, even as the wounds grew more sensitive and anticipating further lashing demolished the man psychologically. The fact that the punishment was given publicly, and by a man of lower rank, was an element in the punishment. Ultimate humiliation involved dressing the convicted man in women's clothing.

Another means of discipline at Wayne's disposal, less humiliating because meted out by equals, was the gauntlet. The offender marched between two lines of men, a soldier walking backward before him with a bayonet at his chest to keep him from running. As he walked, the men bashed his entire body with sticks.

Wayne was Mad Anthony, but such punishments were overwhelmingly common. Everyone commanding European-style armies relied on them. Courts-martial formed to convict and sentence the accused, and methods of punishment were regulated by government. During the War of Independence, General Washington, facing just the sort of desertion problem Wayne faced now, asked the Congress to raise the number of lashes from thirty-nine—it was taken as biblically prescribed, thanks to a reference in Corinthians—to a hundred. British courts-martial had authorized up to two thousand, and Washington believed thirty-nine was tantamount to nothing. His request was granted, but later, when he tried to raise the number to five hundred, he was turned down.

The hope was to deter a host of ruinous infractions from slovenliness to insubordination to drunkenness to sleeping on watch to cowardice in battle to desertion. The hope was also to avoid taking the ultimate measure. But sometimes there was no recourse. Courts-martial also handed down sentences of death by hanging or shooting.

Wayne's growing army was called the Legion of the United States, and "legion" wasn't a decorative name but a term of art. The details weren't fully released until the end of August, but much thought had gone into creating, with the inspiration of ancient Rome, what amounted to four small, complete armies, each with potential to carry out every form of operation on its own. Each was to have a troop of mounted dragoons; an artillery company, to be trained in firing cannon; eight infantry companies, armed with muskets, to be trained in throwing lead in an enemy's general direction; and four companies of riflemen, to be trained in picking off targets. Wayne himself came up with color schemes to distinguish the legions by their caps. Clothing supply was still shaky, but should it ever be fulfilled, the system would provide each soldier with two pairs of blue or brown linen overalls, two wool shirts, two pairs of cobbled shoes, and a long coat, cut down for summer to jacket length. Hats with bearskin crowns distinguished the heavy infantry from the light and artillery companies, who wore flashy multicolored plumes. A flag system distinguished the sub-legions as well.

Army finances had changed too. Supply, accounting, and contracting moved from the War Department to the Treasury Department. Hamilton had always been doing the other cabinet members' jobs whenever he deemed it necessary—he saw Treasury as the top job, himself as first minister—but now he had an important part of what had been Knox's work written into his official position. During the ramp-up for the St. Clair expedition, army contracting, always fertile ground for corruption and inefficiency, had been especially disastrous. The chief army contractor, William Duer, an associate of both Hamilton's and Knox's, had been speculating past the point of no return in land and bonds. One of his advances for St. Clair's supplies amounted to $75,000. Duer kicked $10,000 back to Knox in the form of a personal loan, and he and Knox formed a partnership to speculate in Maine land with the remaining $65,000. They figured the profits would easily refund the army disbursement, but Knox, casually corrupt like so many other men of his day, was also committed to his job, and to success in the field, and he soon began to see where these moves were heading. Duer stopped paying any attention to actually supplying the army. The secretary tried to cover up, and scandal had so far been averted, but those in the know believed the Knox-Duer relationship had contributed to the St. Clair disaster.

Even as Wayne's legion was being formed, Duer was causing a financial panic in New York. He'd tried to use borrowed money to get control of the entire securities market. Duer landed in debtors' prison, but the first national bank, Hamilton's favorite project, nearly failed, and Hamilton was badly embarrassed by his own association with Duer.

Having barely stabilized the market, Hamilton wanted personal control of army supply. All War Department funds, contracts, and purchases were now to be approved by the Treasury Department.

As the men and herds and wagons and supplies came into Fort Fayette, Wayne assigned teams to build and staff new fortifications outside. On Pittsburgh's high points Grant's Hill and Eyer's Hill, commanding the breadth of land between the Monongahela and the Allegheny, he had the men build the simple defensive fortifications known as redoubts, and he staffed the redoubts with sentries.

He began an ambitious regimen of training and drill. The infantry fired muskets dry at first, to save powder. The riflemen used targets nailed to trees, and the men collected the lead and reused it. But soon Wayne had the infantry firing with powder to get cavalrymen and horses used to the loud noise at their front. With musket charges manufactured in a laboratory at the fort, low-proof powder could be used for target practice, the good stuff saved for real operations, and after a while Wayne thought the men were getting less apt to be startled by the sound of their own guns. Meanwhile, he had the artillery teams firing round stones to save on iron. Their rhythm at the cannon remained pretty ragged.

In August, an opportunity to test training in action arose when Wayne received a report that a large body of Indians had crossed the Allegheny and was approaching his fort. He formed his still-partial force and brought it out of the fort, riding along the lines to inspire confidence in the men, and he sent word to the sentries in the two redoubts on the hills above the fort that they were to defend the flanks "with every expense of blood" until he could attack the enemy's rear with dragoons.

On hearing Wayne's orders to expend blood, about a third of the sentries on the hills started east for home. The attack never materialized, but Wayne had to send a party to chase down the deserters. Worse, he had to offer a reward to the locals for his own soldiers' capture.

He knew what he had to do. Two repeat deserters had their heads and eyebrows shaved. The letter *D*, for "deserter," was burned on their foreheads with red-hot iron. They received a hundred lashes and were kicked out of the fort.

Then a court-martial, convened to mete out justice to four of the most incorrigible deserters, sentenced the four to death by shooting, and Wayne approved the sentence. A French priest staying in Pittsburgh gave three of the four men final sacraments of the Catholic Church. Two were already Catholic, and one converted from Protestantism at that moment; all three of those men repented. The sole atheist held out against both unction and repentance.

The priest begged Wayne to spare the men's lives, but the general was determined to end desertion. On the parade ground, with full solemnity of muffled drumroll, and the deserters' fellow soldiers standing in ranks, the squad raised its guns. The priest fainted. Firing commenced.

But only three men were executed. The priest had told Wayne that the atheist was unprepared for eternity. At the last minute the general had changed the order.

Desertions did lessen markedly. Marksmanship improved. The men were learning, with difficulty, the various march steps, synchronized to the rhythm set by drum, marches for traveling long distances and marches for charge and retreat in the field. When Wayne arranged shooting competitions with whiskey rewards, men who had known nothing about shooting became crack shots. He staged mock battles in the woods, one group dressed as Indians, the other in uniform, to practice flanking maneuvers. He was amazed at how enthusiastic the men could get about defeating a fake enemy.

Some of the classic moves Wayne taught his men went back to his days at Trois-Rivières and Monmouth. The flankers and advance guard had to learn how to take fire and stand ground while the main line formed behind it, then fall back when called, firing all the time, spreading to the left and right to let the main line advance. Yet to accommodate woodland fighting, Wayne also departed from standard European practice. He rejected a shoulder-to-shoulder line and taught "open order": the men must not bunch together but hold ranks with space between them, even as they fired and maneuvered as a line in response to orders. That took confidence, and they had to learn it.

It was shortly after that awful day of executions, when Wayne was about four months into what had become the overwhelmingly difficult process of building an army, that he received word from Henry Knox of the fate of the peace emissaries sent to the Indians by President Washington. Both Trueman and Hardin, Knox informed Wayne, had been killed.

Placing undefended men in harm's way went against Wayne's every instinct, and with his appointment those men had come officially under his command. For weeks he'd been worrying over their fates and fearing what to him seemed the obviously inevitable outcome of their assignments.

Confirmation of their deaths filled Wayne with fury. The administration's new policy for diplomacy astonished him: it seemed to arise from inexplicable naïveté. As Wayne saw it, the war was going on. The Indian confederation at the Glaize, whose military control over the great reaches of forest to his west Wayne was preparing an army to end for all time, was fighting him. The murders of the emissaries only further proved it, but in a sense the enemy was always fighting him. Just after Wayne's arrival in Pittsburgh in June, Major David Strong, commander at Fort Jefferson, had ordered a work party of privates out of the fort to cut and stack hay, protected by an armed escort. After an hour or so of hot work, about sixty Indians appeared, fifteen or more of them mounted, and began firing on the guard, driving it back to the fort. Then they started killing the hay-cutting privates. From the fort, one officer led a hastily assembled rescue mission but was instantly cut off by a separate Indian party, deployed in anticipation of just that move. The rescue party retreated to the fort while the Indians killed and captured the men outside, burned the hay, inflicted the usual ritual butchery on the dying bodies they left behind, and rode and ran off with captives. The hot forest resumed its morning sounds, ominously now. The fort stayed on high alert.

As evening fell, soldiers ventured out to find that sixteen men were dead or missing, with only four bodies left to display the terrorizing disfigurements. It was recalled that all the Indians had been wearing tailored white shirts, new enough to suggest they'd been supplied by the British at Fort Detroit. One man wore a coat of blazing scarlet: that might have been Blue Jacket himself. All were well armed, and they had three packhorses. Clearly they'd had Fort Jefferson, thrust farthest north into Indian country, under steady surveillance. That suggested that all the other forts were being watched too.

Strong sent word of the attack down to Wilkinson at Fort Washington, and Wilkinson sent both Knox and Wayne reports. Stuck up at Fayette trying to create an army, Wayne steamed. He didn't have the power to respond to the killing of his troops.

An even more humiliating situation prevailed down the Ohio, in a struggling village at the mouth of the Kanawha River, in a giant bend between Marietta and Cincinnati. Though less well protected militarily than Cincinnati, this town had a name just as ambitious: Gallipolis, city of the Gauls. It had been founded by French settlers induced to buy land actually in dispute between two development companies. The endlessly wily William Duer was the author of this scam, and most of its victims had returned east in disgust, but a few, having been forced to rebuy their land, were trying to make it. The United States had built a small stockade there during the failed treaty efforts, more a way station between Forts Harmar and Washington than any serious obstacle to Indian attack.

Not only had the one lieutenant and the few soldiers left in the Gallipolis stockade suffered repeated attack after the St. Clair defeat, but the small post had become something far other than what it had been built for. The inhabitants had moved in, for protection. Behind the wooden palisade, the ground was now jammed with pens, and the pens were jammed with pigs, geese, ducks, and cows. The so-called parade ground had become an expanse of shit and mud, and everybody was sick. In their threadbare clothing, the troops weren't troops anymore. They'd let the stockade start collapsing. Some of the uprights blew down in high winds.

Nothing could have more physically and morally nauseated Anthony Wayne than reports of conditions at his post at Gallipolis. Yet Wilkinson at Fort Washington lacked the men and security even to try relieving conditions there. Not until late in the year would Wayne have enough of an army to start shaping up Gallipolis, let alone fully staffing and defending it. Life in that post evinced, for Wayne, the success of the Indians' continuous warfare against the United States.

So what was Washington doing, sending undefended men into a war zone? If Wayne considered the enemy from the point of view not of presidential policy but of the European military theorists he loved, defining the conflict in the conventional terms of classical strategy, then "he," the enemy, was still fighting "us," as military manuals refer to the main actors in a war. True, he was fighting us in unconventional ways. Neither seeking pitched battle nor, in European terms, accepting it when so maneuvered, knowing always how and when to work a disadvantage in our position, numbers, and morale, he was able to keep fighting perpetually, even while considering the next big, strategic moves. He sought always to force us into situations overbalanced in his favor. When such conditions were lacking, he wouldn't fight battles but instead degrade our positions in a host of other ways.

Unless absolutely demolished, that is, Wayne's enemy retained per-

manent advantage. In national politics in Philadelphia, the western Indians were often described as fighting an aggressive war of choice, in
violation of accords agreed on at Fort Harmar, but from the point of
view of strategy the Indians occupied an enviably dug-in defensive position, not only strategically, but also politically and morally. To win, all
"he" had to do was send "us" home. Should the United States choose to
withdraw east of the Ohio River, as the confederation demanded, there
was no chance that the western Indians would start pushing that boundary yet farther east. They'd already given up on the 1763 proclamation
line at the crest of the mountains. All they demanded now was the 1768
line at the Ohio. The confederation had no desire, that is, parallel to that
of the United States, to exterminate the Americans, as some parallel
Indian white haters might have had it, or to make Americans the subjects
of a Kekionga regime and train them in Indian ways, as parallel Indian
moderates might, or to bring about any of the other projects that occurred to Americans regarding the future lives of Indians. Victory for
the United States required conquering and subjugating the enemy so
totally that American settlement could occur unmolested in the Northwest Territory. Victory for the Indian confederation only required preventing such settlement, really just making settlement too risky for
investments ever to pay off. That imbalance placed Wayne in a strategically impossible position.

Even more infuriating to Wayne was that he still lacked not only the
army to fight the ongoing war but also the authority. Of course it was a
given that he wasn't ready to invade. Recruits were still coming into
Fayette all summer and fall. Recruitment wasn't strong enough: there
were nowhere near the number of soldiers that the army law allowed
for. Wayne knew he might in the end have to rely in part on militia
and short-term volunteers after all. And the army he did have remained
badly in need of training.

Yet he was constrained as well by policy from Philadelphia. When
Wayne himself had to explain that policy to the western militia lieutenants, he exposed his feelings about it. "The President of the United
States has thought proper to endeavor to come to some explanation
with the hostile tribes": that's how he put it to the militiamen. Then he
did his job, solemnly prohibiting and restraining them, in the president's
name, from forming raiding parties and carrying out freelance attacks

on Indians. When attacked, however, they could do whatever they felt qualified as defense.

If that order seemed possibly self-contradictory, the orders under which Wayne himself operated, given on behalf of the president by Knox, involved a similar problem. He was to wait and see what decision the Indians made for war or peace at their big conference at the Glaize. The western confederation had been gathering an enormous number of branches of an enormous number of nations, it was assumed with the aid of the renegade Alexander McKee, and though scheduled for spring, it now looked as if the conference wouldn't get going until fall. The American emissaries had been killed, but their messages had made it to the Glaize, and Captain Hendrick, Cornplanter, Red Jacket, and maybe even the famous Joseph Brant were supposed to be on their way there too, carrying what the administration presented as its new message for peace. Wayne's orders were therefore to defend the posts as necessary but not to counterattack.

Hence his fury and bafflement. Diplomats had been murdered. Troops had been attacked, with casualties. A real defense always involves offense. It was true that had Wayne been empowered by Washington and Knox to respond aggressively to attacks, he couldn't have done so anyway, but the cold logic of that fact felt only further constricting. He couldn't defend his positions with a good offense, or protect his men, or even keep them clean and clothed in distant posts he'd never yet seen, and despite his incapacity, orders to wait and see what might emerge from the Indians' Glaize conference exasperated and mystified him. The flags were dead, his forts under attack. What did the president imagine the Indians were going to decide, at their big conference, about war or peace?

In early July, before Trueman's and Hardin's deaths had been confirmed, yet another of the president's diplomatic emissaries, Rufus Putnam, arrived down the Ohio at Fort Washington. Putnam, a close connection of Washington's, had a better sense than Wayne of what the president might be thinking. And in the commander at Fort Washington, James Wilkinson, Putnam found a shrewd ally in carrying out Washington's policy.

Putnam was the well-connected New England speculator who had bought, with his partners, almost two million acres of the Northwest Territory on a government grant in the 1780s and founded Marietta, supported by Fort Harmar, upstream from Fort Washington. Now he'd come down the river from Marietta to see Wilkinson on the way to the Glaize, carrying what had become the strictly enforced administration line regarding a peaceful solution for bringing all western Indians into the Fort Harmar accords: the United States didn't want Indian land; all land not ceded by that treaty belonged, of course, to the Indians; if some groups had been left out of the Fort Harmar payoff for ceding the Northwest Territory, that error could be corrected by further payoffs, as long as the Indians acknowledged that the treaty was in force and ceased their attacks; otherwise the United States would have no choice but to attack again, with inevitable victory this time . . . The administration had developed enviable narrative discipline. Whenever planning now, in their official correspondence, for warfare, officials invariably supplied this or some similar qualification: "If all the measures which have been pursued by government to convince the hostile Indians of the just & honorable intentions of the U. States towards them should prove ineffectual . . ." And then they went about planning for warfare.

Putnam's inflammatory message to the Indians even included copies of all of the treaties of the 1780s, which, taken together, had become the cause of war. Yet he did bring one new offer. If the Indians were worried about the forts the Americans had built, the United States would give them up, once the Indians signed a new deal for submission, but if this offer fell on deaf ears, his message concluded, the United States would have no choice but to raise a real army. Even before heading down the Ohio for Fort Washington, Putnam had sent that message ahead to the Glaize.

That a real army was already being raised, by Wayne at Pittsburgh, was something the Glaize Indians could see just by looking. Putnam himself, carrying a message he supposedly believed was for peace, considered invasion so inevitable that he'd pitched Knox and Washington, unsolicited, his own military plan for accomplishing it. In that context, on arrival at Fort Washington Putnam took Wilkinson into a long private meeting, and they emerged to write some documents for the record.

Putnam first wrote to Henry Knox in Philadelphia to review the attack on the hay cutters outside Fort Jefferson. He'd just learned about it from Wilkinson and believed, he said, that he was the intended target of that attack: his advance message to the confederation at the Glaize had said he'd be heading to Fort Jefferson at that time. Yet for the record, he still expressed hope that despite all of what he called the atrocities, which he reviewed in detail, also for the record, the majority of Indians didn't countenance such behavior. He also wrote officially to his host Wilkinson to state his business at Fort Washington and the purpose of his trip. "Should we be so unfortunate as to not effect a peace," Putnam wrote, "yet I have no doubt that such evidence will be given of our united effort to accomplish the wishes of government on this head as will afford a pleasing reflection in our own minds, and convince the nation of the necessity of prosecuting the war with vigor." Wilkinson responded to Putnam in kind, noting for the record that while there had been attacks by Indians, which he too listed again in detail, he was so "anxious to follow the President's course" for negotiating peace that he'd ordered Fort Jefferson's commander, notwithstanding what Wilkinson called the recent outrage, to take only defensive measures. He added that while he doubted it, maybe the attacks had been carried out by some rogue Indians, sadly unaware of the United States' great peace effort.

Wilkinson also formally advised Putnam, in this exchange of official letters, not to go to the Glaize after all. It would be safer and more productive to go out to Fort Vincennes. In that fort near the Mississippi, Colonel Hamtramck had begun making peace with some of the Indians of the lower Wabash, even lining them up to fight the confederation at the Glaize on behalf of the United States. Putnam, in turn, wrote to Knox about this happy eventuality of allying with farther western Indians. If the United States could get other Indian nations to do some of the fighting, the war might shift westward. Country there was grassy and more open, easier for American armies to negotiate than woodland.

These moves to fatally divide the confederation, and rally Indian action against it, were thus rolled neatly into the administration's official record of its effort to gain a negotiated peace with the confederation. President Washington soon wrote to Knox to say he was glad to hear Putnam was going to Vincennes—even if, the president added, nothing should come of it but to show that the executive was doing everything possible to convince the hostile Indians of the peaceful intentions of the United States.

Anthony Wayne had no use for these expressions of peaceful intentions. He'd made his own plan of invasion, and he hoped to get President Washington, through Knox, to approve it in full, well in advance, with as much carte blanche as Wayne could get.

To work up the plan, he had to confront and assess the ideas for an invasion that Rufus Putnam had submitted to Washington and Knox. Knox had forwarded Putnam's proposals to Wayne, noting some reservations and asking for Wayne's evaluation. At first glance, Putnam might have seemed to be making strong points.

Putnam believed that any attack intended to demolish the Indian confederation's will to fight would require not only an advance northward from Cincinnati, as St. Clair had tried, but also a separate advance from the east, using Lake Erie as the avenue. Putnam thus envisioned Wayne's forces, having moved from Pittsburgh down to Fort Washington, starting their march northward toward the Miami towns, just as St. Clair had done, even as a concomitant movement of troops, beginning earlier, left the upper Ohio River near Pittsburgh, traveled overland behind the frontier between Pennsylvania and Indian country, and arrived on the banks of Lake Erie. Putnam identified the Cuyahoga River's mouth at the lake as the ideal point to muster those troops and get them onto the water. This Cuyahoga destination would put the troops within disputed territory; still, at the beach there, Putnam said, the army could build a fort, to be supplied by smaller forts all the way back behind the lines into Pennsylvania. The men could then build enough watercraft to launch sufficient troops, animals, and matériel onto the lake for the westward wing of this concerted attack.

This idea bothered Wayne. The mouth of the Cuyahoga was exposed, in territory controlled by the enemy, thus requiring a very long supply chain. Even if attacking via the lake was a good idea, and Wayne wasn't sure it was, wouldn't that aim be more safely and easily accomplished by building and launching boats from behind the lines, farther east, on Pennsylvania's own Erie beachhead at Presque Isle? A fort already existed there. Putnam's choice of the Cuyahoga wasn't strategically logical.

It was clever, however, in a way not evident to Wayne. A fort at the mouth of the Cuyahoga supported by a string of forts back into Pennsylvania would afford federal military protection and lake access to the entire section of Northwest Territory lying east of the Cuyahoga. That section was known as Washington County, and Putnam and his land development partners had founded it and served as its public officials, on the basis of their having purchased the big grant from Congress. Marietta, their settlement on the Ohio, lay due south of the Cuyahoga's mouth at the lake. The plan of invasion Putnam had devised would place his partners' whole real-estate investment under the kind of military protection that encouraged sales and settlement.

Indeed, Putnam had insisted to Knox that even if a negotiated peace could be made with the Indians, establishing a strong post at the Cuyahoga would be essential to any future American operations in the West. If that much couldn't be done, at least the United States should build a post up the Muskingum from Marietta, a fallback idea that would, he didn't mention, protect at least some of his investment.

And his two-pronged proposed invasion could actually commence, Putnam argued, right away. The two forces could start moving before the end of the year 1792. Left unsaid in that schedule was that win or lose, the proposed action would begin by securing and promoting, at public expense of money, and possibly of life, the Marietta partners' interests.

Wayne was assessing the thing strategically. Aspects of Putnam's plan might look good on paper, but as he sat at Fort Fayette in Pittsburgh and puzzled out the realities of the situation to his west, Wayne came to the conclusion that he didn't buy any of it.

For one thing, Putnam's plan failed to take into account the significance of the British army at Forts Detroit and Niagara. That omission was a strategic and even a diplomatic error of the worst sort. Putnam's proposed American assault on Lake Erie, even if launched from the more logical beachhead at Presque Isle, would have the effect of cutting Niagara off from Detroit and the Glaize, instantly changing the British position. British officers would have reason to assume the attack's target was the fort at Detroit, and they would be under standing orders to repel such an attack. Along with a host of other reasons to avoid war with Great Britain, Putnam's plan would leave the rear of his projected force on Lake Erie open to a British naval pursuit launched from Fort Niagara. Warfare would then rage all along the lake's south bank, not only southward from Detroit toward the lower Ohio, but also eastward from Niagara into Pennsylvania and New York. Putnam's whole idea was out of the question, Wayne determined. He rejected any invasion from Lake Erie.

He had a better idea. Starker, less superficially appealing than Putnam's, it was tougher because it faced squarely the many real limitations Wayne was presented with.

The only practical thing, he calculated, as he worked up his proposal, was a far-from-exciting idea: repeat the basic thrust of St. Clair's effort and get it right this time. Lake Erie was out. Any invasion of the confederation heartland must come solely from the south, from Fort Washington at Cincinnati, just as before.

But this time the force involved would consist of the main body of his regular-army legion, fully trained by then and moving with enormous care in predetermined stages to establish an irreproachably secure supply chain all the way up to Fort Jefferson. Fully stocked and supplied, Fort Jefferson would then become the base of further operations, extending a line of forts beyond Jefferson, one cautious step at a time. The strategic secret of this effort was simply maniacal care, patience, and discipline, Mad Anthony style. Each step of the operation must be fully secured before moving on to the next. Speed was not a factor.

He had a related idea. While this slow, preparatory process of establishing and supplying Fort Jefferson went on, there should be a twist, which would achieve in fact the effect that Putnam's plan only gestured at. Even while the main force supplied and readied Fort Jefferson as an advance position, two squads of mounted volunteers—they could be called up, Wayne had realized, from Kentucky and western Pennsylvania to

supplement his under-recruited force—should range far in advance
of the march toward two widely divergent destinations. This action
could even start soon. One division would circle northeast, all the way to
Sandusky on the Erie shore, and surprise attack the Indian towns there.
The other would surprise attack the core Indian towns, which Wayne
still thought of as Kekionga, not the Glaize.

Those two advance operations—"desultory," in military terminology—
might or might not achieve distinct victories, but even if they left
matters unresolved, the Indian confederation's communications would
be thrown into a shambles and the enemy's main concern would become the safety of women and children. With the enemy thus distracted
from the main army's move to Fort Jefferson, the legion would begin
its real advance. The troops would leave the forward post and move—
again in carefully predetermined stages—against the core of the confederation. "Beware a surprise," Wayne now saw, must in real terms mean
"go surprisingly slowly." To enable those movements, heavy supplies
would have to be laid in at the rear forts, all the way back to Cincinnati, and then upstream all the way to a point just below Pittsburgh.

This idea was getting expensive. Wayne didn't care. It would be in-
calculably cheaper in the long run to do the march right. The Indians
would always refuse to stand and fight unless on ground of their own
choosing and with overwhelming likelihood of victory. Wayne had to
rob them of that advantage. He had to give the enemy no choice but to
move families out of harm's way and keep falling back into the forest.
Once his implacable legion had walked into the Miami towns and established Wayne's headquarters there, he would command the entire
region, using the same caution, the same care, the same constant patrol.
The final showdown might come via Indian effort at surprise attack.
By then, surprise would not be surprising. It would be met, anytime it
might come, with a fully orchestrated response by a legion ever in readiness to fight.

This, then, was the Wayne plan: ambitious, expensive, dependent on
intensive discipline, and very likely, Wayne thought, to succeed. He
couldn't predict exactly how a final showdown would occur. But as he
looked the thing over from every angle, he couldn't see the confederation
holding out long, militarily or organizationally, against a relentlessly
executed plan like this one, the product of an experienced creative

imagination flourishing, to the detriment of every other part of its author's life, in the military mode. While its mounted desultory advances left room for swoop and glitz, the plan in essence relied on nothing more glamorous than heightening to the ultimate every banality of what being military, in essence, just is: supply, patrol, intelligence, march, scouting, bivouac, fighting. The plan was in that sense super-soldierly.

All it would need to succeed was the super-soldierly army it called for. And as eager as Wayne had always been to move forward rather than wait, he was sure there was something else wrong with Rufus Putnam's plan.

Moving the main force in the coming fall was fantastical. Haste would only result in another defeat, and another defeat would be decisive, ending western expansion, the barely breathing military establishment of the United States, and Anthony Wayne's revived career as general. Harvesttime, when Putnam had advised marching, was always the Indians' best time. Winter, however, beat the Indians up, and by spring they were hungry and tired.

Wayne thought he could move at least part of the army down to Fort Washington, call up the mounted volunteers, and even begin the advance desultory operations fairly soon. The big invasion, however, had to wait for spring. He believed he could have his army ready for major combat in early 1793.

9

LEGION VILLE

The big Glaize conference of the whole western Indian confederation, though scheduled for the spring of 1792, was subject to the usual delays. When it got going in September, it turned into a final showdown between the confederation's war party and those on the fence.

Little Turtle and Blue Jacket and other hard-liners knew exactly what they wanted. All delegations must agree that the Fort Harmar Treaty was void, that a new treaty must set a boundary at the Ohio, and that if the Americans wouldn't agree, then all-out warfare involving a host of old and new participants, carried out over a wider range than ever before, would make the victory over St. Clair look like nothing.

By now, Alexander McKee was in close touch with John Simcoe. McKee was pushing the Indians hard to adopt Simcoe's mediation plan. Some ambiguity surrounded Indian opinion on that issue. But there was no ambiguity in the war party's position regarding war.

Still, getting the confederation as a whole to remain on a war footing was by no means a fait accompli. As delegations began gathering and making camp, both at McKee's operation at the rapids and upstream in the Glaize towns, groups held discussions in advance of the formal conference, and not all nations and branches were seeing war as the only solution. Some of the civic and war leaders were fed up with feeling dictated to by the militant Shawnee. Some thought too that the United

States wasn't necessarily as untrustworthy and incorrigibly greedy as the hard-liners claimed. Last winter had been hard. Winter was coming again. There had been a spring famine, and while many were ready to go on fighting, some not living north and west of the Ohio imagined ways of favorably resolving the conflict that might not involve continuous warfare. Others, more local, thought far-western Indians who did hew to the war line might be less warlike if they lived closer to the action. Divisions were complicated.

That was the perception, anyway, of Captain Hendrick, the Stockbridge Mahican who had agreed, at the Six Nations conference in Philadelphia, to carry President Washington's new peace message to the Glaize. He wasn't the only delegate to the Philadelphia conference now carrying messages from the president, but Captain Hendrick arrived early, in July, having taken a complicated journey. Setting out from Buffalo Creek and the Niagara River, his party traveled first by canoe along the north shore of Lake Erie; when the wind made waves unmanageable, they walked overland to Lake St. Clair, north of Detroit; paddled a new canoe into the Detroit River and downstream into Lake Erie; then up the Miami of the Lake to the bottom of the rapids. On the way, Captain Hendrick met with Brant's Grand River Iroquois, delivered bead strings, held discussions. Now hanging around McKee's, he began quietly letting members of arriving delegations, as well as some of those living at the Glaize, in on the president's new message.

Shawnee diplomats had done well: the banks of the Miami of the Lake were starting to get crowded. A partial roster of those in attendance would include—along with the confederation core of Shawnee, Miami, and Delaware of the Glaize—Shawnee from farther west, Cherokee, Creek, Six Nations, Conoy, Nanticoke, Wyandot, Ottawa, Potawatomie, Sauk, Fox, and Mahican. Geographic representation stretched from New York to the South, from the Ohio valley to the Great Lakes to the upper Mississippi. Some delegations numbered in the hundreds. McKee wrote happily to Simcoe to say that this was the biggest gathering so far.

And yet a wide array of nations meant a new variety of opinion. Captain Hendrick's very presence here reflected the potential for division that the United States was hoping to exploit. The message the Mahican carried was identical in substance to those carried by the late American diplomats whose presence, uninvited in Indian country, had

been enough to construe their embassies as acts of war and whose messages, brought to the Glaize, served as outright provocation. Captain
Hendrick, though, was an Indian, if aligned with American interest,
and more or less accepted as a legitimate go-between. Some attendees
even seemed sympathetic to his cause. Big Cat, one of the hard-line
Delaware who had moved from Kekionga to the Glaize, advised him to
talk about the message quietly, in caucus, and build support for peace
before bringing it up for the whole conference.

As crowded as the area was getting, full attendance came slowly,
thanks to hunger during the bad winter, the need for constant surveillance of American forts, and the geographic breadth of the enrollment.
The whole conference was awaiting in particular the arrival of the Buffalo Creek Six Nations delegation, led especially by Red Jacket, along
with Cornplanter from the Allegheny region. The war party viewed
these America-aligned, "tamed" Seneca with suspicion; still, they were
Six Nations, elder brothers to the westerners, and while the western
confederation's military success against the United States had dimin-
ished the Six Nations' status, formally and traditionally the Seneca
remained significant. For one thing, the western hard-liners needed
to know, once and for all, where Red Jacket and Cornplanter really
stood.

At last the opening session was scheduled to begin at Captain
Johnny's Town at the Glaize. That location, testament to Shawnee hard-
line leadership, and especially to Blue Jacket's role in the victory over
St. Clair and the recruiting efforts of the previous winter, gave the war
party a symbolic advantage. On September 27, McKee came up from the
rapids, and on the thirtieth the various delegations walked, single file,
into the Shawnee town and arranged themselves outdoors.

The first day was given over to an opening ceremony. One of the
Shawnee recruiters, Painted Pole, lifted a pipe that Blue Jacket had
personally carried far west. The pipe was adorned with black and red
beads to express both pan-Indian friendship and continued war footing
against the United States.

Six Nations delegates, elder brothers of the Shawnee and Miami
hosts, were among those offered the pipe before others. That was pro-
tocol. Yet despite traditional forms of respect, Painted Pole ended the
opening ceremony with a jab at Red Jacket and the Buffalo Creek Sen-

eca. He warned them publicly against heeding those who would corrupt their hearts and turn them against their real interests.

The next day it rained. The conference was delayed. But the question of Seneca loyalty to the confederation was on the table.

In Philadelphia, Knox submitted Wayne's invasion plan to President Washington. Wayne had written it up in a context of inevitability that peace negotiations would fail and full-on war resume. Washington, however, took all of the ambition and urgency invested in the plan with his usual reserve, even with chilliness.

Washington had never discerned any military brilliance in Anthony Wayne. He'd deployed Wayne successfully at times in the War of Independence, and of the many poor choices for commander of the legion Wayne had seemed the least objectionable. When the cabinet had met to discuss whom to appoint, Washington had said virtually nothing good about anybody, and despite the development that Wayne had once shown as an officer under Washington's aegis, from Monmouth to Stony Point to the battles of the South at war's end, the president's assessment of Wayne was curt. "Brave but nothing more," Jefferson jotted down. Maybe a bit of a drunk, Washington added. But he had that concern about nearly all of his officers.

Ever since Wayne's appointment, Knox had been buffering Washington from most of the general's ceaseless requests, demands, complaints, and opinions about policy. Yet the secretary did have to keep the president informed of certain things, and so he'd also been buffering the prickly Wayne from Washington's utter lack of interest in Wayne's opinions. At the same time, Knox did have to pass on anything Washington told him to pass on. The role taxed Knox's gifts for diplomacy. At one point, Wayne started fiddling with ballistics and musket design—he wanted the muskets to be self-priming, so his light infantrymen could reload on the run and by feel, eyes always on targets—and after getting the Fort Fayette gunsmith to create a prototype with the touchhole redrilled at an oblique angle, he began asking Knox for an especially fine grain of powder to make this new redesign feasible. He sent a sample of the kind of powder he wanted, then complained that what Knox sent him wasn't good enough. Knox got testy and told Wayne that the powder was equal in quality to any used, and "it is to be regretted the grain is not in your judgment sufficiently fine," and he took this one to Washington.

The president advised the secretary to cover himself, all things being equal, by giving Wayne things he asked for, just to obviate blame for any failure later. But in this case, Washington said, he opposed the whole project of tinkering with musket design. The word to General Wayne was to use the standard muskets, cease making innovations, and focus on training and discipline. Knox had to phrase that order carefully for Wayne's consumption. Washington said too that the legality of branding soldiers, as Wayne had done with *D* for "deserter," was questionable: no more of it. Knox wrapped that order in as much verbal batting as possible while making it unmistakably an order.

Now, reviewing Wayne's plan of invasion, Washington thought it looked all right. It seemed largely the same as Putnam's, lacking the Erie attack, a change Washington agreed with: he had his own plans for resolving the conflict with the British over possession of the lake forts, and he'd already determined an Erie attack was a bad idea. Regarding Wayne's advance desultory operations, who could say, so far in advance, whether that was a good idea? Washington had no intention of approving the plan in total now.

Washington's denial of advance approval, though phrased by Knox with a fulsome gratitude unexpressed by Washington, stung Wayne. He'd been here before: Washington was holding him back. In practical terms, the president's refusing to approve the plan formally and set it in stone made no real difference to the plan itself. Wayne knew he had to wait until the spring of 1793 anyway, and Knox more or less concurred in every element of the plan as proposed. The secretary had seen right away that Wayne's ideas were more realistic than Putnam's and assured Wayne that the spring of 1793 would work, "*should there be a need to invade at all*"—Knox underlined, for the record, that qualification nearly reflexive now in all official communication—and that the plan Wayne had presented was likely to be the one approved.

But Wayne couldn't accept anything less than full, formal, immediate approval. He couldn't stand to hear his invasion called provisional. In his letters to Knox, he started nudging Knox into stipulating that negotiations with the Indians would fail, even that they existed only for the purpose of manufacturing public consent for an unpopular war that was in fact inevitable. He took to referring, for the record, to every intelligence of Indian hostility received from any source. He laid out arguments showing that regardless of what came out of the Indians' big conference, this war would have to happen. To Washington and Knox, nothing could be politically less welcome in the official correspondence, yet Wayne piled on, asking for authorization to intervene against and punish any Indian raid and attack. He wanted permission to get at least some part of his force down to Fort Washington and start making those desultory moves with mounted volunteers, creating cover, as he said, for taking supplies up to the forward posts, Forts Hamilton and Jefferson. He was already calling those posts the line of battle. Also, he reminded Knox he would need a lot more grain. In Wayne's letters, if not in real life, he was already on the march.

Because Washington's answer to all of Wayne's requests and arguments must only be an irritated no, Knox found his compositional skills tried to the utmost. He couldn't reassure Wayne that invasion would occur no matter what came out of the diplomacy and the Glaize conference. He reminded Wayne that the army could of course get all the grain it needed later—*if* the war did have to go on—but there could be no forward movement now. "Whatever may be the result of the pacific overtures," Knox insisted, "or however individuals of the frontiers, or among the Indians may regard the said overtures, still, the government of the United States were constrained to make them by a respect to the opinion of probably the great majority of the citizens of the United States."

Wayne, fuming, couldn't understand it. But John Simcoe and other officials in Canada thought they could. From the agent Beckwith they'd been informed that the cabinet knew full well that it couldn't mask its army at Fort Fayette and that it had no expectation of letting its huge buildup of arms stand idle. Yet given the United States' new and unusual form of government, it was impossible to get support for war without creating a sense of absolute necessity. Because popular opinion must be the main stimulus, Beckwith noted, "the most artful measures have been pursued in order to create a pretext, and thereby lead the people into the business," while bamboozling the political opposition. Simcoe knew Beckwith got information from his source in Washington's cabinet, Alexander Hamilton, and he knew that Hamilton had reason to see himself and Washington as being of one mind on these matters.

In further execution of the artful measures, Rufus Putnam had meanwhile traveled down to Vincennes on the Mississippi, and working there with Hamtramck, he did arrive at a separate peace with the Indians of the lower Wabash. Putnam kept the treaty language adroitly vague. He let the Wabash Indians out of declaring existing white settlements north of the Ohio legitimate, and he allowed an article stating that the Indians would retain all the land to which they had a "just claim," a term that neatly fit his instructions, because it could be read by the Washington administration as land not supposedly ceded at Fort Harmar and by the Indians who signed it as all land north and west of the Ohio. Putnam crowed to Washington and Knox about the treaty by letter, calling it a political and military coup. The Wabash signers were brought ostentatiously to Philadelphia to celebrate. While to the Indians at the Glaize the new treaty could only serve as yet another provocative act of war, turning Indians against Indians—Henry Knox noted with satisfaction that it had weakened the confederation by eight hundred fighters—the congressmen viewing the celebration in the capital could mark the treaty down as yet another administration measure to secure peace by negotiation.

When Putnam's Wabash treaty came before the Senate two years later, that body would refuse to ratify it. The treaty was vague to the point of meaninglessness: it failed even to assert a U.S. right to buy land at will in the Northwest Territory. To the majority who voted against its ratification, Putnam's entire effort at Vincennes might have seemed a prime example of government obtuseness and waste. They couldn't discern its real uses.

The rain ended after only a day, and the Glaize conference resumed. Shawnee attacks on Red Jacket and the Buffalo Creek Seneca resumed too. Hard-liners noted in their speeches that the confederation hadn't seen the Seneca in the three years since the last big conference, when they'd all agreed to a collective defense of the West. The Seneca must have been working so hard on the confederation's behalf, it was sarcastically suggested, that they'd been too busy to come west: the allies were happy to see them again and would spread the word of their return to the fold. Buckongahelas, the war-party Delaware, then rose to note that Shawnee criticisms of the Seneca were fully supported by other members.

Cornplanter, largely discredited with the hard-liners, played things pretty quietly throughout the conference: it was Red Jacket who rose to respond. He'd always been closer to the war party than Cornplanter, and now he alleged full Seneca solidarity with the confederation. The Seneca had smoked the pipe that Blue Jacket had sent during the winter, he said, and they did support a collective defense.

But now, Red Jacket announced, he had a message of peace from the United States.

That was a bombshell. In one way, Red Jacket's announcement only confirmed what others had known: Seneca and other Six Nations delegates had attended a conference in Philadelphia. Still, Red Jacket's bringing an American proposal for peace suggested that the Seneca might also have made a separate peace during that conference. Because the Six Nations elder brothers, including the Seneca, had pledged solidarity, going all the way back to the Sandusky meeting in 1783, a separate peace would violate confederation itself, the gathering of one pan-Indian people against encroachment. Red Jacket kept pledging Seneca support for the westerners, yet he and Cornplanter had signed the Fort Stanwix Treaty and now brought a message from President Washington. Which side were they on?

The conference began erupting. Details of the president's message hadn't even been revealed, yet the Seneca's role even in bringing that message drew harsh criticism not only from the western Indians but also from those Six Nations Iroquois who had moved up to Canada and were attending this conference still in the absence of their leader Brant. When the Shawnee Painted Pole accused Red Jacket and the Seneca of double-dealing, there was a sense that a complete break threatened. America-aligned Indians might be classed as traitors and war enemies, not only by the hard-liners but also by all others who had signed on to solidarity.

Painted Pole demanded Red Jacket put down the bundle of messages he carried from the United States and confess everything that the Seneca and the United States had been doing together since the victory over St. Clair. The gathered nations were waiting, he told them ominously.

Red Jacket, flummoxed, could only ask for time. The Buffalo Creek Seneca withdrew. After a hurried huddle they returned to the main conference.

Now they pitched it: the whole message from President Washington, as also carried by the late Trueman and Hardin, and by Washington's friend Putnam, and to this conference by Captain Hendrick. The president wanted no land, the Buffalo Creek Seneca said, not already ceded by treaties summed up at Fort Harmar, and he offered financial satisfaction to anyone who felt the land had been bought from non-owners. If the Indians would agree to this deal, the United States would evacuate all the forts that St. Clair had built forward of Fort Washington, and the confederation was hereby invited to send delegates to a meeting in Philadelphia, or to choose a site more convenient to them, and sign a new treaty to that effect.

The next day, Red Jacket and the Buffalo Creek Seneca went further. They sent a messenger to the other nations' leaders to ask for a private conference, leaders only. When it convened, the Buffalo Creek people came clean. They confessed that President Washington had asked them to serve as his agents, not only carrying his message, but urging the conference to accept the offer. They said that in Philadelphia they'd fairly represented the anger of the western Indians, and they believed the Americans were listening. They took the opportunity of this private, leaders-only conference to suggest that the whole western confederation would be well advised to listen to the president's message.

The final day of formal sessions, October 7, opened with a war dance. That set the tone.

Painted Pole took the floor to castigate Seneca naïveté. The president's offer of further compensation, for land on which he'd already built forts, via a process the confederation deemed illegal, drew the response that anyone in the know could have predicted.

The offer in the message was nonsense, Painted Pole said. The confederation already knew the purpose of St. Clair's failed invasion: American paperwork had been taken from the scene of St. Clair's defeat; the purpose was to build forts at Kekionga, the Glaize, and elsewhere, put the confederation out of business, and either eradicate or remove the western Indians or turn them into farm laborers. Painted Pole now reiterated, as if in words of one syllable, the long-standing, outspoken position of the western Indian confederation and its allies throughout Indian country. The message back to President Washington was simple.

"We do not want compensation," Painted Pole said. "We want restitution of our land, which he holds under false pretenses." The Ohio River was the only boundary the confederation would accept. If the United States really wanted peace, all it had to do was renounce the Fort Harmar boundary and destroy all forts north of the Ohio. Then and only then might U.S. diplomats safely come to a meeting, which the confederation now proposed to schedule for the following spring, at the Sandusky River's mouth at Lake Erie, to formalize a new deal with the United States setting the Ohio as the boundary. Until those conditions were met, and until that deal was made, war was still on.

The hard-liners carried the conference. Leaders overwhelmingly endorsed the militant position. The war party might have won anyway, but exposure of the Seneca's real mission here—its stink of manipulation, the American attempt to turn Indians, with "sweet speeches" of a false peace, as the hard-liners put it, against other Indians—exacerbated the already inflammatory nature of the president's message, which everybody present could see only reiterated, in flowery language, the most destructive terms of the Fort Harmar Treaty.

The Buffalo Creek Seneca copped eagerly to the lesser charge of naïveté. The greater charge would be treason, so they agreed to everything the confederation demanded. Red Jacket reconfirmed his own and the Seneca's commitment to the confederation's aims and promised to take the message back to the United States, reiterate the Ohio boundary, and propose a treaty conference for documenting that boundary, to be held at the Sandusky mouth in the spring. Battered, the Seneca delegation left the conference.

So by the time Joseph Brant, treated by the Washington administration as the most authoritative go-between of all, made it to the Glaize on October 8, all important matters had been decided. The conference was over. War was on. Little Turtle would start a new series of attacks on the forts; they awaited only supplies from McKee's warehouse at the rapids. Blue Jacket handed off a new round of recruiting to Painted Pole, who was to travel south to bring in more Cherokee and Creek fighters. And the very day Brant arrived, Painted Pole met with Alexander McKee and made a formal request, on behalf of the confederation, for British mediation in the event that the United States agreed to come to the Sandusky in the spring of 1793. The Indians had determined they needed the Americans and the Englishmen to meet face-to-face.

Brant had been hoping for a revived role, at this conference, as the voice of reason. He'd sent a message to the Glaize advising the delegations not to trust Captain Hendrick or George Washington, yet he'd also given Henry Knox the impression that peace could be achieved on terms favorable to the United States. Brant still believed a compromise line might be drawn at the Muskingum River.

None of that had any chance of playing now. Some delegations were packing up to head home; all faced a long winter ahead. They'd agreed to continue the war until conditions were met and their land was regained. Joseph Brant's attempts to moderate had become irrelevant to the mounting conflict in the West. He just didn't know it yet.

Blue Jacket was preparing for a final pitched battle with the United States. The Shawnee war leader's vision was influenced on the one hand by Neolin and Pontiac, in whose efforts he'd first come to prowess, and that vision was nativist, fundamentalist, and racially determinist. Yet he was influenced, on the other hand, by a hope more specific to his

own people: Shawnee return to the ancient homeland of the three Miamis, with ultimate reunification, or at least representation, of all Shawnee branches there, shaking off not only white but also Six Nations
oppression. Blue Jacket's strategic thinking was connected to perfecting
the region he loved. And he thought the United States was weakening.

Little Turtle, considering the next phase of warfare, took a charac-
teristically different view. He still believed British artillery would be
critical to success in any further pitched battle, and he remained skeptical of British intentions. Indians didn't have artillery skills: effective
use of the big guns would mean employing not only the guns themselves but also British military advisers for training, even the deploying
of British divisions on Indian behalf. So far, however, British big guns
and troops had not been forthcoming. Minister Hammond and Governor Simcoe, though they'd agreed privately to perpetuate the conflict
in the interest of redrawing the Canada-U.S. boundary line, needed
some degree of deniability, however implausible, about fighting a proxy
war with the United States. Providing the Indians with cannon and
troops, building new forts on U.S. soil, or any other assertive military
move would risk censure from Whitehall. Little Turtle wasn't privy to
their thinking, but he could plainly see that they weren't providing him
with artillery.

He was therefore developing another means of defeating the Americans. It involved neither pitched battle nor attacks on forts but raiding
supply convoys. Less dramatic than outright battle, and slower in its
effects, this strategy had the potential, he believed, to make it impossible for the United States to maintain forts in Indian country. And
without forts, no settlement. This war might be won by attrition and
obstruction. For where Blue Jacket thought the Americans were on the
verge of giving up, Little Turtle discerned a different pattern in American will.

His idiosyncratic way of navigating political complexities enabled him
to see something potentially deflating, which many of his fellow hard-
liners didn't seem to appreciate. Each time the United States attempted
invasion, it sent a bigger and more serious army. Regardless of the antiwar mood of the American people, the current absence of any new
American march up from Fort Washington showed not unwillingness
of the president to fight but only patient buildup for yet another march.

The new fort at Pittsburgh, the convergence there of hundreds of men under Anthony Wayne: it was obvious. From Fort Washington, Wilkinson had been taking every opportunity to provide the forward forts Hamilton and Jefferson with livestock and forage. So despite those forts' weakness, it hardly looked to Little Turtle as if the United States had plans to pull out of them.

An event in his family life gave this perception credence. Little Turtle's beloved protégé William Wells, a white man captured in childhood and raised Miami, now married to Little Turtle's daughter Sweet Breeze, had fought on the Indian side against St. Clair. Now Wells was working for the United States. Looking to reestablish a white life, the young man had taken a job as an interpreter, accompanying Rufus Putnam out to Vincennes and helping Putnam and Hamtramck negotiate the separate peace with the lower Wabash Indians, anathema to the confederation back at the Glaize and in direct opposition to Little Turtle's authority. That treaty alone suggested that the United States was intent on weakening the confederation preparatory to an attack, sooner or later, by the army that Wayne was so visibly building. Indeed, soon William Wells would be working for Anthony Wayne as a scout.

Yet when Wells stayed with Sweet Breeze and Little Turtle at the Glaize, the young man faced no danger. The family situation of William Wells and Little Turtle remained so anomalous, at least to many observers, that stories grew up to explain it. It was said that the two men made a vow that although they had now taken opposite sides, they would never kill each other in battle. It was said they agreed that after a set time they would try to kill each other in battle. It was said that Wells promised Sweet Breeze and Little Turtle that once the war was over, no matter how it was resolved, he would return to live with them. In any event, the recruitment of William Wells gave emotional trenchancy to Little Turtle's perception that the United States was redoubling its efforts to conquer the West.

The Miami war leader nevertheless saw hope. He believed that in the very strengthening of its forward positions the United States was making itself vulnerable. His new idea was therefore to gain a genuine military advantage, not just distraction and harassment, by robbing U.S. forces of their food supply. Desertion would then become rampant, the forts incrementally more difficult to hold. In Little Turtle's projection, victory might come not in a final clash of good versus evil, resolving the West for all time in favor of the Indians, with the United States admitting defeat in the face of a military and moral superior. Victory might come instead from making it persistently difficult for American military power to protect American settlement. The United States might get worn down.

He was reading the situation well. In Fort Washington, Wilkinson was straining every nerve. The forward forts were in desperate shape; it would take very little to make them uninhabitable: Wilkinson was afraid he couldn't even keep hay in stock to feed the horses. Having ascertained that the distance between Forts Hamilton and Jefferson was longer than an average packhorse train could cover in one day, he'd thrown up the way station, Fort St. Clair. Yet virtually no troop reinforcements had yet been sent down from Wayne's force at Pittsburgh, and Wilkinson had fewer than seven hundred privates in all posts, from Fort Washington up to Fort Jefferson and out to Vincennes. Those men had to be steadily fed. In the fall chill, troops were starting to suffer from want of blankets and clothing. Despite light Indian parties always around Fort Washington and the forward forts, Wilkinson had to risk exposure just to get beef cattle and animal forage and other supplies up to Fort Jefferson. He knew how vulnerable he was.

One problem with Little Turtle's strategy was its dependence on discipline. He would have to restrain raiding parties from making attacks wherever they happened on American soldiers. The sole objective must remain supply. No random killing, no trying to take and hold the forts, no waste: just destruction of supply. Little Turtle disapproved, for example, of the late-June attack on the hay cutters outside Fort Jefferson. Men had been killed in that action, yet supply hadn't been seriously interrupted.

Intelligence was therefore key to the strategy. Little Turtle needed to know exactly when supply convoys were scheduled to arrive at the various forts. Taking captives was one way of gaining that intelligence. He began arguing for less killing and more intelligence gathering in service of denying supply.

With the close of the big Glaize conference, Anthony Wayne heard directly from Cornplanter, by express runner to Pittsburgh, that some Indian terms for peace had been sent from the Glaize to the president, via Red Jacket and the Seneca emissaries. Wayne took that news to mean that the Indians had rejected American offers. The Indians' terms sounded manifestly unacceptable, and it was obvious to Wayne that what he'd long predicted had now come to pass: the hard-liners ruled the Glaize conference; the confederation had no plans to submit to a realistic peace.

Since Knox had always told Wayne that all the administration was waiting for, before approving the invasion, were results of the Glaize conference, Wayne's hopes soared. Results were in, winter was falling, and Wayne would have his army ready to move in the spring. He'd continued to send Knox constant thoughts on forward movement, always as if invasion were inevitable, sometimes as if it were already ongoing. He haggled over minutiae, insisting that the invasion would require stationing a minimum of two hundred men in each post, just for security, and that getting generous supplies as far up the line as possible, right now, was critical to the invasion's ultimate success. And it would be absolutely necessary, Wayne said, to advance the troops to what he called the head of the line. He meant St. Clair's field of battle. To Wayne, that place had become no longer a scene of defeat but the most recent position of advance. He wanted to build a fort there in the coming winter, early spring at the latest.

At the Glaize, Little Turtle gathered two hundred fighters, Shawnee and Miami and others, mustered them in battle gear, and led them in single file out of the Miami towns. This was in early November. While the main force readied itself to cross the Miami of the Lake and start upstream in a canoe flotilla, a small party halted outside the cabin of an elderly Mohawk woman taken in by the Shawnee many years earlier. She made her home now on the west bank of the Miami, across from the mouth of the Auglaize, and offered services as a seer. The raiders wanted a blessing for their mission.

The seer went into her cabin. She kept the men waiting outside for almost an hour. They could hear her using a stick to bang her walls, her beds, and her iron pots. Then she started humming.

Finally, she emerged and with wild energy shouted syllables the party took to mean "many scalps, many prisoners, much plunder!" That wasn't the mission Little Turtle had in mind; still, the two hundred fighters crossed the river, many standing in their canoes with muskets and rifles in their hands.

Soon, moving quickly southward, over land now, the raiders bypassed Fort Jefferson and the way station Fort St. Clair and arrived near Fort Hamilton. It was via this fort, next up the line from Fort Washington, that forward supply would be sent. The raiders settled themselves in the woods to await opportunity.

It came late that same afternoon, when two soldiers were captured in the woods. The raiders revealed that a big supply convoy—a hundred packhorses, protected by fewer than a hundred men—had already left Fort Hamilton. The convoy was heading north for Fort Jefferson. Scouts went up the line and returned with good news: the supply convoy was now camped about two hundred yards outside the Fort St. Clair way station. The raiders moved fast. In the darkness just before dawn, they discovered the camp, thanks to fires burning in a ring around where the men lay. Sentries had been posted, and in silence Little Turtle's men encircled the ring of fire.

The camp got ready to move early. Still in the dark, the commander called in his sentries: he was having the whole guard mount up at once. With the perimeter abruptly abandoned, the raiders stepped in silence into the camp.

Then, before the guard knew what was happening, they started shouting and shooting. The guard were Kentucky volunteers, and they ran, completely out of order, for the fort. And yet with the Americans in flight, the discipline that Little Turtle relied on paid off. The raiders didn't give chase, seeking scalps and glory. Only six Americans were killed in the action, five wounded, and four taken captive. But when the Kentucky commander emerged from the fort later that day to survey the scene, everything the convoy had been taking to Fort Jefferson was gone or destroyed. The men found only twenty-three of their horses; most had been captured, some killed and wounded. It was the loss of horses, even more than the theft and destruction of supplies themselves, that damaged the Americans. Without horses they couldn't move or protect supply.

Little Turtle had thus dismounted the guard, disabled supply, and placed the forward forts in more serious trouble than ever, all thanks to one lightweight operation. He'd conceived an easy form of action with devastating consequences for the enemy's ability to fight. His strategy was ideally strategic. All it took was discipline.

Down at Fort Washington, James Wilkinson heard the awful news. He would now have to start deploying dragoons to escort supply trains, and that would further deplete his already scant force, leaving even headquarters vulnerable. The evident impossibility of maintaining security further weakened morale. Wilkinson reported the attack to Knox directly and had the Kentucky commander write up a description to send to Wayne.

Wilkinson had collaborated with Putnam in carrying out the diplomatic measures that had led to the result of the Glaize conference. He would have had reason to think that by this point the administration would be ready to take action against an enemy proven incorrigible, and with his supply ruined and his men killed, he was as angry as Wayne. In his report to Knox, Wilkinson noted that critics might wonder why the garrison at Fort St. Clair hadn't come out to fight the attacking Indians, and for the record, he reminded the secretary that the officers were still under standing orders to engage—and he underlined this, bitterly—"*in defensive measures only.*"

Knox had troubles of his own. The new session of Congress was beginning, and far from having become, during the recess, gung ho for war, the antiwar and pro-militia members of the House were gearing up to diminish Wayne's army just when Wayne believed he was about to receive authorization to start using it.

The Washington administration resorted to a favored technique: submitting to Congress an overwhelming documentary file that placed the administration's positions and activities in a wholly favorable light and responsibility for any failure on Congress. On November 7, two days after the session commenced, Knox sent the House a load of paperwork documenting everything the administration had been doing to achieve peace without invading. The story, painstakingly constructed throughout months of disciplined memo writing for the record, told of bending over backward to achieve a negotiated peace with open diplomacy, just as Congress had insisted, and of endless Indian recalcitrance and violence, with horrific results for the diplomats.

It was all there: instructions to Pond and Steedman and to Trueman and Hardin and Putnam; back-and-forth with Brant; speeches at the Six Nations conference in Philadelphia; Hamtramck's and Putnam's treaty making with the Wabash at Vincennes; the multitude of messages to the Indian confederation at the Glaize, protesting the absence of any U.S. desire for Indian land; the letters between Putnam and Wilkinson and Knox and Washington always averring hope that war could be avoided. Plus much correspondence with Creek, Cherokee, and other southern Indians, trying to persuade them not to join the western confederation.

Then there were Wilkinson's and Putnam's reports from Fort Washington, with news of the Indians' attack on the Fort Jefferson hay cutters and the risk to Putnam's life. Then reports, from many quarters, of the killing of Trueman and Hardin and their parties, with many horrifying details. Plus Wayne's deposition of Private May, an eyewitness behind the lines, showing an implacable Indian intention to fight on, with British support.

These documents were highly effective. The fates of the Trueman and Hardin parties drew especially quick, pained responses from House members. Three days after receiving Knox's file, with members still only partway through all the paperwork, an official House address to the president acknowledged the administration's reiterated peace attempts, the "barbarous sacrifice" of citizens in public service, and the continued hostility of the Indians. Though stopping short of an outright call for achieving peace through invasion—the House reiterated its benevolent regard for Indians generally—the address did refer to Congress's duty to provide for the safety of U.S. citizens in the face of Indian recalcitrance. Washington and his cabinet had reason to think it was succeeding at last in its long effort to pull the House toward a recognition of the inevitable.

But then: narrative collision. On December 6, Washington himself had to send the House further documentation, confusing the trend so painstakingly established for keeping the army at full strength and accepting the need for an invasion.

These were minutes of a meeting held at Buffalo Creek. Red Jacket and the other Seneca intermediaries, having returned from the big Glaize conference, had been debriefed, by both British and American officials near Niagara, on the Seneca's efforts to propose peace and serve as go-betweens during the conference.

And you'd never think, reading what Red Jacket told his auditors at Niagara, that he and other Seneca delegates to the conference had been forced to confess their collaboration with the United States, renounce it, reaffirm loyalty to militant Indian solidarity, and take a confrontational message back to the president. You'd think just the opposite. Red Jacket was famous for rhetoric and theatrical flair, and as he told it, the pivotal figure at the Glaize conference was none other than Red Jacket.

His story had something for everyone. Conjuring possibilities for peace out of thin air, Red Jacket's story made him a sort of new Joseph Brant, the go-between who could see both sides; despite Brant's failures, Red Jacket might really have thought he could trick both sides into avoiding war. Untruth, in any event, was his means.

According to him, the only white man in attendance at the conference was the dreaded renegade Simon Girty. British listeners might have been pleased to hear their high official McKee edited out, because they were denying any official British involvement in the Indian resistance. Red Jacket also alleged that the Shawnee were the only Indians speaking for war: from that, American listeners would receive a pleasing impression that the confederation had been fatally divided on the war question. Captain Hendrick had betrayed his mission, Red Jacket said: the Mahican had given the president's message only to McKee and failed to attend the conference at all. That falsehood positioned Red Jacket as the last go-between standing, sole voice of Indian moderation.

And the western Indians had humbly sought his sage advice as elder brother, Red Jacket told his auditors. Gratefully, they'd concurred in his suggestion that the confederation meet with the Americans at the mouth of the Sandusky in the spring and discuss reasonable terms for peace. He implied that at such a conference the confederation might be willing to give up, for cash, much land north of the Ohio River. Declaring himself eager to travel to Philadelphia to discuss all of these matters further, he shoved both Cornplanter and Brant out of the traditional role of Six Nations mediator—a role already fatally compromised anyway—and adroitly conjured an impression that a negotiated peace was still possible, and that the one man who could make it happen was Red Jacket.

Red Jacket left out of his report the conditions the confederation had set for a meeting in the spring: the Americans must destroy the forts before any Sandusky meeting convened; the Ohio River must be the agreed-upon boundary. The one thing he chose to render faithfully was the confederation's tone. Its harshness suggested a need for the supposedly steady, calming hand of Red Jacket. The chamber's doors had been closed when the message was read aloud, and many members expressed outrage at what they heard.

And yet by no means would Congress want to reject such clear progress toward peace. Here was an invitation to a face-to-face meeting between the western Indian confederation and U.S. commissioners, with no evident conditions and an implication of Indian concession of land, to talk terms for a peace treaty. This was just what Senator Hawkins and the other moderates had been hoping for when insisting on sincere diplomacy for peace.

The administration might readily have countered, on the basis of what it had long known was the impossibility of meeting the Indians' real demands, that Red Jacket was disingenuous or just wrong. The cabinet had Cornplanter's message to Wayne, with its more accurate description of the dire point things had reached at the Glaize conference. But that argument would have thrown a harsh light on the real nature of the administration's peace efforts. Arguing that peace was impossible might have made war seem a fait accompli, the negotiations a sham, the deaths of Trueman and Hardin in vain.

Preternatural patience was Washington's mode, and as soon as Knox and Washington saw the minutes of the Niagara debriefing, it was clear that the Sandusky meeting proposed for the spring of 1793 would have to be a go, and that any military movement by Wayne's army in the meantime would be taken by the Indians as an excuse for war, and by Congress as evidence of administration insincerity about peace. Knox would have to hold Wayne back, yet again. He would have to make him wait until a new conference arrived at the inevitable.

That was no easy task. Knox had already written to Wayne after hearing Cornplanter's report on the Glaize conference, and the secretary had then mentioned, as casually as possible, the notion of a peace conference at the Sandusky in the spring, telling Wayne that no decision had yet been made about that. But Red Jacket's testimony tore it. The day after receiving the minutes, Knox sent them to Wayne and gave him the bad news, in the form of new orders.

There was to be no invasion in the spring of 1793. An American commission was to be appointed by the president, Knox told Wayne, to negotiate directly with the Indians at Sandusky. The public, Knox said, demanded this fair experiment for peace: only if the last effort failed could it be presumed that public opinion would support making war. Wayne's new orders from the president therefore took two parts: one, it was more necessary than ever that no offensive operations be undertaken; two, it remained essential that the troops maintain the height of vigilance.

When he received these orders, so devastating to his hopes, Wayne had just learned of Little Turtle's raid on supply outside Fort St. Clair and had been writing to Knox in a mood pretty much the opposite of the restraint Knox was now ordering him to exercise.

"Be not therefore any longer bemused or deceived with ideal hopes of an honorable and lasting peace," Wayne tried to thunder, via the written word. The destruction of his supply capability bore out everything he'd been saying for months about what he saw as a wrongheaded policy for negotiating peace. "Let us be in a condition to take the field in force in the spring," he demanded, with a sudden access of martial charm, and he, General Anthony Wayne, would pledge success.

But now came Knox's new orders to hold back. At first, Wayne thought he could argue. He wrote again, reminding Knox of the attack on supply, which showed the Indians' real intentions. Congress must, Wayne insisted, see through this transparent ploy of asking for a meeting at the Sandusky.

But soon Wayne became, for him, nearly speechless. He was reduced to cold, disdainful understatement.

"I shall not comment," he wrote to Knox, "further than to observe that it is a most humiliating and disagreeable situation to remain with our hands tied, whilst the enemy are at liberty to act upon the offensive, and have done it with some effect." There was nothing for him to do but continue training his men.

Knox knew what Wayne didn't: their entire army remained at risk from a source other than Indian. In Congress, the apparent willingness of the western confederation to negotiate terms favorable to the United States, as presented by Red Jacket, was giving the antiwar and pro-militia factions further inducement to reduce the army's size. On December 20, John Steele of North Carolina, introducing a bill to strip the army back to only two regiments, attacked the military institution as a whole.

Army expenditures, Steele claimed, now amounted to two-thirds of the federal budget and had bought nothing. Steele called Washington's policy inefficient, ignorant, foolish, ambitious, and disgraceful. The army was being built up for its own sake, he argued, as unchecked power will do; the budget was financed by Hamilton's debt, hiding the immense expense. The American people wouldn't take it. Steele cited examples going back to Braddock's defeat to demonstrate the uselessness of regular troops and the virtues of militia. This war, Steele said, could be fought at minimal public expense and far greater effectiveness via guerrilla raids carried out by militia on the scene, instead of by funding a huge, lumbering, unequipped, hungry, outrageously expensive deployment of regulars. Like many other southerners and westerners, Steele wasn't pro-Indian or antiwar, just anti-army. He'd been horrified by the bill passed in the previous session and hoped to undo it now.

Pro-army members fought hard to save the fledgling institution. They recounted episode after episode in which militia had failed. They noted the insolent language of the confederation's message to the United States. They argued that the upcoming Sandusky meeting had been made possible only by a show of force, that laying down arms in advance of negotiation went against every lesson of history, that the House had just learned of the destruction of the Kentucky volunteers' supply convoy, that the Roman legions had always defeated the barbarians until the latter adopted Roman discipline.

Steele came back by hymning the Revolutionary militia in a series of rhetorical questions, naming every famous and not-so-famous battle: Who won the Battle of Bunker Hill? The battles of New Jersey? Of Cowpens, Kings Mountain, Hanging Rock, Blackstock's Farm? The answer, according to Steele, was the American freeholder, not the trash who compose regular armies.

Now, for the first time, James Madison spoke against the regular army. Senator James Monroe, Madison's Virginia ally, had bridled especially hard at the appointment of Anthony Wayne, and Monroe's opposition to what he saw as overreaching by the Washington party in Congress tracked with Madison's own developing critique. And yet Madison wasn't ready to oppose Washington wholeheartedly. His compromise was to propose an amendment to Steele's motion: an appropriation of funds to shift frontier defense away from the army and back to the militia. He failed to argue strenuously for his own amendment or Steele's bill, voted in favor only of a grammatical revision to the motion, then abstained from the final vote.

So after all that, on January 5, 1793, the House retained full troop strength. Wayne's army was saved. Still, political dissent was clearly alive and active, the margin close.

Wayne, learning of Steele's attempt on his army, accused the anti-army faction in Congress of undermining his officers' morale. He was looking at a long winter stuck upstream with restless men, with no way to reinforce the vulnerable forward forts and prevent attacks, and with no approved plan for maneuvers. He doubted the Congress's support for his troops and remained infuriated by the presidential orders that rendered his men so vulnerable.

The United States had never had an army before. Now it was facing the stuff of crisis between military and civil power.

Knox wrote to the Indian confederation at the Glaize to confirm a spring meeting, as proposed by the confederation, to discuss peace. His letter put the Indians instantly on guard.

Knox didn't mention one of the main conditions for meeting, which the confederation had clearly instructed Red Jacket to communicate to the president: demolition of all U.S. forts in Indian country. Nor did Knox acknowledge the other a priori condition: the Ohio River boundary.

And while the confederation had given the mouth of the Sandusky as the meeting place, Knox's letter switched it westward, without explanation, to the rapids of the Miami of the Lake, McKee's operation, one of the confederation's headquarters. This change raised the suspicion that the American commissioners would really be spies, seeking to count troop strength and assess enemy operations in advance of an invasion. Nothing about Knox's letter seemed right.

The confederation leaders wrote back. They wrote not to Knox but to George Washington himself. For the first time, direct communication was established between the western Indian leaders and the man they'd been fighting for so long. And where America-oriented Indians like the Buffalo Creek Seneca called Washington "Father," the western confederation leaders now addressed him as "Brother," an equal.

Dissociating the killings of the Trueman and Hardin parties from confederation policy by labeling them acts of foolish young men, the Indians nevertheless made the blunt statement, directly to the author of U.S. policy, that messages carried by those late emissaries, as well as messages brought to the Glaize conference by Captain Hendrick and the Buffalo Creek Iroquois, exposed the president as duplicitous, with no sincere intention of making peace, only of dictating terms for taking land north and west of the Ohio. The recent letter from Knox, they went on, found the president refusing even to acknowledge confederation demands and conditions for a meeting; meanwhile, thousands of new American soldiers were visibly preparing for war. The young Indian men might be foolish, the confederation admitted, but there was no way for cooler heads to prevail under conditions created solely by the president.

Still, the members of the confederation promised they would do their best—no guarantees—to call in their war parties in advance of the spring meeting. They reiterated that the mouth of the Sandusky at Lake Erie, not the rapids of the Miami of the Lake, must be the meeting place. They sent three strings of beads, white, for friendship, not war.

Washington didn't respond.

During a cabinet meeting in February, all members were now openly agreed that the Sandusky meeting would go forward only to gratify public opinion, not with any expectations of success. Jefferson especially pushed the idea that even as preparations for the conference went on, military preparations must go on too: he suggested the American commissioners be given a certain date, prearranged, after which any talks must end and invasion begin.

Washington told Knox to exert every nerve in preparing for invasion. Considering the setting of a negotiation end date, Knox said he thought invading in the winter after the Sandusky conference might be effective. Counting back from that season, he advised setting the end date accordingly. Knox, not Washington, got back to the confederation. He confirmed the Sandusky as the meeting place; the error had been his, he said. He made no mention of the other conditions.

So the Indian confederation determined to approach the spring negotiation with extreme caution. Prior to meeting with the American commissioners at the Sandusky, they would gather the nations at Roche de Bout, a massive rock formation at the top of the rapids of the Miami of the Lake. There they would consider their options.

New tensions meanwhile developed between the United States and Britain regarding preparations for the Sandusky peace meeting. John Simcoe was in charge for the British side, and as he got involved, during the winter of early 1793, the whole thing started to make him angry.

The Simcoes were no longer in Quebec. After the ice had broken up, they'd finally moved west in the summer of 1792. They lived now across the Niagara River from Fort Niagara, on the legitimately British side, in the town once called Niagara and now named Newark, by Simcoe, for Britishness. From here the governor was developing the institutions that would make Upper Canada a province. He had plans to build a provincial capital at a settlement he would rename York, directly across the western end of Lake Ontario from Newark, a place the Indians there called Toronto.

In the meantime, the Simcoes' Newark quarters still stood on the west bank of the river, near its mouth at the lake, and they weren't much. Newark itself was primitive, only twelve or so cabins. A compound called Navy Hall, having served British ships on the lake, now served as the governor's residence. The main attraction of the position remained the British garrison in Fort Niagara across the river, in U.S. territory.

Fort Niagara was a prize. It was no wonder Simcoe didn't want to give it up to the Americans. Originally built by the French, this was no spartan wilderness outpost, no wooden stockade, but a statement of command, written in stone. The big feature was a huge, three-story house, nine windows wide with multiple chimneys, nearly top-heavy with its peaking roof rising to flatness. The house stood on a point at the river's mouth, right at water's edge, gazing in lonely grandeur upon a seemingly limitless expanse of lake and sky. The grounds around it, sprawling and rolling, could be accessed from the road only by clattering over a stone floor via a stone gate, and then over more stone floor, and then through another stone gate, and all that only after having crossed broad fields cut with deep earthwork redoubts. The whole big enclosure was built on top of a long, zigzagging stone wall that put anyone approaching it deep in a ravine, subject to the fort's looming power. Even after one passed through the second gate under its high stone arch, the parade ground loomed as yet another hill to be climbed.

Within this impregnable construction was a busy city of officers and men in bright red and gleaming white living mainly in stone barracks. Social life bustled among the officer class: many of the officers' wives and children lived in the fort.

So the Simcoes made do. While Navy Hall was being renovated, they lived in tents, in the breeze from the river, looking across at their fort, so nearby, and they were rowed and sailed across at will. They traveled as well to the great falls of the Niagara River, its white mist visible miles away, so Elizabeth Simcoe could sketch them. She found Navy Hall cramped, but she was fascinated by the natural features around her, and by the Indians, and she made good friends among the women at the fort.

Simcoe himself was busy creating a province, and as plans developed in early 1793 for the Sandusky meeting of the Indian confederation with U.S. commissioners, his hopes became complicated. He had a multitude of reasons, including reports from the agent Beckwith, for believing that the Washington administration was pursuing this meeting only to create political justification for an invasion. Simcoe had always seen George Washington as nothing but a grubby land jobber possessed by avarice. "There is no person, perhaps, who thinks less of the talents or integrity of Mr. Washington than I do," he once announced. Even if, at the upcoming meeting, the Indians were to surprise everybody by relinquishing all the land that had already been settled in the West, Simcoe was sure Washington would never give up anything in return.

The Indians had asked for British mediation at the upcoming Sandusky meeting. That caused Simcoe some logistical and political headaches. The governor himself wouldn't travel west to Lake Erie for the meeting, but the privilege of hosting lay by default with the British, because the region was still under British control, and yet both British mediation and British hosting, on what was technically U.S. soil, pressed some tender areas. Minister Hammond had made it clear to Secretary of State Jefferson that both Alexander McKee and the commander at Fort Niagara would be present at the meeting, per Indian request. The United States had to live with that, but the British, trying to avoid rubbing American noses in it, didn't refer to their role explicitly as mediation. The main controversy devolved instead on proper ways of handling food, drink, and entertainment for an event possibly involving five thousand people and lasting six weeks. Whichever power supplied food and fun would be displaying closer Indian ties.

When Alexander Hamilton asked George Hammond for permission to buy and move supplies for the meeting in British-controlled territory, Simcoe bristled. As much as he resented the expense, supplying the Indians out of the forts had traditionally signified that the British held their forts by Indian permission; at this tricky moment, maintaining that formality was crucial. The fact that the United States was asking for permission to transport supplies underscored, for Simcoe, the Americans' lack of sincerity in undertaking the meeting. He denied permission.

Washington needed to bring prestige and seriousness to this bootless errand. The American commission to the Sandusky had to look real.

Any sense in Congress that negotiations were sham would be fatal to the invasion and to the newborn military establishment of the United States.

To give the commission proper prestige and integrity, Washington asked Charles Thomson, a Pennsylvanian, to accept an appointment as commissioner. As secretary of the Continental and Confederation Congresses, Thomson had helped keep the country together before the accession of nationhood and enjoyed credibility with Pennsylvania Delaware Indians. Washington also appointed Charles Carroll, the fabulously wealthy Maryland planter and signer of the Declaration of Independence. Both men declined.

Accepting appointment instead were Benjamin Lincoln of Massachusetts, a former Continental army general and the Confederation Congress's secretary of war before Knox; Timothy Pickering, also of Massachusetts, postmaster general of the United States and a famous Anglophile; and Beverley Randolph of the Virginia Randolphs, related to Lees and Jeffersons and other planter families, a former governor of his state. Washington described the trio as immune to any suspicion of hoping to continue the war. To the same end, he'd even considered appointing John Steele, the most vociferous antiwar congressman.

The three commissioners left for Simcoe's temporary capital, Newark, in late April, carrying orders from the president: they were to make contact with Simcoe and await, under Simcoe's auspices at Newark, an invitation from the Indian confederation meeting now at Roche de Bout, at the top of the Miami rapids. When the commissioners were invited westward, Simcoe was to arrange safe passage by water, through regions now under British and Indian control, along the south shore of Lake Erie and into the Sandusky Bay.

The commissioners' orders for negotiating with the western Indians involved offering the usual deal, with a few twists. For an Indian promise to end attacks and resistance, an Indian admission of American sovereignty, and an Indian acknowledgment of the exclusive right of the United States to buy western land, the commissioners would confirm the Fort Harmar Treaty line, offer $50,000 in supplies and $10,000 per year on top of the Fort Harmar money, and promise to demolish the forts forward of Fort Washington.

The commissioners were also authorized to admit an error on the part of the United States. Indian land had been claimed by the United States per right of conquest, a fruit of victory over England. That was wrong. The United States now claimed Indian land only as freely bought and sold, as enshrined in the Fort Harmar Treaty.

There was one fallback position. Because the administration had no intention of achieving a negotiated peace, it was only for public consumption, a sign, once invasion began, that the United States had bent over backward to avoid war. If necessary, the commissioners were authorized to cede a small further portion of land. Even this theoretical cession would exclude 150,000 acres to serve as bounty land for the soldiers of George Rogers Clark, who had wreaked such havoc in Indian country during the Revolution.

The commissioners were also instructed not to strike any deal with the confederation as a whole. They must make separate treaties with individual nations.

And the orders also contained an end date for the negotiation: August 1. Whatever situation prevailed on that date, the commissioners were to communicate it immediately and directly to General Wayne, who should by then be in position down the Ohio and ready to invade. If they'd been unable to get the Indian confederation to submit, they must send him these words: "We did not effect a peace." That would be Wayne's signal to move.

Wayne hadn't yet taken his army all the way down to Fort Washington, the invasion's launching point, when the commissioners left for Niagara, but he wasn't still in Pittsburgh. In December 1792, even while Knox was throwing cold water on the plan of invading in the spring, Wayne had moved nearly the whole army, with Knox's approval, to winter quarters.

Pittsburgh was too much the rowdy frontier boomtown. The men and officers were improving, in Wayne's view, and to improve further, they needed a rugged woodland situation with no access to vice. The new place was about twenty miles downstream and north of Pittsburgh, on the west side of the river, a broad, level bank. It had been known as Logstown: Tanacharison had lived here when a young George

Washington tried to collaborate with him in seizing Fort Duquesne
so long ago.

Wayne called it Legion Ville, and in early November he'd sent a
work crew to ready the place for the army. Although for some weeks the
Ohio remained too low for travel, Wayne started sending arms, animals, uniforms, and baggage downstream as soon as he could, and at
the end of the month the general and the bulk of his army boarded big,
flat barges. Giving Pittsburgh a fifteen-gun salute, they drifted on
sluggish current away from the point. Four hours later, they were moving
into their winter home.

And it was at Legion Ville that Wayne's army really became something of an army. The general began by showing his officers and men
what securing an area, the Mad Anthony way, really called for. He had
no officers with what he thought of as the scientific knowledge to build
a fort, so he supervised everything himself, and the intensity of his supervision brought to a high point everything he'd ever learned about
military preparation and discernment. He'd chosen the Legion Ville
site in part for natural protection. Deep ravines lay to its north, east,
and west. He'd laid out the huge camp on the east-west axis, with four
earthwork enclosures circling it, redoubts but big ones, each capable of
containing thirty-six men to defend the whole place in protected cover
behind parapets. Routine at Legion Ville involved ceaseless attention to
security. A hundred and twenty men were always stationed at guard
posts for a strong perimeter. Beyond the perimeter, a defensive ditch
more than a mile in circumference surrounded the whole camp; it too
was closely patrolled, and guard duty at Legion Ville was no joke. Twenty-
four hours every day, that duty employed an unusually high number of
troops. Falling asleep on duty warranted brutal punishment. In only about
a month, Legion Ville was transformed into a hyper-developed version of
the temporary camps Wayne intended to build, every night without fail,
and then guard with hypervigilance, during his projected march into
Indian country.

Within those many rings of protection were rough wooden barracks
for the men, one story high, basically winter huts; a two-story barracks for the officers; and for Wayne himself a two-story, two-chimney,
four-fireplace house. Construction hit an immediate snag when the
temperature dropped below freezing for days, icing the Ohio so supplies

couldn't travel. Snow fell thickly and piled up deeply in camp, stopping everything but the constant guard duty. The men slept in tents, and Wayne and his officers didn't seek out homes for their own bivouac: Wayne had the officers sleep in tents too, Wayne in his own big marquee. It was a sign of the efficiency of the growing army, and of the men's desire to get inside, that by the end of December all men and officers were housed. With recruits still arriving in Pittsburgh and coming down to camp, soon there were nearly three thousand men stationed at Legion Ville.

The routine was demanding. Men coming off watch began long hours of drill; those exhausted from drill took up posts as guards. Desertion continued, courts-martial convened, flogging went on, and one repeat offender was executed by firing squad. The army improved.

The chance of full-scale attack on Legion Ville itself was remote. Wayne even left his redoubts lacking the bastions that made it easier to defend forts without firing across and inward on one's own men. Still, there was always the possibility of attack on parties outside the camp gathering forage or traveling, and the general was inculcating in men and officers his own relentless approach to caution. Soon Wayne believed that even if all the Indians were to come in a single force, they couldn't dislodge the legion from Legion Ville.

The men practiced tactics too, and the legion structure held up. Wayne's redesigned musket had been approved after all by Washington and Knox: on attack, his light infantry could maintain steady fire, running among the big trees ahead of the main body and discharging self-primed buckshot, eyes on targets. Infantry lines followed, leveling with standard muskets to put out blasts of balls and buckshot. Howitzers designed for quick woodland movement launched shells, and the fearsome dragoons followed up on horseback with sabers. That's how Anthony Wayne, in frustration, passed the winter.

Now it was spring, and the Sandusky meeting, to Wayne's disgust, was still on. The three American commissioners were on their way to Governor Simcoe at Newark, and from there, they were to take a British-provided ship west to negotiate with members of the confederation.

Wayne groused that he'd prefer to lead about two thousand "commissioners" west and decide the issue by force.

He had new orders from Knox. They did involve movement, at last, and the good news was that the invasion plan was on. Wayne was to make appropriate deployments for securing all of the frontier forts as fully as possible and get the main body of his army down the Ohio to join Wilkinson at Fort Washington. Wilkinson would move up to take command of Fort Hamilton, and the moment Wayne heard "We did not effect a peace" from the commissioners, he was to start marching the main army northward against the Indians.

Wayne took this order to move downstream and get into position as identical to an order to invade. The invasion wasn't about to begin, as far as he was concerned; it was actually beginning. The American commissioners were still in transit to Newark when Wayne began the big move out of Legion Ville. To the consternation of the locals, Wayne left Fayette, Legion Ville, and all of the Pennsylvania posts barely staffed; he needed almost everyone. The Indians were watching, and what they saw, on the eve of what was supposed to be a negotiation for avoiding war, was Anthony Wayne's Legion of the United States coming down the Ohio River with all martial ostentation. Behind a pilot boat way out front, Wayne's thirty-boat armada, most of the craft freshly built, rowed with the current in single file, a hundred yards between each boat in as straight a line as the boatmen could manage, each in the wake of the one before. Wayne came in his own boat, the *Federal*, and guard boats followed the whole line, about three hundred yards behind. Every night along the way, riflemen disembarked before everyone else and moved half a mile inland to cover the landing of teams to build overnight breastworks. Only when the breastworks were built would the full force land.

The river was high with rain, and the armada moved fast. It passed weakly staffed forts at Wheeling and Steuben and other posts, passed Fort Harmar at Marietta, passed the beat-up stockade at Gallipolis. Rounding bend after bend, men and officers were astonished by the obvious arability of these hundreds of miles of untapped bottomland along the river, thick with lush, high vegetation and towered over by trees of a size they'd never seen before: sycamore, elm, beech, hickory, maple, and more. The wealth was astonishing.

It took only seven days to reach Cincinnati. Wayne didn't like what he saw there. Fort Washington, Harmar's pride and joy, was the one impressive construction; the rest looked like log cabins, mud, and more frontier-town vice. Wayne moved his whole force slightly downstream from the fort and encamped two thousand men and most of the baggage, matériel, livestock, and stores at a point of high ground he named Hobson's Choice, because he had, he determined, no choice about where to put his camp: he had to keep the army away from the roistering of Cincinnati, and yet for convenient supply, he had to remain close to Fort Washington.

Here Wayne's men broke up the boats to build stables, set out white tents in long rows, and moved in. New recruits in smaller armadas were coming down to join them. Wayne went to Fort Washington to see Wilkinson, whom he'd known since the Revolution and had been commanding for more than a year but hadn't yet seen in the West. Hamtramck was soon on his way up from Fort Vincennes to make a plan for invasion with Wayne and Wilkinson. The legion was downstream at last.

When the American commissioners, Pickering, Randolph, and Lincoln, arrived at Newark in mid-May, Simcoe insisted they stay as his guests at Navy Hall. Mrs. Simcoe had a bad cold and found the commissioners' presence in her cramped quarters unwelcome; she fled with her children to the fort across the river to stay with the wife of a lieutenant.

Simcoe held bachelor's hall. Though he considered them at once dishonest and stupid, he wined and dined the Americans with relentless charm. Not two weeks earlier, he'd received some unsettling news. France and England had yet again declared war. Much pro-France sentiment prevailed in the United States, though not in the Washington administration: Jefferson, not long for the cabinet, was again odd man out on that issue. Still, with no known American position on the England-France war, Simcoe could imagine the United States using the Indian war as a pretext for attacking the contested forts, maybe even moving beyond them into Upper Canada, on behalf of the old American ally France. He did his best to beguile the American commissioners.

Simcoe was assessing a host of other challenges. Intelligence had it that Anthony Wayne had moved down to Cincinnati. Wayne was nearly the only Revolutionary general for whom Simcoe had any respect. They'd both come into their own at the Battle of Monmouth, and Wayne, unlike Washington, was actually capable of doing some damage, Simcoe thought. Meanwhile, Lord Dorchester was on his way back to Canada from London, and Dorchester was bringing more specific orders from the Home Office. Simcoe couldn't predict what his wet-blanket boss might try to do to his own plans and maneuvers. He was therefore hoping that the Sandusky meeting would go on, and go as slowly as possible, and with as much irresolution as possible, delaying any potential American military move on Indian country and possibly even into Canada. He wrote to his subordinates Alexander McKee and the Niagara commander, who would attend the upcoming Sandusky meeting, that ceaseless kindness and urbanity toward the American commissioners would avoid any appearance of actively mediating while retaining control of the Indian relationship. Advise Indians secretly, he instructed them, and treat the Americans with nothing but affable ceremony.

Pickering, Randolph, and Lincoln, for their part, had nothing to do at Newark but await word from the Indian confederation, now in pre-meetings at Roche de Bout at the top of the Miami rapids, that the nations had gathered and were ready to proceed to the Sandusky to treat. At Newark, the king's birthday came; there was a splendid ball at the fort, and Simcoe invited his American guests. After dancing came a late-night supper. The commissioners were impressed, especially by the food. But they heard little from the West, aside from a chilling rumor that should negotiations fail, the first act of war would be the killing of the commissioners.

When Simcoe took the opportunity to pass on to the commissioners a report from Alexander McKee that Wayne's moving the American army down the Ohio boded ill for the meeting, the commissioners wrote to Knox. Wayne's move, they reported, was arousing suspicion in the Indians.

Knox knew that. How could Wayne's move not alarm the Indians? But there was nothing he could do. Washington and Knox needed Wayne ready to move as soon as negotiations failed. The risk they were taking, both with their commissioners' safety and with Congress's skepticism about the administration's sincerity, was an audacious but calculated one.

The commissioners at Newark gave Knox another warning. With Wayne now down the river, any armed guard accompanying supply from Fort Washington up to the forward forts Hamilton and Jefferson would be taken by the Indians as military aggression, and they would ditch the meeting, for cause. Knox wrote immediately to Wayne. The general must be poised to move against the confederation, Knox said, at the exact moment the commission inevitably failed, and yet in order for the commission to collapse on its own, Wayne must make no forward movement. He couldn't use armed guards to supply the forward forts.

Received at Hobson's Choice, these warnings and instructions sent Wayne into a tailspin. He couldn't follow orders to remain in readiness for an immediate march without securing, staffing, and supplying his forward forts. He couldn't follow orders not to secure, staff, and supply those forts without risking defeat in an engagement that he had orders to do everything to win.

He couldn't follow orders.

He determined to make what he called, in a letter to Knox, a provisional arrangement. He sent a detachment of troops under a veteran lieutenant to widen the road between the advance forts. This detail would fell trees to create easy passage for the many ox-drawn wagons and livestock herds necessary to heavy supply. The team cut hay outside Fort Jefferson as well, bivouacking every night under a breastwork made of the felled trees. And contrary to orders, the convoy was guarded: sentry duty was of course constant.

The Indians watched. They found stealing horses impossible now, surprise attack unlikely to succeed. The American crew drove more than eighty head of cattle up that wood road to Fort Jefferson, and soon Wayne had put heavy supplies of grain in the most forward fort, the head of the line.

At the great rock formation at the head of the rapids of the Miami of the Lake known as Roche de Bout, delegations convening for the first time since the Glaize conference, again from many nations and branches, discussed the tone and meaning of Knox's communications with them. There was lack of compliance with the prior condition of demolishing the forward forts. There was ignoring the demand for an Ohio River boundary. There was trying to change the proposed meeting location. A large army under Anthony Wayne had made a move from the Ohio head-waters to Fort Washington and built a giant camp near the Great Miami.

Joseph Brant was at this Roche de Bout pre-meeting, heading the Grand River Iroquois delegation. In the face of much hard-line disdain, he was still trying to jockey himself back into what had become, since at least the Glaize conference, the nearly irrelevant position of tradi-tional Six Nations go-between. Simcoe himself no longer had any use for Brant. Alexander McKee was under orders from Simcoe to oppose any compromise Brant might propose at Roche de Bout.

Brant nevertheless kept trying to revive the old idea of a boundary line at the mouth of the Muskingum River. This wasn't something Simcoe would have rejected on its face—a Muskingum line com-ported with the buffer zone he hoped for—but it was Simcoe's policy now to do anything to keep the Indians together and attached to the British forts. McKee, for his own reasons as a Shawnee militant, wanted the Ohio boundary line or war. Again and again, he shot Brant down in debate.

Yet Brant seemed to remain one of the few people involved who really thought the upcoming Sandusky conference offered a chance for a negotiated peace. Against dissent from both McKee and the Indian hard-liners, and despite all signs of American duplicity, he kept advis-ing the confederation to attend the Sandusky meeting as planned.

Then came new intelligence. Wayne's army had moved forward.

When Mrs. Simcoe came home from her sojourn at the fort, she was surprised to find the American commissioners still in her house, awaiting word from the West. They really weren't as bad as she'd feared. Pickering gave her a recipe for a twenty-minute salmon chowder with sea biscuit and pork.

And that was a parting gift. The trio had finally decided there was nothing to do but sail west, even without an invitation. Simcoe had fitted out the schooner *Dunmore*, ready for the commissioners' trip to Detroit. The commissioners arrived at the landing on June 26.

But the wind changed. Waves crashed on the Fort Erie beach, blown persistently from the west. This trip wanted a following wind. There was no way to sail.

Then, on July 5, with the commissioners stuck on the beach at Fort Erie, a British sail appeared against that gulf of sky. A ship was traveling quickly toward them on the west wind.

It turned out to be carrying a delegation of fifty Shawnee from Roche de Bout. They'd been sent to forestall the commissioners' trip west. They had some bones to pick; the whole Sandusky meeting might be off. And accompanying this Shawnee delegation was none other than the famous Mohawk Joseph Brant.

Bewildered, the three commissioners trooped back to Navy Hall to begin an unexpected preliminary round of discussions with Brant and the Shawnee delegation. The Simcoes' son was ill, and Mrs. Simcoe had taken him to an open-air camp on a hillside, away from the river's buggy humidity, so she missed the unexpected return of her American guests and the appearance of so many Indian ones.

Wayne's road crew had moved forward of Fort Jefferson. That's what the Indian delegation reported to the commissioners at Navy Hall. The crew had cut about six miles of road northward. Running into swamp, it had stopped and cut trail back to the fort. Wayne had thus advanced beyond the head of the line. On the very eve of peace talks, the United States was invading.

The commissioners wrote urgently to Knox. They did their best to spin the preemptive arrival of Brant and the Shawnee delegation as a positive: discussions under Simcoe's aegis might be useful, they said. And they'd done what they could to allay Indian suspicions: they'd shown Wayne's orders to stay put to the Indian delegation; they'd stated, falsely, that their instructions contained no predetermined boundary, only that concessions would be needed from both sides.

Still, they expressed to Knox intense upset regarding Wayne's advance. They underlined in the letter that Wayne had moved *"six miles beyond"* Fort Jefferson into Indian country. Furthermore, Wayne was said to have lavishly stocked all of the posts with horses, cattle, forage, and other provisions, well beyond the needs of the garrisons there and clearly in preparation for supplying an invasion. These maneuvers— rogue, as far as the commissioners were concerned—placed Wayne within three days' march of the Glaize itself, according to Brant. The general had, the commissioners told Knox, taken an unwarrantable action.

Anthony Wayne saw nothing but red. Receiving urgent orders, which Knox sent explicitly "in the name of the President of the United States," to withdraw any and all extra men from the head of the line and hold the army at Fort Washington until the outcome of the treaty was known, with an enclosure of the commissioners' report castigating his activities, Wayne began writing back with grim, barely controlled politeness to refute every charge.

But after a page or so, he realized he was going too far, at least for the record. He took up a clean piece of paper. He scribbled "private" at the top. He let fly at Knox.

He began by citing, exhaustively, by date, all of the letters he'd sent Knox laying out his plan to widen the road as a *"preparatory arrangement,"* a term he underlined. He called the commissioners' alarms and apprehensions unnecessary, called the commissioners themselves credulous, implied they were physical cowards. He called the Indians disingenuous, the British aegis poisonous.

Just the facts: he'd cut road only up to Fort Jefferson, going beyond only to get around bad terrain. Supplying the forward forts had been neglected before his arrival at Hobson's Choice; having received positive orders from Knox to do so, as documented in official letters, each of which he cited by date, he'd made appropriate efforts to supply them. He only wished it were true that the forts were as well supplied as the Indians had frightened the timorous commissioners into claiming they were. They weren't, thanks to Knox's and Washington's orders to hold back, and Wayne feared the upcoming invasion would thereby be badly hampered. Because, despite their protestations, the Indians were still raiding supply, Wayne could readily understand why they didn't like his cutting grass outside forts and guarding livestock: the Indians used long grass as cover for killing troops and stealing animals. He gave exact numbers of men in each fort and noted, citing the record in detail, that Knox had approved every one of those deployments.

It was unfortunate, he apologized rhetorically, that from what he called the idle and fallacious reports of what he underlined as *"Hostile Savages,"* he was forced to detail with such extraordinary minutiae the men's enlistment terms, and the challenging measures he was taking to keep well-trained soldiers who, because of the delaying tactics of the peace policy, were about to leave the army. But he did go through all of that minutiae, just for Knox's information.

Then he really lost it. What especially galled him, in the orders "with which you have been pleased to honor me 'in the name of the President of the United States'"—and Wayne meant this blast for Washington himself—was the absence of trust not only in Wayne's conduct but also, even more outrageously, in his honor. At great risk to his army, he'd lived up to his promise not to advance until the treaty result was known. False intelligence from hostile Indians and complaints by hysterical commissioners were believed instead, and by default. Wayne hoped that Knox would inform the commissioners that he had never forfeited his word or his honor to any living man. He hoped the worried minds of hostile Indians and American commissioners alike would be eased by news that he'd just withdrawn all men and wagons from the advance posts, in obedience to the president's orders.

Then the zinger. Wayne had one favor to ask of Knox. He would like all future orders to be as clear and consistent as the most recent one.

It was a serious accusation, if only implicit: military inconsistency in the commander in chief himself. Having laid down his pen at last, Wayne picked it up again. He scratched out the word "private." He put the first batch of pages together with the second and made them into a single letter. He was going on the record after all.

For the final copy, he did calm the tone slightly. He removed the section with scare quotes around "in the name of the President," as well as some exclamation points, and he moved passages around for flow. Still, his letter exposed the issue. Orders from the President of the

United States, as commander in chief, were self-contradictory. They couldn't be followed.

Wayne signed off by expressing hope that the legion wouldn't fail in the field due to a lack of—underlined again—*"timely supplies at the head of the line."* And in a P.S., he added news he'd just received: the woods and roads up the line were "infested with savages." Would to God, he signed off again, and again for the official record, that his hands were untied.

At Newark, the commissioners assured the Shawnee delegation that the president had sent a special message to General Wayne, ordering him in no uncertain terms to stay put. That news had the right effect on Joseph Brant. Clinging to his self-appointed role as mediator, Brant chose not to remind the American commissioners that the Indian confederation was insisting on the Ohio River boundary, and he somehow persuaded the grudging Shawnee delegation to accept Washington's orders to Wayne as a sign of good faith. Brant told the commissioners they could now come on to Detroit.

The Indian delegation sailed west from Fort Erie toward the mouth of the Miami of the Lake, to make a report at Roche de Bout, and on July 14 the American commissioners boarded the *Dunmore* and sailed west on Lake Erie too. After a week, they reached the mouth of the Detroit River. They'd arrived at last in the American West.

Five weeks later, after much activity on all sides, the inevitable finally came to pass. On August 23, the commissioners wrote directly to Wayne, as ordered, underlining the exact words: "We did not effect a peace."

Nobody ever got to the mouth of the Sandusky. In late July, the commissioners were put up across the Detroit River from the fort, on the legitimately Canadian east bank, by Alexander McKee's associate Matthew Elliott. Simcoe had prohibited them from visiting the fort itself: the contested installation was a restricted area, and especially given war with France its vulnerabilities were nothing American eyes should see. Elliott kept a farm and house, much nicer anyway for the Americans than De-troit's few mud streets, packed with roistering French and Indian trad-ers and embittered loyalists; the Americans stayed on Elliott's grounds in tents. Where the Simcoes were abolitionists, and held nobody in slavery, the former Pennsylvanian Elliott was a notably harsh slave master, and as Elliott followed the Simcoe plan of killing the commissioners with kindness—food, drink, charm—the New Englanders Pickering and Lin-coln might have been discomfited by the brutal system Elliott's hospi-tality depended on. Randolph would have been right at home in that sense, but the weather was uncomfortably hot, the river breeze sluggish, the mosquitoes nearly unbearable. All three commissioners remained anxious for their personal safety in what to them seemed a creepily re-mote loyalist outpost.

Soon, on Bois Blanc Island, in the Detroit River off Elliott's farm, a delegation from the Indian confederation at Roche de Bout arrived and made camp. The delegation had come to present the Americans with a message. This time, no Brant. His grip on the impossible role of media-tor had slipped for good. Reporting back at Roche de Bout on his trip to Newark, he'd been asked with much sardonic comment why he hadn't made the confederation's real position clear to the Americans before allowing them to come all the way to the Detroit River. At one session, leaders of the Shawnee, Delaware, Miami, and Wyandot showed up with pistols in their belts. The point was clear. When Brant proposed bringing the American commissioners at Elliott's up the Miami of the Lake to address the meeting, the huge Shawnee Captain Johnny led the hard-liners in rejecting that proposal. Instead, he and other leaders composed a message to the commissioners, telling them up front and point-blank what Brant had kept from them: the Ohio River remained the only acceptable boundary. Brant refused to sign it. He persuaded other Iroquois to withhold their signatures too.

But all of the other leaders signed the statement, and crossing to El-liott's from their camp on Bois Blanc on July 30, a delegation brought it to the American commissioners. The statement repeated the position the confederation had been stating for many years, whenever asked, and had killed hundreds of Americans to defend. The delegation sat down with Pickering, Lincoln, and Randolph. At last, the Americans and the western Indian confederation met face-to-face.

There was no room to move. The Indians' signed statement, as now delivered directly to the commissioners, claimed that no valid treaty had been made since the first Fort Stanwix Treaty, back in 1768, when Indians had given up the great hunting ground Kentucky for an Ohio River limit on white settlement. The statement also asked the commissioners a blunt question: Were they empowered to set an Ohio boundary or not?

The delegation stared down the commissioners, in expectation of a straight answer at last. The commissioners asked for the night to confer.

The next day, they spoke to the Indian delegation at length. They explained why they could not set the boundary at the Ohio. They put forth their various offers for compensation. They went to their fallback position: ceding some land west of the already settled areas, along with an acknowledgment of the Indian right to sell, not as a conquered people, though only to the United States. None of it came close to acceptability.

Nor did Indian demands come close to acceptability. The simple truth had finally become as clear as it could be.

And yet it took nearly two more weeks for the commissioners to send Wayne the signal. There was further back-and-forth, again leading straight to the obvious conclusion, before a slight feint backward. The commissioners were preparing to leave when Elliott persuaded them to wait for one more Indian response.

Simcoe, McKee, and Elliott were only trying to buy time now. The longer they could delay the commissioners, the less time Wayne would have to prepare for invasion. If they could push the timing for Wayne's march up to the fall frost, the grass would die; moving horses and livestock would become difficult. The commissioners, for their part, remained under orders to negotiate until absolute failure was reached. They were well past their August 1 cut-off date. But if they walked out with an offer supposedly pending, Congress would withdraw support for the war. They felt they had no choice but to stay for one more round.

While they waited for this supposed last-ditch attempt, enough discord was prevailing among the confederation at Roche de Bout that working everything out took days of heated debate. Brant tried one more time for his Muskingum line, but now that the Americans had expressed themselves clearly, his position made even less sense to the others than it had before: the commissioners were under strict orders to reject a line at the Muskingum. McKee and Brant meanwhile exchanged stinging letters—both men possessed greater command of English than most non-Indian officials—accusing each other of influencing Indian decisions to Indian detriment.

Brant gave up, this time it might appear for good. Given the likelihood of war, all he could do, he told the confederation, was get as many exposed Iroquois people as possible off U.S. soil and up to Canada. The leading diplomat of the Six Nations, the elder brothers, broke up with the western confederation, left Roche de Bout, and went home.

The American commissioners had meanwhile been waiting miserably at Elliott's for some final answer, suffering pouring rain, 100 percent humidity, and swarming mosquitoes. They received visits from various Indians but no official statement from Roche de Bout. Blue Jacket himself, well known by reputation as one of the authors of St. Clair's defeat, came to dinner in a laced hat and a scarlet jacket with gold tassels. He wouldn't discuss terms.

At last the commissioners did receive a final message from the confederation. Two Wyandot brought another written communication from Roche de Bout to Elliott's. Regarding the money offered in compensation for the Northwest Territory, the western Indians had one last suggestion. Because they didn't want money, and they did want their land, the United States might instead take the money and divide it among white settlers in Indian country as compensation for moving out. Furthermore, if the United States would not now agree to the Ohio boundary, there was no point in further discussion.

Look back, the Indians wrote to the commissioners, at lands from which Indians had been driven to the place they now stood. They could retreat no further. There was already barely enough food to sustain their lives. "We have therefore resolved," they said, "to leave our bones in this small space to which we are now confined."

The American commissioners called the speech contemptible. Indians weren't capable of expressing themselves in such elevated terms, they believed, and they concluded that the British must now be in total control. As they prepared to sail homeward, Lincoln sent the news of the commission's failure to Knox, and now he didn't bother covering up the sham, causing a Quaker observer some consternation by confiding that this was "just such an answer as he could have wished." During the westward trip across Lake Erie, Lincoln had taken in for the first time the vastness and value of the great West. He'd come to the conclusion that the savages' way of life was destined to become extinct.

The war party at Roche de Bout celebrated by passing the hatchet and war dancing. The truth the hard-liners had been expressing for so long—Anthony Wayne had too—was finally out in the open. It was a truth that went back to the proclamation lines of 1763 and 1768. It went further back, to the great investments of the Ohio Company of Virginia and other land companies, which those proclamation lines and the Quebec Act had been intended to tame. There had never really been, for George Washington or for the nationhood of the United States, any alternative to a war of conquest. After all this time, the true lines were drawn.

General Wayne, appointed to carry out in actuality what had been his hope for so long, received the signal code from the commissioners he so despised, and he also saw that the commissioners were continuing to articulate, for the review of Congress, the administration narrative. They wrote to Wayne that despite their failure, they hoped some good might come of their mission to seek peace, and they gave him their unqualified thanks for his care of their safety.

To Wayne, no good could conceivably come of their errand. It wasn't until September 11 that he received their message with the signal to move, and the loss of time, potentially disastrous, that the commissioners and the political process they represented had caused his mission overwhelmed him with anger. He got in gear.

PART III

THE
BLACK SNAKE
MARCH

10

RECOVERY

Under a spreading oak, General Richard Butler's bones had frozen three times and warmed twice. The flesh of hundreds of bodies lying on the forest floor had been broken down by bacteria, ripped by wolves, pecked by birds, tunneled out by bugs and worms. Spring rain sank the bones, long since clean, in mud. Summer sun dappled them. Fallen leaves blew past and settled against them.

It was the afternoon of Christmas Eve 1793, and Captain Edward Butler, his breath steaming, had returned to the scene of St. Clair's defeat and the death of his elder brother. General Wayne had been close to Richard Butler during those years in the Continental army's Pennsylvania Line, and Wayne had been keeping young Edward under his wing to the point where some said the general played favorites. Having been made acting assistant adjutant general and acting inspector of the army, the youngest Butler brother had been given much responsibility.

Now Edward rode up to a lieutenant and a sergeant major and instead of giving an order asked a difficult favor. He described the impressive size of the oak where he'd last seen his brother, the propped-up position Richard had been left in, the pistol in each hand. The men surveyed the scene. There were skulls everywhere: deep eye sockets, teeth possibly intact. A skull could be anybody's.

Richard's skeleton might help identify him. Edward asked his two subordinates to inspect any thighbone under any such oak. The bone might show a breakage and reknitting that Richard had experienced years earlier. Clearly Edward had been thinking this over.

A somber Christmas. Bone spread for five miles, marking the paths of the beaten soldiers' panicky flight. There were muskets lying about too, with broken-off locks and barrels the enemy had bent double, and other detritus not taken after the victory more than two years earlier. So much bone crowded the site's central area that just to make room to pitch tents, the men were ordered to gather and stack all the remains. Some of the skeletons held together while being moved.

About three hundred men were on the scene, eight infantry companies and an artillery detachment. Taking control of the position had long been one of Wayne's main objectives, and he intended to hold it. While the bones were moved and the tents were pitched, the major in command started other men clearing ground for a fort. Under protection of patrols ranging in the woods and a guard under quickly constructed timber redoubts, the fort went up fast.

When Wayne himself arrived later that day with an infantry detachment mounted on packhorses, he was pleased to see his precise instructions so well followed. Under strict protection of the guard details, the construction crew was building four twenty-foot-square blockhouses to form the fort's corners, each with embrasures on three sides to enable howitzer fire, and building them simultaneously, so that in a matter of hours at least partial protection from attack existed on the site of the defeat. Even while the building was going up, troops moved within its boundaries and set up operations.

For this, Wayne had turned down Christmas dinner at Fort Jefferson with General and Mrs. Wilkinson. Now the general's tent too was pitched. He would sleep with his men on cold ground where his old rival St. Clair had lost so many men, women, and children.

The next morning, Wayne ordered the troops to dig a pit within the unfinished fort grounds, gather in the skulls, and inter them in the pit. Edward Butler's lieutenant and sergeant had identified Richard Butler, and Edward took personal charge of his brother's remains. A rough service was said over the mass grave. Soon the living were picketed above the dead within a palisade fifteen feet high. On all sides, trees and brush were cleared for a thousand feet to give the fort command of the whole area. The doors had musket-proof barricades made of multi-ply reinforced timber; the embrasures had shutters. Wayne loved this fort. He'd named it before it existed: Recovery.

A long year of disappointment and exasperation came to an end with the construction of Fort Recovery. Back in September, upon receiving word of the failure of the negotiations near Detroit, Wayne had made every effort to do as quickly as possible what he'd finally been authorized to do. He started giving orders: officers were to divest themselves and their men of any heavy baggage, assemble only what would be necessary, and prepare to march against the enemy at a moment's notice.

That sounded good, but a number of problems had held Wayne back until October. The readiness of troops, for one thing, remained a serious concern. Hobson's Choice had seen constant drill, maneuver, inspection, those day-to-day activities that Wayne and his men and officers had been carrying out together, many hours every day, for well over a year, but the results remained imperfect. Again and again the general had to issue his officers orders of correction. The men formed up imprecisely, without what Wayne called velocity, exhibited sluggishness in following signals, and had difficulty holding open order instead of grouping together, especially the cavalry when charging. Wayne reminded officers, with asperity, to forget their standard British texts on infantry and dragoon charge, which taught only how to ride down on an enemy across an open plain: this was the American woodland.

Courts-martial had kept handing down sentences. Worse, the ranks had never been filled. Because of all the delays, certain enlistments had ended, robbing Wayne of some of his best-trained men; others were sick and invalid. Congress had created a five-thousand-man army, but three thousand was the reality, and Knox had therefore authorized Wayne to call out the Kentucky militia as a volunteer adjunct. Knox also advised him that calling out the new state's infantry would yield only paid substitutes: Kentuckians didn't like serving, but they did like showing off on horseback, so Wayne should call out a mounted force. Wayne was loath to use men he hadn't trained himself. But he had no choice, and in the militia call-up, the oddball state-versus-federal relationships prevailed. Kentucky militia officers agreed that Wayne, as the federal authority, could commission and rank them, as long as he didn't lower them more than one rank below their Kentucky ranks, and they wanted to be engaged against the enemy, insofar as possible, separately from the regulars. It was by no means clear that they had the power to dictate terms: the latest militia law gave the president power to call up the militia at will, and both the Constitution and that law placed the militia under federal control.

But Wayne wanted the best men. Getting them out meant negotiating. The Kentucky recruiting began weakly, but by late September he knew he could expect fifteen hundred mounted Kentuckians to meet him at the head of the line, Fort Jefferson.

Wayne also faced persistent problems with contractors in charge of supply. Thanks to his army's presence at Hobson's Choice and Fort Washington, the contracting firm had become the biggest employer in the Northwest Territory: its agents were charged with buying and moving not only food and a host of other necessities but also the packhorses and wagon oxen themselves, as well as the horse masters and teamsters who worked and cared for the animals. And yet supplies were persistently delayed and, according to Wayne, disgracefully subpar.

Nevertheless, he had to march. Teamsters and horse masters would form an important part of the forward movement, but Wayne, unlike St. Clair, would advance with no noncombatants unnecessary to operations. Wives, girlfriends, and children were to stay with the remaining garrison in Fort Washington. Women who worked there would get food, that's all.

Finally, on October 7, 1793, one cannon fired, the fifers and drummers played a march, and at the head of what would soon be a long column, scouts left Hobson's Choice on the road already widely cut, thanks to Wayne's preparatory measures. The assembled units moved out in smart order and began marching along the course of a creek. Oxen hauled wagons filled with baggage and tents, livestock were driven in herds, and packhorses plodded under supply. On all sides of this lengthening column, rifle companies moved through the woods providing security. Scouts ranged widely in front of the line. The pioneer detail, armed with axes and implements of destruction and repair, cut trail to make passage easier. The weather was ideal: crisp and clear, with low humidity.

And yet because this was the army's first real march, it took two days to reach Fort Hamilton, and the men were exhausted by the quick trek on rough trail under heavy accoutrements. When they camped, Wayne put into operation the techniques he'd been planning and practicing for so long. His entire army spent that night under a temporary, disposable breastwork, with sentries posted in redoubts quickly built at all corners. There was no easy opportunity for attacking the men, no chance for a Little Turtle–style raid on horses and supply. This was Wayne's plan for the entire advance.

Two days later, the men were breaking down under the strain of the hike. Wheels bent on rough road. Sick men unfit for active combat were on the march to garrison the forward forts; they straggled. The column stretched for five miles. Wayne received word that well to the rear, men of a supply convoy from Fort Washington to Fort St. Clair had broken into the stores and gotten drunk, and had the enemy shown up, they would have been overwhelmed in minutes, their whole supply taken.

Then, on October 13, the sound of shooting abruptly filled the forest. Just as the army was drawing, at last, within a few miles of Fort Jefferson, the men heard gunfire ahead of the front of the line.

This might be it. In the ranks, orders were given, signal music was played, musket loading began. The men began forming, and the rear guard, hearing the distant shots, moved quickly forward to help with the engagement.

It turned out to be troops at Fort Jefferson, in a practice battle. The next day, the line of march passed that fort, and many of the marchers looked away from the men in the post, refusing to acknowledge them. The army had been badly scared.

They camped that night where the cut road ran out, six miles ahead of Fort Jefferson. The legion had arrived ahead of the head of the line. No U.S. construction existed forward of this position.

Yet they were anything but deep in the woods. This camp lay on the edge of a beautiful prairie, spreading to long-range views. Its high grasses still green, the prairie displayed goldenrod, yarrow, and other fall wildflowers as far as the eye could see; birds swooped and cicadas buzzed. To men unused to the Indians' practices for shaping the woodland, this seemed a natural paradise, evidence of God's bounty, an augury of success.

And here, to the general's dismay, the advance got stuck. While on October 14, newly camped beside the prairie, Wayne expressed satisfaction with the quality of the march to date—the difficult movement had been accomplished through the attentive duty of the officers, he noted in a general order, with only one officer having to be escorted back to Fort Washington for drunkenness—his worst fear soon materialized as fact. The president had required Wayne to stop supplying Fort Jefferson beyond the immediate needs of the garrison, and Wayne found the fort so poorly supplied that it could barely sustain the men already stationed there, let alone support his march. Convoys would have to bring heavy supplies all the way up from Fort Washington while the army waited here beside the prairie.

Nor had Wayne solved the supply problem caused by Little Turtle; indeed, by marching, he'd aggravated it. Back down the line, a convoy was ambushed on October 17 between Forts St. Clair and Hamilton. At the first shots, all but about twenty of the guard had panicked and run—and these were Wayne's trained regulars—leaving the few others to follow orders and be killed or captured. The raiding party quickly unhitched seventy horses and drove them off.

So two weeks after arriving at the prairie, still awaiting supply, Wayne held a meeting with his top officers and the Kentucky volunteers' commander. He read aloud his orders from Knox, as well as lists of troops, supplies, and estimated enemy strength. Then he posed the key question: Would a forward movement under present conditions enhance the safety and protection of the frontier, the reputation of the army, and the honor and dignity of the nation?

The consensus was no. The officers believed the only realistic place to make a stand, for now, was right where they were. They were more than seventy miles ahead of headquarters at Fort Washington. Supplying the troops would require convoys to travel great distances, without enough protection from an intrepid, focused enemy with good intelligence and command of the ground. It might take months to get the forward forts heavily enough supplied to support further invasion. This prairie campground, just forward of Fort Jefferson, was only about halfway to Wayne's objective, the Glaize, and no road had yet been cut in that direction. The country before them was controlled by the Indian confederation, patrolling ceaselessly in full war mode. The Kentucky volunteers had built their own camp on the prairie, within sight of the legion's camp, and at night both camps were forever erupting with gunfire as guards overreacted to shadows and sounds. There had already been one big, wet snowfall. Clothing supply, too, would have to be brought up: uniforms were already failing. Guards trying to keep warm in high winds had started a wildfire on the prairie. Smallpox and flu were loose; treatment demanded quarantine, inoculation, nursing.

So Wayne's officers advised the general to winter here. Even the Kentucky volunteers, when asked by Wayne whether they could at least carry out desultory operations at the Glaize, expressed skepticism. The frost had killed the grass. Forage was low. The horses were ailing.

Wayne listened. He confronted his own drive to push on. He mastered his rage at having been held back until it was too late.

The entire secret of his strategy was maniacal carefulness. It was the last thing he wanted to report to Knox, but he did: he would turn this prairie camp into a fort, far more secure than the camp at Legion Ville ever was, and make his winter headquarters only six miles ahead of minuscule, vulnerable Fort Jefferson. The Kentucky volunteers could go home: all they could do here was use up precious supplies; they might try a raid on the way home. The regular dragoons would also go to Kentucky for winter quarters: the horses could more reliably eat there.

Wayne ordered construction to begin. He would name the new fort Greene Ville, after his old mentor and friend. Then he got the flu.

So when Wayne, barely recovered from that illness, saw Fort Recovery go up in late December, at the end of a road cut more than twenty miles forward of the prairie and Greene Ville, and saw the skulls of the fallen

Americans interred within it, he had reason for satisfaction at the end of a difficult year.

He sent a detail to search for St. Clair's cannon, taken by the Indians after the defeat. A soldier who had been held captive at McKee's operation had told Wayne that the victors hadn't been able to remove the cannon, so they'd buried them here at the victory site. The men found a three-pounder and a six-pounder, and Wayne used them to replace two of the howitzers in Fort Recovery, which could now be spared to return to Greene Ville or Fort Jefferson. In a ceremony to inaugurate the new fort, both of the recovered guns were fired, and although some loose powder severely burned the major in charge and his servant, Wayne remained upbeat. He placed Captain Alexander Gibson in command of Recovery, staffing it with a rifle company, an infantry company, and twenty-six artillerymen, and gave Gibson orders that were all Mad Anthony: make constant and proper patrols; reconnoiter up to the Glaize for intelligence regarding not only enemy numbers but also topography, distances, directions of river flow; defend the fort with every expense of blood. Wayne went back down to Greene Ville with strong confidence in his new forward position.

Greene Ville, headquarters now, was bigger and stronger than Recovery. Having gone up on the prairie in November to house the entire army, the post had eight blockhouses, and Wayne was pleased with its defense: elevated loopholes in the stockade, too high for the enemy to reach, enabled firing muskets and rifles; two-foot earth banquettes below the loopholes allowed the shortest man to fire on the attacking enemy's center. Still, Fort Recovery would always be closer to Wayne's heart. He expected great things from his forward position, built on the site of his rival's defeat, and he kept in constant touch with Captain Gibson.

At Greene Ville on New Year's Day 1794, the army celebrated with a grand review of troops, many of the men wearing new uniforms. Then Wayne and some of the officers rode down to Fort Jefferson and ate a huge dinner, hosted by the Wilkinsons: meats and fowls, game, every kind of dessert, with wines and fortified wines. Greene Ville stood where only prairie had recently been. Fort Recovery commanded a bend in the Wabash, with forest cleared for a thousand feet in every direction.

Anthony Wayne was putting the United States, in prototype, into the Ohio Country.

The New Year's dinner in the forest fort was a jolly occasion. And yet between Wayne and his second-in-command, James Wilkinson, divisions had formed. Wayne didn't know about them yet.

Other things Wayne didn't know: two James Wilkinsons existed, and both Wilkinsons hated Anthony Wayne.

Wayne knew only one of the James Wilkinsons, the official one, and he'd known him since the War of Independence. Their relationship went all the way back to the days immediately following Wayne's first battle command, in 1776, in the failed attack on Trois-Rivières. As American forces withdrew southward in that retreat, young Wilkinson appeared on a dangerous overland mission to ask for help in covering General Benedict Arnold's retreat from Montreal and found in Wayne the only commander with the position—maybe the willingness—to respond to Arnold's request. Wilkinson and Wayne, sharing enthusiasm for action, got along right away. Their mission became pointless when Arnold sent news that his retreat had been effected anyway, but by then Wayne and Wilkinson had developed mutual admiration.

The James Wilkinson Wayne knew had a big, sharply etched military personality. He was decisive, possessed of good judgment. Like Wayne, he was a firm believer in the benefits of discipline, but unlike Wayne he was approachable, not mad for discipline, and never irascible. His paperwork was clear and intelligent. Militiamen, regular troops, and fellow officers liked him. For all of his background as a scion of Maryland's planter elite—its younger generation was infamous for indolence and vapidity—Wilkinson had become an early settler in the Kentucky Territory of Virginia, a hands-on frontiersman with the common touch. And he was a medical doctor.

This James Wilkinson represented all that seemed respectably innovative about the emergent leadership of the United States. Wayne wasn't alone in liking him. Everybody did. Unlike Wayne, Wilkinson went out of his way to be liked.

That's one of the things that made him such a good spy. And spying was only one of the things the other James Wilkinson, the man Wayne had never met, did with himself. The other Wilkinson had come into existence only five or six years before the official Wilkinson's appointment as Wayne's second-in-command in the new national regular army. And the other Wilkinson had other allegiances.

In the late 1780s, many Kentucky settlers had become fiercely attached to independence from Virginia, James Wilkinson among them. They felt unprotected by distant Williamsburg against Indian attack and unfairly constrained from launching their own attacks on Indians. Kentucky looked west, not east, for business. That mainly meant tobacco business, with enormous potential profits, but Kentuckians were barred from those profits. The Mississippi River flowed down to the great international trading hub New Orleans; that's where the real tobacco money could be made. But Spain controlled the Mississippi, and Spain was rich, mighty, and stubborn. Nobody in Virginia's government seemed to be doing anything about negotiating with Spain for access to that trade route.

Opinion among the Kentucky secessionists differed as to what the region should become, once it shook off the Virginia yoke. Some wanted the region to become a self-contained, unaffiliated republic, like Vermont. Others wanted annexation by the United States, which was making noises, but only noises, about negotiating with Spain for river access: ultimately such a plan would mean statehood for Kentucky. Many investors of the George Washington type wanted Mississippi trade to remain blocked, sending western products eastward on their own roads and canals to seaboard entrepôts, warehouses, and ships.

James Wilkinson had his own opinion. Just as Anthony Wayne had hoped to grow rich on rice in coastal Georgia, Wilkinson had moved to the Kentucky interior to gain wealth by flipping land well suited to forcing enslaved Africans to grow tobacco in almost unbelievably rich soil. Backed by investors in Philadelphia, he'd accumulated tens of thousands of acres for his backers and himself; his commissions sometimes amounted to half the land he purchased. Steadily supplied with goods by a Philadelphia businessman, Wilkinson also opened a store in the jumping-off village of Lexington on the Ohio, offering tobacco growers and land seekers a chance to stock up before heading up to the forest or out to the bluegrass. He sold precious things like salt and fabric and set up a trade with nearby Shawnee for fur. And he built a tobacco warehouse. There he stacked bale upon bale in appropriate conditions and issued paper chits backed by product; the chits circulated as currency.

Merchant, real-estate investor and agent, tobacco factor, even banker, James Wilkinson deployed all the charm and appeal he'd demonstrated during the war to build a political network of like-minded business friends. He and his cronies advertised, to eastern audiences, the beauty and easy money to be had in Kentucky.

Their advertising was false. Despite the bestselling exploits of the arch-Kentuckian Daniel Boone and the Kentucky businessmen's descriptions of an Eden of profitability south of the Ohio, when poorer people arrived in Kentucky, they were painfully disappointed. Many were making good on promises of bounty land offered as payment by Virginia for war service, but they found the local land office so out of touch with the home government, so dominated by well-financed interests already established, and so thoroughly corrupt that they had no way of taking possession without crippling deal making and loss of promised property. The richest land was already taken. Meanwhile, Indians came across the Ohio at will, attacking and killing confused, unready new settlers.

Many ordinary people in Kentucky blamed the home government in Virginia, far more than they blamed the local elites, for all of these problems. And few in any social class had any regard for what was still the Confederation Congress. Populism and secessionism among ordinary Kentuckians played into the ambitions of the better-off, politically connected, eastern-backed Kentuckians, like Wilkinson, who formed the local governing class. For despite his high status in Kentucky, Wilkinson wasn't doing so well either.

Like so many others caught up in the real-estate bubble, Wilkinson had taken to borrowing on precarious margins to finance a search for fabulous wealth. He took loans from partners to buy land, then used that land as collateral for loans for buying more land. While developers on the ground in Kentucky and investors back in Philadelphia might look rich in estimated value on paper, posting actual profits by selling land was always slower than desired, and selling slowed with each new disappointment in sales, each Indian attack, each obstacle for new settlers. The developers' and their creditors' investments were secured more by hope than by value.

Wilkinson believed the solution for Kentucky was to get its tobacco, grain, and whiskey onto the Mississippi and down to New Orleans. That was the only hope, potentially a marvelous one. But Spain still banned from the river any ship not flying its flag, and Spain controlled the Gulf Coast. The empire had become an ally of the American Congress during the war—that's how Spain had taken the Gulf Coast from the British— but the Spanish minister in Philadelphia was by no means eager to give up control of the Mississippi. Spain was committed to protecting silver, the biggest lode in the world, in the region it called Mexico. Vast Spanish landholdings in North America—one known as Texas, and the other that region from the Mississippi to the Rockies still known by the old French name Louisiana—served Spain not as space for settlement but as an impenetrable barrier between its silver and any other empire's greed.

That's the context in which the unofficial James Wilkinson, the man nobody knew or at least acknowledged knowing, began making his first moves. Wilkinson wrote to Francisco Cruzat, the Spanish commander at Fort St. Louis on the west side of the Mississippi. In his letter, Wilkinson didn't ask for a pass to New Orleans; he'd already been denied one, both by the governor of Virginia and by the Spanish minister to the Congress. Instead, he made Cruzat a free gift: intelligence of impending attacks on Spanish forts. He knew about the planned attacks because when rallying support for Kentucky independence, Wilkinson himself had proposed that Kentucky attack Spain's Mississippi forts in an effort to open the river by force. Now, having learned that certain Georgia men were planning assaults on forts as far south as Natchez, he told Cruzat the name of their leader, called them "desperate adventurers," and suggested Cruzat mention the danger of attack to Don Esteban Miro, the governor of all of Louisiana.

Meanwhile, Wilkinson was advertising in Kentucky for consignments. Regardless of the Spanish ban and his lack of a passport, he proposed to carry tobacco, ham, and butter down the Ohio and onto the Mississippi, bound for New Orleans. He hyped the mission as a blow against necrotic mercantilism on behalf of free trade and American liberty, hired a crew of twenty, and at a dock below the Ohio's falls at Louisville had the crew load up a fifty-foot flatboat. In April 1787, he defied the laws of at least three governments by ordering the crew to shove off. As he floated away, an enraptured crowd cheered.

Soon Wilkinson came ashore on the western bank of the Mississippi at St. Louis. The fort commanded both banks of the river and all transportation north and south: Cruzat was in a legal and physical position to fire on Wilkinson's boat, seize its cargo, and prosecute its crew, but he didn't. Spanish America was vast by now, run in two gigantic chunks out of Havana and Mexico City, and Cruzat wasn't an especially high official. When the dashing Kentuckian, so aristocratic, adventurous, and enthusiastic, made himself known to Cruzat as the man who had tipped him off to the plot against Natchez, he also presented the commander with two horses, mighty Virginia thoroughbreds brought on the flatboat from Kentucky.

Cruzat gave Wilkinson a passport to Natchez and a letter of introduction. When Wilkinson got to Natchez, Cruzat's superior wrote an effusive reference to Don Esteban Miro in New Orleans. Wilkinson was getting pretty high up—Miro reported directly to Havana—and at the end of June his flatboat was tied to a dock in New Orleans, his product in warehouses there, and his emerging other self deep in discussions with Miro and some lesser officials. Ostensibly, they were talking terms of sale for his cargo.

This was only a sample, Wilkinson told them. He wanted to bring long flotillas of flatboats loaded with products of far greater value, including that most valuable of commodities, African human beings. Miro and Wilkinson got thick fast.

But the Spaniards in New Orleans had a plan of their own. They thought James Wilkinson might be just the man to bring it about. Spain had been getting worried about Americans, newly independent and looking westward. The American land bubble kept expanding, and Louisiana—it remained, from the Mississippi to the Rockies, virtually empty of settled Europeans—attracted both American investors and the American squatters those investors hated, and neither group had ever shown respect for legal boundaries. A nervous Spanish official could imagine even the arid plains of Texas appealing, one day, to these land-hungry, unruly Americans. Security for the Mexican silver mines was getting shaky.

Miro and his finance minister had come up with a solution: block American border crossing by settling Louisiana with people loyal to Spain. Such settlers would take up a lot of room on the west bank and

resist any adventuring not under Spanish aegis. Western Americans
disenchanted with eastern establishments seemed ideal candidates
for this settlement project: the appeal for them would be free land in
Louisiana and free trade on the Mississippi. Spain had the money and
the land to make that happen; what it needed was the people. Wilkinson, seeking political and economic independence from his home governments, and Miro, seeking new adherents to the Spanish flag, made
a deal.

When Wilkinson sailed out of New Orleans for Charleston, they'd given
him a number and taken away his name. Thirteen: the number began
as the name of a complex code that Wilkinson and Miro would use for
all future communication, but Wilkinson started wearing it like a veil. He
insisted that his Spanish counterparts address him only by that number. The new Wilkinson had a knack for espionage: the code itself would
never be fully broken. Thirteen nevertheless came to think in it.

The deal was this: James Wilkinson, granted an exception to the
Mississippi ban, was allowed to bring Kentucky products and commodities down the Mississippi to New Orleans. Because nobody else, for now,
enjoyed this grant, Wilkinson gained an invaluable monopoly. Miro, in
turn, would get a nice taste of each shipment's profit.

But their long-range plan was far bigger. Under Wilkinson's direction,
Kentucky as a whole was to leave not only Virginia but also the United
States. It would become a Spanish possession east of the Mississippi
River, with river trade to New Orleans and new settlers moving across
the river to live there under Spanish aegis. To bring this plan about,
Wilkinson began advising Miro regarding strategy against the United
States. Britain, he informed Miro, also had designs on an independent
Kentucky. The Spanish minister in Philadelphia should therefore make
a definitive statement: Spain would never, under any circumstance, agree
to give the Congress access to the big river. Because Britain couldn't
offer river access, and the United States would appear blocked from
the river in perpetuity, Kentuckians would see joining Spain as their
only realistic hope of prosperity. Spain should also build and staff a
strong fort below the Ohio's mouth at the Mississippi, Wilkinson advised

Miro, and invite Kentucky investors and settlers to cross the river below
that fort and under its protection, for free land and free trade.

All of this was to be managed by James Wilkinson. He was on track
to becoming a big man in a rearranged American West and on the international scene. He executed a secret document transferring his allegiance from the United States to the king of Spain and arrived home a
folk hero. His trip had brought about a steep rise in the price of Kentucky goods.

Anthony Wayne had no way of knowing that his second-in-command
had been living a double life since 1788 and that despite the officer's
oath of allegiance to the United States was serving as a sworn agent of
a foreign power. Wayne liked the Wilkinson he knew.

Wilkinson's feelings about Wayne, however, had changed since the
good old days of the Revolution. Nothing about the secret activities of
Thirteen made the official James Wilkinson any less put out about having
been passed over by President Washington for commander in chief of
the new army. The administration had considered Wilkinson, of course.
Why wouldn't he seem a nearly ideal candidate for command? By then,
he'd performed admirably not only in the Revolution but also in both
the Harmar and the St. Clair expeditions and had now taken the difficult command of Fort Washington. He'd built Fort St. Clair and kept a
skeletal army intact in the Northwest Territory after the awful defeat
on the upper Wabash.

Still, the cabinet had passed over Wilkinson with surprising speed
and little comment. In the meeting to discuss candidates for command,
the president and his secretaries behaved as if they didn't know quite
enough about Wilkinson to form a judgment. That was peculiar, because
they suspected a lot about him: there were credible rumors of his relationship with Spain. But there was no proof, and the army's very existence had come to depend on Wilkinson. Indeed, none of Wilkinson's
secret activities—they would one day go totally over the top—would be
fully proven for well over a century. In the cabinet meeting, the idea
that Wilkinson was a double agent didn't get a mention. Instead, when his
name came up, everybody just got vague. They only hoped any wounded

feelings over the Wayne appointment might be salved by offering Wilkinson the rank of brigadier general.

They were wrong. When Anthony Wayne was wounded by a slight, he made everybody aware of how he felt about it. Wilkinson, schooled in secrecy now, saw no percentage in seeming to be other than the amiable and able officer people wanted to see. When Wilkinson and Wayne first established communications between Fort Fayette and the key post down the Ohio, Fort Washington, where Wilkinson was in charge, the subordinate showed nothing but the old charm, polish, respect, and efficiency in making the clearest sort of reports to his old comrade, now his superior. While Wilkinson did also continue to report directly to Knox, and he collaborated with Rufus Putnam in furthering the administration's policy regarding negotiating for peace, he put nothing on the record that would give Wayne pause.

The fact was that Wilkinson was in the American army only because Thirteen's activities hadn't been enough to save him from financial disaster. Even as he'd begun sending load after load of Kentucky cargo down to New Orleans, with gross sales for producers and shippers routinely amounting to tens of thousands of dollars in Mexican silver, secessionism in Kentucky faltered. The region now enjoyed, thanks to Wilkinson, the Mississippi trade that investors and settlers had always wanted, and few Kentuckians wanted their region to become a Spanish subsidiary. Meanwhile, the new American nation had formed: Virginia had ceded Kentucky to the federal government; Congress and the president might be getting serious about admitting Kentucky and Vermont as states, negotiating Mississippi access for the United States as a whole, and defeating the western Indian confederation that had been crossing the Ohio to raid Kentucky. Certain upscale Kentuckians were getting lucrative appointments as federal officials. As Wilkinson took business losses—there were the usual inefficiencies and a shipwreck, and then one of his key partners killed himself—and finally went broke, Kentucky was on its way to statehood, and while in coded messages Wilkinson tried to cover up the Kentuckians' reluctance about entering Spain, Miro came under pressure too. His bosses in Havana and Spain denied any further funds for supporting Thirteen.

The entire plan had failed, yet James Wilkinson's search for gain in the West, status in the U.S. Army, and a pivotal role in international intrigue had only just begun. That's why he'd taken a commission as a lieutenant colonel in Harmar's flying strike on Kekionga and made himself indispensable to U.S. efforts to possess the Northwest Territory.

Recently, he'd been bringing personal charm and Thirteen-like skills to a new campaign: the destruction of Anthony Wayne. Wilkinson had begun writing from Fort Washington to the anti-army faction in Congress with lurid tales of Wayne's supposed erratic behavior, incompetent command, and drunken irascibility. Worst of all for Wayne, Wilkinson used his own popularity with junior officers to form a faction in the army that mocked the commander behind his back and complained bitterly about what they saw as his draconian measures of cultivating discipline. Wayne could sense this movement against him, and he knew how destructive it could be to the army's morale and effectiveness, but Wilkinson remained irreproachably friendly and respectful to Wayne in person. Though perpetually outraged by the malcontents' mutters and complaints and resistance to orders, Wayne couldn't identify the instigator.

Division was meanwhile deepening between Blue Jacket and Little Turtle, and between the Blue Jacket and the Little Turtle ways of thinking. Soon the two greatest collaborators in the victory over St. Clair would not be speaking.

It would become easy, in later years, to take up the position of one man and claim for him the importance that opponents were forever claiming for the other man. This fight would allow the Little Turtle–Blue Jacket competition to live on long after the men themselves and the parties that surrounded them had died. Conflicting stories that later writers told regarding what happened in 1794 to make the personal enmity so bitter, and the two parties' mutual disregard so rank, had something to do with strategy, something to do with personality, something to do with the inclinations of writers, and something to do with Blue Jacket's controversial decision, made in collaboration with others, to attack Wayne's new forward post, Fort Recovery.

All fall and winter, the confederation had watched as Wayne advanced to the prairie and built Greene Ville there. Then, in late December, they saw Fort Recovery going up. They watched soldiers stationed at Recovery continue to search the woods for the missing cannon and find two more.

To the confederation's scouts, security for both the fort itself and the crews outside it seemed preternaturally tight. Soldiers at Recovery could meanwhile be observed making improvements: the blockhouses now stood a truly commanding two stories, allowing troops to fire from above on attacking parties. Wayne's main army might be stopped for the winter just north of Fort Jefferson, but there was no question, for the confederation, about what Fort Recovery meant and what Wayne had in mind for spring and summer.

Wayne, for his part, had quickly recognized the potential of Little Turtle's supply-raid strategy for destroying his campaign. The general's response to that possibility gave Little Turtle a sense of what Mad Anthony was all about. The army was deploying super convoys now: up to five hundred men protected each supply train, as if on an aggressive march by an entire sub-legion, with dedicated front and rear guards, flankers, and wide-ranging patrols. They'd built permanently fortified camps between the forts, where packhorses could be corralled within breastworks and the guard could occupy bastions. Officers were ordered to bayonet or half pike to death any man who turned away from attack without an order to retreat.

These were unconventional measures for supply. The man didn't sleep: that's how Little Turtle came to think, with semi-admiring frustration, of Anthony Wayne.

Given an enemy who didn't sleep, and no British artillery, Little Turtle was growing skeptical of victory. Defeat was a possibility he found hard, but not impossible, to face.

Blue Jacket, however, had reason to believe that the British would now support Indian war efforts in a newly decisive way. He was again traveling and sending runners to nations distant from the Glaize, asking them to come to the confederation headquarters there. This time the gathering would be for decisive maneuvers to destroy the American advance for good.

The best news for the Blue Jacket approach came from an unexpected quarter. Lord Dorchester had returned from England to Quebec in September 1793. John Simcoe, Alexander McKee, and others eager for success against the United States hadn't been looking forward to the return of a man whose support for Indian allies had always taken uninspiring, ultimately untrustworthy form. But something new was happening. It took everybody aback.

Dorchester returned to North America in an uncharacteristic mood of anti-American aggression. He'd somehow changed from a complacent elder statesman offering platitudes into a hotheaded youngster spoiling for a fight, alternately belligerent for action and terrified of imminent American attack. Everywhere he looked, he saw grounds for conflict with the United States, and he wasn't alone. Vermont had been lost, and American militias in that new state, as well as in New York and Pennsylvania, now posed a threat to the Canadian border. The Pennsylvania militia had been threatening to occupy Presque Isle on Lake Erie; that was against federal policy, but the British war with France was magnifying any such threat. Far away on the high seas, England was seeking to restrict American shipping of French goods and keep U.S. ships out of the West Indies. Meanwhile, in the U.S. Congress, anti-British elements behind Madison and Monroe, formerly critical of the deleterious effect of war on republican liberty, were beginning to get war fever over British aggression.

In February, Lord Dorchester met in Quebec with some Six Nations delegates. The delegates were curious about Whitehall's ideas regarding the future of all Indians in English-speaking North America, and they got a surprise. In evident contradiction of stated British policy, Dorchester made the unsolicited observation that he wouldn't be surprised if England found itself at war with the United States in the current year.

"I believe our patience is almost exhausted," Dorchester told the delegation.

That was a bombshell, and for the Blue Jacket party, it would come as thrilling news. Even Joseph Brant was reenergized: he envisioned the western Indians getting into a position, with British aid, to stop Wayne's forward march, and he revived his idea of a total pan-Indian unity, imagining the Six Nations again leading it. Alexander McKee, for his part, envisioned a great boost to the confederation's size and unity:

Dorchester's new attitude would promote Shawnee militants within the confederation and justify McKee's own advice to the confederation, as both a Shawnee and a British official, that it remain on a war footing. John Simcoe received perhaps the most gratifying jolt. British policy had long been to defend the forts. That had always meant readiness for action if attacked, and mild support of the Indians, but eschewal of any aggression farther into U.S. territory. Now Dorchester's definition of defense abruptly changed.

He ordered Simcoe to go west and get a new fort built. In anticipation of Wayne's march, this new fort was to command the Miami of the Lake below the rapids, about seventy miles forward of Detroit. That was well into U.S. territory ceded in Paris.

Simcoe was authorized to select the exact spot. His dreams were coming true. He sent Dorchester an ambitious plan of military action: Simcoe would lead three regiments from Fort Niagara all the way to Pittsburgh, then go down the Ohio and take Fort Washington and Cincinnati, thus shutting off supply for Wayne's advance and holding Wayne's rear. It was already March, however, and even Simcoe saw the risk in what he was proposing: should Wayne start moving out of Greene Ville, the new fort on the Miami of the Lake might not get built in time to hold him back. The new fort would have to come first.

Simcoe got onto Lake Erie, and the wind cooperated. He arrived at McKee's operation up the Miami of the Lake by April 10. In consultation with McKee, whose dreams were coming true too, Simcoe sited the new fort on high ground on the west bank of the river, a place where the British had demolished a fort when evacuating in 1783. This was just the plan McKee had been pushing on his superiors since at least as early as 1791: the site could be readily supplied by Detroit to its north while controlling passage out of the Miami into Lake Erie and the Detroit River. On April 18, 120 infantry and cavalry and an artillery detachment were installed in the construction site that Simcoe named Fort Miamis. The eight cannon Simcoe chose for Fort Miamis were bigger than anything he thought Wayne would be able to travel with.

Simcoe was looking forward to the new contest. Wayne was the one American general he believed possessed some competence. The British strategic assumption, underlying the building of Fort Miamis, was that Wayne's real mission was to conquer not Kekionga and the Glaize but Fort

Detroit itself, seizing that disputed post and throwing out the British garrison. Simcoe's hope was that Wayne would try tracking around the new Fort Miamis on his way to Detroit, exposing his communications for miles.

What the British didn't know and couldn't imagine: as much as Wayne would have relished evicting the British from Detroit, he had express orders not to march on Fort Detroit when taking the Indian heartland. The British thought it was about them. It was really about the western Indians. John Simcoe was building a provocative fort on what, according to the Peace of Paris, was American soil, in order to protect a strategic objective that the Americans didn't have.

Simcoe sailed back for Newark with Fort Miamis in good progress. Before leaving, he'd made McKee's dreams come further true. British forces were stationed along the Miami of the Lake from the rapids to the lake: a detachment of soldiers, though only under a corporal, at Roche de Bout below the top of the rapids; a stockade on Turtle Island, in the Lake Erie bay of the Miami. The British army was now openly occupying key river points on American soil south of the disputed forts.

Before he left, Simcoe made one other move. He had McKee assemble the Indian confederation leaders at McKee's operation on the rapids, nearly in view of the British fort rising just downstream. When McKee read them Dorchester's comments about an ensuing Anglo-American war, British support for the Indian cause seemed to come to life before the confederation leaders' eyes.

Fort Miamis, they were given to understand, was being built for their protection from Anthony Wayne. There was still no mention of the one thing Little Turtle deemed necessary to Indian victory: artillery.

To Blue Jacket, this seemed the perfect time for mounting a decisive attack on Wayne's army. Delegations and war parties were beginning to arrive at the rapids and the Glaize, ready for all-out final war on the American advance. This was the most militarily assertive gathering of nations ever seen in the West, the largest Indian war party ever formed against Americans, flush with evidence of revived British support not only in words but also in the visible fact of the well-garrisoned, well-cannoned Fort Miamis rising on the west bank, along with the British troops at Roche de Bout and on Turtle Island.

Blue Jacket's effort now was to pressure all whites on the scene—British officials and agents, and even traders—to prove their commitment by joining the military effort, actively, as fighters. Confederation leaders demanded that McKee shut down the traders' liquor selling—it was something he and Simcoe were always trying to do anyway—and they made an especially stark move on McKee's associate Matthew Elliott, who had hosted the American commissioners. They presented Elliott and a group of traders with the black beads. That was a demand for participation as fighters. The only move was to accept or reject the beads, and Elliott and his crew accepted them. So did Alexander McKee's son, Thomas. They would dress as Indians and join the force.

Mainly under the leadership of Blue Jacket, by May a big, concerted move against Wayne's positions was in plan. The nations most fully involved were branches of the Shawnee, Ottawa, Potawatomie, and Ojibwa. Delaware led by Buckongahelas were supposed to provide reinforcements, but they'd been plied with rum by the Wyandot wife of a French interpreter and were running behind. Little Turtle, increasingly skeptical that a single climactic battle, especially without artillery, could win this war, would not join this operation that Blue Jacket believed would be decisive. Yet a small group of Miami did join.

Beginning in mid-May, about twelve hundred fighters, a huge force, moved out of the Glaize in waves, with predetermined rendezvous points and a system of fast-running messaging, heading generally southwest toward Wayne's army. And yet the exact objective had not yet been determined. Reconnoitering, the leaders believed, would reveal the appropriate action. The force's immediate plan was to get into the vicinity of Wayne's two most forward positions, Fort Recovery at the head of the line and the even stronger headquarters Greene Ville, not far behind.

On June 25, the whole force had gathered in a camp about sixty miles south of the Glaize, only twenty miles or so northeast of Fort Recovery.

They began riding and walking southwestward through the big trees in wide-open formation: twelve columns long and loose, about fifty yards between each column. Ideally, each man carried a rifle or a musket, ammunition, a war hatchet, bow and arrows, and little else. So large was this advance, however, that firearms had become scarce. More than a hundred men went without guns. The movement of this entire gigantic operation was nearly silent.

Supply problems quickly emerged. Ranging widely to the front and sides of the advance, sometimes for miles, parties of scouts also served as hunters; food supply was thus created on the move. That system obviated long communications but had drawbacks of its own. To feed so many men, maybe two hundred deer and two hundred turkeys had to be killed and brought into camp every day. That used up ammunition.

On June 28, the front of this force arrived at the stretch of Wayne's wood road between Greene Ville and Fort Recovery. Here the advance paused.

The men made camp with close attention to security. A guard was posted facing down the road at Greene Ville. The horses were hobbled, and the bells normally used to alert the men to their horses' nighttime movements were removed.

That night the leaders held a planning meeting. They'd lacked a specific objective; now they tried to come up with one. Blue Jacket proposed moving south, circling past Greene Ville, and taking control of the road below it. That would cut off the American headquarters' communications and disable its supply. If Wayne turned out his army, weakened by poor supply, in hopes of removing the confederation's blockade, he would find twelve hundred fighters ready to make the final battle site.

Others proposed moving instead up to Fort Recovery. Intelligence reported movement there, possibly in anticipation of the arrival of a supply convoy.

Blue Jacket objected: he thought attacking a single convoy at the front of the line was pointless: it would leave the main army at Greene Ville untouched. His plan, by contrast, would cut off both Greene Ville and Fort Recovery, potentially disabling the army.

A dispute broke out. Those wanting to hit a possible convoy at Recovery—mainly Ojibwa, Potawatomie, and Ottawa—argued that the forward fort was weaker, easier to attack. Blue Jacket and those favoring his plan—mainly Shawnee, Miami, and Wyandot—were outnumbered, or at least out-argued. Maintaining unity in the western confederation had been Blue Jacket's overriding concern since the 1760s. The decision was to leave Greene Ville alone and move on Fort Recovery.

Later the next day, the force camped a few miles below Recovery. Intelligence reported that a train of about 350 animals and wagons, with a guard of ninety riflemen and fifty dragoons, had arrived there the night before and was now camped outside the fort.

There could be no immediate interruption of food delivery: flour had already been loaded in. But the animals, the most important element in supply chain, were the most valuable targets.

The plan was to attack the train as it left the fort in the morning and started back down the road to Greene Ville. The hope was for another devastating triumph, right here on the site of victory over St. Clair, in defiance of Wayne's fort building. Should troops deploy from the fort in defense of the departing train, Blue Jacket's fighters would get a crack at them too.

Twelve hundred men stripped down to their breechcloths, painted themselves black and red, and at dawn were moving toward the fort, weapons ready, again in silence. Some small parties took to spots in the woods around the fort, while most of the force lined the road, out of sight, some on horses, some on foot. Some were hidden behind the bank of a creek. They waited to ambush the departing convoy.

At about 7:00, every Mad Anthony rule was violated when the horse masters and ox drivers, without the least protection, began moving their herds across the cleared ground outside the fort and onto the wood road: the guard was still inside finishing breakfast. Thus fully exposed, the herds were coming quickly down the road toward the ambush, and when they were about two hundred yards into the woods, the attack force made its move. One party charged the train, shooting and yelling. The main force was still waiting out of sight. As herds stampeded, the drivers turned and started trying to push their way through the rush of panicked, noisy animals running back toward the fort. The attacking party pursued them, shooting.

The major in charge of the guard had run out of the fort and mounted in haste, shouting orders; flanked by riflemen, he and his dragoons rode through the chaos and onto the road. Now the main force down by the creek bed rose as one and fired at close range, killing the major and felling other dragoons and horses while the rest tried to run or gallop back to the fort.

The American riflemen had meanwhile taken positions on a rise in the woods above the road. But the Indians' smaller attack parties flanked them, and the main attack force, having dispatched the dragoons, turned to charge the outnumbered riflemen. The rifle captain, Asa Hartshorn, tried for an orderly retreat to the fort, and his men did better under fire than the Indians were used to seeing, but the Indians had cut off the way back. Captain Hartshorn was hit and fell. His soldiers tried to drag him toward the fort, but that was no way out. He ordered the men to leave him and scatter.

In this melee, Alexander McKee's son, Thomas, accompanied by an enslaved African servant and one of the Indian fighters, rode up to the injured Hartshorn and demanded surrender, offering good treatment in return. The captain swung his half pike upward and knocked McKee from the saddle, rose on his one good leg, and started swinging the pike at the black man and the Indian.

The Indian shot an arrow into the man's chest. The black man ran forward and killed Hartshorn with the war hatchet.

Meanwhile, many of the drovers, dragoons, and riflemen who had made it out of the woods and back onto the cleared ground outside the fort were shot down and hatcheted to death in full view of the fort's garrison. A detail had come out in support of the convoy and its escort, and fierce gunfire spat from the fort's loopholes. Some of the supply convoy's dragoons tried to make a stand under cover of that fire, but the Indian force quickly sent them all in retreat to the fort.

The action was a confederation success, in the sense that hundreds of animals had been captured or killed, dozens of men killed or wounded, the enemy once again put to rout, the garrison's incapacity revealed. Then again, an entire Indian force had been deployed against a small forward position, leaving the main enemy force to the rear intact. The action's strategic legitimacy might have become a subject of debate, regardless of success.

But a bad decision now rendered the topic moot. As Blue Jacket and other veteran fighters watched in bafflement, the Ojibwa and Ottawa who had pushed for this action started running toward the fort. Dodging behind stumps on the cleared ground, they were trying for a full-scale assault to seize the fort itself. Musket fire and cannonballs quickly cut them down, and the attackers had to pull back to safer ground.

And yet they kept up the attack, firing steadily on the fort. There was nothing for Blue Jacket to do but lead his men forward in support of their allies.

It made no sense. They had no targets. The men in the fort were firing from behind musket-proof barricades through loopholes, some from the second story of the blockhouses. The shooters were invisible as they swept the cleared ground with lead, and the attackers were fully exposed on the ground. Fort Recovery was smart but not strong. With cannon, the assault could have put big holes in the wood, but for all of the renewed British support, including the presence here in the field of Matthew Elliott and of McKee's son, no British artillery had been forthcoming.

This undisciplined attack on a well-defended fort was just what Little Turtle had been warning against and why he hadn't joined the operation. Blue Jacket hadn't been hotheaded: he'd tried to focus on cutting off the whole army at Greene Ville, then on limiting the action at Recovery to disabling supply. Still, the operation had gotten away from him. Consequences for the future of the Indian confederation would be dire.

The futile shoot-out went on all day. At nightfall, the attackers gave up and withdrew to their campsite of the night before. Late that night, some snuck back to collect their dead, in hopes of keeping them from being scalped by the Americans, but they couldn't retrieve bodies lying close to the fort: even in the dark, sentry fire held them back. The next morning, they shot at the fort again for a while, but by early afternoon they withdrew for good.

Many had died, mostly among the lake Indians who had led the assault. Their bodies would be carried back to the Glaize, then taken home in mourning.

Blue Jacket himself had lost seventeen men. Only three had died in the highly effective ambush of the convoy, the rest in support of a foolhardy attack. That fact played painfully into the crisis that would now grip the confederation back at the Glaize.

Blue Jacket had pushed for a far more strategic operation. Nobody could say what might have happened if the whole force had cut Greene Ville off from rear supply. Still, he'd led the force out of the Glaize and toward Wayne's positions without any specific, agreed-upon objective: the plan to destroy the convoy had developed on the fly, more opportunistically than strategically. Decisions about operations were always made in conference, and Blue Jacket had no special power to order anyone to do anything. Unity had always been his grandest strategy. Breaking off with the obstinate Ottawa and Ojibwa on the eve of battle would have accomplished nothing.

Postmortems like that, under emotional pressure, worsened the mood as the force fell back in frustration to a position at the headwaters of the Wabash. The Shawnee and others criticized the lake Indians for attacking the fort. The lake Indians claimed that the Shawnee and others had not only failed to support them but actually fired on their rear. There wasn't much to say in response to that.

The lake Indians went home. That move reduced the attack force by about half. With the force now camped at the Wabash headwaters, Buckongahelas and his Delaware fighters finally showed up, and the group considered putting Blue Jacket's plan into effect after all, cutting off Greene Ville, but supply problems persisted and numbers were now too low. There was nothing realistic to do but go back to the Glaize in failure.

The failure wasn't only to take Fort Recovery or to engage Wayne in final battle. The failure was of confederation itself.

At the Glaize, Alexander McKee was unhappy to hear a report by his son on undisciplined behavior at Fort Recovery. Still, he had to believe that further British support would soon be forthcoming, and he urged the Glaize inhabitants to hang together and rely on the newly built Fort Miamis. From within that fort, the commander had sent to Simcoe asking for reinforcements, and Simcoe wrote back to say that he too now considered war with the United States inevitable. He had McKee tell the fighters at the Glaize that in August he would come in person to Fort Miamis, take command, and meet with them in a war council.

Little Turtle was still thinking. McKee and Simcoe had never given the confederation the big guns he was sure it needed. Now, amid mutual vituperation over the failure at Fort Recovery, the confederation itself might be collapsing.

So Little Turtle went around McKee. He traveled to Fort Detroit and got a meeting with Colonel England, the fort's commander.

The Miami leader made a simple and forthright request of Colonel England. He wanted two big cannon and twenty soldiers. If the British could supply him, he would lead another campaign against Fort Recovery: planned in advance, with artillery and British troops, such an attack would be capable of success.

But if the British wouldn't supply the battered confederation with cannon and men, Little Turtle told England, the Indian confederation simply could not prevail against the United States. It would have to give up the campaign to stop Wayne's progress.

Colonel England was impressed by Little Turtle's calm, forthright manner. The British army did fear that Wayne was about to march, and they thought his objective was Fort Detroit. England and many others wanted to keep the Indians fighting Wayne.

Yet despite Alexander McKee's deepest hopes, despite John Simcoe's imperial ambitions, even despite Lord Dorchester's recent, hard-to-figure blast of militancy and remarkable move forward on U.S. soil, the British army's Indian policy remained firmly against fighting an overt, direct war. If there was to be outright warfare between the United States and Great Britain within the year, as Dorchester had predicted, that war would have to be declared by the Crown. Until then, McKee's and Simcoe's busy machinations could only go so far.

So Colonel England promised Little Turtle nothing more than continued British support. He wouldn't commit artillery or troops. As the Miami leader left the fort, the commander thought this gentlemanly Indian, so much easier to deal with than the rowdy Blue Jacket, felt satisfied. Little Turtle thought it was all over.

11

FALLEN TIMBERS

Wayne felt more than ready to march the legion out of Greene Ville, head toward the Glaize, and meet the enemy in final battle. Contractor chicanery, supply fluctuations, looming end dates to the men's enlistment terms, and the largely untested nature of both officers and men still plagued his every moment. He was forced to dedicate his own quartermaster's horses to transporting supplies that should have been delivered, and the quartermaster had to buy supplies directly from suppliers: Wayne was basically supplying the army himself, he said, the contractors being criminal liars. In early May, the army had gotten down to eight days' worth of meat.

And yet by June, thanks to his constant focus on supply, Wayne had 250 cattle at Greene Ville and 800 more on the way, plus much new supply from the east. To make up for losing trained regulars at the end of their enlistment terms, he'd been authorized again to call up the mounted Kentucky volunteers. While he couldn't understand who was inspiring the malcontent officers to utter damning falsehoods against him, he retained confidence in both the Kentucky commander and James Wilkinson, and Wilkinson responded in kind. He wrote to Wayne pledging instant fidelity to the general's every order.

Wilkinson also wrote to Knox to inform him that Wayne's incompetence was putting victory at risk. Under such leadership, the army had nothing to gain and everything to fear, Wilkinson told a friend. Wayne was a blockhead, he said. The officers around Wilkinson reveled in these displays of disrespect for the commander by the second-in-command.

Wayne, meanwhile, delighted by the successful repulsion of attack at his forward fort on June 30, sent praise up to the men and officers at Fort Recovery, and he sent Knox the good news, expressing approval of the men and officers and singling out Gibson, the fort commander. On the Fourth of July, every soldier in the army was issued a gill of whiskey, and at Greene Ville there were fireworks.

By now, Henry Knox had begun urging Wayne to get moving. All the restraint imposed on Wayne the year before was replaced by polite pushing for forward motion. British presumption in building Fort Miamis on U.S. soil had combined with republican rage over the British shipping restrictions and republican fondness for revolutionary France to make the antiwar faction in Congress militantly anti-British, and as hard as he could, President Washington was leveraging this brief moment of seeming alignment with his opposition. Anti-British sentiment in Congress had temporarily quieted criticism of Washington's war policy—even of his professional army. The prospect of war with England undermined congressional objections to military buildup. Administration allies in the House took advantage of the anti-federalists' anti-British sentiment and pushed through Congress a host of emergency defensive measures, with appropriations for everything from fortifying harbors to deploying engineers to erecting armories to building ships.

The moment couldn't last long. Washington was in fact working quietly to resolve evacuation of the forts and other conflicts with the British, without getting into a war with England. In April, he'd sent John Jay, chief justice of the Supreme Court, to Paris to achieve a new treaty. The president knew that resolving those conflicts would further irritate his anti-British opposition, so he hoped to get as much of a military establishment erected as possible, as permanently as possible, before his efforts at resolution became public. He'd deployed his extraordinary gift for patience in playing out, to its bitterest end, the political show of negotiating for peace with the Indians, leaving Congress with nothing further to say against invasion. At the same time, he'd kept General

Wayne in a state of impossible tension over contradictory orders, necessary to gaining that effect on Congress, even while barely avoiding the
military-versus-civil crisis that would have ruined everything. As a result, Washington was at last in a position to take the old Illinois and
Ohio Countries from the Indians. The president had used implacabil-
ity, adroitness, and extreme yet calculated risk to join his two oldest
precepts—nationhood needed the West; nationhood needed a regular
army—in a single political and military action. It was time to turn
Anthony Wayne loose.

Being urged to move galled Wayne. It wasn't his fault he hadn't been
able to make his moves a year ago: had he been authorized to march
then, the ending of enlistments could have been avoided, and that's
what was now forcing him to wait for the arrival of the Kentuckians.
More than once he wrote to Knox in the "would to God" mode, noting
the exceedingly unfortunate situation that, he couldn't help reminding
Knox, Congress and the administration had placed him in.

On the other hand, Washington had now expressed, through Knox,
great satisfaction in all decisions Wayne had made so far: the attempted
advance in September; the discipline and judgment involved in facing
reality and stopping the advance in November; the retaking of St. Clair's
battleground in December. It was up to Wayne to make the decisions, Knox
told him. The general was on the ground, in charge, in enemy territory,
and basically on his own.

There were some new orders, however, and for a change they gave
Wayne heart. They regarded the new British Fort Miamis. It hadn't
existed when Wayne had received orders to avoid threatening Fort Detroit. Knox told him now that if, in the course of the operation against
the Indian confederation, it became necessary, in Wayne's judgment,
to dislodge the British garrison at the new fort on American soil, he
had authorization to do so, as long as he was confident that he would
succeed.

Those were good orders to get. The Miami American William Wells,
Little Turtle's son-in-law, was working for Wayne now, with an honor-
ary rank of captain, leading scouting parties far up into enemy country
and taking prisoners for intelligence, and intelligence had it that John
Simcoe was in Fort Miamis, with four hundred British troops, making
militant speeches about a showdown with the United States. In fact

Simcoe had returned to Newark, but Wayne now imagined that in an engagement to seize the offending fort, he might encounter Simcoe at the head of a line of British troops and loyalist militia from Detroit. He'd known for a long time that the British were supplying his enemy. Now there was proof: one-ounce balls dug out of the pickets of Fort Recovery were of the kind used in the British Brown Bess musket. Wayne relished the prospect of failing to distinguish in battle between John Simcoe and the Indians. He had carte blanche, and he was ready to march.

On July 28, 1794, the morning gun aroused the men at first light in weather already hot and sticky, and the fife and drum got them ready to move. They waited anxiously in formation for an hour; then came the usual single cannon blast, this time from a Greene Ville redoubt, to start them off. Again the creak of the overloaded baggage and food wagons, the cattle complaining, the clanking hardware. The force was nearly thirty-five hundred strong. Each soldier carried, along with his weapon, five days' ration of bread, two rations of beef and whiskey, and twenty-four rounds of ammunition. The speed of march was to be quick, despite the hot weather and the weight of provisions, because stopping early, every day, was critical to Mad Anthony's approach to establishing proper security, without fail, at each camp.

The route was tricky. Wayne's objective was the Glaize, north of Greene Ville but also very slightly east, and he wanted to fool enemy scouts, so he began by heading toward Fort Recovery, which might suggest that his further course would be more northwesterly, in the direction of Kekionga. The first day was hell on the men. They slogged through thick brush on swampy ground to the sides of the cleared wagon road, the dragoons in spurred boots struggling to lead their mounts. Wayne was on the cleared road, making time, and he expected the army to keep up as it fought its way across ravines and through thickets. Water in the muddy creeks was barely potable. Mosquitoes swarmed.

The next day, the long, sweating line of men and animals and matériel passed Fort Recovery, the head of the line. The garrison in the fort gave the march a fifteen-gun salute from two blockhouses. The army camped shortly ahead of Recovery, and Wayne went back to the fort to congratulate the men there personally on holding it against Blue Jacket's attack. He shook their hands and grasped their shoulders and called them the bravest boys in the world. The following day, the Legion of the United States entered uncut forest.

The Indian confederation force was still gathered at the Glaize and the rapids. There were frequent meetings regarding strategy, and despite the failure at Fort Recovery many of the fighters expressed continued eagerness to attack and defeat Wayne. Blue Jacket and Captain Johnny were largely in charge now, and McKee remained committed to the Shawnee hard-line position and to the idea that British military support would be forthcoming from Fort Miamis. Little Turtle, certain after his meeting with Colonel England that British support was a fantasy, had stepped back.

On August 4, a deserter from Wayne's army showed up at McKee's storehouses. Wayne was on the march, the man told the confederation leaders. The U.S. objective was to build a string of posts all the way to the Glaize towns, destroy the towns, hold that ground, and from there start coming down the Miami of the Lake toward Fort Miamis, thus establishing control over the entire Land of the Three Miamis.

So confrontation was imminent. McKee urged the leaders to stay in the Glaize towns to form an obstacle to Wayne. Yet the families were clearly vulnerable to destruction. Women, children, and the elderly had to be made as safe as possible. The whole set of towns around the confluence, occupied by the confederation Indians for more than two years, with their thriving cornfields, fruit trees, and artisan shops, had to be evacuated quickly.

Over McKee's worried objections, dismantling the Glaize became a chaotic flight. In canoes and on foot, people carried all they could take, old people and children straining under massive backpacks, anything not easily moved left behind. Little Turtle's Town, Big Cat's Town, Captain Johnny's and Blue Jacket's Towns, the seer's home, and the French bakery: it all became, nearly overnight, a long set of riverbank ghost towns, littered with disused possessions. A hurried migration came in huge numbers down the Miami of the Lake to set up camps, beginning under the protective walls of Fort Miamis and running north down the river almost to the banks of Lake Erie. Thousands of people were involved, and the camps quickly became miserable. The refugees had left food behind. They expected not only British military protection but also British food supply.

This new situation overwhelmed McKee. He sent an express rider to Fort Detroit to get a schooner full of provisions up the river as fast as possible.

Yet the desperate condition of the people and the courage of the war leaders and fighters drew sympathy from distant nations. Even the lake Indians, who had gone home in disgust after the Fort Recovery debacle, were subject to diplomatic entreaties, by fast runners, and many returned to the banks of the rapids where the new British fort stood. By mid-August, a thousand fighters had gathered there. White loyalist militia from Detroit came down and joined the force too. And McKee kept insisting British regulars would join as well.

A schooner from Detroit soon landed at Fort Miamis with a hundred barrels of food supplies for the refugees and fighters in the camps. The schooner also brought two small, rolling howitzers. But they were for the fort, not the Indians.

Wayne's army had turned northeast ahead of Fort Recovery and was now headed straight for the Glaize. Here things got really tough. A detail of more than fifty soldiers spent ten hours building a bridge fourteen feet wide and three hundred feet long, just to cross a deep swamp. Pioneers meanwhile cut road by felling trees and trying to clear brush. Still Wayne kept up the pace. He rode ahead of the line with only a small escort—recklessly, some officers groused—as far as the pioneers, and even beyond them.

As the men moved through what was turning out to be a vast wetland, they found themselves in the dark, under growth so thick that it blocked sunlight, and aside from their splashing and grunting there was a strange silence. In here, birds weren't seen or heard. The water tasted

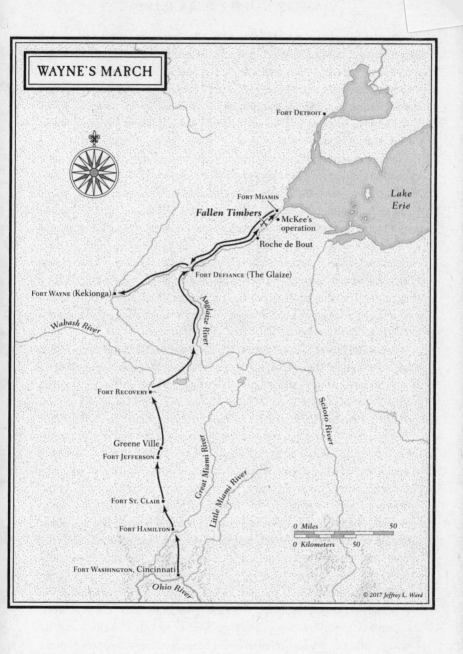

WAYNE'S MARCH

FORT DETROIT ▪

Lake Erie

FORT MIAMIS

Fallen Timbers

▪ McKee's operation

Roche de Bout

FORT DEFIANCE (The Glaize)

FORT WAYNE (Kekionga) ▪

Wabash River

Auglaize River

FORT RECOVERY ▪

Scioto River

Greene Ville
FORT JEFFERSON ▪

Great Miami River

Little Miami River

FORT ST. CLAIR ▪

FORT HAMILTON ▪

0 Miles   50

0 Kilometers   50

FORT WASHINGTON, Cincinnati ▪

Ohio River

© 2017 Jeffrey L. Ward

sulfurous. After hours of that, they emerged into an explosion of sunshine: a vast, beautiful prairie, stretching for miles around, studded with groves full of birdsong. Everything about these landscapes, from the horrible to the beautiful, seemed unutterably strange to men who had never ventured so far into woodland.

At every bivouac, without fail, the army built breastworks, corralled animals, and set sentries in what had now become, for the legion, a standard practice. The Indian scouts confirmed Little Turtle's assessment: Wayne's army did not sleep. No horses or supply could be taken. Wayne could not be surprised. With respect for such preternatural vigilance, the scouts took to calling him the Black Snake.

One afternoon Wayne was surprised. While he was having a small fort quickly built on the bank of the St. Marys River, he retired to his tent about 3:00 p.m., and as he lay on his cot a tall beech tree toppled onto the tent; it missed killing him by inches. Men pulled Wayne from the tent. He was unconscious and had to be revived by smelling salts. His right leg and ankle were bashed in. The tree had missed his vitals only because its impact had been deflected by a stump.

In terrible pain, Wayne mounted up and rode around the camp yelling orders of march. There had been a rumor that the general was dead.

The tree, it turned out, seemed to have been deliberately set to fall: it was burned partway through on one side. An Indian ploy to assassinate the Black Snake? Something even more sinister? Wilkinson, as second-in-command, was on the march as well, and officers under his influence had been raging against Wayne's command: the march struck them as unbearably fast, as if they were in hot pursuit, day after day, of a fleeing enemy. In fact, they groused, they didn't know where the enemy was or what he was doing, and they were miles into enemy territory ahead of any food supply, and the general had cut the men down to half rations of flour. It was as if he were afraid the enemy would melt away, the Wilkinson faction said, as if his personal glory might never be achieved.

Wayne meanwhile had been coming to a realization of Wilkinson's toxic effect on officer unity. He understood now that his second-in-command was working against him. Wilkinson had written a long, scurrilous, anonymous screed and had it published in a Cincinnati newspaper, a fake report from the field attacking Wayne for everything from theft to favoritism, from warmongering to drunkenness. Wilkinson had hoped the letter would force Washington to relieve Wayne of command, but instead, Washington had Knox write to Wayne to assure him of full support, that the attacks were discredited on their face and passionately denied by other officers. Wilkinson then sent Knox formal charges in his own name. Knox advised Wilkinson to settle down.

Now, with the tree incident, Wayne suspected Wilkinson not only of insubordination but also of attempted murder. But he had no proof, Wilkinson was critical to his operation, there was nothing to do, and it was time to move. Forward movement had become Wayne's only plan, only focus. He left another unhappy officer and crew to finish building a small fort on the St. Marys, and he pressed on—his leg and ankle radiating pain—filled with darkest suspicion, yet with ever-narrowing intent: battle.

By August 7, the army was already moving down the Auglaize River toward its confluence with the Miami of the Lake: they were nearing the Glaize. While the men were building camp that afternoon, scouts returned with news of an enemy war party camped nearby. Wilkinson got excited. Here was opportunity, he urged Wayne, and he asked the general to detach him with a mounted unit to attack the party. Wilkinson's resentment reached a high pitch when Wayne denied the request. The general would not divide his army to chase one enemy party. Of such impulses defeat was made. Impetuosity lay far behind Wayne now. This was Mad Anthony. His leg and foot were bashed, swollen, and throbbing, but impervious to suggestion, he knew what to do now. Move forward.

Row upon row of high green corn stretched for thousands of acres under big sky on both sides of the Miami of the Lake. The men could not believe what they were seeing. Wayne's army had arrived at the Glaize.

It wasn't just the beauty that so astonished the Americans, but the prosperity and tranquillity, expressed by undulating rows of corn, orchards, neat log cabins with kitchen gardens. Here was the magnificent fertility of the western bottomland in glorious display.

And yet nobody lived here. Everyone was gone. To get to this confluence, the army had marched through towns hastily abandoned, cooking fires recently in use, household items simply dropped. Some of the storehouses, having been burned, smoldered. A civic complex abruptly depopulated, a heartland uninhabited.

Clearly Wayne's objective had been discovered. He'd sent the mounted Kentuckians ahead, and the downstream flight of the Glaize refugees had preceded those volunteers' arrival by mere hours. There would be no battle here at the Glaize.

Still, the general now had control of the headquarters, plantation, and civic center where the confederation had been operating with impunity against the United States ever since defeating St. Clair. He camped his army at the abandoned stockade on the point at the confluence. He made an order of congratulations and had a gill of whiskey given to each man. The next morning, fort building commenced, on the Recovery model. This one, replacing McKee's stockade at the confluence, was to be named Defiance. Wayne held the Glaize.

Abandonment suggested to Wayne that the confederation might finally be willing to surrender without a fight. This impulse ran contrary to the caricature, drawn by the Wilkinson faction, of a general in pursuit of nothing but personal glory in the field. As much as he would love an excuse to attack Fort Miamis, Wayne knew he'd have to win such an engagement hands down or cause new problems, and he knew John Jay was negotiating in Paris for a treaty between the British and the Americans. His army was low on food. He was deep in enemy territory, with poor supply and no communications back with headquarters at Greene Ville, let alone with Fort Washington or with Henry Knox. Felled to his cot by a sudden attack of gout—it had begun in a foot and advanced to his knee—Wayne sent a message downstream to the rapids. This was the last chance he would give the enemy.

Wayne told the Indian confederation that the British had neither the power nor the inclination to help them. He announced that he was in the midst of their towns. He invited them to meet him halfway between the rapids and the Glaize and settle preliminaries for a lasting peace.

❖❖❖

He wasn't waiting for a reply. On August 15, with Fort Defiance near completion, the columns resumed their advance.

The gout had grown so bad that the general had to be lifted onto his horse. He insisted on riding, not being carried in a wagon, and he continued to go impatiently ahead with little protection. He waded the whole army and all of its wagons and animals across the Miami of the Lake, with a good bit of chaos, to the west bank, then turned the columns downstream toward the rapids. The way narrowed. Wayne kept moving. The army marched in an uncomfortably tight passage, the floodplain of the river to its right and a rising wooded ground to its left.

Food supply, at least, had been temporarily solved. Reducing the flour ration by half had meant privation and strain. Given the abundant produce of the Glaize towns, however, the men could now live off the land. Marching out of the Glaize after seven days, they left miles of broken cornstalks, vegetables smashed, fields trampled by horses and cattle, cabins burned to the ground. With black smoke rising from a landscape demolished as far as the eye could see, Wayne's legion moved forward behind its general. He rode anguished by gout and fatigue, implacable.

In the spring of 1793, while still seething with rage at being restrained by Washington's and Knox's orders, Wayne had received word, first, that his wife, Mary, had died and, shortly afterward, that his mother had died. While moving the army from Legion Ville to Hobson's Choice, he underwent days of inner turmoil, less over the death than over the life of his long-estranged Polly. It had been a disappointing life, and he knew that his own penchants, failures, and weaknesses were responsible for her misery.

In the interim, his son, Isaac, had become an upstanding young man. Having hacked about for a long time, he'd suddenly become serious, not because of his father's disparagement and criticism from long distances via intermediaries, but because, somehow, he'd grown up. And as Mary Wayne reminded her son in one of her last letters, he'd had to do so without a father. She took no credit; she gave credit to God and to Isaac himself. His merit should be more esteemed, she assured him, than that of those who always had both parents with them.

Wayne had written to Isaac just this past spring, mainly to express astonishment that his own mother had cut Wayne out of her will. Wayne had almost never paid her the annuity that had been a condition of his inheritance from his father, so she not only disinherited him but also made her bequests to grandchildren subject to collection of what Anthony owed her. Wayne's only explanation, which he communicated to Isaac, was that the old lady had been infirm with age; the whole thing, he said, could probably still be worked out. As fatherly advice, in closing he recommended his son give serious perusal, thought, and attention to the advice of Polonius to Laertes. Isaac would find the passage, Wayne said, in the Shakespeare play *Hamlet, Prince of Denmark*.

Just before moving out of Greene Ville to begin this march on the Glaize, Wayne made his own will and wrote again to Isaac. Land in Pennsylvania and Georgia he left to Isaac, the house in Philadelphia to Peggy. He crossed out his description of the fifteen hundred acres of bounty land he'd received from Congress as a trifling compensation; instead, he called it "retribution" for the loss of blood he'd sustained in "the defense of the liberties of America in many a well-fought field from the frozen lakes of Canada to the burning sands of Florida." He explained to Isaac that he was dealing with all this now because he was planning to march against the biggest body of Indians ever assembled in America, combined with British troops and Detroit militia under Simcoe (he still expected to meet him). The issue would be determined, Wayne noted, before Isaac received the letter. He charged Isaac with burning what he called his idle and juvenile letters: he'd meant to do it himself. He wished blessings and God's protection for "my only son and daughter. Adieu, my dear friend," he wrote, "give your amiable and lovely sister a last embrace from your

"Affectionate father,
"ANTY WAYNE"

Little Turtle spoke first. The confederation leaders were meeting under an elm on the riverbank outside Fort Miamis to discuss the message

they'd received from Wayne for negotiating a peace. Intelligence had it that Wayne's army would arrive within a day or two.

The Miami leader saw no likelihood of success. All hope for victory was at an end, he argued. There would be no end to this long, bloody trail. Every time the Americans came, they came with more men. The confederation had defeated them twice: How many more times was that likely to happen?

And the Black Snake was different. He didn't sleep. It was time to talk peace with him: anything else was unrealistic. While Little Turtle didn't say he'd asked Colonel England point-blank for artillery and British troops and had gotten nowhere, it was clear he didn't believe British support would be there when it counted.

But Little Turtle was alone. The tone of the meeting was gung ho. Some would say it was Blue Jacket, Little Turtle's partner in the great victory over St. Clair, who now made the speech chastising the Miami leader for cowardice and accusing him of wanting to cozy up to the Americans. The leaders described Anthony Wayne as just another St. Clair, and the war cry went up. The confederation had more fighters coming in every day. Runners were combing the countryside asking for even more help. Even Joseph Brant was supposed to be bringing a hundred Mohawks.

Little Turtle tried one last time. He felt old, he told the others. He made official what had been true at least since his meeting with Colonel England at Detroit. He relinquished leadership. He wasn't backing out of fighting. He would, he said, now only follow.

With the meeting concluded, the war leaders began their preparations to ambush Wayne's advance. All noncombatants were to be moved well downstream, past Fort Miamis, near the lake. The entire fighting force would gather just forward of the fort and jump the Americans when they arrived there. The British commander at Fort Miamis, in anticipation of the ambush, pulled the troops upstream at Roche de Bout back down to the fort. Wayne would come unopposed until surprised by the confederation.

The Indians chose a place of concealment w
blown down a mile or so of timber to create a huge
bers, about two miles south and downstream of Fort
that Wayne's force, in attempting to establish control

the Miami of the Lake, would have to get through Fallen Timbers, and the place offered excellent cover for a large ambush, hiding more than a thousand men.

On August 18, the fighters began forming their hidden line. Blue Jacket placed the confederation's core—Shawnee, Delaware, and Miami— in the center. The right was formed by a few British regulars dressed as Indians; loyalist militiamen from Detroit; Wyandot; and the few Six Nations Iroquois who had agreed to fight. On the left were Potawatomie, Ottawa, and Ojibwa, back in the fight but still impetuous. As they waited at Fallen Timbers, the men were semi-fasting. They'd eaten only one meal the day before. It was common practice: empty bowels were safer in the event of being shot.

After a long wait that day, however, most of the fighters vacated the spot and fell back to the camp outside the fort. Again they ate only one meal. The next day, the nineteenth, they returned to the ambush position and re-formed their line. Still Wayne didn't appear. The leaders agreed that the fighters could eat another meal in the morning.

Wilkinson, writing for the record just in case he made it out alive, described Wayne's march as a total disaster; he expected defeat. In the progress down the narrow riverbank, his infantry kept getting crowded by the center, causing what he saw as total disorder. And Wayne, he'd concluded, was actually insane. The army was way too far ahead of its food and ammunition, with no possibility of reinforcements. Gout worsened the commander's dementia, Wilkinson thought, and he imagined an Indian attack producing an outright fit. As long columns struggled along the riverside, on trail barely passable by wagons, Wilkinson hoped to live through the battle, someday present his journal to Henry Knox, and renew formal charges against Wayne for incompetence.

Wayne was far past caring. Through illness and exhaustion, all he knew was punctiliously vigilant forward movement toward final victory. Arriving at Roche de Bout on August 18, the army still met no resistance. There were signs not only of recent military presence but also of major trading operations: empty storehouses, ledger books and trade s left behind. Here the confederation had met to send messages to the commissioners. The British had maintained a small force here as well. Now Roche de Bout was abandoned.

The men were amazed by the beauty of the beginning of long falls and the great rock formation in its midst, but Wayne had no concern other than security and intelligence. He'd received a letter from the confederation: it was deliberately vague, with a general tone of challenge. The battle was coming. Wayne was advancing directly toward wherever it would take place. The time was getting short. Wayne's own pace would set the schedule.

So reversing his usual insistence on quick forward movement, Wayne stopped the army for two full days at Roche de Bout. He ordered a breast-work fort of deposit built to hold all accoutrements not needed in the coming battle. He held a meeting with top officers and proposed sending five hundred of the mounted Kentuckians forward to reconnoiter.

Their commander averred that such a move might only provoke the final engagement, leaving the main army too far to the rear. Wayne swore loudly. He needed to know, he shouted, the ground and the enemy position. His best scout, William Wells, had skirmished with a party of Delaware; he was wounded, and Wayne had come to depend on Wells's knowledge. Even officers not in the Wilkinson faction began wondering whether the commander was losing his grip.

The next day, the Kentucky battalion went forward to reconnoiter. This was a large force. The scouts marched in detachments spread about a hundred yards apart in the woods: if one detachment walked into ambush, the others would not. Behind them came the mounted volunteers. With every mile they proceeded, the men became more expectant that the forest was about to explode in gunfire. All they found was the eerie quiet of the woodland, birdsong, wind, the rush of the nearby rapids.

They discovered a place that might have been prepared for an ambush: a mile or so of fallen, blowdown trees toppled everywhere, thickly overgrown. Then they spotted an enemy party. It bolted toward Fort Miamis.

Back at Roche de Bout, the scouts reported to Wayne that all evidence suggested a massive gathering of enemy fighters in the vicinity. The big thicket of fallen trees looked like a place of ambush, and they'd seen Indians near there.

So the day and place of battle were now known: tomorrow, and amid those fallen timbers, unless that was a trick. Wayne prepared for both eventualities. He was ready to be surprised.

In the darkness before dawn on the morning of the twentieth, the American camp at Roche de Bout arose in the rain. In a move that might as well have been intended to send the commander around the bend, the drums had been left out overnight in the downpour. When the rain stopped a little after 7:00, the big day began with Wayne's having to send staff officers around the camp verbally ordering commanders to assemble their men.

Heat and humidity quickly became oppressive. Before 9:00, the army moving downstream in the steamy air, spread across thick, high woods above the river and down onto the riverbank floodplain, had covered almost five miles.

The order of march was unusual. Wayne's whole attention was on refusing to be flanked and on turning the enemy flanks. Battle orders therefore had to do with initiative. The enemy made a fearsome opponent when charging and pursuing those in flight, Wayne reminded his officers, but not when being driven back, because the enemy normally relied not on making firm stands against attack but on falling away, disappearing, returning unexpectedly. The critical tactic of advance was thus to move forward no matter what. They'd practiced it hundreds of times. Orders to both artillery and infantry officers were to fire on any forward soldier giving way without an order to withdraw.

At the front of the march were seven units of Kentucky horsemen: they'd scouted the enemy position the day before and would locate it again. Well out in front of them, two riders served as the advance of the advance, having volunteered for this most dangerous duty of all. Four hundred yards behind the Kentucky squads, a detachment of infantry regulars marched in reserve of the advance units, a squad of dragoons behind them. After them, the entire bulk of the army, and so broad was the whole advance that while the right wing moved through six-foot-high grass on the river's broad floodplain, the center and left were moving through forest on the ridge above the river. Lighter artillery rolled in the center, with Wayne himself.

Wilkinson thought the arrangement idiotic. He was sure the army would never be able to concentrate quickly when attacked: some of the horsemen were too far down by the river; the two main infantry columns were marching three hundred yards apart, widely dispersed to an unconventional degree. But Wayne, riding with the artillery, was satisfied. He had about thirty-three hundred men on the move, more or less impervious to surprise. He believed the scouts had found the site where attack could be expected, but he also knew the enemy could come from any direction at any time. In addressing that problem, the sub-legion structure was proving its worth: Wayne could quickly transform an attack from left or right into an attack on a new front. Turning to face left, right, forward, or back, the whole army would retain structural integrity, with the ability, he hoped, to form and hold lines and, ultimately, charge: light infantry and riflemen up front, supported by muskets; dragoons with artillery always in the center. If enemy fighters tried to defeat that structure by running in from the corners, they'd be automatically flanked and overwhelmed.

The terrain, however, cut up by ravines, posed a challenge to forming strong lines under pressure. On the march that morning, the left kept falling behind. Wayne halted the army periodically to review and practice moves for getting into formation.

After about two hours of march, the forward Kentucky scouts saw that they were within about half a mile of the area they'd identified the day before as the probable place of ambush. They paused and drank water. The two front men then proceeded slowly, walking their horses, picking their way around the debris. At about 9:45, they were the first Americans to die, shot at close range by the first enemy volley.

At Fallen Timbers earlier that rainy morning, some of the Indian fighters had taken a quick trip downstream to eat, returning to the ambush position around the time Wayne had begun his march out of Roche de Bout. They now formed a strong barrier, hidden among the high tangled overgrowth and fallen trees, across the main thrust of Wayne's advance line. Their formation wasn't as broad as Wayne's—nobody was down in the high river grass—and with the entire force at the front there was nothing in reserve. Largely because of the food problem, the position was understaffed this morning: some thought maybe only five hundred confederation fighters were in position; others thought about eleven hundred. But the formation held up, about seven hundred yards across and two men deep: Shawnee, Delaware, and Miami in the center of the line; the motley of British regulars, Detroit militia, Wyandot, and Iroquois on the right; Potawatomie, Ottawa, and Ojibwa on the left.

It was the Ottawa and Potawatomie on the farthest left who first saw the two advance Kentuckians walking their horses. About a hundred yards behind those two, squads of Kentucky scouts came slowly too, some working their way along the difficult ridge terrain, some coming more easily through the high river grass. When the advance drew within range, the Indian fighters rose from hiding and fired. They ducked, reloaded, and rose and fired again.

"No fight," sniffed Wilkinson, in part because the Battle of Fallen Timbers, as it came to be known, lasted only a little over an hour. As with every battle, and perhaps even more so with this first victory in the field that the United States of America ever achieved, disagreement would prevail among the victors about what happened. The reason for one side's victory and the defeat of the other, who ordered what, and when, who went out on their own, and why: certainty about issues like that would remain impossible to attain, and only in part because it all happened so fast.

Anthony Wayne believed two things happened at Fallen Timbers. Each had to do less with change in ground than with change in belief. The Indian confederation came to believe the United States enjoyed military superiority. U.S. troops came to believe they could prevail in battle. Regardless of all the competing stories and judgments, those results made Wayne's victory strategically, politically, and historically decisive.

What didn't happen: everything clicked and Wayne's army performed perfectly. The Kentucky scouts at the front, fired on, moved forward to within about twenty yards of the enemy in the thicket, took a huge roar of musket fire, and fell back quickly. The Ottawa and Potawatomie

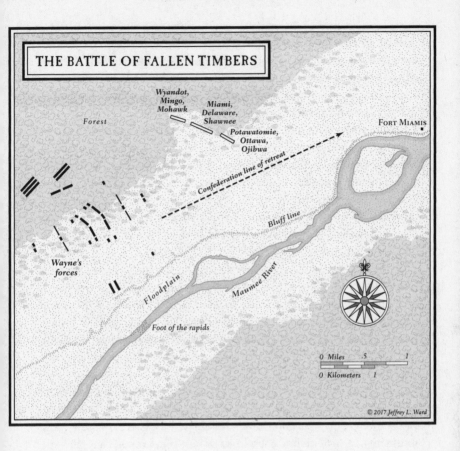

THE BATTLE OF FALLEN TIMBERS

Forest

Wyandot,
Mingo,
Mohawk

Miami,
Delaware,
Shawnee

Potawatomie,
Ottawa,
Ojibwa

FORT MIAMIS

Confederation line of retreat

Bluff line

Wayne's
forces

Floodplain

Maumee River

Foot of the rapids

0 Miles .5 1

0 Kilometers 1

© 2017 Jeffrey L. Ward

charged them, and while for a moment the Kentucky riflemen were able to hold off the attackers, a huge number of Shawnee from the center then charged the riflemen's left. The Kentucky militiamen then did just what George Washington, Anthony Wayne, and other proponents of a regular army said militia always did. They turned and fled in disorder, with the enemy in triumphant pursuit.

Behind the Kentuckians, the supporting regular-infantry advance men, two sets of thirty-seven, had been halted by their commanders at the sound of fire and successfully formed in lines. But the fleeing Kentuckians were now galloping on horseback straight toward them, threatening to break up the formation. Captain John Cooke followed the order to fire on fleeing Americans. An infantry volley sent the mounted Kentuckians racing around the line and all the way back toward Wayne and the main army.

So it was regular infantry now facing the charging enemy. The infantry did fire a volley in what Captain Cooke thought was very good order, but the enemy kept coming, and the men on the left, in danger of being flanked, began to give way; some started to run. Cooke put his remaining men together with the line on his left, under Lieutenant John Steele, and together the advance guard now did hold ground. It delivered three solid volleys.

The charging Ottawa and Potawatomie were undeterred, however, so Cooke ordered a firing retreat. The men executed it for about a hundred yards. The enemy kept coming. Cooke ordered the men to scatter back to the main army and find their units as best they could. That moment couldn't have felt anything like victory. But it did see regular army following orders under fire.

Meanwhile, well to the rear, with the Kentucky advance arriving in panic, Wayne had halted his main army and was bellowing the order to prepare to receive the enemy, in two lines. Because the drums weren't working, his staff officers had to run around the woods and down to the river relaying the order. Not everybody got it.

Up front, the Ottawa and Potawatomie were still advancing, and now it was up to forward light infantry to hold them off, buying time for Wayne's main army to form. But the light infantry was suddenly disrupted by Cooke's men, fleeing, though on orders, right through them. Some of the light infantrymen began joining that flight, but their

commander chased them down, shouted orders, and managed to regroup the whole force in a line. That line began exchanging heavy fire
with the attackers.

Behind all of that action to the front, Wayne and the commanders
were still shouting orders. Fife, bugle, and staff officers relayed them.
The main army was taking its assigned positions with all deliberate
speed: rear-line battalions, being smaller, formed more quickly than
the full-strength battalions, which took up to five minutes to get into
the lines they'd practiced, while the dragoons and artillery waited to
move up to their flanks. Everything would depend on the success of the
light infantry up front in buying time. The report from up front: all is
confusion.

Forces under Blue Jacket were not at their best today, and they were
finding themselves having to cope with an enemy relatively competent,
in comparison to anything they'd seen from the United States before.
By now, the whole confederation line was involved. Even as the Ottawa
and Potawatomie who had begun the firing had charged well forward,
and were now exchanging fire with the American forward light infantry,
the Indian left and right moved forward too. Blue Jacket and the other
leaders hoped to turn the enemy's flanks and encircle Wayne's whole army.
Ojibwa and Ottawa therefore moved down onto the river grass and advanced against light infantry, while up in the forest, Shawnee, Delaware,
and Miami from the center joined the right wing in probing the woods
in search of the American left.

The Indian force down by the river met with stiff resistance. The
American company there was defending its position with rhythm and
intensity, and now the attackers found themselves dangerously exposed
in the high grass. American cannon had moved into position above
them: suddenly the attackers were taking howitzer shells and grapeshot
from the ridge. Too, rifle companies from the main American army were
advancing on the floodplain in support of the forward light infantry, firing
balls with accuracy.

The advancing American right simply could not be turned. The Indian left therefore retreated from the grass and moved up to the relative

protection of the woods on the ridge, where the center was still exchanging fire with light infantry. That move gave the Americans a chance to
move units forward along the floodplain, advancing on the riverbank
beyond the Indian line, thus flanking the Indian left.

Still, at what had become the center up in the woods, Ottawa and
Potawatomie seemed to be making good ground against the light infantry there. The American troops kept falling back, on orders, and now
they'd fallen so far back that they'd reached the infantrymen of the
main army. And yet their attackers, moving forward so confidently, found
themselves suddenly trapped. The howitzers that had bombarded their
comrades on the riverbank had been turned ninety degrees, and now
from their left the Indian fighters, so far and so confidently advanced,
were taking cannon fire, and regular-infantry lines were also firing on
them from their right.

Meanwhile, out of sight of that action, the Indian confederation's
center and right, probing the forest, had finally found the Americans.
The Wyandot, Iroquois, and Canadian forces were swinging far to the
enemy left, moving fast and hoping to get all the way around the entire
main force and flank it.

But to its surprise, this flanking force found the enemy fully prepared for that maneuver. A force of 550 Kentucky militia, dismounted,
had been kept out of the main action and sent from the rear to range far
left into the woods. It would have been nearly impossible to anticipate a
commander's holding such a huge fraction of his force for such a purpose, but there they were, in position, ready to resist the Indians' flanking effort. Another Kentucky brigade was already moving around the
Indian fighters. The Indians were being flanked on both sides.

From his more or less central position just behind all the heat to his
left, right, and front, Wayne was in a heat too. He shouted orders, received information from the action, revised orders, sent his staff back to
give the orders and get more information. To Wilkinson and other officers, the whole thing seemed chaos. Yet Wayne was getting ready not to
defend but to attack.

His young staffers were worried about something else. The general was straining in his saddle, all pain evidently forgotten, seemingly on the verge not only of ordering a charge but also of digging in his spurs and galloping to the front of it. The staffers were taking turns watching. They were ready to grab his reins.

Finally, one of them, Captain William Henry Harrison, was bold enough to caution Wayne.

"General Wayne," Harrison said, "I am afraid you will go into battle yourself." He feared the general would leave him without any field orders.

"Perhaps I may," Wayne told him, with evident enjoyment. "And if I do, recollect that the standing order of the day is 'Charge the damned rascals with the bayonet'!"

The Indian confederation fighters began a retreat, at first in orderly fashion. Hearing American bugles from left and right, those in the center believed they'd been flanked even before they really were, and the Indians' center units withdrew, carrying the dead and wounded. They gained cover, turned and fired to cover their retreating comrades, then withdrew further, in organized stages.

Soon, however, there was nothing to do but leave the bodies and sprint. They were being subjected to a classic bayonet charge. Wayne watched as the center of his heavy infantry now stepped out in nearly perfect synchronization on a quickened version of the common-time pace, seventy-two steps per minute. Some of the men charging were hit and fell, but the rest went on, holding the pace, bayonets fixed and ready, and they went so fast, so implacably, that the retreating Indians soon had no time to stop and reload. They fled.

Watching, Wayne suddenly reined up his horse, as if to dash out and join the march, and two staffers grabbed his reins. They tussled with horse and man, the animal urged to move while being held.

"Let me go!" Wayne yelled. "Damn them, let me go!"

Then, cheering on his bayonet charge, he shouted, "Give it to them, boys!" Meanwhile on the flanks, the dragoons, riflemen, and light infantry had shot up the Indian line, and the Indian left and right were now in flight too, converging with their former center, on the run across open ground, pursued by Wayne's bayonets. Indian fighters arriving late met this retreat and turned to join and swell it. Some of the fighters tried to flee on the floodplain, others crossed the river, but their main objective was to reach the safety of Fort Miamis.

On high ground just forward of Fort Miamis, Alexander McKee had been waiting and hoping with his associates Simon Girty and Matthew Elliott. Suddenly hundreds of their Indian allies appeared, running toward them away from the battle.

McKee couldn't believe he was seeing a rout. With outraged disappointment, he shouted to rally the fighters, trying to stop them in their tracks, begging them to turn and fight.

They paid no attention. Rushing past the Shawnee British official, they sought only escape. They ran for the safety of the fort.

Arriving in full flight at the Fort Miamis stockade wall, more than five hundred beaten men found the gate closed. They piled up against it, demanding entrance.

The commander of Fort Miamis was Major William Campbell. He had no specific orders. He knew he had no authority to start a war with the United States, and he knew he had to defend the fort.

He'd heard the sounds of battle, and around 11:00 a.m., seeing a few retreating Indian parties nearing the fort, he'd realized the United States was victorious. He'd put the fort on battle alert and cut off all communication with the outside.

Now, with hundreds of Indian fighters clamoring for entrance, Campbell made a critical decision. He couldn't, he thought, let them in.

Blue Jacket, Buckongahelas, and the others, panting from their exertions amid hundreds of fighters, couldn't believe what was happening. Little Turtle might have been less surprised than others that the western Indian confederation's lost battle was ending in a moment even worse than the defeat, a betrayal they would never forget. The British were locking the Indians out of the fort supposedly built for Indian safety.

The situation was now impossible. Presuming an American pursuit, the fighters finally gave up their outraged demand for entrance to the fort. They gave up on the British too. There was nothing to do but keep moving. They turned and resumed flight, down the river, toward the places where their families were camped near Lake Erie.

Alexander McKee kept following them. He kept exhorting them to stop, turn back, fight the United States.

Wilkinson couldn't understand it. Wayne wouldn't follow up his victory. Instead of pursuing five hundred beat-up, fleeing Indians with his entire excited, victorious army, the general had the recall sounded. Forward movement stopped dead. Wilkinson decided he would describe that decision as an ignominious retreat.

It was hot and humid, and the men were at the edge of exhaustion, but that wasn't it. Wayne understood what he'd just accomplished. The Indians believed in U.S. might. The men believed, as Wayne put it, in the bayonet. However things went now, with whatever bumps and setbacks, he was sure American possession of the Northwest Territory was a fact.

He had a half gill of whiskey issued to each man. Then he made a series of moves far more strategic than pursuing the fleeing Indians. After a four-hour break—during it, Wayne sent scouts to reconnoiter all the way to Fort Miamis—he ordered the army up for a march downstream to the British fort.

He rode along with the marching ranks now, giving the men his congratulations. Wherever he went, he told his men, he always flogged Indians and British. Gaining a view of Fort Miamis, the soldiers could see the Union Jack flying above the river, claiming passage to Lake Erie. They knew the British garrison could see them too. Here, less than a mile and a half from the gates of the fort, Wayne camped the Legion of the United States.

Within Fort Miamis, all afternoon Major Campbell watched Wayne's troops spreading out over ground near his post as if in total disregard of his presence. He had only 160 regulars plus 24 Canadian militia. He watched American cavalry units feed herds of horses on the islands and at what had been McKee's operation across the river. Wayne's main force was busy making a bivouac with high security. His commander's marquee was pitched. His men ostentatiously beat drums and blasted out bugle calls.

Campbell had no intention of surrendering, but he had no idea what Wayne was up to. Intelligence had it that Wayne possessed only twenty small howitzers, nowhere near big enough to tear open the fort. Yet England and France were at war. Simcoe and Dorchester had said they expected war with the United States. The fort stood on U.S. soil. Campbell didn't have orders.

The next day, his tension worsened. He could see hundreds of American cavalry in the woods near his fort. From an island, American officers were peering at him through spyglasses. Infantry units had been posted on the high ground so audaciously nearby that they were within cannon range. Campbell began to understand that this whole operation amounted to a gigantic, complicated insult. That got to him.

At 11:00 a.m., he sent a captain under a flag to ask in what light he was supposed to take such a near approach to his fort. The captain met outposts of Wayne's force, and they took the message but sent the emissary back: they feared for his safety, they told him.

It wasn't until 4:00 p.m. that Campbell received an answer. Wayne told the major that the most full and satisfactory answer to his question had already been given by the sound of the muzzles of Wayne's arms in the rout of the Indians the day before. The fort hadn't existed before the war began, Wayne pointed out, and it stood illegitimately on U.S. soil. Had the action continued to the fort, he told Campbell, he wouldn't have been impeded.

In fact, Wayne had already determined that he couldn't take Fort Miamis. He was low on food, and his howitzers weren't big enough. There was a more important strategic objective anyway: make the Indians overwhelmingly aware, if they weren't already, that there was no help for them in the British army.

To bring that point home, the next day he made two moves. First, under the eye of an increasingly infuriated Campbell, Wayne posted four companies of light infantry and four of dragoons in a perimeter at the edge of the woods about a hundred yards from the walls, completely surrounding the fort. In response, Campbell put the garrison at its posts and trained cannon on the American men.

Then the coup de grâce. Leaving the woods, General Wayne himself rode out, alone, onto the open ground between the woods and the fort.

The British soldiers in the fort stared in amazement. The general was within easy pistol shot.

He rode slowly around the entire fort, inspecting it with ostentatious minuteness. Within the fort, one officer begged Campbell for permission to dispatch the American bravo, but despite his own outrage Campbell refused. He could defend the fort, but he couldn't fire the first shot in a war with the United States. He was forced to observe the American commander inspect his post at will.

Finally, Wayne withdrew, and the two commanders exchanged escalating notes accusing each other of aggression. Wayne ordered Campbell to withdraw to Fort Detroit, offering him safe passage. Campbell said if Wayne didn't desist, honor would force him to fire. But Wayne's real work here was almost done. He was readying the men to withdraw to Fort Defiance and regroup.

Before marching the army out, he made his final move. For six days, cavalry squadrons rode about the countryside putting to the torch everything of value within view of the fort. Indians' houses, McKee's storehouses, piles of hay, and other supplies all went up in flames. Major Campbell could only watch as another cloud of black smoke sent up by the Legion of the United States hung everywhere, day after day, in the humid air above the foot of the rapids of the Miami of the Lake. Downstream where they camped, Little Turtle and Blue Jacket and the other leaders and fighters watched too.

12

BLACK GRANITE

This story took place, of course, mostly in what today is called the Midwest. It was near modern-day Toledo, Ohio, that John Simcoe and Alexander McKee built Fort Miamis. Fort Wayne, Indiana, lies where the western Indians had their heartland Kekionga. The lovely, long falls of the Miami of the Lake—the Maumee River, today—where Alexander McKee once had his storehouses, flows past Grand Rapids, Ohio.

Some of the forts important to this story have long since been demolished, but others are preserved. Eventual British evacuation of the contested lake forts on American soil led to the city of Detroit, Michigan, and all that that's entailed, but also less famously to Youngstown, New York, where Fort Niagara has been continuously operated as one kind of military facility after another. Now restored in a state park, its four-chimney, top-heavy French mansion looms in lonely splendor against the sky over Lake Ontario. Leaving that park, a traveler on the trail that Anthony Wayne made safe for the first great wave of American commercial development can take a 450-mile drive generally southwest and arrive at the site of Fort Recovery, where St. Clair's army was destroyed, Richard Butler died, and Anthony Wayne built the post he so loved. The town has the same name: Fort Recovery, Ohio, near the ‸na border.

‸es to the south, on the Ohio River, where Wayne began his er-
‸onquest, wide tangles of rail bed and rusty, disused warehouses

lie along the banks, and nuclear and chemical and coal plants' stacks
rise along the water route all the way from Pittsburgh to Cincinnati.
Thanks to direct highways, nobody has to go that twisty way, and while
hundreds of thousands of people live along it, few others have reason to
visit. When these towns thrived on iron and steel production and
other big manufacturing, the factories that belched smoke supported
main-street clothing and appliance stores, diners and groceries, porched
homes of managers and bankers on quiet, elm-lined streets and cookie-
cutter workers' housing on company plots. But a stinking cloud no longer blots out the sky. Boarded-up downtowns and weed-sprung parking
lots make clear that there's little to buy or sell there now, and even fast
food can be hard to come by.

At the Ohio mouth of the Muskingum, across from West Virginia,
lies Marietta, Ohio, the first certified development in the Northwest
Territory. On both sides of the river, much is physically broken. Much is
simply abandoned. None of that is unique, of course, to southern Ohio.
That's how much of our former industrial heartland is. But Marietta has
special importance to this story. At the Muskingum's mouth, a sprawl
of mobile homes, some displaying Confederate symbols, leads to Harmar
Elementary School, where during math or social studies a kid looking
out a window at the Ohio River might see, but probably no longer register, the flagpole that rises on school grounds. A small stone with a brass
plaque at the foot of that pole, barely legible for rust and dirt, notes the
former presence of Fort Harmar.

Treaty terms were dictated and rejected here, leading to the first war
the United States ever fought to gain an empire. From that war came
agricultural and industrial Ohio, denuded of high forests, sky exposed
to the horizons. In a shift of dynamism from the seaboard to the Midwest, Anthony Wayne's conquered territory superseded the world that
produced George Washington. Most U.S. presidents throughout the
nineteenth century and into the twentieth came not from Virginia, as in
the brief founding generation, but from Ohio, the first state cut from the
Northwest Territory. Washington himself had always seen Ohio as the
site of explosive American wealth and glory, and thanks to some complicated actions that he and others took, he turned out to be right. Battle
lines in the war that started that shift were drawn where Harmar Elementary now stands.

High on the pole outside the school, a flag barely dangles. Even in a high wind, it can only barely dangle. All but one clasp having failed, it's more of a rag, faded and shredded not from battle, of course, but from years of exposure. Its limpness too would be visible from schoolroom windows, and while evidently nobody is responsible for the flag's care, squinting up from the ground, one can still identify, barely, the stars and stripes.

In the summer of 1795, American flags were waving high over forts throughout the Northwest Territory, thanks to Anthony Wayne and his legion, and if Wayne could have looked ahead and seen an industrial boom that would last, with ups and downs, approximately two centuries, he would have been pleased. When he won the Battle of Fallen Timbers, fewer than 5,000 white people were living in what would become the state of Ohio. Less than fifteen years later, 230,000 Americans would live there; a decade later, more than twice that. In 1795, the Ohio that Marietta no longer is was soon to be, and it was up to Anthony Wayne to get it going.

While everything didn't go as smoothly as he might have hoped, Wayne made quick progress. After leaving Major Campbell unmolested at Fort Miamis in August 1794, and destroying everything within view of that fort, Wayne marched back up the river to his quickly built fort of deposit at Roche de Bout. He found he had only thirty-three dead, plus a hundred wounded, and while Indian casualties might be only around forty, the legion had not only put its enemy to rout but also demonstrated, at long last, the faithlessness of the enemy's so-called British allies. Pulling back from Roche de Bout in five days of dreary march in the rain, managing nevertheless to light up acres of cornfield all the way, Wayne brought his men to the post they'd built so quickly at the abandoned Glaize: Fort Defiance.

Here Wayne wrote to Knox, "with infinite pleasure," to report the victory at Fallen Timbers, which Wayne called, understandably enough, the "brilliant success of the federal army." He praised his men for following orders and for bravery and praised his officers for leadership, even singling out Wilkinson, along with Hamtramck and a few others, for special merit.

Then Wayne's men began hyper-fortifying Defiance in true Mad Anthony style: leveling the ground to give artillery field of fire, digging trenches to prevent surprise, raising the height of the fences. Wayne had received intelligence that the enemy might, in fact, make an effort to regroup and attack him here, in hopes of retaking their towns. Confederation forces had indeed been shadowing his forces back upstream, and he would have loved what he believed would be a more exciting final showdown, right here where they'd sent operations against him for so long. But while bands continued to harass Wayne's army—they ambushed patrols and tried to off small deployments—there was no concerted attack. Indian fighters around Fort Defiance made menacing sounds at night, but sentry duty remained tight, and having experienced a victory, the troops were no longer so easily intimidated. Wayne remained in a state of furious hostility toward his contractors; still, supply was now feasible along the route he'd taken and cut from Greene Ville to the Glaize, and back at Greene Ville supplies were coming up without significant incident all the way from Fort Washington. Wayne controlled the strategic confluence that had once been the Glaize, and he controlled the entire length of the route he'd established in getting there.

Harassment by the enemy nevertheless demonstrated a need to demoralize the confederation into final submission. Leaving Fort Defiance under Major Thomas Hunt, in September Wayne marched the main body of his army southwestward, up the Miami of the Lake, to its source at Kekionga, the original heartland of the Land of the Three Miamis, emotional center of the western Indian confederation. Here in 1791, Josiah Harmar had come from the south, burning fields and dwellings before being forced to withdraw. St. Clair, expecting to build a fort at Kekionga, had never even gotten that far. Wayne had gone much farther, and now he came down on Kekionga from above.

He met no resistance. Arriving on September 17, 1794, and of course immediately fortifying his camp with breastworks, Wayne soon had his men doing at Kekionga what they'd become accustomed to doing everywhere they went: building a fort. This fort would be, the general wrote to Henry Knox, the most important post between the St. Lawrence River and the Gulf of Mexico. He chose a high point facing the confluence of the two rivers forming the headwaters of the Miami of the Lake. Enjoying direct communication with both his rear and his forward posts, this new post at the former Kekionga connected command of Lake Erie to command of the Ohio River. The fort would thus control the future of Indian trade throughout the Land of the Three Miamis and put the entire Northwest under American control. It was by the will of his men, Wayne said, that he named it Fort Wayne.

Having put his name on the enemy's former strategic center, the general dismissed the Kentucky volunteers, with official praise despite the endless irritation they'd caused him; sent messages to the Indians, now camped in impoverished retreat downstream from Fort Miamis, that he would parley for peace and new boundaries; and made plans to leave Hamtramck in charge of Fort Wayne and withdraw the main army to the headquarters at Greene Ville for the winter. There he hoped to gather all the western Indian nations and establish American possession of the West not only in fact but also on paper.

In December 1794, George Washington emerged from the President's House in Philadelphia to observe a strange parade. As crowds mobbed the sidewalks to jeer and gawk, mounted officers marched prisoners, brought over the mountains from western Pennsylvania, through the streets of Philadelphia. These men were trophies of federal victory over the whiskey rebels.

Two years earlier, even while General Wayne was building his army at Fort Fayette in Pittsburgh, an uprising had begun roiling that area. Its sources were in the radical economic populism that everybody in federal government had written and ratified the Constitution to put an end to. Small farmers in the West had long been objecting to eastern landlords' and investors' pull on the region's wealth: the government-connected canal projects launched by Washington and others; governmental delay in pursuing American access to the Mississippi; what western settlers saw as government's failure to protect them from Indian attack. These radicals were rank-and-file veterans of the War of Independence, sent home with nothing when the officers were made federal bondholders, and their communities had long been resisting wealth concentration and trying to get ahead their own way. Western juries refused to convict debtors. Debt prisoners were broken out of jails. Boycotts were enforced against foreclosure sales. Trees were felled to block the steep, narrow passes and keep officialdom out. Militias were formed to kill Indians.

Yet many of these radicals weren't anti-federalist. Many had hoped that national government would foster economic fairness. Hence the explosiveness of their disappointment in Alexander Hamilton's revenue measures, passed by the First Congress.

The crux of those measures was a tax on whiskey, the first federal tax ever laid on a domestic product, earmarked for making regular interest payments—tax free—to the small group of wealthy public bondholders. Whiskey was the small western farmers' only cash crop, hence their only means of gaining incremental profits. Seasonal distilling helped them avoid the debt penury that robbed them of independence and sometimes of land itself, making them tenants of and laborers for big planters, merchants, and speculators, those very bondholders who would benefit from the tax. Yet Hamilton carefully calibrated minutiae in the whiskey tax to favor big distilling and shut down small farming, and while his Jeffersonian opposition in Congress didn't understand those mechanisms or their purposes, ordinary westerners certainly did.

Hamilton and the western radicals understood each other. The tax clamped down hardest at the Ohio headwaters, where the best whiskey was made and radical populism flourished. Hamilton's taking over supply to Wayne's army from Henry Knox played an important role: Hamilton placed whiskey sale to Fort Fayette, an essential service advertised politically as a boon to small western farmers, in the hands of the few, rich locals with connections to Washington and other eastern politicians, those same families who had been sewing up business around the headwaters for years. Hamilton assigned members of one of the biggest planting and distilling families in the region both to collect the tax that directly benefited it and to serve as army whiskey contractors; another family member served as quartermaster in Fort Fayette, buying the product. Hamilton also got Congress to pass a measure for removing anyone accused of nonpayment of the tax all the way over the mountains to Philadelphia for trial. Removal of that kind had long been viewed as the exercise of tyranny.

Each of these stinging measures served as incitement to an uprising. Hamilton labeled the ensuing events "the whiskey insurrection" in order to erase its critique of his economic plan, but the armed militias didn't call themselves whiskey rebels: they called themselves regulators, in the sense of breaking up monopolistic power, and by the summer of 1794 they'd effectively taken over the whole region, tarring and feathering tax collectors, bullying tax-compliant fellow citizens, and coercing regional loyalty to their cause. Marching in military order under veteran Revolutionary leaders, they exchanged gunfire in battle with a federal officer. They marched against Fort Fayette, but they didn't attack it; instead, thousands met late that summer, armed, at a regional congress on a high bank of the Monongahela, where five western counties of Pennsylvania, plus delegations from western Virginia, flew their own regional flag. These radical militias announced that the West was independent of the United States. Sharpshooters, they defied any force to come through the mountain passes to enforce U.S. sovereignty in the West.

So financial investment and U.S. sovereignty in the West had come again under threat. This time the threat came not from the indigenous inhabitants but from American citizens. Washington had told Hamilton that military force against the citizenry must come only as a last resort, and here that resort was.

Yet the army was busy. By the time the rebellion turned to secession, Washington and Knox were urging Wayne to start his march out of Greene Ville, and Washington warned Hamilton that, anyway, if they used regular troops against the citizenry, the anti-army crowd would howl that suppressing the populace was the real purpose of forming a standing army.

What they had to work with was the new Militia Act that Congress had passed in 1792. In contemplation of just such disturbances, the act gave the president the power to call out and federalize state militias to put down insurrection. Hamilton faced little effective opposition in the cabinet: Jefferson had at last resigned his office, and encouraging Knox to request a leave to inspect his troubled Maine investments, Hamilton raised a huge militia from New Jersey and eastern Virginia and Maryland and placed himself at the organizational center of planning for a military operation against western Pennsylvania, managing supply, contracting, recruitment, uniforms, and rendezvous. Rich city bravos, too young to have served in the Revolution and eager for a taste of easy glory, signed up as officers and began squabbling over their ranks and spending heavily on uniforms, swords, and horses. The backdoor draft meanwhile filled out the soldiery with the kinds of insubordinate, ir-regular novices that Washington and Hamilton had always complained about. In the end, they raised about twelve thousand troops, more than double the legal limit of Wayne's regulars, more than had beaten the British at the Battle of Yorktown, to march against American citizens.

The president was to lead this operation personally, and Hamilton wrote anonymously for the papers, too, ginning up a powerful outburst of nationalist fervor. Westerners were soon being denigrated by the eastern public as "white Indians" and worse. Some congressmen would later grouse about all of this, but in the face of popular opinion few were eager to oppose the executive in putting down an insurrection of grubby western settlers.

The administration was meanwhile employing a technique borrowed from its Indian diplomacy: sham negotiations with the rebels to placate Congress, confuse the enemy, and buy time for military buildup. A set of commissioners went west, empowered to give nothing but a promise to hold off invasion under the condition that an overwhelming majority of people in the region expressly submitted to federal authority.

The most militant rebels had already fled the region, and the head-waters citizenry, petrified at the prospect of federal invasion, did offer complete submission. On a day of referendum dictated by the federal commissioners, white adult males throughout the region went to polling places to put their names on a loyalty oath supposed to hold off the in-vasion or, if invasion must come anyway, guarantee the signers' amnesty. But Hamilton and Washington weren't really about to halt the invasion now, regardless of what the populace might agree to. Hamilton was al-ready changing dates on military orders to disguise the buildup's timing and preserve the fiction of good-faith negotiations. At the last minute, he asked Washington for permission to go along, and in September, the commander in chief, mostly riding in a coach, was commanding in the field, with Hamilton back in his Revolutionary role as chief of staff.

Yet having led the army to the steep, remote mountains around the village of Bedford, Pennsylvania, President Washington turned back for the capital. He never, in the end, returned to the headwaters where he'd first seen the great wealth of the West and first made his name, but left the operation to Hamilton and Governor Henry Lee of Virginia. While the president sent them instructions, for the record and from a distance,

against looting and pillaging the poor farms of the region, Hamilton and
Lee came down out of the Alleghenies with astonishing force. The
mask was off. Hamilton was no longer accompanying the mission or
serving as the president's chief of staff. He was in charge.

Subjecting the general public to roundups, rough interrogation, and
indefinite detention, the riled-up officers carried out warrantless, door-
kicking late-night mass arrests of hundreds of people against whom both
Hamilton and Washington knew they had no evidence, in near-total
disregard of the supposed amnesty. Adept in the art of rationale, Hamilton wrote to Washington to justify such measures for the record: as a
lawyer, he noted that any citizen is empowered to arrest a traitor. Meanwhile, he tried to get detainees to name names, less of rebel leaders than
of political enemies he hoped to see hanged on trumped-up charges of
fomenting the rebellion. He'd brought a federal judge along, but per
Washington's orders, as composed by Hamilton, the civil judiciary was
subordinated to military authority, and the judge fully cooperated with
the executive branch.

There wasn't much legal work to do anyway. As Hamilton and
Washington discussed by letter, they were seeking to make intimidating examples, not achieve convictions based on evidence. A gaggle of
detainees was sent eastward over the mountains, in chains and on foot
in the harshest conditions—it was winter now—under an officer known
for taking pleasure in demeaning and abusing prisoners. Hamilton
meanwhile subjected the entire headwaters region to military occupation. Citizens signed loyalty oaths delivered by armed dragoons, and
Hamilton and Lee established, for the foreseeable future, a federal
soldiery at Pittsburgh and in towns nearby.

The skinny, bedraggled prisoners in the parade the president was
watching in Philadelphia that December day hadn't been indicted,
in most cases, for a crime. None had been convicted of anything.
Indeed, only three of these captives would ever be convicted. Even
eastern juries could perceive the lack of evidence, and adding to the
public's sense of presidential largesse, Washington would pardon those
few convicts. Indictments and convictions were beside the point.
This parade was the point. Blame for the operation's extremity—really,
its total unconstitutionality—would forever rest on Hamilton, not
Washington.

It was when he'd been with Hamilton on the march that Washington had received news of Wayne's victory at Fallen Timbers. With that victory over the western Indian confederation, and now with the suppression of western Pennsylvania, there could be no doubt in the American public mind, or the mind of the world, that the United States possessed the West. And Wayne's victory had been achieved by a regular, federally organized army. It thus represented a world-changing success for the nation and for Washington.

He'd long been hoping to sell much of his western properties and gain the rewards, so long obstructed and deferred, of a lifelong investment amounting to decades of complicated headaches. Management at a distance, in letter after letter, both of his western claims and of Mount Vernon, took up many hours during the presidency and contributed to Washington's often evincing stoic, barely contained beleaguerment. He'd begun speculating in the West in his energetic teens. Now his energy, hearing, and memory were flagging. Together, Wayne's march and the suppression of western Pennsylvania not only established U.S. sovereignty west of the Alleghenies and in the Northwest Territory but also increased the value of Washington's western land portfolio by about 50 percent.

He rarely showed emotion, of course, and Philadelphians watching the president stand outside his house had come to project on the great man whatever they imagined he might be feeling. Still, the story goes that on the day of the prisoner parade in Philadelphia, the public saw a look of immense, calm satisfaction pass over the face of the American Cincinnatus. He was halfway through his second term. Setting a tradition unbroken until 1940, and later enshrined in law, he wouldn't accept a third. He returned to his farm.

In January 1795, an unsettling rumor came to Alexander McKee in Detroit. He'd been keeping the faith all fall and winter. No sooner had the Battle of Fallen Timbers ended than McKee began trying to stop members of the western Indian confederation from even thinking about breaking away and making deals with the Americans. With more than twenty-five hundred Indians encamped as refugees downstream from Fort Miamis, their homes and cornfields burned, their strategic positions captured, and winter yet again holding them in its grip, McKee had been in ceaseless movement between Fort Detroit, the new Indian camps, and Fort Miamis. He promised the refugees from the Glaize British provisions, tried to talk confederation leadership out of migrating to Spanish territory, hectored his superiors for supplies and support.

Much of British officialdom didn't share McKee's concern for the Indians. After Fallen Timbers, many officers were taking the position that the Indians had given up any claims to reliability. They'd only lost about forty men, yet they seemed abruptly washed up, Colonel England complained after the battle. All he took away from the situation to which the great western confederation had been reduced, in part by his refusal to provide artillery, in part by the lockout from Fort Miamis, was a notion that Indians could no longer be depended on to defend Fort Detroit against Americans.

But McKee's best sponsor, John Simcoe, still believed in the old plan. The way Simcoe had reported Fallen Timbers to his bosses, Wayne had retreated upstream from Fort Miamis, pursued by the Indians. In late September, the governor showed up at the fort, having again sailed across Lake Erie from Fort Niagara. Indians lined the banks of the Miami of the Lake to greet him. He went to Fallen Timbers to inspect the battlefield. He called a big meeting near the Erie mouth of the Detroit River. The purpose was to revive the Indians' spirits and get them focused on attacking Wayne, and Simcoe had even brought Joseph Brant west, yet again, hoping he might put the confederation back on a war footing, but Brant's relationships on all sides had crumbled. The Mohawk had decided at the last minute to bring Six Nations fighters to aid the confederation against the last leg of Wayne's march, but he'd been too late. And Brant still believed that McKee had egged the Indians on to a showdown without getting them the support they'd needed.

Now Brant demanded publicly of Simcoe, in full conference at the Detroit River mouth, what Little Turtle had demanded before Fallen Timbers: a commitment of artillery and men. Simcoe couldn't respond. The governor's dream was dying at last. He would never reestablish

British control of the Northwest and upstate New York, via Indian proxy, let alone retake the city of New York or threaten Philadelphia. He sailed for Niagara, already angry and discouraged enough, and en route he took delivery of some decisive dispatches from Whitehall.

Now it really was all over. The Jay Treaty was soon to be signed, resolving outstanding disputes between Great Britain and the United States. The lake forts would be evacuated.

So John Simcoe turned, if not on a dime, then with impressive dispatch. Lord Dorchester, he began to allege, had really been the driving force behind the building of Fort Miamis and the warlike efforts of the summer of 1794. Whitehall had begun an investigation of Dorchester's behavior, leading to an official censure, and Simcoe said that while he'd been reluctant to engage in such aggressive operations in the West, he'd had no choice about following his boss's orders. Meanwhile, he tried to keep news of the Jay Treaty from the Indians camped below Fort Miamis.

Blue Jacket soon knew better. In October, only weeks after Simcoe sailed away, members of the Indian confederation made direct communication with Wayne at Greene Ville, seeking parley. The Sandusky Wyandot were the first to break from the confederation's unity against peace, when an agent wrote to Wayne inquiring on the Wyandot's behalf about American terms for peace, and four Wyandot fighters brought that letter personally to Greene Ville.

The shift toward Wayne was far from unanimous. Each nation, branch, and family began splitting over this dire issue of making peace with the United States. At first the militant Shawnee seemed, as usual, the toughest holdouts. The towering Captain Johnny was dead set against submission. Yet when the Wyandot and others, returning from Greene Ville to the cold and hungry camps, told of good treatment by Wayne, attrition more than argument began making the point. Soon whole groups were surreptitiously leaving the camps every day to travel to Greene Ville and discuss preliminaries with Wayne for a big summer meeting, already set for mid-June 1795. In January, leaders of many Chippewa, Ottawa, Potawatomie, Sauk, and Miami signed, at Greene Ville, preliminary documents acknowledging that the negotiations set for June would have a basis in boundaries set out in the Fort Harmar Treaty and agreeing to cease all hostilities and return all prisoners.

Still, the most famous leaders were hanging back. Then things changed. The rumor Alexander McKee heard in Detroit late in January devastated his last hopes, and he hurried down to the Indian camp to stop it from coming true. Too late: Blue Jacket himself had left for Greene Ville, with a Shawnee retinue, and in a hurry, hoping to avoid any confrontation with McKee. Blue Jacket had said he was going only to talk prisoner exchange with Wayne, but McKee, facing the flight of a fellow Shawnee who had served as the most charismatic force for pan-Indian unity, knew what was happening.

Like McKee himself many years earlier, Blue Jacket was making a life-changing decision. He was switching sides. That made him, in McKee's terms, a turncoat. At Detroit, McKee's son, Thomas, exploded at the news, threatened to kill Blue Jacket, and threw a pair of gold epaulets, intended as a gift to the Shawnee leader, into the fire.

Alexander McKee, in line to be promoted to the position of deputy superintendent of Indian affairs, came down with rheumatic fever that spring and went out of commission for a long time. Fever was raging as well through the garrison at Fort Miamis in which McKee and Simcoe had placed such hopes; anyway that fort was preparing for evacuation. Detroit, a scene of massive preparations for British exit, and thus of Indian and loyalist bitterness and privation, began a descent into anarchy. At Niagara, Elizabeth Simcoe fell ill to the point of wasting away, and John Simcoe, sick too, became barely able to function; he requested a leave to take his family back to London. With Lord Dorchester facing recall in the wake of his censure, and even, as a sop to American feeling, George Hammond, the British minister to the United States, scheduled for replacement, all of the British promoters of Indian rights, never very reliable anyway, were down and out.

On February 7, 1795, with his usual flair, Blue Jacket made an entrance into the fort at Greene Ville. Having sent a small party ahead with a flag of truce, he'd traveled first to Fort Defiance with twenty Shawnee and Delaware, among them some famous leaders, as well as his sister. Ostensibly, the mission was to deliver four white prisoners to Defiance, but after being welcomed there, Blue Jacket got the commander Major Hunt to assign him an escort of twenty soldiers for a trip to see Wayne.

The famous Shawnee leader, known to American troops as the architect of the confederation and a destroyer of St. Clair's army, entered Greene Ville wearing a regimental British red coat with gold epaulets, a fine wool shirt, and all the usual accoutrements, with his sister beside him also dressed to the nines, attended by the party of Indian dignitaries and the twenty soldiers from Fort Defiance. Anthony Wayne greeted Blue Jacket in full dress uniform with sword. He had his men on the sharp, clean display that he always set such store by.

Amid polite expression of mutual regard, discussion between these two enemies now went quickly. Wayne made clear that the basis of any peace would be the terms of the Fort Harmar Treaty. Blue Jacket attested to the faithlessness of the British and expressed willingness to abide by a new boundary line based on those terms.

While this was obviously a surrender, Blue Jacket was eager to construe his new relationship with Wayne in terms of realignment. He therefore showed Wayne the commission issued, signed, and sealed by the British superintendent of Indian affairs in 1784, naming Blue Jacket an official war leader under British authorization. Wayne, bemused by what he took to be a savage's naive faith in a silly piece of paper, showed Blue Jacket an example of a highly decorative American commission, on parchment, not, like the British version, on paper. Blue Jacket asked to receive one in June as part of the new treaty.

Wayne wouldn't have viewed his own commission in light of a superstition. The Shawnee leader was simply making the switch from British to American connection official. Wayne agreed to issue him an American commission, and on February 14 Blue Jacket started back for the camp downstream from Fort Miamis. Formerly the most militant of militants, rejecting any thought of seeking peace, and even after the failure to take Fort Recovery expressing ever-greater certainty of victory, Blue Jacket now intended to sway as many holdouts as possible to attend the June meeting and sign Wayne's new treaty. He'd proven expert at persuading Indians far and wide to gather and fight. In the spring of 1795, he would use those skills to galvanize Indian submission to the Americans.

❧⸻❧

Wayne's respectful dealings with Blue Jacket reflected the approach he was adopting for the negotiations scheduled for June. In tone, it was to be the exact opposite of the dictatorial approach taken earlier by his old nemesis Arthur St. Clair. The Indians had viewed St. Clair and the others as presuming victory without winning it. Having beaten his enemy in the field, Wayne saw no need to humiliate his enemy verbally: he knew the enemy acknowledged him as victor. Any diminishment of his forces by a faithless Congress, Wayne worried daily, might still turn things around—he'd been doing his usual thundering on paper at Knox about that—yet as Indian delegations came piecemeal into Greene Ville to make overtures, he could see that the confederation was broken.

Taking a respectful tone allowed the general to be perfectly blunt, with all of the Indian leaders who reached out to him, about the terms for peace: an end to all attacks; acceptance of U.S. sovereignty in the Northwest Territory; a new boundary for western Indian reserve, based on the Fort Harmar accords. Yet he also honored and feted his former enemies, fed them, offered warm clothing for themselves and their families. He promised the Delaware that he would build a fort to protect them. He planned to allow Glaize Indians to replant some corn in their old fields. Some of the more important Indian leaders would need houses, cash, commissions. Wayne knew he needed to secure not only submission but also a sense of approval, even if both sides remained guarded.

In this effort, he had a new boss and collaborator. Henry Knox resigned his cabinet position in early January and moved his family to his big house on the remote Maine coast. Never a believer in the importance of the West, in his final report to the president regarding Indian affairs, Knox described the years leading up to Wayne's victory at Fallen Timbers as a series of unethical incursions by whites onto sovereign Indian land. The West, according to Knox, was nothing but a mess: Indians responded violently to white encroachments; whites, for the most part worse, in Knox's terms, than Indians, responded to the responses; all was forever bloody. Of course it was good that Wayne had won—Knox believed firmly in the regular army—but ultimately he feared the victory would become pointless. This war against Indians, doing more harm to the Native people, he said, than anything ever perpetrated by the Spanish in Mexico or Peru, could only degrade the American people themselves.

The only practical solution for the West that Knox could therefore recommend, on departure from office, was the establishment of a string of forts, filled with regular army empowered to sit not on the Indians but on the whites, meting out harsh military justice to any white person who broke any law in the Northwest Territory. With that somewhat startling renunciation of the policy he'd been carrying out for years, Washington's most loyal subordinate left public office.

The new secretary of war was Timothy Pickering. A Massachusetts man like Knox, and politically a creature of Hamilton, Pickering had given Elizabeth Simcoe a chowder recipe when serving as one of the commissioners stuck at Niagara and now served as Wayne's main channel of communication with the president's policy. The communication was mutually sympathetic. Arguing strenuously yet diplomatically with Congress for maintaining troop strength, and using a letter from Wayne as evidence of necessity, Pickering kept Wayne's army at full force.

Now Pickering in Philadelphia and Wayne on the ground began planning for the June meeting. They had a new aim. Deploying the friendly, respectful approach that Wayne was taking with the Indians, they hoped to expand the Indians' land cessions well beyond what had been set out in the Fort Harmar Treaty. In devising this demand for even more land, Pickering showed a Hamiltonian talent for rationale. Wayne's victory, he noted, had altered the circumstances since Fort Harmar. The defeated confederation must compensate the Americans for blood and treasure expended in achieving that victory by giving up all land from the mouth of the Cuyahoga at Lake Erie to the mouth of the Great Miami at the Ohio. This new line would not only push the Indians even farther westward but also, within land reserved for Indians, include exceptions chopped out for white settlement, as well as a major federal corridor through the whole reservation, giving easy access to U.S. authority.

In considering how to pay for this great shift of western Indians westward, Pickering again showed shrewd judgment. Where Wayne, with characteristic brusqueness, had asked for what he called trinkets with which to placate and bedazzle the natives, Pickering authorized $25,000 to be spent on what the Indians really needed: huge numbers of shirts, cloth, axes, knives, wire, blankets, shoes, thread, thimbles, and so on. Once a treaty was arrived at, $10,000 more in merchandise was to be paid, per year. That payment was to be made to the confederation as a

whole. Pickering and Wayne had abandoned the old insistence on dealing with the nations individually, an approach that had insulted Indian
unity to no good end. Dealing with confederation leaders on behalf of
all of the nations would more efficiently reduce the members' ability
to resist. Pickering had calculated the matter closely. The amount of
the annual payment, he figured, would be just enough to keep the western Indians, as a whole, forever dependent.

Pickering also coached Wayne in bringing off the trickiest part of
this process: telling the gathered nations that they must agree to this
deal while maintaining a fiction that it was voluntary. To achieve this
potentially self-contradictory aim, Pickering wanted Wayne to explicitly
renounce the earlier U.S. claim, based on the Peace of Paris of 1783,
that the United States had sovereignty over Indian land. According to
Pickering, that claim, advanced in the 1780s by Richard Butler, George
Rogers Clark, and other commissioners, and further advanced by St. Clair
even when offering to buy the land in the Fort Harmar Treaty, had inspired the Indians to form and grow their confederation and ally with
Britain. The construction could thus not be over-renounced. At the
same time, Wayne was to maintain the underlying, preemptive right of
the United States to all of the land that the Indians must now cede.

Some delicacy, Pickering admitted, might be needed in addressing
this issue. The Indians might well ask, if the land really was theirs, why
they couldn't decline to sell it. Denial of American coercion, assertion
of Indian consent—here's where the veil had always worn the thinnest.
Knox, never able to think past the contradiction, had just gone ahead
and carried out policy, but Pickering had a solution, Hamiltonian in its
ingenuity. Collective federal control of western land had the purpose,
Pickering said, of protecting the Indians from efforts by nefarious individuals to take it from them. He suggested Wayne try out that line of
thought on the gathered nations.

Not until June 23, 1795, did Little Turtle arrive at Greene Ville, accompanied by a retinue. Of the famous confederation leaders, he alone had
made no direct overtures or held any preliminary meetings with Anthony
Wayne. He'd signed no papers, acknowledged no terms for peace.

Blue Jacket had meanwhile been working hard, all spring and into the summer, to bring about wholesale acceptance of the new terms, and he'd had much success, but it wasn't total. While many Shawnee, Miami, and Delaware leaders agreed to abide by the preliminary articles for peace, and in fact sincerely intended to do so, Blue Jacket could get only about two hundred Shawnee to commit to appearing at Greene Ville for the conference. And while many of the Miami branches had come on board with Blue Jacket in submission to Wayne, Little Turtle himself was reserving judgment.

Little Turtle's holdout wasn't military. Nobody had less faith in a revived Indian assault on Wayne's army. He'd warned the rest of the confederation leadership, when Blue Jacket was still at his most militant, that Wayne didn't sleep; that the British army didn't live up to promises; that no victor remains forever victorious. Derided by Blue Jacket as a weakling and even a traitor, Little Turtle had relinquished strategic leadership in advance of Fallen Timbers yet remained a war leader in that battle, and he'd seen all of his predictions come miserably true. The United States had indeed regrouped after its devastating defeat. Wayne was a general of another order than St. Clair. American soldiers had learned how to hold ground and advance. British officers locked the fleeing Indians out of Fort Miamis and were now evacuating the lake forts. Little Turtle and his people had spent a hungry, cold winter.

The Miami leader maintained his philosophy. Yet again resisting Blue Jacket, but now from the opposite angle, he kept his eye on Anthony Wayne. The Miami leader's arrival at Greene Ville in late June presaged another showdown. It wouldn't be military this time. Yet it would put Wayne to a new test.

With the slow arrival at Greene Ville of the various nations, Wayne kept having to postpone the meeting. He hosted the delegations nicely, holding ceremonies and giving them places to sleep in the fort's outer redoubts, but he was concerned about Blue Jacket. All-important to concerted Indian submission, the man hadn't shown up yet. Some of the Potawatomie, far from home, were already expressing boredom and a yearning to leave, and now even Little Turtle had arrived. Blue Jacket did finally appear at Fort Recovery, on June 29, and sent messages to Wayne at Greene Ville assuring him of attendance. Then he left to round up further attendees. On July 15, Wayne decided he had to begin treaty discussions without Blue Jacket.

As he opened proceedings, the general had a new role to play, in certain ways a more difficult role for Anthony Wayne than leading a long march into Indian country. While he'd proved himself beyond any doubt the first U.S. army man par excellence, the current task demanded the very skills he'd so visibly lacked in civilian life: consistency, delicacy, credibility. He'd beaten the Indians, but to shore up the confidence of Congress and the American people, things had to go smoothly here. And his gout had worsened.

Yet Wayne had become more sure of success than even Pickering or the president seemed to be. Pickering had passed on the president's express warning, again, to beware surprise: the Indians might be at Greene Ville to attack. Wayne was sure they weren't. He knew the old enemy better now than any American in Philadelphia could; anyway, in the unlikely event that an attack was planned, the general reassured Pickering, the redoubts where he'd given the Indians sleeping quarters were always under the guns of the fort's bastions.

He felt no physical exposure to worry about. The diplomacy necessary to political success—that was another thing.

After engaging in the usual ceremonial smoking and acceptance of beads, Wayne made his first move. Referring to himself not as father but as brother to the Indians, he invoked the Fort Harmar Treaty, calling it an equitable agreement, satisfactory to all parties at the time, and the natural basis for any future peace. Giving the Indians a few days to chew on that, he put the meeting in recess.

Wayne's calling the Fort Harmar Treaty generally satisfactory couldn't possibly resonate with his auditors. Their war with the United States had been precisely over the illegitimacy of that treaty. It was harsh reality, not any change of position on the Fort Harmar accords, that had brought the defeated nations to Greene Ville. Partly thanks to Blue Jacket's leadership, yet also for many reasons of their own, all of the gathered leaders were ready to agree to whatever Wayne would propose. All were ready, as well, to overlook any absurdity in the rationale.

All but Little Turtle. When the meeting resumed on July 18, the

Miami war leader rose to object to Wayne's characterization of the Fort Harmar Treaty.

He reminded Wayne that most of the Miami people, and certainly Little Turtle himself, had boycotted the Fort Harmar negotiations, which had involved mainly America-aligned Seneca, not the western Indians whose lands the treaty had "disposed of without our knowledge or consent," as Little Turtle noted. Obviously, only the Miami could cede Miami land.

He wasn't questioning Wayne's military superiority. He was questioning Wayne's facts, Wayne's narrative, and Wayne's credibility. An earlier Anthony Wayne might have exploded into a series of thundering threats. Wayne the conqueror just called another recess.

On July 23, the conference resumed. Blue Jacket had finally arrived: now he addressed the nations, praising Wayne and those willing to make a deal with Wayne. Then Wayne resumed his speech. Having noted that while the United States had already paid the western Indians twice for their land, such was the magnanimity of the American people that they were willing to pay again, he turned to Little Turtle's objections. No, Wayne argued, the Miami had no exclusive claim to the land that Little Turtle referred to. At least six other nations also claimed it, and remains of forts there suggested that Miami forefathers had long since sold the land to Europeans. Wayne's men had discovered, for instance, the ruin of an old French fort on the Great Miami.

Accusing Little Turtle of "bad grace" in defeat, Wayne then resorted to the oldest of American arguments, supposedly long since abandoned. He pulled out copies of both the Peace of Paris and the Jay Treaty—the latter not yet ratified—and presented them as proof that the Indians' former "fathers," the British, defeated by the United States, had forfeited the Indians' land. This assertion contradicted Pickering's even less logical official line, that the Indians were now required to freely cede their land. But Wayne, in piling on this way, was pretty sure that few of the other leaders had much interest in Little Turtle's critique. Because the Miami people no longer had any real claim to the land in question, Wayne announced, the United States could have taken it all. In its benevolence, the United States had chosen not to. Then he ordered a double ration of rum for the attendees and closed the day's proceedings.

Little Turtle didn't stop objecting, but just as on the eve of Fallen Timbers, his objections didn't matter. In succeeding sessions, Wayne presented the attendees with the new, farther-western boundary line, plus the exceptions for white settlement and federal access within the reservation, thus taking far more than St. Clair had tried to take at Fort Harmar, and still the attendees not only expressed compliance but also played along with the narrative, fulsomely praising Wayne's fairness.

On July 29, Little Turtle pushed back one last time. He noted that the hunting ground left to his people would be inadequate and again denied the validity of Wayne's account of events in the region. For one thing, the ruin of the old fort on the Miami that Wayne had mentioned "was not a French fort, brother," Little Turtle said, "it was a fort built by me."

That's how the translator rendered it on the scene. Little Turtle really meant that his father had built it, or that his people had, or that they'd permitted the French to build it, back in the days when European powers competed for Indian favor in the fur trade. The point was that Wayne's history, serving as a cover for outright coercion, was bunk. Little Turtle then proposed a compromise boundary, farther east.

Wayne wasn't having it. He knew there was no need for compromise. All of the other leaders were submitting, and he was more or less done here. All he had to do was keep his cool, go on putting forth an argument that the leaders could pretend to buy, and remain firm on the boundaries.

Wayne announced that the other leaders' decision should be reason enough for Little Turtle to submit too. He said he would reward those who had submitted early, like the Wyandot, and punish Little Turtle's recalcitrance by giving his people a place with a crooked boundary, conducive to all kinds of problems. The $8,000 annually—Pickering had reduced it at the last minute—should be more than adequate to compensate for any supposed hunting losses.

Wayne then preempted further discussion by calling for a voice vote on the treaty terms. The nations, polled individually, made it unanimous for submission, with Little Turtle abstaining. On August 3, everybody but Little Turtle put a mark on a drawn-up document. It was over. Wayne,

aided by the Indians' own realpolitik, had played his new role with
aplomb.

On August 12, Wayne and Little Turtle had a private meeting. The
Miami leader's tragic sense had always made him practical. He knew
better than anybody else that he couldn't realistically remain the only
holdout.

Still, he told Wayne yet again that he could never approve of the
treaty terms. He said that it was his duty to speak the truth on behalf of
his people, and he hoped the United States wouldn't look on him with
disdain for doing so.

As the last to sign it, Little Turtle told Wayne, he'd be the last to
break it. He put his mark on the treaty.

That's one way of looking at what Blue Jacket and Little Turtle did at
Greene Ville in the summer of 1795. There's no good way to look at it,
because it was during and after those proceedings that the controversy
between Blue Jacket and Little Turtle really took off. The document
that became known as the Greeneville Treaty may be the most decisive
treaty ever made between the United States and indigenous people in
North America. Its proceedings launched what would become known
as "the treaty period," beginning a new relationship between the United
States and the first nations of the continent, prevailing throughout a
succeeding century of white expansion.

Yet accounts of the proceedings that created the document have been
infected, to the point of manifest distortion, by the biases of the partisans
of Blue Jacket and Little Turtle. Historians on one team have called the
other team's protagonist a sellout, Little Turtle presumably for advising
the confederation leadership to seek peace while Wayne was on the
march, Blue Jacket presumably for organizing compliance with Wayne
after Fallen Timbers. Each side emphasizes the degree to which the
other's protagonist accepted cash payments and related inducements—
both men did so—while de-emphasizing its own man's self-interest in

taking them. Each camp seems to want its hero to have been at once the most fearsome and powerful leader of the confederation; the first to face reality, at precisely the right moment to face it, and seek peace with Wayne; the less corruptible and more ethical person; and the shrewder negotiator. Sometimes instead of openly attacking the other's favorite, each side writes him out of the narrative, making Blue Jacket or Little Turtle just another chief hanging around the edges while the real man does his work. Little Turtle's people can thus characterize Blue Jacket as disastrously hotheaded, and the author of what is sometimes called the confederation's most decisive turn toward failure, the effort to take Fort Recovery, and yet somehow at the same time not especially significant. Blue Jacket's people manage to accuse Little Turtle of having caused the collapse of the confederation by urging peace with Wayne before Fallen Timbers, even while treating him as a sideshow to the main drama in which Blue Jacket plays the hero.

Most Americans are in neither camp, of course. Even those interested in the nation's early history haven't heard much about Blue Jacket and Little Turtle. Or about dozens of other confederation leaders, perhaps equally significant; or about the fighters of many nations and branches, unnamed in the historical record; or about the American officers and soldiers, also unrecognized by history, who took part in the war that turned such a big national wheel. This blank spot in America's public history isn't just any blank spot. Together Blue Jacket and Little Turtle participated in leading the only confederation that had a chance of obstructing the westward expansion of the United States; they thus came close to damaging the whole American project in its fragile infancy, perhaps fatally. Little Turtle was cursed with the ability to imagine something he found painful, which came true: the confederation's victory over Arthur St. Clair's troops on the upper Wabash is the worst defeat the United States ever suffered at Indian hands, the high-water mark in resistance to white expansion. No comparable Indian victory would follow. When the Shawnee Tecumseh led a renewed resistance in 1809, and gained renewed British military support in 1811 and 1812, he won no battle against the United States.

Yet Tecumseh remains far better known than Blue Jacket and Little Turtle. The victory of Sitting Bull and the Sioux over General George Custer's Seventh U.S. Cavalry at the Little Bighorn in 1876 involved

about three hundred American casualties, less than a third of those in
the victory over St. Clair, and Sitting Bull's victory caused no fundamental change in American life, as Little Turtle and Blue Jacket's victory
did, and yet the Battle of the Little Bighorn is far better known than the
confederation's victory over St. Clair or Wayne's success at Fallen Timbers,
as are the Plains wars generally. That the more decisive war, and thus
the more important people, has lapsed into obscurity points to a vacancy
in American memory when it comes to what is perhaps the longest-
lasting legacy of George Washington's career, and to the political, moral,
and existential burden his career, and its national indispensability, will
forever carry. That legacy is the formation of a permanent military
establishment, via the conquest of indigenous people, in pursuit of the
industrial and imperial power that, with victory in its first war, the United
States did go on to achieve.

As for America's national military establishment, first created during
the war with the western Indian confederation, it was to have a bumpy
and veering future. Its existence, however, would never again be seriously threatened. Resorting mainly to his own towering will—his worst
enemy during his civilian enterprises—Anthony Wayne had formed the
first army from nearly nothing, led it to decisive victory over the Indians
of the Northwest Territory, and forced them to agree, after more than
forty years, that Americans possessed the old Ohio and Illinois Countries. From the bitterest failure that a hero of the Revolution can be
imagined experiencing, Mad Anthony became in many obvious ways the
author of the United States of America as a military power, from which
much, in the future not only of North America but also of the rest of
the world, would follow. That decisive phase came to its climax with
Little Turtle's signing the Greeneville Treaty.

In a larger sense, the formation of a regular American army under
direct federal control represented the satisfaction of George Washington's and the other nationalists' long-standing desire, going back to the
Revolution, to create a military establishment that would gain the former colonies what all nations enjoy, perhaps by definition, at least at the
time of the American founding: wealth in legitimate military power,

military power in concentrated wealth. By the time Wayne got signatures on the Greeneville Treaty, America possessed not only a regular
army but also national naval operations. Thanks to Wayne's operations
against the Indians and to those anti-British coastal-defense measures,
pushed through Congress before ratification of the Jay Treaty, an administrative network had come into being, by 1795, of a size and complexity
unimaginable by anyone assessing the United States' military capabilities only five years earlier. Strings of forts, supported by complicated
supply networks run out of the War Office in Philadelphia, stretched
from the seaboard to the lakes and along all the major western rivers.
The bureaucracy, as well as the force itself, was in place.

Not only astonishing, the speed and size of that military bureaucracy: horrifying, to the many legislators who had long opposed such
institutions for America. The executive branch had dragged them step
by step toward a result they hated. Every incremental development
that made the military more regular and more federal also made it more
potentially permanent, yet each development came not from consensus,
determining that the nation needed a professional military after all, but
because one horrific emergency after another during the war for the
Northwest called for urgent response, politically inexpedient to refuse.
At every turn and to every degree, Washington had carried out the plan
he'd commenced after the destruction of St. Clair's army: tightening
the screws that made it impossible for the anti-army congressmen to
resist.

But what now? If those steps had really come only from necessity, the
army could no longer be called necessary. Wayne had gained signatures
on the Treaty of Greeneville. The U.S. Public Land Survey was moving
freely through the Northwest Territory. Development could boom on
great western tracts. The Jay Treaty, though abominated by anti-federalists
as truckling, dissolved any immediate threat of war with Britain. The
legislators had been told that the military buildup had represented a
series of emergency measures. If the emergency was over, why field an
army, except as an excuse for enhancing executive power?

To James Madison, more and more a leader of the Jeffersonian opposition party now calling itself Republican, the whole buildup had
amounted to nothing more than a "game behind the curtain . . . the old
trick of turning every contingency into a resource for accumulating

force in the government." Yet Madison was for it before he was against it. He'd introduced the regular-army bill in the House in 1792, based on the need for invasion of Indian country. Now he was among those hottest to reduce, at least, the army's size.

To the pro-army contingent, Madison and the anti-army faction were at best paranoid—there was no real threat of military suppression of the citizenry—and impractical: it's easier to have an army ready in peace than to build one from scratch under threat. It was clear to the pro-army faction too that keeping the West under control required full strength.

In the face of such arguments, the Republicans began calling the Federalist Party militarist: pursuing not national strength but power in government via military buildup. This division in the nation's elite was becoming scabrous.

Division rose to a crisis following Washington's retirement. In what became known as the Quasi-war with France, a group of Federalists led by Hamilton proved themselves militarists indeed. Hamilton was out of office by then, yet hardly retired. His men, including Pickering, formed the cabinet of President John Adams and worked, under Hamilton's direction, against the president at every turn. Adams's Federalism at times seemed a party of one, with the president trying nearly alone, and without much success, to leaven high finance with touches of agrarianism. Hamilton's Federalism, by contrast, represented an effort to perfect the concentrations of economic and military power begun under Washington. The two chief men of the party thus came at odds and sought to destroy not the Republican opposition but each other.

The creative part of Hamilton's career was over, and now his inveterate martial enthusiasm knew no bounds. Inspired by the suppression of western Pennsylvania in 1794, he began longing, among other things, to put the whole state of Virginia to a military test, as he put it, and as tensions with France developed in 1798 over the old war debt to the French and French privateers' attacks on American shipping, Hamilton wanted to push it to a full-on war.

Hamilton and his camp had begun dismissing the army formed by Wayne as "the old army," a mere "frontier constabulary." What Hamilton called the New Army would be the real thing, taking U.S. power to the next level by fighting a great European power. France now seemed to be providing the right enemy. Dispensing with Washingtonian step-by-step patience, so politically effective in building Wayne's army, the Hamiltonian Federalists in Congress managed to expand the naval budget tenfold in one year, quadruple the army's infantry regiments, and sextuple the cavalry. That swelling of military operations and funding, far beyond any necessary response to a visible threat, made military establishment seem the sole, overwhelming purpose of national government. The Republicans made gains from the public reaction.

The Federalists' preparations for the supposed French war meanwhile began breaking down in a squabble over rank. Trying to ensure the war's occurrence, Hamilton urged President Washington out of retirement to put a beloved face on it as commander. Hamilton naturally expected to be second-in-command and actually run the New Army, but Washington had the feelings of Knox and other veteran officers to consider, and Adams wanted nothing now but to squelch Hamilton. When Hamilton's men in the cabinet got Hamilton to the top of the officer list anyway, Adams left town, pretending he'd forgotten to sign the officers' commissions, and from his home in Massachusetts the president now tried to defy his cabinet by placing Hamilton below Knox. Hamilton refused to serve in such a capacity. Washington, bombarded by appeals from the Hamiltonians, threatened to walk out too, humiliating Adams. Adams had to back off, but he backed all the way over to the Republicans he so despised. He began calling the army unnecessary, the war with France a chimera.

Then Adams did the one thing he could, as executive, do. He made a deal with France for peace. That frustrated Hamilton by denying him the big foreign war he'd been so gung ho to fight.

That was it for the Federalist Party. In 1800, the Republicans, with an anti-army, pro-militia ideology, won the presidency and both houses of Congress.

Yet it was during Thomas Jefferson's presidency that the national military establishment, as created by Washington, Hamilton, Knox, Wayne, and their allies in Congress, came into its own. While often described as an irony, intertwined projects of expanding the nation and solidifying the army may represent the apotheosis of Jeffersonian politics.

Even before taking power, the Republicans had realized that militia couldn't fight wars. While Federalists had always said that too, it was the acquiescence of Republicans that made the regular army a done deal: dissent from the army's existence had now come to an end. A famous objective correlative, the officer training academy that President Jefferson established at West Point in 1802, reflected this tacit Republican acceptance of permanent regular army.

Jefferson himself reconciled the apparent contradiction by drawing on his fantastical mode. Militia, he mused, might now be revived and made a national force. Then, should an invasion occur, regulars could relieve the militiamen. He wanted, that is, professional soldiers. But he wanted them to form the reserve. That's Jefferson.

While that imagined invasion didn't occur, national military action had to go on anyway. The army solidified not in overweening Hamiltonian displays of aggression but in the way it had begun: preventing resistance by people who lived in places where the United States declared itself newly sovereign. Not long after the Revolution, Jefferson had asked George Rogers Clark if he'd like to lead a mission to explore all the way to the western end of the continent. As president, Jefferson doubled the nation's territorial size by buying 530,000 acres across the Mississippi from France, which had gained the land in a treaty with Spain and now flipped it. Clark was no longer a viable choice for the expedition: he'd fallen into disgrace for collaborating with France in a private military scheme to end Spanish control of the Mississippi. Once the biggest landowner in the Northwest Territory, he'd also fallen into debt, drunkenness, near landlessness. Jefferson turned instead to Clark's younger brother, asking William Clark to join Meriwether Lewis in an expedition to explore what was now known as the Louisiana Purchase. Jefferson's empire of liberty was becoming a reality.

That empire required forms of military action that Jeffersonians couldn't, given their precepts, construe as conquest. With forts going up on the other side of the Mississippi, a rhetorical distinction emerged between the "standing army," still theoretically hateful, and a "frontier constabulary," what Hamilton had denigrated but Republicans cherished, innocuous to Republican fears of tyranny. On both sides of the big river, "defense" became the word American authorities now used for taking ground, making settlements, intimidating European powers, and pacifying indigenous inhabitants. To all of those ends, a regular army was obviously needed. It was to be modest yet permanent, even in what this ethos defined as peacetime, and expansible in a pinch by recruitment of volunteer citizen soldiers, with the whole thing managed not at the state but at the federal level. It was to be a professional national army.

So while he couldn't have envisioned U.S. bases bigger than cities one day girdling the globe, it was Thomas Jefferson who made the American military permanent and construed it as a peacekeeping force enabling beneficent projects. President Washington had federalized state militias in response to the Whiskey Rebellion, and that function of militia would one day be modernized and formalized in the National Guard; the regular army might forever be amplified, when necessary, by call-ups and drafts. But the state system would never have any officially central role as the nation's fighting force, and regular forces, of varying sizes and structures, would be permanent.

In 1812, Jefferson's successor, Madison, engaged, with Jefferson's approval—and with the out-of-power Federalists suddenly going antiwar—in a war of choice with England. Tecumseh's coinciding effort to revive the Indian confederation gave new explicitness to an idea that Jefferson had been harboring at least since 1776. By 1812, he'd long been trying to get the Indians on the civilization-assimilation plan, and in that context, taking their land was seen as good for them, because too much land encouraged hunting, not farming. Given their perennial recalcitrance, however, as now demonstrated by Tecumseh, Jefferson determined that the only humane way to pacify, civilize, and assimilate the treaty Indians might be to move them across the Mississippi, for their own good, as he wrote to William Henry Harrison in 1813.

Andrew Jackson possessed enough blameworthy qualities to fill a demonology, and great relish is often taken, and maybe some anodyne achieved, by placing blame solely on him for the crime against humanity that is Indian removal. Yet the sources of Jackson's policy lie in urges, at once territorial and military, that were inherent in creating the American nation. From Washington's claims of desiring only peace and no Indian land, to Jefferson's defining conquest as peacekeeping and removal as assimilation, much thoughtful official rhetoric regarding Indian rights marked the early national period, contradicted at every turn by the political and entrepreneurial actions taken by national officials.

Jackson only collapsed that contradiction. His hustling age was tonally blunter than that of the founders, and he wouldn't pretend to view Indian nations as sovereign. No president has ever put forth a policy of genocide. Yet thirty years after Andrew Jackson left office, General William Tecumseh Sherman, reporting to President Ulysses S. Grant on their efforts against the Plains Indians, felt free to put the policy this way: "even to their extermination, man, woman, and child."

After signing the Greeneville Treaty, Little Turtle and Blue Jacket eschewed each other's company. In 1796, with Detroit evacuated, the leaders who had signed the treaty were to travel to Philadelphia and meet with the president, and at the last minute Little Turtle refused to go: he wouldn't travel in company with Blue Jacket. The architects of the greatest Indian victory over the United States were never again on speaking terms.

Blue Jacket moved to a comfortable house on the American side of the Detroit River and continued his business enterprises and his enjoyment of European conveniences. In 1805, via Jefferson's policy, carried out by William Henry Harrison, the Greeneville Treaty was superseded by a new boundary line, pushing the western Indians still farther west, and Blue Jacket signed it. In 1809, however, a treaty signed with Harrison at Fort Wayne, taking another three million acres, sparked the Tecumseh resistance. Tecumseh's brother Tenskwatawa had been preaching a fundamentalist, pan-Indian spiritual and political revival, in the old "drive them out" manner of Neolin, and Tecumseh, taking the Pontiac role, began recruiting for a revival of military confederation. He could offer, in the end, only a mournful echo of Blue Jacket's unifying military successes of the 1790s, yet the aging Blue Jacket gave Tecumseh and Tenskwatawa moral support and lent their effort prestige. He died shortly before Tecumseh's failure at the Battle of Tippecanoe in 1811.

After Greeneville, Little Turtle returned to the Eel River near was now Fort Wayne and tried to take up and promote the a ist lifestyle, hoping to foster Indian-white harmony have surprised both his former enemies and his for

Fallen Timbers, it was Little Turtle who had conceived the only practical plan, in the absence of sincere British support, for preventing white settlement west of the Ohio: deny the American army supply, via many repetitive, small-scale operations focused not on glory, not on numbers killed, not on seizing territory, but on destroying selected targets again and again. But the necessary discipline and patience were too hard to achieve, and when the Miami leader lost hope for success, he never looked back. Washington presented him with a ceremonial sword. Later, Little Turtle traveled more than once to the nation's new capital of Washington, D.C., and there met two U.S. presidents, Adams and Jefferson. Little Turtle tried without success to get Adams to widen the boundaries of Indian country, but in the Fort Wayne Treaty of 1809, Little Turtle supported Harrison's position, a decision that alienated other Miami, as did his characteristic rejection of Tenskwatawa's nativist plan of universal Indian purification and his refusal to ally militarily with Tecumseh.

In July 1812, having suffered from gout for years, he lay dying on a bed in the home of his son-in-law William Wells at Fort Wayne. He asked to be carried outside and placed beneath a tree. Little Turtle died on the ground that had been Kekionga, and he was buried there, with valuable possessions, in traditional Miami style.

As for Anthony Wayne, his final battle was with James Wilkinson. After Fallen Timbers, their mutual animosity grew open, intense, even nationally dire. Wilkinson amplified his complaints about Wayne, writing to Knox and to allies in Congress to call the general a liar, a drunk, and a fool, militarily incompetent to a degree literally never seen before in history. Wayne had meanwhile come up with a theory about Wilkinson that, while possibly all wrong in its specifics, got at a truth: the man had been working secretly with the Canadians, Wayne alleged, to defeat and obstruct American military efforts. Wayne still had Wilkinson in command at Fort Washington on the Ohio, where the action decidedly no longer was. Presenting Knox with some fuzzy evidence of Wilkinson's double agency with Canada, he told his superiors he wouldn't be giving Wilkinson any further significant role to play in army affairs.

While Washington and Knox had been hoping to keep Wilkinson's slanders from Wayne, this rising conflict caused them to fear for the future of their regular army, and they forwarded Wayne all of Wilkinson's

voluminous accusations; then, shortly before resigning his cabinet position, Knox privately wrote to both men to ask them to settle things.
Pickering, on taking over, took a harder line with Wilkinson, and the
second-in-command withdrew his demand for an inquiry into Wayne's
command while continuing to conspire against him.

Kept out of any important army role by Wayne, stuck in Fort Washington handling logistics, Wilkinson harbored big plans for restructur-
ing continental sovereignty. While the Wilkinson everybody knew and
liked lived high, along with Mrs. Wilkinson, at Fort Washington—they
flew in their coach down Cincinnati's mud streets and tried to get ahead
in Ohio land, ballooning in value after Fallen Timbers—Thirteen was
reviving his secret relationship with Spain. He passed Wayne's plans
to his Spanish handlers across the Mississippi and suggested ways of
keeping the United States from turning its military attention southward. Spain was already building two forts on the American side of the
Mississippi, and Wayne was demanding they be removed. Wilkinson's
Spanish contacts told Thirteen that if he could get Kentucky and Tennessee connected to the Northwest Territory and then detach the whole
thing from the United States, the president of that new western world
would be none other than James Wilkinson. He assured his handlers
that to those ends his immediate plans were to destroy Wayne, play up
to the emerging Republican opposition, get the size of the American
army reduced, and become its commander.

By now, Wayne was tired and ill. Along with worsening gout, he had
a deepening, painful ulcer, and he hadn't been home in more than three
years. The general applied for a leave, and before taking it, he summoned
Wilkinson up to Greene Ville and coldly handed his subordinate a long,
involved list of chores to be done in the commander's absence, allowing
Wilkinson no discretion to depart from orders. Pickering had approved
that move. With no plans to comply, Wilkinson took the insult as it was
intended.

Even Arthur St. Clair, still governor of the Northwest Territory, sent
Anthony Wayne good wishes and high compliments in advance of the
general's departure for the capital. Wayne had left Philadelphia in the
spring of 1792 with his affairs in disorder, thrown out of Congress,
reputation in tatters. In January 1796, after having traveled a thousand
miles from headquarters in the West, he found himself greeted outside

Philadelphia by an honor guard and escorted into town to artillery thunder, clanging bells, and the shouts of massed thousands, including many of his men, in uniform, from the Continental army. He paid an official visit to President Washington, went on a round of parties, accepted honors. He saw Isaac, now doing well as a lawyer. After a couple of weeks, he even went back to Chester County and paid Peggy a brief visit. Then he stayed in Philadelphia until May. He took up again with Mary Vining, and it was rumored that they planned to be married.

Before he went west again, Wayne had a meeting with Pickering's replacement as secretary of war, James McHenry, and learned that the administration believed that James Wilkinson was indeed a spy, but in the pay of Spain. In July, having arrived at Greene Ville, Wayne relieved Wilkinson of command of Fort Washington and got busy seeking evidence of the espionage. Wilkinson, still in possession of his rank and number-two position, went straight to the capital to work with the Republican opposition on demolishing Wayne's reputation and reducing the size of the army. He reasserted his demand for a court-martial to investigate Wayne. Washington and McHenry tried their best to tamp down the political embarrassment.

Anthony Wayne never got his full-on throw down with James Wilkinson. Weakening steadily, Wayne moved up to Fort Detroit to oversee the American takeover there. In making that fort his new headquarters, he completed American control of its sovereign territory gained in the War of Independence. Fever soon began raging through him, and in December 1796, en route to Pittsburgh, Wayne died in great pain at Presque Isle.

As Wayne's second-in-command, James Wilkinson now became the army's senior officer. He was reduced to third place during the Quasi-war with France, when Hamilton wanted the number-two spot, but reclaimed the top position in 1800, and the Spanish spy would command the U.S. Army for twelve more years. But that's another story.

For a long time Anthony Wayne's name remained well known to the American public. Towns and sites named for him throughout the Midwest are thanks to his conquest. Theodore Roosevelt, looking back at

Wayne's campaign, celebrated it as critical to America's booming nationhood: Wayne's victory, Roosevelt said, transferred in one move the
great wealth of the continent from an inferior race to a superior one.

Such muscular, racist American imperialism, associated with ideas
about manliness, remained connected to Wayne's name as late as 1930,
when the actor born Marion Morrison changed his name to John Wayne.
Military glory, energetic expansion, great nationhood, white supremacy—
for many years that brand of romance burnished the name of the
gruff, beat-up soldier, fighting off gout on his last slog from Greene Ville
to Fort Miamis, punctiliously securing his positions every night in search
of some kind of vindication.

Nowadays, public memory of Wayne's legacy seems largely limited
to the locales where he performed. In northwestern Ohio and north-
eastern Indiana, better-thriving towns like Greeneville, Defiance, and
Fort Recovery offer visitors a feeling of persistence of that prosperous
American Midwest of the nineteenth and early twentieth centuries, the
leafy, small-town Ohio and Indiana of Sherwood Anderson and Booth
Tarkington that have largely been demolished down around the Ohio
River. Wayne's legacy is lovingly preserved up there too. In Fort Recovery, Monument Park boasts a soaring obelisk, erected in 1912, in memory
of Americans killed under command of Arthur St. Clair and Anthony
Wayne. A sculpture at the obelisk's base evinces the celebratory style of
its period: a frontiersman in deerskin, with powder horn and musket,
gazing toward lands that Wayne's victory opened. The great shift that
Teddy Roosevelt celebrated persists in that monument.

Defiance, Ohio, offers a different way of imagining the effect Wayne
and his men had at Fallen Timbers. On a lawn outside the Defiance
County Courthouse stands the county war memorial, with names of
those killed in modern wars, and while of course many towns have them,
the memorial in Defiance, relatively recently created, installed, and
dedicated, involves an unusually arresting and satisfying design. Bounded
by an open circle on the ground, the memorial invites the viewer to
step in and look closely. Beside an eternal flame stands a big, simple,
symmetrical form spanning nearly twenty-five feet and reaching a
height of over seven: two scalloped wings of polished black granite, one
on each side of a central arch.

Within the arch, in realistically modeled bronze, a modern male soldier, helmeted, kneels over a fallen comrade, holding the dead man's dog tags. A female nurse kneels beside them, hair hanging, one hand cradling the dead man's head, the other resting on the living man's shoulder. Their heads are bent together in grief, or in mutual devotion, and their knees, in fatigues, seem to obtrude beyond the bottom of the frame, where a big inscription, in lighter granite, runs all the way along the ground. "Dedicated to those who paid the supreme sacrifice," the inscription reads. Without comment or bathos, the sculpture captures the pain of that sacrifice.

Yet it's the swooping symmetry of the black wings on either side of the sculpture that makes the memorial so eye-catching and satisfying. The symmetry comes from an artist's organizing historical fact in expressive form. On the left, the heading "Korea" sits low: names of the dead listed there are relatively few. The wing widens upward toward the central arch: under the heading "World War I" there are more names to accommodate. The right wing mirrors the left: the widest section, close to the central arch, is headed "World War II," and the right wing then narrows and lowers to embrace, under "Vietnam," the smallest batch of names, from here in Defiance County, of those killed in a modern war.

Two big, declared wars, bookended by two limited, undeclared wars: the sweep offers a narrative unity concluding with Vietnam, a story that might thus seem to have an ending, perhaps in its somber way even a happy one, at least when tallying, as American memorials do, only American casualties of wars. For the monument's two big slabs are full, and the whole winged form, with the realistically modeled soldier and nurse at its center, expresses subsidence, completion. When the memorial was dedicated, the wars it memorializes were history, their epoch done.

That was in 2000. Unity and symmetry have since been shattered by the addition of a separate stone, standing alone and placed, within the surrounding circle, off to the right of the main structure. It's made of black granite too. It echoes the main memorial's winglike form. Yet nothing can bridge the jarring division between the completeness of the main monument and the new stone's add-on abruptness.

Our first war, fought by Anthony Wayne and Blue Jacket and Little Turtle, and by all of the fighters, fallen and surviving, for possession of the ground where this memorial sits, remains nearly unmemorialized. Our founding war of conquest doesn't have a name, and the conflict memorialized by the add-on slab at the Defiance courthouse doesn't have one either. The new heading, obviating any need in the future to break history down in periods, is "Global War."

Under that heading has been inscribed the name of a sergeant in the U.S. Army, killed in action in Afghanistan, when he was twenty-seven. Below his name, only black expanse, empty the last time I looked.

NOTES

PROLOGUE: THE RUINS OF AN OLD FRENCH FORT

3 *The Ruins of an Old French Fort*: Paraphrased from an argument between Anthony Wayne and Little Turtle, discussed in chapter 12, drawn from Carter, *Life and Times of Little Turtle*, 151–52.

3 *the Illinois Country*: Alvord, *Illinois Country*, 34 and elsewhere, emphasizes the importance of the Illinois River route to the Mississippi; Barnhart and Riker, *Indiana to 1816*, 9, emphasize the Wabash, but both sources call the region the "Illinois Country," as do other scholars of the region and period: see Hinderaker, *Elusive Empires*, for example, chaps. 1 and 2.

3 *unlike the English speakers*: Alvord, *Illinois Country*, 2, 61, 226, and Barnhart and Riker, *Indiana to 1816*, 9–10, for differences in how the French and the British viewed and used the region.

4 *transmarine*: Alvord's term, *Illinois Country*, 92.

4 *three types of peculiarly French boats*: Ibid., 192–93.

4 *The Illinois Country, in between and pulled administratively*: Hinderaker, *Elusive Empires*, 92, referring to administrative struggles between New France and Louisiana, calls the Illinois Country "the linchpin."

4 *Smooth, warm fur*: For the French trade, see Alvord, *Illinois Country*, chap. 6; Carlos and Lewis, *Economic History of the Fur Trade*; and Hinderaker, *Elusive Empires*, 32–39. On the importance of hats, the role of beaver in fine hatmaking, and the resource's decline in Europe, see Feinstein, *Fashionable Felted Fur*, citing Crean, "Hats and the Fur Trade," which also see; and Carlos and Lewis, *Economic History of the Fur Trade*.

4 *usually with the permission*: Hinderaker, *Elusive Empires*, 14, 47. For fort and village lifestyle, see Barnhart and Riker, *Indiana to 1816*, 76.

5 *nearly one hundred years*: The French trade is usually dated ca. 1670–1763; see Carlos and Lewis, *Economic History of the Fur Trade*.

1. THE DEATH OF GENERAL BUTLER

11 *On a November morning in 1791*: The fabled death scene presented in sections throughout this chapter is drawn from a number of more and less credible primary and secondary sources: Sword, *President Washington's Indian War*, 185, 191; Gaff, *Bayonets in the Wilderness*, 6; Calloway, *Victory with No Name*, 122; Ward, *When Fate Summons*, 114–15; Kopper, "Arthur St. Clair and the Struggle for Power in the Old Northwest," 185; Sargent, *Diary*, 44–45; *American State Papers: Indian Affairs*, 1:137; Butler, Butler, and Butler, *Butler Family in America*, 158–61, 285; Denny, *Military Journal of Major Ebenezer Denny*, 17; Lytle, *Soldiers of America's First Army*, 103; *National Cyclopaedia*, 84.

12 *The Indians . . . knew Butler*: Calloway, *Victory with No Name*, 222; Winkler, *Wabash 1791*, 19.

12 *particularly good stories*: The only full-length biography of Richard Butler is by Ward, *When Fate Summons*, detailing Butler's jobs and enterprises yet ignoring without comment some of the interesting stories found elsewhere.

12 *he'd fathered a child*: Winkler, *Wabash 1791*, 19; Howe, *Historical Collections of Ohio*, 301.

12 *Nonhelema*: Cook, *Women and War*, 434; Sword, *President Washington's Indian War*, 39.

13 *Shawnee vocabulary and grammar*: Richard Butler to George Washington, Nov. 30, 1787, http://founders.archives.gov/documents/Washington/04-05-02 -0419-0001.

13 *another Indian vocabulary book*: *Denny's Vocabulary*; Calloway, *Shawnees and the War for America*, 80.

13 *Little Turtle and Blue Jacket*: The major biographies are by Carter, *Life and Times of Little Turtle*, and Sugden, *Blue Jacket*, each evincing partisanship for its subject at the expense of the other's. For background on both leaders and on conflicts in interpreting their importance, see chapters 10 and 12.

14 *these leaders' names*: Carter, *Life and Times of Little Turtle*, 42–44; Sugden, *Blue Jacket*, 27.

14 *The way many Shawnee . . . looked at it*: For notes on both the Shawnee and the Miami, see ensuing chapters.

14 *the Indians had encircled*: Winkler, *Wabash 1791*, 57–64.

16 *In the ensuing battle*: Gaff, *Bayonets in the Wilderness*, chap. 1, is the exhaustive secondary source for the battle at the Wabash; Calloway, *Victory with No Name*, chaps. 4 and 5, is the most compelling. See also Sword, *President Washington's Indian War*, chap. 16. Those accounts draw in part on the eyewitnesses Denny, *Military Journal of Major Ebenezer Denny*, 165–69; Sargent, *Diary*, 30–39; and St. Clair to Knox, Nov. 7, 1791, in St. Clair, *Papers*. For lucid battle maps and strategy analysis, see Winkler, *Wabash 1791*, 62, 69, 86. For casualty figures, see Calloway, *Victory with No Name*, 127–28.

16 *"The Butlers and their five sons!"*: "Sketch of Career," 60.

16 *"Sinclair's Defeat"*: *United States Songster*, 123. (Roger McGuinn performs the song at http://ibiblio.org/jimmy/folkden/php/music/Sinclairs_Defeat.mp3.)

17 *He'd been served*: Sword, *President Washington's Indian War*, 191; Kelsay, *Joseph Brant*, 457. While some earlier sources had it that Brant led Mohawk forces against St. Clair, Calloway, *Victory with No Name*, 114, cites Alexander McKee

on Brant's absence; Kelsay, *Joseph Brant*, 457, places Brant at home in Grand River and discusses western Indian resentment. For more on Brant and his background, see chapter 4.

2. THE TURNIP FIELD

19 *George Washington was famous*: The story told here draws on accounts by Rush, *Washington in Domestic Life*, 65–69; Custis, in George H. Moore, *Libels on Washington*, 7.

21 *The United States was not at war*: The policy, the treaty process, and other events leading up to St. Clair's defeat are covered in chapter 4.

23 *The Ohio Company of Virginia*: For origins, see Bailey, *Ohio Company of Virginia and the Westward Movement*, 23–24; James, *Ohio Company*, chap. 2. For differences between Northern Neck speculators and competitors south of the Rappahannock, see Philyaw, *Virginia's Western Vision*, 47–48, and Egnal, *Mighty Empire*, 88–96; Bailey, *Ohio Company of Virginia and the Westward Movement*, too emphasizes this regional aspect of Virginia's land speculations. Hinderaker, *Elusive Empires*, 37–52, masterfully handles a further multitude of complexities glossed over in this chapter. Note that Boyd, review of *The Ohio Company*, by Kenneth P. Bailey, 126, objects to the focus on Virginia at the expense of Pennsylvania in discussions of colonial western speculation.

23 *Every member was somebody*: Bailey, *Ohio Company of Virginia and the Westward Movement*, 59–60.

23 *He wasn't a member*: The first petition—see James, *Ohio Company*, 18—names Lawrence and Augustine Washington as petitioners but not George, unsurprisingly given the youngster's status at the time (but note that the petition also fails to mention others named as members by James and Bailey). Knollenberg, *George Washington*, 143n46, states that no evidence exists that George Washington ever became a partner.

23 *The idea the petition expressed*: James, *Ohio Company*, 20.

24 *The real attraction*: Higgonet throughout "Origins of the Seven Years' War" and Gage, in Chalmers, *Queries of George Chalmers*, emphasize the company's promotion of commerce, development, and the territorial ambitions of Virginia over the goals of Crown and empire. Egnal, *Mighty Empire*, chap. 5, analyzes the role of what he calls the "self-interested goals of the Ohio Company" (98) in connecting the expansion of Virginia with the imperial struggle against France. Boyd, review of *Ohio Company*, by Bailey, 126, suggests that even the commercial element served as a screen for the settlement and development plan. Evidence as granular as the company's instructions to its chief scout, in Gist, *Gist's Journals*, 1, as general as the sheer size of the grant request, and as anecdotal as outcomes discussed in this chapter and throughout this book suggest that the Ohio Company bent imperial aims to the service of the commercial and real-estate speculation that were always part and parcel of the Northern Neck gentry's pursuit of greater Virginia expansion.

25 *a tough business*: For tobacco in Virginia, see Salmon and Salmon, "Tobacco in Colonial Virginia."

26 *The search was always on*: See Holton, *Forced Founders*, chap. 1, for the develop-

ment of tobacco planters into real-estate speculators, and his "Ohio Indians," 456, for the financial importance of land speculation to the richest Virginians.

26 *begun as tobacco planters*: Washington, for one, stopped growing tobacco at Mount Vernon in the mid-1760s, even as he expanded his western land speculations. See Flexner, *Washington*, 49.

26 *The soil where George Washington was born*: All biographers cover the material presented here, as well as adventures covered later in this chapter, in varying degrees of detail. That Augustine was known as Gus is widely mentioned. See, for example, Freeman, *Washington*, 37. Regarding the Home Farm, some biographers refer to the place as Ferry Farm, as does the Mount Vernon website (http://www.mountvernon.org/digital-encyclopedia/article/ferry-farm/), but the website for the Washington Foundation restoration of the farm site, among others, notes that the Washington family used the name given here.

29 *In 1749, the governor of Virginia*: Philyaw, *Virginia's Western Vision*, 48–49.

30 *Dunk Halifax was rising to power*: Greiert, "Board of Trade and Defense of the Ohio Valley," 3–4. On newly assertive British policies, see Alvord, *Mississippi Valley in British Politics*, vol. 1, chap. 4.

33 *Dinwiddie had seen*: The Dinwiddie story in this chapter relies on Higgonet, "Origins of the Seven Years' War," 61–67. Also see Philyaw, *Virginia's Western Vision*, 37–38, 53; and Egnal, *Mighty Empire*, 96. Note that Greiert, "Board of Trade and Defense of the Ohio Valley," dissenting from Higgonet's criticism of Dinwiddie and the Virginia speculators, emphasizes Dunk Halifax's own expansionism.

34 *the majority of Virginians*: Holton, "Ohio Indians," 456, states that land speculation was a major source of income for Virginia's richest 2 to 5 percent.

35 *He took the long, hard trip*: Washington's formative western trip with Gist is covered in all biographies, drawing mainly on Washington, *Journal*. Philyaw, *Virginia's Western Vision*, 34, notes that Dinwiddie would have viewed Washington as "competent, but expendable."

38 *Trouble began even before*: Adventures at Great Meadows and Jumonville Glen are discussed by all of Washington's cited biographers. Clary's lively and thoughtful full-scale study of Washington in the Seven Years' War covers these episodes in much illuminating detail. *George Washington's First War*, 68–120.

39 *Or not*: For various and conflicting accounts, see ibid., 85–88. Both ibid., 112, and Ferling, *Ascent of George Washington*, 25, note the episode's importance in launching Washington's tendency to take credit for unearned victories and blame others for failures. Parkman's classic rendering in *Montcalm and Wolfe*, 146–50, dismisses all criticism and defends Washington. "I have heard the bullets whistle": George Washington to John Augustine Washington, May 31, 1754, http://founders.archives.gov/documents/Washington/02-01-02-0058.

44 *"The primary causes"*: Chalmers, *Queries of George Chalmers*, 369, also cited by Philyaw, *Virginia's Western Vision*, 61. Read in full, Gage's contemporary analysis supports Higgonet's modern argument that English speakers' aggressive land speculation incited French territorial aggression in the Ohio Country.

3. DRIVE THEM OUT

45 *Confederation wasn't a novel idea*: The Iroquois longhouse is widely discussed; for example, Kelsay, 1–5. Richter, *Facing East from Indian Country*, 167–68, clarifies conditions that made Ohio valley and Great Lakes life especially multicultural by the eighteenth century. Calloway, *American Revolution in Indian Country*, 1–3, gives a compelling sense of "cultural cacophony" (1) in the variety of indigenous and European people living and working throughout the Ohio valley.

46 *having conquered many of them*: Hinderaker, *Elusive Empires*, 13–22; Alvord, 36–38. Yet Mann, *George Washington's War on Native America*, 112, describes the upper Ohio and the Great Lakes region as defended by the Iroquois confederation in alliance with nations living there. Sugden, *Blue Jacket*, 23, by contrast, says the Iroquois had "flushed" the Shawnee from the Ohio in the seventeenth century and refers to the returning Shawnee's historical resentment (67). Mounting tension between an emerging western confederation and a long-dominant Iroquois confederation seems borne out by events related in this book.

47 *Fundamentalist religious movements*: For the totality of indigenous people's dependence on European goods and indigenous constructions of that relationship, see Richter, *Facing East from Indian Country*, 174–79; Calloway, *American Revolution in Indian Country*, 11–14, places the phenomenon in the context of "consumer revolution." On spiritual resistance and revival, Dowd traces with much nuance the many roots and branches. See especially *Spirited Resistance*, introduction and chap. 1; also Hinderaker, *Elusive Empires*, 153, and Richter, *Facing East from Indian Country*, 181.

47 *An Ohio valley Delaware named Neolin*: Dowd, *Spirited Resistance*, 33–35; Hinderaker, *Elusive Empires*, 154; Richter, *Facing East from Indian Country*, 193–201. The original source is Burton, *Journal of Pontiac's Conspiracy*, 20–32; see also the recollections of John M'Cullough in Loudon, *Selection of Some of the Most Interesting Narratives of Outrages Committed by the Indians in Their Wars with the White People*, 252.

48 *Neolin's story . . . was in certain ways novel*: Hinderaker's reading, *Elusive Empires*, 154.

48 *eager listeners*: Ibid., 155.

49 *The young Blue Jacket heard those stories*: Sugden, *Blue Jacket*, 28, relying on logical conjecture, given the weakness of the record.

50 *British political and military monopoly*: Downes, *Council Fires on the Upper Ohio*, 105–19; Hinderaker, *Elusive Empires*, 144–52; Richter, *Facing East from Indian Country*, 187.

50 *the Treaty of Easton*: Downes, *Council Fires on the Upper Ohio*, 113; Richter, *Facing East from Indian Country*, 192.

51 *Pontiac began recruiting*: For Pontiac's War, see Dowd, *Spirited Resistance*, 35–36; Hinderaker, *Elusive Empires*, 156; Richter, *Facing East from Indian Country*, 198–99.

51 *Blue Jacket responded*: Sugden, *Blue Jacket*, 30, noting the weakness of the record, says that Blue Jacket "almost certainly" fought in the Pontiac uprisings. Young people reacted to Neolin's message as a "Great Awakening" (Dowd, *Spirited Resistance*, 23), and Blue Jacket's evident lifelong interest in Shawnee return and pan-Indian unity suggests that his first mature actions would have come in response to the Neolin-Pontiac message.

52 *Amherst made the suggestion*: Parkman, *Conspiracy*, 39, for example, cites the famous exchange between Amherst and Colonel Henry Bouquet in which both refer to their desire to "extirpate" what Amherst calls "this execrable race."

53 *settlers began defining all Indians*: Hinderaker, *Elusive Empires*, 161.

53 *George Washington had come back*: Clary, *George Washington's First War*, 111, shows Washington becoming "the toast of Williamsburg" for his supposed defeat of Jumonville, even as the Virginian first became known in England as a failure, even a figure of fun (89). All cited biographies cover Washington's social, military, marital, and economic rise after the Great Meadows battle, as related here.

54 *He'd become fastidious*: Ford, *True George Washington*, 185–90, gives entertaining details regarding Washington's clothing, hair, and accessories.

54 *He was adding cunning*: For the Forbes road story, see Knollenberg, *George Washington*, 64–70. See also Egnal, *Mighty Empire*, 98; Philyaw, *Virginia's Western Vision*, 59–60.

55 *violence and chaos persisted*: Downes, *Council Fires on the Upper Ohio*, 123–42; Hinderaker, *Elusive Empires*, 161–70.

55 *big land-investment companies*: Alvord, "Virginia and the West," 22–23, brings to life the mad multiplicity of competing ventures now baffling the ministry.

56 *the little town growing up*: Hogeland, *Whiskey Rebellion*, 13–15. For pronunciation of the name, see, for example, "What's in an H?" http://popularpittsburgh .com/whatsinanh/.

56 *policy of withdrawing*: Alvord, *Mississippi Valley in British Politics*, vol. 1, chap. 8; Alvord, *Illinois Country*, chap. 4; and Barnhart, "New Evaluation of Henry Hamilton and George Rogers Clark."

57 *a royal proclamation froze*: See Richter, *Facing East from Indian Country*, 208, for the proclamation as a repudiation of Amherst's Indian policies and a reflection of Gage's. See Del Papa, "Royal Proclamation of 1763," for the edict's impact on Virginia speculators' prewar companies.

58 *Ohio Company was in trouble*: Del Papa, "Royal Proclamation of 1763"; Bailey, *Ohio Company of Virginia and the Westward Movement*, 146–49.

58 *Washington kept at it*: All biographers cover the Mississippi and Great Dismal plans; see, for example, Knollenberg, *George Washington*, 87–90. Curtis, *Jefferson's Freeholders*, 49, places Jefferson and Henry in the Mississippi venture.

58 *the incoherence of Crown policy*: Downes's chapter title "A Decade of British Muddling," in *Council Fires on the Upper Ohio*, is well put. For a blizzard of detail, see Alvord, *Mississippi Valley in British Politics*, vol. 2, chap. 4, and *Illinois Country*, chap. 12.

60 *Washington offered William Crawford*: Washington to Crawford, Sept. 17, 1767, http://founders.archives.gov/documents/Washington/02-08-02-0020.

61 *in 1768, at Fort Stanwix*: Richter, *Facing East from Indian Country*, 211, notes both Shawnee and Cherokee resentment. Holton, "Ohio Indians," 458, argues persuasively that while the Fort Stanwix Treaty did not repeal the 1763 proclamation, many speculators were delighted to think it would; their disappointment became a cause of resisting British policy.

61 *Blue Jacket was a Shawnee war leader now*: Sugden, *Blue Jacket*, 38–39, noting the dearth of direct evidence, places Blue Jacket in this role by this time. For Blue Jacket's life and lifestyle, contrasted here with the attraction to pan-Indian

revivalism, see ibid., 30–34, drawing on Spencer, *The Indian Captivity of O. M. Spencer*, 89–92, and other primary sources. Sugden also lays to rest the story that Blue Jacket was a white man captured as a child (*Blue Jacket*, 1–4).

64 *the more practical idea was warfare*: Sugden, *Blue Jacket*, 39.

64 *Thomas Jefferson was in his twenties*: Jefferson's schooling, relationship with Wythe, and so on are widely covered. Holton, "Ohio Indians," 458, underscores the young Jefferson's eager involvement in land speculation.

65 *He followed that chain of history and logic*: Jefferson, "Summary View of the Rights of British America." Though presented to the Continental Congress in 1774, the paper expresses ideas Jefferson had been working up for some time. Curtis, *Jefferson's Freeholders*, 36–37. Williams, *American Indian in Western Legal Thought*, pt. 3, details Jefferson's thinking with specific regard to the status of Indian land.

66 *the Norman Yoke*: The classic treatment of the Norman Yoke is Hill, *Intellectual Origins of the English Revolution*, chap. 17. Curtis, *Jefferson's Freeholders*, pt. 3, connects the concept to ideas about land tenure in America; connects Jefferson's ideas to speculators' resistance to a Crown role in land grants (36–58); and mentions Bland's influence on Jefferson's interpretation (62). Williams, *American Indian in Western Legal Thought*, 272, finds in Jefferson's thought a basis for speculators' hope to define Indian land as easily available.

67 *Camden-Yorke*: Williams, *American Indian in Western Legal Thought*, 275–78. For Washington's carrying a copy in his diary, see Sosin, "Yorke-Camden Opinion and American Land Speculators," 43.

68 *tantamount to . . . slavery*: Jefferson, "Summary View."

68 *This latest scheme*: Knollenberg, *George Washington*, 91–97.

71 *Dunmore had arrived*: Alvord, "Virginia and the West," 126.

71 *the governor used his position*: Knollenberg, *George Washington*, 98–99.

72 *Patrick Henry*: As Dunmore's close adviser on defeating home-government regulations, see Alvord, "Virginia and the West," 29. On Henry's role as Dunmore's real-estate lawyer, and on his belief in an absolute liberty to purchase Indian land, see Williams, *American Indian in Western Legal Thought*, 274–75, drawing on Wharton, "Selections from the Letter-Books," 444–45. There Henry admitted the legality of the Vandalia project, and Mayer, *Son of Thunder*, 314, notes that Richard Henry Lee would soon warn him off that position.

73 *The Dunmore cousin*: Williams, *American Indian in Western Legal Thought*, 288–89.

73 *new royal colonies*: Complexities of the various Dartmouth plans are distilled well by Curtis, *Jefferson's Freeholders*, 53–54, 56–57; and Williams, *American Indian in Western Legal Thought*, 262–63, on Vandalia. Alvord, *Mississippi Valley in British Politics*, vol. 2, details the many convoluted ins and outs and ups and downs of the new-colony approach (149–65); the Vandalia plan (180–85); and the auction plan (214–15); Alvord also notes, as does Williams, 266, that Jefferson's "Summary View" came in direct response to those schemes.

74 *the Quebec Act*: Alvord, *Mississippi Valley in British Politics*, vol. 2, 227–37, details its substance and passage. Barnhart, "New Evaluation," argues that if the act hadn't served as a cause of rebellion—a big "if"!—it would have represented the ministry's first cogent and effective policy for managing the West.

75 *he started a war*: In the grand scheme of things a tempest in a teapot, Dunmore's War is complicated enough to have challenged cogent explanation. Even before passage of the Quebec Act, Dunmore was beginning to pursue warlike measures against Pennsylvania at the headwaters and the Shawnee down the river. Curtis, *Jefferson's Freeholders*, 59–62, distills the war; Alvord, *Mississippi Valley in British Politics*, vol. 2, 188–94, details it, while admitting that Dunmore's motivations for starting it have been "thrown into obscurity" (192).

75 *Blue Jacket led men*: He enters the record here, if faintly; see Sugden, *Blue Jacket*, 41–45.

76 *the Virginia Convention*: Curtis, *Jefferson's Freeholders*, 59–62, clarifies nicely the irony of the Dunmore-patriot relationship, covering the proroguing of the assembly, and so on. McGaughy, *Richard Henry Lee of Virginia*, 106, quotes the convention's accolade to Dunmore.

76 *Rancor exploded*: Morrow, *"We Must Fight!"* argues that the breakup was personal and quotes Washington on Dunmore as a "monster" (65). "A certain Patrick Henry": "Proclamation by Lord Dunmore."

77 *he would form a black regiment*: Widely noted, for example, in ibid., 46.

77 *Richard Henry Lee*: On his background and goals, McGaughy is a realistic and comprehensive biographer. For the relationship with the Adamses, the schemes to overthrow Dickinson, and so on, see Hogeland, *Declaration*, esp. chaps. 3 and 8.

78 *the action for him*: McGaughy's narrative, *Richard Henry Lee of Virginia*, 121–22, makes clear that Lee's focus throughout 1776 was on stymieing Vandalia competitors and getting land policy into the hands of his Northern Neck speculating circle. The burden of Alvord, "Virginia and the West," is that it was British curtailment of land investment that made the Virginia gentry partisans of independence. Holton, "Ohio Indians," 455, says the same thing.

79 *removed or exterminated*: Jefferson to George Rogers Clark, Jan. 1, 1780, http://founders.archives.gov/documents/Jefferson/01-03-02-0289.

80 *"the pursuit of happiness"*: Both Curtis, *Jefferson's Freeholders*, and Williams, *American Indian in Western Legal Thought*, linking Jefferson's ideas about liberty to speculators' desire for Indian land, stop just short of pursuing that linkage explicitly into the declaration's famous preamble. Yet their readings of "A Summary View of the Rights of British America," taken in conjunction with common understandings of the causes and effects of the proclamation line, the Vandalia colony, and the Quebec Act, make the interpretation presented here seem nearly inescapable. As a thinker, Jefferson was by no means so limited; he hoped, for example, that people everywhere would rebel against what he saw as the oppression inherent in holding land by tenure and not freehold (Curtis, *Jefferson's Freeholders*, 64). Such characteristic mental expansiveness only adds strangeness to the real expansion, and the real resistance, that form the subject of this book, a struggle in which Jefferson himself would play an important part (see chapters 6 and 12).

4. AN INQUIRY INTO THE CAUSES OF THE LATE UNFORTUNATE DEFEAT

81 *thousands of delegates . . . held a conference:* Sword, *President Washington's Indian War,* 20–21; Downes, *Council Fires on the Upper Ohio,* 283–84.

81 *Alexander McKee:* See chapter 5.

82 *Washington's general Daniel Brodhead:* Calloway, *American Revolution in Indian Country,* chap. 1, brings to life the ways in which the conflict in the West was a civil war, for both Indians and whites, and details the U.S. terror and scorched-earth policy (46–56). Mann, *George Washington's War on Native America,* 2, notes that in the Western Department the war was fought solely between the United States and indigenous people, not the United States and Britain—an overstatement, perhaps, given British army presence in the Mississippi and lake forts, yet consistent with Riker's discussion, "A New Evaluation of Henry Hamilton and George Rogers Clark," of the military effects of British military withdrawal from the forts.

83 *The Moravian Delaware:* The incident is widely discussed; see, for example, Mann, *George Washington's War on Native America,* 155–66.

84 *He'd also changed his base:* Sugden, *Blue Jacket,* 52–54.

86 *the Land of the Three Miami Rivers:* The term has been revived in Barbara Mann's *Land of the Three Miamis* and in Leonard Hill's *John Johnston and the Indians in the Land of the Three Miamis.* The river here called the Miami of the Lake was sometimes then known by that name, sometimes as the Maumee, as it is today; also as the Miamis, the Miamia, the Tawa, the Ottawa, the Omee, and sometimes simply the Miami.

86 *Kekionga:* Sword, *President Washington's Indian War,* 101–3.

87 *Miami attitudes about white incursion:* Anson, *Miami Indians,* chaps. 1 and 2, explores the differing Miami branches' alliances with and against the French and the intensifications of trouble after the English takeover.

87 *Exploits of . . . George Rogers Clark:* Alvord, "Virginia and the West," characterizes Clark's and Henry's joint effort as a continuation of land speculation and expansion of greater Virginia, connecting Clark to the Dunmore cousin mentioned above. Riker argues, in "A New Evaluation of Henry Hamilton and George Rogers Clark," that thanks to the British army-withdrawal policy, Clark's success in seizing the understaffed western forts reflects no great military prowess.

88 *Little Turtle prepared to meet La Balme:* Carter, *Life and Times of Little Turtle,* 72–78, covers the battle.

89 *Joseph Brant:* Much of the factual background is drawn from Kelsay's exhaustive biography, *Joseph Brant.* Taylor, *Divided Ground,* 253–54, analyzes the tendency of both British and U.S. officials to construct Brant, in the face of much evidence to the contrary, as the dominant force of Native unity and thus a credible go-between. For his role at the Sandusky conference, see Kelsay, *Joseph Brant,* 345–47.

92 *why Lord Shelburne . . . gave away so much:* Ritcheson, "Earl of Shelbourne and Peace with America," details the development of Shelbourne's thinking, the vicious infighting prevailing within the ministry, and the great gulf between what Shelburne might have hoped to accomplish in the treaty negotiations and what was possible.

92 *assaulted the honor of many British military men*: See, for example, Taylor, *Divided Ground*, 112, on General Frederick Haldimand.

92 *by offering bounty land*: Hutchinson, "Bounty Lands of the Revolution in Ohio," 5–16, on the Congress's various means of paying soldiers with land.

93 *The line that the ministry and the Congress arrived at*: *Definitive Treaty of Peace*, Article 2.

93 *The states' western borders*: Hutchinson, "Bounty Lands of the Revolution in Ohio," 21–31, on bitter conflicts between states with western land claims, on the one hand, and states with fixed borders, on the other.

94 *an American nation in embryo*: Ray Allen Billington insisted in 1959 that the 1787 Northwest Ordinance did more to perpetuate the Union than anything other than the Constitution (quoted by Shriver, "America's Other Bicentennial"). Lynd, "Compromise of 1787," 225, notes the coinciding meetings of the Congress writing the ordinance and the convention writing the Constitution and explores cross-pollination between the two bodies. Onuf, *Statehood and Union*, xviii–xix, points to the tension inherent in the Congress's writing a kind of constitution for a public domain when the body was not itself constitutionally created and associates the Ordinance of 1787, if not explicitly with nationhood, then with a robustly expanding union (xiii). Hinderaker, *Elusive Empires*, 227, sees the states' cessions of western lands as an act of incipient nationhood, indeed incipient empire.

95 *the Congress passed an ordinance*: This is the 1784 ordinance, superseded in 1787 by the more celebrated act. Few major historians of the Northwest Territory place territorial development in the context of confronting, or failing to confront, the reality of indigenous habitation and possession there. That development began in 1784 and in part inspired the first ordinance.

95 *the Congress established a military presence*: Kohn, *Eagle and Sword*, 60–72; Lytle, *Soldiers of America's First Army*, 16–17.

95 *Josiah Harmar*: Brown, "Role of the Army in Western Settlement," deftly covers Harmar's background and brings to life his activities in the territory, as related here, including the escort for the Hutchins survey team. See Sword, *President Washington's Indian War*, 89, for Harmar the stickler.

97 *the Congress appointed three commissioners*: For the three ensuing meetings, as related here, Sword, *President Washington's Indian War*, 24–26, 28–30, gives the most detailed descriptions. Downes, *Council Fires on the Upper Ohio*, 292, sees the Fort Stanwix Treaty as the beginning of the end of Six Nations hegemony. For Butler's satisfaction with the process, see Sword, *President Washington's Indian War*, 30.

102 *fallout from the treaties*: Downes, *Council Fires on the Upper Ohio*, 298; Sword, *President Washington's Indian War*, 31–41, with the Logan raid and the fate of Moluntha.

103 *he went all the way up to Kekionga*: Sugden, *Blue Jacket*, 79–80.

104 *The militants told the moderates*: For the gathering at Fort Detroit and the letter to the Congress, see Sword, *President Washington's Indian War*, 41–42; Downes, *Council Fires on the Upper Ohio*, 299–300. Hinderaker, *Elusive Empires*, 235, underscores the insistence of the "United Indian Nations," as the confederation called itself in the letter, on being treated as a single entity.

105 *The nationalists remained state partisans too*: Onuf, *Statehood and Union*, 15, notes a potential contradiction in that fact.

105 *slavery . . . was prohibited in the Northwest Territory*: Lynd, "Compromise of 1787," arguing for the constitutional centrality of the three-fifths clause, asserts that southern leaders believed states formed from the territory would vote with the South and that they expressed no fear of antislavery measures' ever extending south of the Ohio; Lynd sees as a compromise what is often called the contradiction, regarding slavery, between the 1787 Constitution and the 1787 ordinance: "In legislating against slavery in the Northwest Congress tacitly legislated for it in the Southwest" (232).

106 *disorganized flood*: Washington to Richard Grayson, April 25, 1785, http://founders.archives.gov/documents/Washington/04-02-02-0375; also quoted in Onuf, *Statehood and Union*, 42.

106 *Washington was hoping for sales*: Flexner, *Washington*, 365.

106 *Armstrong across the Mississippi*: Harmar to St. Clair, Feb. 20, 1790, in St. Clair, *Papers*.

107 *Arthur St. Clair*: Hawke, *In the Midst of a Revolution*, 78–79, succinctly and realistically covers St. Clair's early career as a western exponent of Pennsylvania. William Henry Smith, editor of St. Clair's *Papers*, paints an admiring portrait. Thanks to his service as president of the Congress, an Internet search on his name will return, high on the list, the initially bewildering assertion that St. Clair was the ninth—some say the eighth—president of the United States. That view is held by those who maintain that the Congresses meeting in the years preceding ratification of the U.S. Constitution formed the governments, under the Articles of Association, the Declaration of Independence, and the Articles of Confederation, of three successive U.S. republics.

108 *This was Marietta*: Sword, *President Washington's Indian War*, 47–49, details the deal that gave the Marietta partners an inside track and linked public policy to enormous private benefit. For St. Clair's Ohio Company acreage and "the greatest land deal ever made": Calloway, *Victory with No Name*, 52; for Harmar's involvement, ibid, 56. While those and other accounts make clear that Rufus Putnam was hardly alone in settling Marietta, Putnam is especially important to the story told here. For Fort Harmar and the picnic and toasts, see Brown, "Role of the Army in Western Settlement," 169–72.

110 *St. Clair named the settlement Cincinnati*: For Harmar's pride in Fort Washington, see Harmar to St. Clair, Jan. 14, 1790, in St. Clair, *Papers*. For a succinct account of the land grants around Cincinnati, see Sword, *President Washington's Indian War*, 60–61, 84.

110 *Brant proposed setting a new boundary*: For the Fort Finney pre-meeting, see Downes, *Council Fires on the Upper Ohio*, 34. Sword, *President Washington's Indian War*, 61, says that it was Little Turtle who shrugged off the belt; the original source—St. Clair to Henry Knox, Nov. 4, 1788, in St. Clair, *Papers*—says only that it was the Miami's "principal chief." For Brant and St. Clair before the Fort Harmar meeting, see Sword, *President Washington's Indian War*, 61–62. For Brant's move to Grand River, see Taylor, *Divided Ground*, 121–22.

113 *They began by announcing*: Downes, *Council Fires on the Upper Ohio*, 307–9, and Sword, *President Washington's Indian War*, 74–75, describe the Fort Harmar

negotiations. Regarding their effect, Sword, *President Washington's Indian War*, 67, says the western Indian confederation "had been gleaned of its more pacific elements" and that St. Clair had succeeded only in putting the confederation in militant hands.

114 *had been planning an operation*: Sword, *President Washington's Indian War*, 85–86.

114 *resist Harmar's invasion*: For much detail on the Harmar expedition, see ibid., 94–119; Heath, *William Wells and the Struggle for the Old Northwest*, 110–24; Calloway, *Victory with No Name*, 34–38. Warner, "General Josiah Harmar's Campaign Reconsidered," blames the expedition's failure largely on the vague strategic goal of punishing an enemy and the lack of time for training troops.

115 *Washington, choosing to blame Harmar*: Washington to Knox, Nov. 19, 1790, http://founders.archives.gov/documents/Washington/05-06-02-0323.

115 *The youngest Butler brother, Edward*: St. Clair's retreat is detailed in Sword, *President Washington's Indian War*, 189–91, and Heath, *William Wells and the Struggle for the Old Northwest*, 146–48. Primary sources include Sargent, *Diary*, 39–41, and St. Clair, *Narrative*, 50–58.

119 *an inquiry into the causes*: Steele's motion was tabled and never taken up, but an inquiry did later commence. See editor's note at http://founders.archives.gov /documents/Washington/05-09-02-0166.

119 *In plain language, he described*: St. Clair to Knox, Nov. 7, 1791, in St. Clair, *Papers*.

5. STANDING ARMIES

123 *"the greatest character of the age"*: Boston 1775's John Bell, http://boston1775 .blogspot.com/2015/10/panel-on-washington-in-roxbury-24-oct.html, runs down a set of quotations that were perennially confused in nineteenth-century journalism and remain confused today on the Internet. Cincinnatus comparisons mentioning Washington's return to his farm range from that of a 1788 visitor to Mount Vernon (http://www.mountvernon.org/digital-encyclopedia/article/cincinnatus/) to the famous statue by Horatio Greenough to the thoroughgoing analysis by Wills, *Cincinnatus*. Napoleon's remark is widely quoted, poorly sourced.

124 *the retired commander in chief*: The Washington projects related here are mentioned in all of the biographies. Ferling, *Ascent of George Washington*, xx, dissents from portrayals of Washington as rising above politics and argues throughout his book for seeing Washington as a relentless political and commercial actor, including in the immediate postwar years.

126 *A standing army . . . a tool of tyranny*: Kohn, *Eagle and Sword*, 2–6, 81–83, distills the classic line of thought.

126 *what they called the militia*: This discussion of militia and provincial and state troops relies largely on Carroll and Baxter, introduction to *American Military Tradition*; Kohn, *Eagle and Sword*, 6–8; and Shy, "New Look at Colonial Militia." For Virginia troops in the Continental army, see *Virginia Revolutionary War Records*, 1.

128 *The inexperienced commander in chief*: On the failures of militia, see Washington to Samuel Huntington, Aug. 20, 1780, http://founders.archives.gov/documents /Washington/99-01-02-02978.

129 *The nationalists' worst fears of what peace might bring*: The story beginning here, of stymied efforts to get a peacetime army, relies largely on Kohn, *Eagle and*

Sword, chap. 3, with reference to Washington, "Sentiments," and Hamilton's "Report," June 18, 1783, http://founders.archives.gov/documents/Hamilton/01 -03-02-0291.

132 *ineluctable Hamiltonian connection*: Howell's across-the-board objections are noted in Ferguson, *Power of the Purse*, 153, 172.

133 *even state sovereigntists had gotten scared*: Hogeland, *Founding Finance*, chaps. 1 and 6.

134 *fought about . . . military authority*: The most heated debate, with Gerry's "drill sergeants," occurred on August 23, 1787; see Farrand, *Records of the Federal Convention of 1787*, 380–94.

135 *"His Electoral Highness"*: See Bartoloni-Tuazon, *For Fear of an Elective King*, 8, on John Adams's preferences.

136 *made Patrick Henry, for one, sick*: Maier, *Ratification*, 226–27; Henry, "Speech."

137 *widespread objections to a standing army*: Kohn, *Eagle and Sword*, 48–60. On the hodgepodge approach, see ibid., 62–72, and with regard to "levies," see ibid., 109–10.

138 *From the bank of the Wabash*: Calloway, *Victory with No Name*, 125–26.

138 *the confederation's core . . . faced significant challenges*: Sword, *President Washington's Indian War*, 197–99; Alexander McKee to John Johnson, Jan. 28, 1792, in *Michigan Historical Collections*, 24:365.

139 *As the man . . . Alexander McKee*: Facts in this discussion of McKee's background are drawn largely from Larry Nelson, *Man of Distinction Among Them*, introduction through chap. 6.

142 *McKee's wife was Blue Jacket's sister*: Ibid., 63.

143 *the Girty brothers*: For the myths and realities of Simon Girty, see Colin C. Calloway, "Simon Girty: Interpreter and Intermediary," in Clifton, *Being and Becoming Indian*.

145 *Filled with optimism*: McKee to John Johnson, Dec. 5, 1791, in *Michigan Historical Collections*, 24:335.

145 *The Indians were meanwhile facing*: McKee to John Johnson, Jan. 28, 1792, in *Michigan Historical Collections*, 24:366. In the record, the Glaize is also called "Grand Glaize."

147 *Little Turtle was enigmatic*: Characteristics described here combine some later, often patronizing white impressions, documented by Carter, *Life and Times of Little Turtle*, 4–9 (he participates in them as well); the speech discussed in chapter 11, which is also revealing of Little Turtle's concerns about the inevitability of U.S. escalation and the danger of expecting repeat victories; and his focus on pragmatic action in both victory and defeat, as seen throughout.

148 *He wanted British artillery*: While Little Turtle made an outright request for artillery on the record only once, to Colonel England at Fort Detroit in 1794 (see chapter 11 herein), Carter, *Life and Times of Little Turtle*, chap. 12, places Little Turtle's entire post-victory strategy in the context of the confederation's lacking artillery and British troops.

6. METROPOTAMIA

149 *"It is with great concern"*: Washington to the Senate and House, Dec. 12, 1792, http://founders.archives.gov/documents/Washington/05-09-02-0166. The communication also included copies of reports from St. Clair and a list of dead and wounded officers. *American State Papers: Indian Affairs*, 1:136–38.

150 *reports of sheer terror*: Gaff, *Bayonets in the Wilderness*, 10–11; Sword, *President Washington's Indian War*, 199–200.

151 *"General St. Clair shall have justice"*: Rush, *Washington in Domestic Life*, 68–69.

151 *Wilkinson took over*: Gaff, *Bayonets in the Wilderness*, 11. On the suffering of the army, see Sword, *President Washington's Indian War*, 199–200; Gaff, *Bayonets in the Wilderness*, 12–14. McKee, writing to Johnson, Jan. 28, 1792, in *Michigan Historical Collections*, 24:365, gives testimony to the plight of Fort Jefferson.

152 *From Pittsburgh came an official memorial*: For the memorial and the back-and-forth among Knox, the Pittsburghers, the militia lieutenants, and Mifflin, see *American State Papers: Indian Affairs*, 1:215–20.

154 *Jefferson was already expanding America*: For Jefferson and western land cessions, see "Editorial Note: Virginia Cession of Territory Northwest of the Ohio," http://founders.archives.gov/documents/Jefferson/01-03-02-0289. For the proposal to Clark, see http://founders.archives.gov/documents/Jefferson/01-06-02-0289. Rashid, "Plan Is the Program," 615, notes Jefferson's fondness for New England's rectilinear approach.

156 *Jefferson dissented from Washington's army project*: Kohn, *Eagle and Sword*, 117.

156 *another key tool for Hamilton was the standing army*: See the discussion of Hamiltonian nationalism in chapter 4.

157 *"There is a western country"*: Hamilton to St. Clair, May 19, 1790, http://founders.archives.gov/documents/Hamilton/01-06-02-0298.

157 *Such uses of military power*: Hamilton's excitement of the prospect of using military power against the citizenry is explored by Hogeland, *The Whiskey Rebellion*, chapter 2, and p. 240. Also see Kohn, *Eagle and Sword*, chapters 2 and 8.

157 *Henry Knox*: For Knox's views on Indians and the West, see "Enclosure," Knox to Washington, June 15, 1789, http://founders.archives.gov/documents/Washington/05-02-02-0357-0002.

158 *passionate opposition to forming a regular army*: Kohn, *Eagle and Sword*, 121, 141–43, shows the opposition's multi-partisan nature.

158 *Washington's supporters called them simply "anti's"*: For example, Fisher Ames to George Richards Minot, April 4, 1789, in Ames, *Works*.

158 *Not every American citizen*: Onuf, *Statehood and Union*, xv, 19.

159 *an egalitarian intellectual commune*: For more on what the poets called their Pantisocracy, see White, "Pantisocracy and Pennsylvania," 72–75.

159 *Benjamin Franklin Bache*: "Minutes of Debate" includes an extract from the March 1792 edition of Bache's *Aurora*, not only passionately antiwar, but also passionately pro-Indian.

159 *assimilating the Indian people*: The Knox reference above is typical. Parsons, "Civilizing the Indians of the Old Northwest," cites mutually positive exchanges on the matter between Knox and Cornplanter and other Seneca and makes a case for the humanitarian sincerity, at least, of the "civilizing" effort during the Jefferson administration, also discussed in chapter 12.

160 *Quakers sent the president a letter*: Quakers to Washington, Dec. 16, 1791, http://founders.archives.gov/documents/Washington/05-09-02-0181.

161 *They built it from the ground up*: The discussion that begins here, of the creation and submission of "A," "B," and "The Plan," with supporting material, is extrapolated from those documents as presented to Congress. *American State Papers: Indian Affairs*, 1:139–215.

164 *the Glaize*: McKee's efforts to gain British support are discussed above. The description given here of life at the Glaize is distilled from Tanner, "Glaize in 1792," 84–85, 95–96, who offers a wealth of fascinating detail, drawing in part on Spencer's memoir.

165 *What bothered McKee*: On threats to confederation unity, see Alured Clarke to Henry Dundas, Feb. 11, 1792, with enclosures from McKee and others, in *Michigan Historical Collections*, 24:373–78. Frustration over the failure to follow up victory is reflected in McKee to Johnson, Jan. 28, 1792, in *Michigan Historical Collections*, 24:365, with a complaint that the Glaize Indians must hunt instead of supporting their more distant allies by destroying St. Clair's forts. For Dorchester's policy, see Taylor, *Divided Ground*, 358; Sword, *President Washington's Indian War*, 158–59. For Dorchester's speech to the Indians, see *Michigan Historical Collections*, 24:309.

168 *officers cleared the public galleries and closed the doors*: *Annals of Congress*, House of Representatives, 2nd Cong., 1st sess., 327–28; also noted by Kohn, *Eagle and Sword*. The story of the bill's progress told here relies on the editor's note to Washington's submission of the documents, http://founders.archives.gov/documents/Washington/05-09-02-0253.

168 *James Madison*: Kohn, *Eagle and Sword*, 121, notes the seeming contradiction in Madison's authoring the bill even while becoming a leading administration antagonist. Ketcham, *James Madison*, 275–77, reviews Henry's not only barring Madison from the Senate but also engaging in gerrymandering in hopes of keeping him out of the House.

169 *Over Knox's name, this op-ed*: Though not officially submitted to Congress, the article is published in *Annals*, 2nd Cong., app., 1046. For its development and backdating, see "Editorial Note," http://founders.archives.gov/documents/Washington/05-09-02-0296-0001.

170 *The House . . . threw open its doors*: *Annals*, House, 2nd Cong., 1st sess., 337. It is Kohn's assertion, *Eagle and Sword*, 121, with footnote 125, that the event was staged, because the speeches are summarized in the *Annals* without attribution, a highly unusual procedure.

170 *allies in the House also requested new paperwork*: *American State Papers: Indian Affairs*, 1:215.

171 *The House held the vote*: *Annals*, House, 2nd Cong., 1st sess., 354.

171 *The return of John Simcoe*: Riddell, *Life of John Graves Simcoe*, is the exhaustive yet badly dated biography. Fryer and Dracott's lively, modern treatment, *John Graves Simcoe*, follows Riddell in taking at face value too much of Simcoe's self-serving construction of his activities regarding the military conflict of 1791–1794. Discussion here of Simcoe's goals and dreams is largely extrapolated from Taylor, *Divided Ground*, 268–70, with reference to Simcoe's letter to Joseph Banks, in Simcoe's *Correspondence*, 1:17; to Henry Dundas, June 30, 1791, 1:27; and to Dorchester, 2:336. For the formation of Upper and Lower Canada, see

"Constitutional Act, 1791," also known as the Canada Act. Taylor, *American Revolutions*, 323–34, discusses the act in terms of the loyalists' plight and the British administrators' ambitions.

174 *Marquis de Lafayette's military capabilities*: John Simcoe, *Remarks*. On Lafayette, ibid., 42; on Greene, ibid., 44; on Washington, ibid., 40–41.

176 *Shawnee diplomacy . . . organization*: Sugden, *Blue Jacket*, 128–29.

176 *an attempt to reform the old militia system*: This discussion closely follows Kohn, *Eagle and Sword*, 133–38.

178 *Benjamin Hawkins . . . began playing an important role*: For Hawkins's overall role in the Senate, see Pound, *Benjamin Hawkins*, chap. 4. It is Kohn's speculation, *Eagle and Sword*, 123, that Hawkins and Washington struck the private bargain described here. An examination of the record in light of ensuing events fully supports that idea. See Hawkins to Washington, Feb. 10, 1792, http://founders.archives.gov/documents/Washington/05-09-02-0328, and Washington's line of thought in response in editor's note 2. Hawkins's reversing his vote following the exchange points to the deal, and the administration's new policy regarding peace negotiations followed directly from passage of the bill (see chapter 8).

182 *Washington, too, wanted St. Clair cleared*: For Washington's handling of St. Clair, from St. Clair's arrival in Philadelphia to his resignation in April: St. Clair to Washington, March 26, 1792, http://founders.archives.gov/documents/Washington/05-10-02-0095 (with the editor's note on background); March 31, 1792, http://founders.archives.gov/documents/Washington/05-10-02-0107; April 7, 1792, http://founders.archives.gov/documents/Washington/05-10-02-0132; Washington to St. Clair, April 4, 1792, http://founders.archives.gov/documents/Washington/05-10-02-0123.

182 *to supply certain documents*: Editor's notes on Knox to Washington, March 30, 1792, http://founders.archives.gov/documents/Washington/05-10-02-0104; and Jefferson's "Memoranda of Consultations," March 9 to April 11, 1792, http://founders.archives.gov/documents/Jefferson/01-23-02-0219.

183 *mulling over . . . a poor set of choices*: Jefferson, "Memorandum of Consultation on Indian Policy," March 9, 1792, http://founders.archives.gov/documents/Jefferson/01-23-02-0205; Washington, "Memorandum on General Officers," March 9, 1792, http://founders.archives.gov/documents/Washington/05-10-02-0040.

7. MAD ANTHONY

185 *Anthony Wayne*: Much biographical fact in this chapter is drawn from Paul David Nelson's judicious study *Anthony Wayne: Soldier of the Early Republic*. Wildes's affectionate portrait, *Anthony Wayne, Troubleshooter of the American Revolution*, has a lot of dated charm yet is at times bewilderingly sourced. Tucker's sometimes fanciful biography, *Mad Anthony Wayne and the New Nation*, includes some good stories not readily verified. H. N. Moore's patriotic, nineteenth-century *Life and Services of Anthony Wayne* makes good use of primary sources, drawing in large part on "Biographical Memoir." Especially telling facts, direct reference to the primary record, original reflections, other secondary sources, and related observations are noted below.

188 *staging drills and battles*: "Biographical Memoir," 17; also cited by Paul David Nelson, *Anthony Wayne*, 7, noting the weakness of the record regarding Wayne's early life.

189 *Wayne never really went home*: The remark seems borne out by the ensuing story.

189 *to learn how to be led*: This feature of Wayne's early military career relates to the mature military frustration and threat of crisis described in chapter 9.

190 *his first battle*: This discussion relies largely on Paul David Nelson, *Anthony Wayne*, chap. 2. Wayne's idea that St. Clair had merely stubbed his toe comes from Tucker, *Mad Anthony Wayne and the New Nation*, 40, possibly apocryphally.

195 *Near Paoli*: For Wayne's eagerness for action, see Paul David Nelson, *Anthony Wayne*, 65–68. Nelson refutes the common notion of Paoli as a massacre, expressed at the site by the monument of 1817 and the obelisk of 1877, both still standing (54–58).

196 *Monmouth Court House*: For Wayne at the Battle of Monmouth, see Paul David Nelson, *Anthony Wayne*, 77–83. The museum and preserved site at Monmouth Battlefield State Park give strong aid to understanding the overall event.

199 *Wayne achieved the signal victory*: Ibid., 94–102. The Stony Point Battlefield State Historic Site and museum bring to life the nature of the action.

201 *Mad Anthony*: Moore, *Life and Services of Anthony Wayne*, has the most detail on the nickname's origins, quoting a letter from Wayne to family members expressing affection for "Jemy [sic] the Rover" (132); the account closely follows "Biographical Memoir," 498. Wildes, *Anthony Wayne*, 236, blames the author Washington Irving, in his *Life of Washington*, for spreading the idea that the nickname referred to rashness in the field and even to insanity, and notes that Wayne's real military strengths involved intense regard for discipline; Tucker, *Mad Anthony Wayne and the New Nation*, 13, concurs. Paul David Nelson, *Anthony Wayne*, 125, dissents, asserting that the name did refer to impetuosity in battle. From Jemmy's original remark, if it was really made, through the events related in chapters 10 and 11, tensions between critics' presumptions of derangement and foolhardiness and Wayne's nearly maniacal attention both to discipline in his troops and security on his advance lend the nickname strange resonances.

202 *Wayne bucked*: Ibid., 145–46.

203 *a gregarious man*: Wildes, *Anthony Wayne*, 309–12, details with brio the nature of Wayne's romantic relationships. Paul David Nelson, *Anthony Wayne*, 103–4, discusses the relationship with Mary Vining. The intensity and intimacy of the Wayne–Catharine Greene connection are revealed in Catharine Greene to Anthony Wayne, Nov. 15 and Dec. 30, 1789, Wayne Papers, Historical Society of Pennsylvania.

203 *Mary felt a passionate longing*: Mary Wayne to Anthony Wayne, Jan. 29, 1776, Correspondence, Wayne Family Papers, Clements Library. His to her, July 22, 1784, Wayne Papers, as discussed in the text, is typical of his tone.

205 *Wayne joined in an elite movement*: Paul David Nelson, *Anthony Wayne*, 188–90, explores Wayne's antidemocratic attitudes and efforts in revising the populist constitution, as well as his methods for getting elected.

205 *Rice production*: Ibid., 198–200; Daniel C. Littlefield, "The Varieties of Slave Labor." For numbers on enslaved blacks in Pennsylvania, see "PA Civil War 150,"

http://pacivilwar150.com/Understand/SlaveryandFreedom.html. For "the curly heads" quotation, see Wildes, *Anthony Wayne, Troubleshooter of the American Revolution*, 305.

206 *He sent an application for a loan*: Paul David Nelson, *Anthony Wayne*, chaps. 9 and 10, deftly organizes the welter of detail exploding for years from the financial detonation that Wayne set off with this application.

206 *presented on a standard ledger sheet*: June 30, 1785, Wayne Family Papers.

207 *the brothers Willink were reviewing*: In Wayne Family Papers, see Willinks to Robert Morris, March 26, 1784 (extract hand copy); Willinks to Wayne, March 26, 1785; Wayne to Sharp Delany, June 7, 1785, reading the Willinks' letter as promising loan approval any minute; Wayne to the Willinks, June 9, 1785, announcing that he's drawing on them.

208 *Penman now wanted his money from Wayne*: Penman to Wayne, Sept. 29, 1785; Wayne to Willinks, Dec. 20, 1785, on the bounced check; Willinks to Wayne, Oct. 31, 1785, and Jan. 6, 1786; Wayne to Jacob Cohen, Feb. 5, 1786; Wayne to Willing, Feb. 13, 1786, Wayne Family Papers.

210 *a classic bubble always threatening to burst*: Hogeland, *Founding Finance*, 142–44.

210 *build a sufficiency for his children*: Wayne to Sharp Delany, May 24, 1787, Wayne Family Papers.

210 *Wayne's proud and wounded tone*: Examples abound in the Wayne Family Papers: Wayne to Penman, for example, Feb. 10, June 13, Aug. 12, 1787. One of Wayne's lawyers, Aedanus Burke, tries to no avail to get Wayne, Nov. 10, 1787, to moderate his tone with creditors: "Harsh terms irritate the man in whose power you are."

211 *"pardon me, my dear girl"*: June 28, 1786, Wayne Papers.

211 *His daughter, Peggy*: Margaretta Wayne to Anthony Wayne, date illegible, Wayne Papers.

212 *"the man Penman"*: Wayne to Burke, Oct. 2, 1787, Wayne Family Papers. Elsewhere Wayne simply underlines Penman's name for disgusted emphasis.

212 *he might actually face arrest*: At times, Wayne seems worried about being arrested anywhere *but* Pennsylvania; for example, Wayne to Delany, Oct. 23, 1787, Wayne Papers.

212 *stuff the bank's hungry maw*: Wayne to Delany, May 24, 1787, Wayne Family Papers. For the depreciation of paper and Hamilton's efforts to fund the debt, see Hogeland, *Founding Finance*, 76–78, 163–72.

213 *sue him for dower rights*: This discussion of dower rights is based on an e-mail correspondence with Mary Ann Hallenborg, J.D., Clinical Assistant Professor of Real Estate, Shack Institute of Real Estate, New York University.

213 *legally bound to pay her an annuity*: Paul David Nelson, *Anthony Wayne*, 11.

213 *an offer that, he informed Penman, was so good*: Wayne to Penman, Oct. 2, 1787, via Burke; Penman to Wayne, Nov. 7, 1787, Wayne Family Papers.

214 *Wayne faced the fact*: Anthony Wayne to Mary Wayne, May 30, 1789; Anthony Wayne to Elizabeth Wayne, June 28, 1790, Wayne Family Papers.

214 *he'd had his eye on federal appointments*: Wayne to Washington, April 6, 1789; and to Catharine Greene, Feb. 4, 1790 (with first pages, probably more personal, redacted), Wayne Papers.

215 *Wayne reveled*: Paul David Nelson, *Anthony Wayne*, 217–19.

215 *He took part in the secret debates on the army bill*: See *Annals*, House, 2nd Cong., 1st sess., 348. Because *Annals* departs from the usual practice of ascribing speeches to individual members, and only lists names in the groups speaking against and in favor of augmentation, Wayne's inclusion in the list speaking against raises questions. Nothing in the speechmaking against augmentation, as reported, accords with any position Wayne ever held. Paul David Nelson, *Anthony Wayne*, 222, states without qualification that Wayne spoke in favor of augmentation, and that he had advance word, possibly directly from Knox, that the appointment as commander was imminent; yet Nelson doesn't address the report in *Annals*. Wildes, *Anthony Wayne, Troubleshooter of the American Revolution*, wishfully ascribes to Wayne a sardonic remark in favor of troop augmentation, uncredited as reported. Kohn, *Eagle and Sword*, 122–23, pointing to the showcase nature of the debate, notes that others speaking in favor of cutting troop strength were also Federalists and quotes an observer on the idea that insincere grandstanding in favor of militia may have been in play as a tactic. Kohn also notes that Wayne was critical of the administration's war efforts in the West and speculates that he may have changed his position on the promise of being appointed commander (ibid, 126). In any event, per *Annals*, 355, Wayne voted with the majority on January 31 against cutting out the augmentation portion of the bill.

216 *denouncing his chicanery*: Jackson's lengthy and passionate speech is given in full in *Annals*, House, 2nd Cong., 1st sess., 458.

217 *Wayne received news*: Paul David Nelson, *Anthony Wayne*, 226.

8. THE PEACEFUL INTENTIONS OF THE UNITED STATES

218 *John Simcoe learned with pleasure*: Simcoe to Henry Dundas, Feb. 16, 1792, in *Michigan Historical Collections*, 24:377. Fryer and Dracott, *John Graves Simcoe*, 138, cover the house rental, the trip to Montreal, and so on.

219 *George Beckwith*: For his role as a gatherer of intelligence and his relationship with Hamilton, see Reuter, "'Petty Spy' or Effective Diplomat." Boyd, *Number 7*, makes a passionately pro-Jefferson criticism of Hamilton's secret interactions with Beckwith.

219 *Stevenson traveled southwesterly*: Stevenson's lively letters are revealing of the intense interest of certain colonial officials in regaining big parts of territory ceded in 1783. See John Simcoe, *Correspondence*, 1:100, 109, 116, 123, 127.

222 *Washington convened the cabinet*: Jefferson, "Memorandum of Consultation on Indian Policy," March 9, 1792. For background on the Steedman-Pond mission, see *American State Papers: Indian Affairs*, 1:227, 235.

226 *meetings with members of the Six Nations*: For the Six Nations meeting in Philadelphia, see *American State Papers: Indian Affairs*, 1:229. For Brant's move to Grand River, see Kelsay, *Joseph Brant*, 369–71. Knox's invitation to Brant, in *American State Papers: Indian Affairs*, 1:228.

228 *the administration's line*: For Washington's speech to the Six Nations, see *American State Papers: Indian Affairs*, 1:229. Kohn, perhaps the leading scholar of the politics of forming the army, shows that in December 1791 the administration fully committed itself to attacking the western Indian confederation, winning the war, and establishing a fort at Kekionga: "force was now mandatory," regulars a necessity

(*Eagle and Sword*, 108). In January 1793, as Kohn asserts and shows, all cabinet members openly referred to peace negotiations as a mere ruse for manufacturing public consent for war (149). Yet Kohn takes at face value the administration line of 1792, described here, and presents the suddenly renewed effort at negotiations as somehow temporarily sincere (144–45). In accommodating that idea, his narrative becomes uncharacteristically elaborate and self-contradictory: at the Six Nations meeting, "the administration learned to its surprise" that there had been a misunderstanding; yet on p. 123 the ensuing negotiations were undertaken "mainly for political reasons." Kohn himself has the simpler and far more logically applicable explanation for the new policy: the deal he suggests Washington and Hawkins made to get the army bill passed. Diplomatic policy beginning in the spring of 1792, with its seemingly self-contradictory nature—"dual policy," as Kohn puts it—flowed from the administration's desire to satisfy Congress that sincere and energetic efforts to start peace negotiations were under way and to have those efforts dramatically fail—just as Kohn notes the administration expected in 1793—in order to rally support behind the military agenda that Washington had become implacably committed to, as Kohn shows, at the end of 1791. Wayne, meanwhile, got time to build the army. Not enough attention has been given, generally in the history of this episode, to the starkness of difference in sending Pond, Steedman, and others in disguise as spies, before the Hawkins deal, and sending the Trueman and Hardin parties and others undisguised and in uniform after the deal was made.

229 *By May 29, Trueman*: For the fates of the two parties, see Sword, *President Washington's Indian War*, 211–12.

230 *General Anthony Wayne arrived in Pittsburgh*: Wayne to Knox, June 14, 1792; to Delany, June 22, 1792; to Knox, June 29, 1792, Wayne Family Papers. Wayne to Wilkinson, June 16, 1792, Wayne Papers.

231 *the whole setup at the headwaters*: Wildes, *Anthony Wayne, Troubleshooter of the American Revolution*, 358. For frustrations in building Fort Fayette, see Hogeland, *Whiskey Rebellion*, 101.

232 *a flurry*: For example, Wayne to Knox, July 13 and Aug. 10, 1792; Knox to Wayne, June 20, 1792, in Knopf, *Anthony Wayne*.

233 *Desertion was Wayne's*: Sword, *President Washington's Indian War*, 232. Ward, *George Washington's Enforcers*, chap. 15, details the lives and duties of army musicians and their special role in enforcing discipline. For Washington's request to raise the number of lashes, see Maurer, "Military Justice Under General Washington," 11–12.

235 *the Legion of the United States*: Gaff, *Bayonets in the Wilderness*, 64. On the Duer-Knox scheme as background to the finance change, see Sword, *President Washington's Indian War*, 148–51.

236 *he had the men build . . . redoubts*: For training efforts, see Gaff, *Bayonets in the Wilderness*, 60–64; Sword, *President Washington's Indian War*, 234–35. For the threatened attack in August, the brandings, and the executions, see Gaff, *Bayonets in the Wilderness*, 61–62.

238 *Placing undefended men in harm's way*: See Knox to Wayne, Aug. 3, 1792, Wayne Papers, giving news about the emissaries' deaths. For Wayne's outrage at the policy, see Wayne to Sharp Delany, August 24, 1793, Wayne Family Papers. For the at-

tack on the hay cutters, see Putnam to Knox, July 5, 1792, Wayne Papers; Gaff, *Bayonets in the Wilderness*, 17–18. For Gallipolis, see Gaff, *Bayonets in the Wilderness*, 18–19; Sword, *President Washington's Indian War*, 49.

240 *"he," the enemy, was still fighting "us"*: In letters of 1792 not only to Knox but also to others, Wayne repeatedly expresses the view that the war was actually ongoing, and while still refraining from openly criticizing Washington, he castigates Congress's insistence on peace measures. For example, Wayne to Irvine, July 20, 1792, and Wayne to Delany, Aug. 24, 1792, Wayne Papers.

241 *"The President of the United States has thought proper"*: Wayne to the Militia Lieutenants, June 23, 1792, Wayne Papers.

242 *Rufus Putnam, arrived*: Putnam to Wilkinson, July 3 and 5, 1792; Wilkinson to Putnam, July 5, 1792, and July 6, 1792 (copy of extract); Putnam to Knox, July 5, 1792, Wayne Papers. Putnam followed up those exchanges with further letters to Knox and Washington, for the record, retailing Indian atrocities while expressing fervent hopes for peace.

243 *"If all the measures which have been pursued"*: Washington to Knox, Aug. 22, 1792, http://founders.archives.gov/documents/Washington/05-11-02-0008.

243 *Putnam's inflammatory message*: *American State Papers: Indian Affairs*, 1:234–36.

245 *his own plan of invasion*: Wayne to Knox, Aug. 24, 1792, in Knopf, *Anthony Wayne*.

245 *Putnam's proposals*: For Putnam's invasion plan, see Putnam, *Memoirs*, 279.

9. LEGION VILLE

250 *As delegations began gathering*: Sugden, *Blue Jacket*, 132–33; Sword, *President Washington's Indian War*, 213. For Hendrick Aupaumut's journey and take on the gathering, see his *Narrative*.

252 *The first day was given over*: For the opening of the debate, see Sword, *President Washington's Indian War*, 223–26, and Sugden, *Blue Jacket*, 134–35, drawing in part on Aupaumut, *Narrative*.

253 *Knox submitted Wayne's invasion plan*: Knox to Washington, Sept. 1, 1792, http://founders.archives.gov/documents/Washington/05-11-02-0031; Washington to Knox, Sept. 7, 1792, http://founders.archives.gov/documents/Washington/05-11-02-0041.

253 *"Brave but nothing more"*: Jefferson, "Memorandum of Consultation on Indian Policy," March 9, 1792.

253 *At one point, Wayne started fiddling*: For the ballistics and powder flap and the branding issue, see Wayne to Knox, July 13 and Aug. 10, 1792, in Knopf, *Anthony Wayne*; Knox to Washington, Aug. 17, 1792, http://founders.archives.gov/documents/Washington/05-11-02-0003; and Washington to Knox, Aug. 26, 1792, http://founders.archives.gov/documents/Washington/05-11-02-0016.

255 *he started nudging Knox*: Growing tension can be traced, in Knox to Wayne, Sept. 1, 1792; Wayne to Knox, Sept. 14, 1792; Knox to Wayne, Sept. 21, 1792; Wayne to Knox, Nov. 16, 1792; Knox to Wayne, Nov. 24, 1792, in Knopf, *Anthony Wayne*.

256 *"the most artful measures have been pursued"*: Beckwith to Dorchester, Jan. 14, 1792, in John Simcoe, *Correspondence*, 1:298.

256 *a separate peace*: For the Wabash treaty, see Putnam, *Memoirs*, 363–66. For Putnam's satisfaction with his efforts, see ibid., 379–80. Sword, *President Washington's Indian War*, 217–18, notes the later failure of ratification.

256 *the Glaize conference resumed*: In the blowup between the Seneca and the confederation, both Sword, *President Washington's Indian War*, 226–28, and Sugden, *Blue Jacket*, 135–38, make clear that that conference was a hard-line victory. For Brant's late arrival, see Kelsay, *Joseph Brant*, 481. On Painted Pole's role as a recruiter, see Sugden, *Blue Jacket*, 138, also noting there the British mediation role.

260 *Blue Jacket was preparing*: His enthusiasm is borne out by Sugden, *Blue Jacket*, 38. Little Turtle's doubts are explored by Carter, *Life and Times of Little Turtle*, 125.

262 *William Wells*: The modern biography of Wells is by Heath, *William Wells and the Struggle for the Old Northeast*.

262 *robbing U.S. forces of their food supply*: Carter, *Life and Times of Little Turtle*, 125, implying Little Turtle's disapproval of the attack on Fort Jefferson. On U.S. supply problems, see Wilkinson to Wayne, Oct. 4, 1792, Wayne Family Papers.

264 *He'd continued to send*: Wayne to Knox, Nov. 9, 1792, in Knopf, *Anthony Wayne*. For Cornplanter's message to Wayne, see Wayne to Knox, Nov. 16, 1792, in Knopf, *Anthony Wayne*.

264 *Little Turtle gathered two hundred fighters*: This account of the expedition is based in part on Spencer, *Indian Captivity of O. M. Spencer*, 115–77, in part on Wilkinson to Knox, Nov. 4 and 6, 1792, Wayne Family Papers, as also related by Carter, *Life and Times of Little Turtle*, 125–26, and Sword, *President Washington's Indian War*, 220–21. That the expedition was led by Little Turtle is evidenced by Colonel England to Simcoe in John Simcoe, *Correspondence*, 1:270.

266 *gearing up to diminish Wayne's army*: Kohn, *Eagle and Sword*, 146–47. For the load of paperwork, see *American State Papers: Indian Affairs*, 1:225–318.

267 *"barbarous sacrifice"*: *Annals of Congress*, House of Representatives, 2nd Cong., 2nd sess., 678.

267 *narrative collision*: Red Jacket's report on the Glaize conference is in *American State Papers: Indian Affairs*, 1:323–24. While Red Jacket is not named as the speaker, Sword, *President Washington's Indian War*, 227, attributes the speech to him, logically enough.

270 *no invasion*: Knox to Wayne, Nov. 24, 1792, with the vague idea of a conference; then Knox to Wayne, Dec. 7, 1792, bringing the hammer down, in Knopf, *Anthony Wayne*.

270 *"Be not therefore any longer bemused"*: Wayne to Knox, Dec. 13, 1792, followed up by Wayne to Knox, Dec. 21, 1792, Wayne Family Papers.

271 *"I shall not comment"*: Wayne to Knox, Dec. 28, 1792, Wayne Family Papers.

271 *John Steele . . . attacked the military*: For the debate, see *Annals*, 2nd Cong., 2nd sess., 773, with Steele's speeches, 795–97. For Madison's opposition, see Kohn, *Eagle and Sword*, 148, also tracking the debate process through to resolution.

272 *Knox wrote to the Indian confederation*: For their rocky exchange, see John Simcoe, *Correspondence*, 1:283–84.

274 *only to gratify public opinion*: Kohn, *Eagle and Sword*, 149, quoting Jefferson's notes.

274 *The Simcoes were no longer in Quebec*: Fryer and Dracott, *John Graves Simcoe*, 148–50. For Simcoe's denial of Hamilton's request, see Sword, *President Washington's Indian War*, 229.

277 *give the commission proper prestige*: Kohn, *Eagle and Sword*, 151; Sword, *President Washington's Indian War*, 238–39. For commissioners' instructions, see *American State Papers: Indian Affairs*, 1:340–42.

279 *Wayne called it Legion Ville*: Gaff, *Bayonets in the Wilderness*, 74–76, describes the site in detail.

281 *Wayne's thirty-boat armada*: Ibid., 110–14, details the trip downstream and the camp at Hobson's Choice; pp. 123–26 describe issues and routines there. Wayne to Delany, April 7, 1793, Wayne Family Papers, makes clear that Wayne saw this move as the beginning of his inevitable march: "Peace is out of the question." See also Knox to Wayne, March 5, 1793, in Knopf, *Anthony Wayne*, more or less admitting the same thing.

282 *the American commissioners . . . arrived at Newark*: The story that begins here, with the back-and-forth that threatens to rise to crisis among the commissioners, Simcoe, the confederation, Knox, and Wayne, and ends in the breakdown of discussions, is drawn from Sword, *President Washington's Indian War*, 239–41, Elizabeth Simcoe, *Diary*, 164–76, John Simcoe, *Correspondence*, 1:330–32, 333–34, 345–51, and Lincoln, *Journal*, 122–37 (for the commissioners' time in Newark); from the Wayne Papers, May 27, 1793, June 28, 1793, July 2, 1793, July 20, 1793, Aug. 8, 1793, Sept. 3, 1793 (for the commissioners' warnings and Knox's and Wayne's responses); and from Sugden, *Blue Jacket*, 143–46, 149–55, Sword, *President Washington's Indian War*, 241–43, 245–48, John Simcoe, *Correspondence*, 2:34, 17–22, Lincoln, *Journal*, 137–69, Jacob Lindley, "Expedition to Detroit," in *Michigan Historical Collections*, 17:565–666, and Heath, *William Wells and the Struggle for the Old Northwest*, 173–78 (for the meeting at Roche de Bout, the confederation's response to Wayne's movements, and the final breakdown near Detroit).

285 *twenty-minute salmon chowder*: Elizabeth Simcoe, *Diary*, 172.

287 *Anthony Wayne saw nothing but red*: Wayne to Knox, Aug. 8, 1793, Wayne Papers. Knopf's version edits this document in bewildering fashion by including some parts of the first drafts yet not all of the final, thus eliding the construction described here.

292 *"We have therefore resolved"*: The full text of the message is in John Simcoe, *Correspondence*, 2:17–20; quoted by Sugden, *Blue Jacket*, 154; and Heath, 176, also describing the commissioners' responses and conclusions. Taylor, *Divided Ground*, 280, sees the suggestion that the United States divide the payment among settlers as an attempt to disrupt a system by which Americans attempted to manage class conflict via expansion into Indian land.

293 *"just such an answer"*: *Michigan Historical Collections*, 17:628; and quoted by Heath, *William Wells and the Struggle for the Old Northwest*, 176.

293 *Lincoln had taken in for the first time*: Lincoln, *Journal*, 138–39; and quoted in part by Taylor, *Divided Ground*, 278; and Heath, *William Wells and the Struggle for the Old Northwest*, 176.

293 *The war party at Roche de Bout celebrated*: Sword, *President Washington's Indian War*, 248.

293 *General Wayne . . . received the signal code*: Commissioners to Wayne, Aug. 23, 1793, Wayne Papers.

10. RECOVERY

298 *A somber Christmas*: Gaff, *Bayonets in the Wilderness*, 184–87, and Sword, *President Washington's Indian War*, 255–56, provide details on building the new fort, and cover the Edward Butler story, drawing in part on Buell's diary, in *Journal of the Military Service Institution*, 106.

299 *He'd named it before it existed*: Gaff, *Bayonets in the Wilderness*, 184.

299 *A long year of disappointment*: Poor supply, unreadiness, Kentucky recruitment, and so on, are detailed in Gaff, *Bayonets in the Wilderness*, chaps. 9–11, and distilled in Sword, *President Washington's Indian War*, 249–50. For the march northward and the decision to stop at Greene Ville, see Gaff, *Bayonets in the Wilderness*, chaps. 12 and 13; Sword, *President Washington's Indian War*, 251–53; Buell, in *Journal of the Military Service Institution*, 104–6.

305 *two James Wilkinsons*: Wilkinson's background, as related here, is drawn largely from Linklater, *Artist in Treason*, chaps. 7–11.

306 *Spain was rich, mighty, and stubborn*: See Philyaw, *Virginia's Western Vision*, 102, 107, for Spain's concerns about American river access and the desire of George Washington and other members of the commercial elite to keep the Mississippi closed in favor of the East. On Spain's focus on protecting its silver, see Linklater, *Artist in Treason*, 83.

308 *Wilkinson wrote to Francisco Cruzat*: Linklater, *Artist in Treason*, 79. A highly nuanced view of the mission is found in Whitaker, "Wilkinson's First Descent to New Orleans in 1787." It is Linklater's insight, *Artist in Treason*, 81–82, that the size of the empire made Miro less powerful than one might have expected.

310 *name of a complex code*: Linklater, *Artist in Treason*, 333–34, provides an analysis.

311 *The administration had considered Wilkinson*: Jefferson, "Memorandum of Consultation on Indian Policy," March 9, 1792; Washington, "Memorandum on General Officers," March 9, 1792. Wilkinson's appeal to the cabinet, in light of what he was suspected of, remains a mystery; Linklater explores it in *Artist in Treason*, 117.

313 *a faction . . . that mocked the commander*: Sword, *President Washington's Indian War*, 266; Gaff, *Bayonets in the Wilderness*, 180–81.

313 *Division was meanwhile deepening*: Writers who advance Blue Jacket over Little Turtle—in part by justly criticizing early overreliance on William Wells's exaggerations and self-promotion—include Blue Jacket's biographer Sugden, debunking the "Little Turtle myth" (*Blue Jacket*, 4–6), and Jortner, *Gods of Prophetstown*, 90, describing Little Turtle but not Blue Jacket as "bought off." Such readings tend also to promote the Tecumseh story, with its eschatological prophet Tenskwatawa, as the watershed moment in indigenous defense of the Ohio and Great Lakes Countries, with reference backward to Neolin's and Pontiac's similarly paired prophet-warrior resistance. In that reading, the western Indian confederation that fought St. Clair and Wayne is but a precursor to the real story, and because a young Tecumseh served with Blue Jacket, and Blue Jacket would later ally with him, the Shawnee leader, as viewed from 1811, is axiomatically not only the more important but also the more virtuous leader. For other views, see Sheehan, in review of Dowd's *Spirited Resistance*, arguing that the spiritual unification that Dowd and others call "nativism" is only a superficially integrative force, really a sign of internal collapse, and arguing that Little Turtle's lack of a prophet

partner made him more, not less, effective; Skaggs, in review of *Tecumseh: A Life*, by Sugden, questioning reading backward from Tecumseh to make Blue Jacket the most important 1790s confederation leader; and Eid, "American Indian Military Leadership," arguing among other things that a fatal attraction to the Tecumseh story leads writers to misunderstand not only Little Turtle but also what occurred in the West in the 1790s, and thus in the nineteenth century as well.

314 *The man didn't sleep*: For Wayne's defensive measures on the move, see Gaff, *Bayonets in the Wilderness*, 159, taking issue with comparisons between Wayne and Julius Caesar. "Super convoys" is Gaff's term, ibid., 176, 202.

314 *Blue Jacket . . . was again traveling*: Sugden, *Blue Jacket*, 158–60.

315 *Dorchester returned to North America*: For the speech, see Downes, *Council Fires on the Upper Ohio*, 330. Simcoe's biographers follow Simcoe himself in his efforts, later, to dissociate himself from the Fort Miamis project, but the plan fulfilled everything he'd been hoping for, as noted by Sword, *President Washington's Indian War*, 260, and Taylor, *Divided Ground*, 283, 287. Simcoe did express doubt, but only in worrying that the fort might not get built before Wayne marched; see Sword, *President Washington's Indian War*, 261–62. For Simcoe's plan—or dream—of total military action against the United States, see Taylor, *Divided Ground*, 287. For McKee's gathering wrongly that the U.S. objective was the Great Lakes forts, see Sword, *President Washington's Indian War*, 292.

316 *the one American general*: John Simcoe, *Remarks*, 42–43.

317 *mounting a decisive attack*: The attack on Fort Recovery is often seen as a turning point in the war—"the beginning of the end" (Downes, *Council Fires on the Upper Ohio*, 334)—and in that sense at least as important as the Battle of Fallen Timbers. The account given here is drawn from Sugden, *Blue Jacket*, 159–71; Sword, *President Washington's Indian War*, 273–78; Gaff, *Bayonets in the Wilderness*, chap. 19; Winkler, *Fallen Timbers*, 51–53; Alder, *Captivity of Jonathan Alder by the Indians in 1782*, 110–12; and Buell's diary, in *Journal of the Military Service Institution*, 110. Proponents of Little Turtle over Blue Jacket tend to blame the failure on the expedition's not being guided by Little Turtle (Carter, *Life and Times of Little Turtle*, 132), and on Blue Jacket's supposedly poorer strategic judgment (Sword, *President Washington's Indian War*, 271). Larry L. Nelson, "Never Have They Done So Little," argues that the Fort Recovery battle represents the confederation's collapse.

324 *Little Turtle went around McKee*: Carter, *Life and Times of Little Turtle*, 132; John Simcoe, *Correspondence*, 2:333–34; Horsman, "The British Indian Department and the Resistance to General Anthony Wayne, 1793–1795," noting that if Little Turtle were as sensible as England said he was, the Miami leader could have had no doubts about British insincerity (279).

11. FALLEN TIMBERS

326 *Knox had begun urging Wayne*: See Knox to Wayne, May 16, 1794, and Wayne to Knox, May 30, 1794, with "would to God," in Knopf, *Anthony Wayne*.

326 *Congress militantly anti-British*: Kohn, *Eagle and Sword*, 155–56.

327 *new orders*: Knox to Wayne, June 7, 1794, in Knopf, *Anthony Wayne*.

327 *William Wells . . . working for Wayne*: Heath, *William Wells and the Struggle for the Old Northwest*, 185.

328 *Wayne relished the prospect*: Wayne to Knox, July 16, 1794, Wayne Family Papers, shows him planning his campaign in part against Simcoe.

328 *On July 28, 1794, the morning gun*: The narrative of Wayne's march, broken in sections throughout this chapter, is drawn mainly from Gaff, *Bayonets in the Wilderness*, chaps. 21–23; Sword, *President Washington's Indian War*, 279–86; Winkler, *Fallen Timbers*, 54–59; the surprisingly upbeat *Precise Journal*, signed only "Randolph"; Quaife, "General James Wilkinson's Narrative of the Fallen Timbers Campaign"; and "General Wayne's Orderly Book," in *Michigan Historical Collections*, 34:341.

329 *He shook their hands*: Winkler, *Fallen Timbers*, 55.

329 *The Indian confederation force was still gathered*: The narrative of confederation and British response to Wayne's march and formation at Fallen Timbers, broken in sections here, is drawn largely from ibid., 36–37; and Sword, *President Washington's Indian War*, 288–98.

329 *dismantling the Glaize became a chaotic flight*: For the evacuation, the stress on McKee's resources at Fort Miamis, and logistics of supplying the fort with howitzers, see Sword, *President Washington's Indian War*, 288–89, with reference to John Simcoe, *Correspondence*, 2:334–45, 362, 373–74.

332 *the Black Snake*: That this became an appellation for Wayne is widely reported and is accepted by Sword, *President Washington's Indian War*, 296, and Heath, *William Wells and the Struggle for the Old Northwest*, 200–201. Because William Wells was sometimes known as "Black Snake," Heath also suggests that it might have been Wells, not Wayne, to whom the name referred. The earliest published reference and explanation of the term's application to Wayne appears to be Heckewelder, *History, Manners, and Customs of the Indian Nations Who Once Inhabited Pennsylvania and the Neighbouring States*, 192n1: originally published in 1818, Heckewelder's account is based in part on its author's experiences in Vincennes and Detroit at the time.

332 *a tall beech tree toppled onto the tent*: Gaff, *Bayonets in the Wilderness*, 389n21, points out that despite Wayne's suspicions, dropping a tree on him would have been an overly complicated means of assassination. Wilkinson's anonymous screed is described by Paul David Nelson, *Anthony Wayne*, 256.

335 *his wife, Mary, had died*: William Hayman to Wayne, April 28 and May 31, 1793, Wayne Family Papers. For Wayne's emotional turmoil, Wayne to Knox, April 19, 1793, in Knopf, *Anthony Wayne*. For the Isaac story, see Mary Wayne to Isaac Wayne, n.d., 1792; Anthony Wayne to Isaac Wayne, May 9 and July 14, 1794, Wayne Family Papers.

336 *Little Turtle spoke first*: Sword, *President Washington's Indian War*, 289–91; and Sugden, *Blue Jacket*, 174–76, on the question of whether it was Blue Jacket himself who attacked Little Turtle directly. As Sugden notes, those who present this scene as one in which Little Turtle abdicates solo command, in the face of resistance to his policy, in favor of Blue Jacket—Sword does so—are constructing confederation leadership in an unrealistically top-down manner. That reading enables the Little Turtle contingent—Sword and Carter throughout, and Winkler, *Fallen Timbers*, 21—to position their man as the author of victory over St. Clair and his absence from leadership as a reason for confederation defeat at Fort Recovery and Fallen Timbers.

337 *Fallen Timbers*: For the confederation's line, see Sugden, *Blue Jacket*, 172–73, 176–80; Winkler, *Fallen Timbers*, 58, 62; Sword, *President Washington's Indian War*, 301–3. The British withdrawal from Roche de Bout is mentioned in a report by Simcoe, *Correspondence*, 3, 19.

338 *Wilkinson, writing for the record*: Quaife, "General James Wilkinson's Narrative of the Fallen Timbers Campaign."

340 *on the morning of the twentieth*: For the final U.S. approach, the ensuing battle itself, and the back-and-forth at Fort Miamis, see Sword, *President Washington's Indian War*, 299–311; Sugden, *Blue Jacket*, 176–80; Gaff, *Bayonets in the Wilderness*, 299–327; Winkler, *Fallen Timbers*, 61–67, and maps, 63, 69, 85. The confederation's preparations are recalled by Alder, *Captivity of Jonathan Alder by the Indians in 1782*, 113–115, with the reason for fasting, 114. For Wayne's order of battle, see *Michigan Historical Collections*, 34:532. For Wilkinson's condemnation, see Quaife, "General James Wilkinson's Narrative of the Fallen Timbers Campaign," with "no fight," 84. Wayne's "Perhaps I may": Gaff, *Bayonets in the Wilderness*, 306. For McKee's efforts at persistence, see Sword, *President Washington's Indian War*, 305. Sugden, *Blue Jacket*, 179, underscores Blue Jacket's personal sense of betrayal by the British at Fort Miamis, lending support to Wayne's view of what the battle accomplished.

12. BLACK GRANITE

354 *fewer than 5,000 white people*: Statistics are from Sugden, *Blue Jacket*, 204. In "The Meanings of the Wars for the Great Lakes," in Skaggs and Nelson, *Sixty Years' War*, 375–89, Andrew Cayton notes that the transformation of the entire continent enabled by U.S. victory in the Northwest Territory occurred "with a speed and a thoroughness virtually unmatched anywhere in the history of the world" (376) and considers the ironies involved in such a critical war's having been forgotten.

354 *Wayne made quick progress*: The march back up the river and the building of Fort Wayne are detailed in Gaff, *Bayonets in the Wilderness*, chaps. 26–28, and distilled by Sword, *President Washington's Indian War*, 310–11. Sword says it was raining; Wayne reports lighting fires and expresses "infinite pleasure," in Wayne to Knox, Aug. 28, 1794, in Knopf, *Anthony Wayne*. That confederation Indians followed Wayne is reported by Simcoe, *Correspondence*, 3:19, based on reports from Major Campbell and Colonel England, 20–21. For fortifying Defiance, see Gaff, *Bayonets in the Wilderness*, 344. Sword, *President Washington's Indian War*, 319, notes the strategically commanding position of the fort.

356 *In December 1794*: This section distills Hogeland, *Whiskey Rebellion*. Washington's gain in land value is deduced from discussion of land prices between James Ross and George Washington in June and September 1794 and January 1795: http://founders.archives.gov/documents/Washington/05-16-02-0193, http://founders.archives.gov/documents/Washington/05-16-02-0439, http://founders.archives.gov/documents/Washington/05-17-02-0267. For Washington's exhaustion and hearing and memory loss, see Flexner, *Washington*, 261, 337.

361 *He returned to his farm*: Washington's correspondence after leaving office makes clear that his persistent project remained land development.

362 *British officialdom didn't share*: For England's remarks, see Gaff, *Bayonets in the Wilderness*, 326. For McKee's efforts during this shaky period, see Larry Nelson, *Man of Distinction Among Them*, 173–74; for McKee's and Simcoe's attempts to carry on, see Sword, *President Washington's Indian War*, 312–15. Simcoe's calling Wayne's march upstream a retreat is in Simcoe, *Correspondence*, 3:19.

363 *the Indian confederation made direct communication*: This issue plays into scholarly controversies over credit and blame and conflicts between Blue Jacket and Little Turtle fans. Jortner, for example, in *The Gods of Prophetstown*, says the Miami were "first to fall," and "the Miami arrived in December." Yet he cites references that don't support that conclusion. Heath, *William Wells and the Struggle for the Old Northwest*, 219, quotes Wayne, *American State Papers: Indian Affairs*, 1:567, on a Miami leader called the Soldier asking for terms at Greene Ville as early as September. Yet the document cited says, in parentheses in the text itself, that "the soldier" (lowercase in the source) refers to the Wabash people, who had indeed made an earlier peace and are listed in the transcript as attendees. Wayne himself further states, in that same document, that the first to sue for peace, in September, were the Sandusky Wyandot; Horsman, "The British Indian Department and the Resistance to General Anthony Wayne, 1793–1795," cites England and McKee on Wyandot priority. By putting the Miami first, Heath, following Carter, *Life and Times of Little Turtle*, 145, is advancing their importance; Jortner puts them first to characterize them as eager sellouts. Blue Jacket's biographer Sugden, for his part, presents Wayne as having failed to break the confederation until Blue Jacket showed up at Fort Defiance and lent the negotiation process support (*Blue Jacket*, 186–87). All are bending the record out of shape to fit a preference. Sword, *President Washington's Indian War*, 318, seems to have the process of interaction between Wayne and the various Native groups more or less right.

364 *Blue Jacket himself had left for Greene Ville*: Sword, *President Washington's Indian War*, 318; Sugden, *Blue Jacket*, 180–87; Horsman, "The British Indian Department and the Resistance to General Anthony Wayne, 1793–1795," 287. For the younger McKee's rage, see Sugden, *Blue Jacket*, 194. Sword, *President Washington's Indian War*, 319–21, tracks the winding down of McKee and Simcoe. For Blue Jacket's entrance, see Sugden, *Blue Jacket*, 188, with reference to Buell's eyewitness account (268). Sugden, *Blue Jacket*, 192, notes that Blue Jacket saw the event less as a surrender than a shift in alliance and covers his new effort at recruitment, in this case for Wayne (195–200).

366 *Knox . . . final report to the president*: Kohn, *Eagle and Sword*, 170–72, with reference to "Preservation of Peace with the Indians," *Annals*, 3rd Cong., app., 1400.

367 *Pickering*: For Pickering and Wayne, see Sword, *President Washington's Indian War*, 325, and Pickering to Wayne, April 8, 1795, in Knopf, *Anthony Wayne*.

368 *Not until June 23, 1795, did Little Turtle*: In describing the progress of the overall discussions and Little Turtle's pushback, Sword, a Little Turtle man, calls Little Turtle "the champion of Indian rights," while Blue Jacket's biographer Sugden, *Blue Jacket*, 200–207, remarks that "Little Turtle's fight was not a model of tact." Little Turtle's biographer Carter, *Life and Times of Little Turtle*, 148–51, goes overboard, claiming in the face of all evidence to the contrary that the Miami leader was the overwhelmingly dominant presence at the meeting and ascribing all of Blue Jacket's efforts to a selfish desire to supplant Little Turtle. For more on

the partisans of Blue Jacket and Little Turtle, see related notes above and the notes for chapter 10. For Wayne's confidence that there would be no attack, see Sword, *President Washington's Indian War*, 327.

372 *"was not a French fort, brother"*: This quotation is widely cited. Carter's interpretation of its meaning, *Life and Times of Little Turtle*, 151–52, is followed here.

374 *Tecumseh . . . won no battle*: Eid, "American Indian Military Leadership," 72n, points with asperity to ironies involved in the relative fame of a leader who "died in one defeat," when the unknown "army that defeated St. Clair represented in practice what Tecumseh was never able to achieve."

375 *America's national military establishment*: Much of the discussion that begins here is based on Kohn, *Eagle and Sword*, chap. 9.

376 *But what now?*: This discussion of the struggles of the permanent military establishment in the balance of the Federalist period relies on ibid., chaps. 9 and 11–13, which offer much compelling detail not included here. Kohn locates the fracture and fall of the Federalists in the serious military-policy issues and the embarrassing squabbles that arose from the Quasi-war with France, with special attention to the Adams-Hamilton showdown.

376 *"game behind the curtain"*: This has been widely quoted; see, for example, ibid., 175. The Federalists' view of the anti-army faction as paranoid can be seen in Fisher Ames, quoted by ibid., 277: "[Government military takeover] is quite a Utopian dread."

378 *it was during Thomas Jefferson's presidency*: Ibid., 286–303, explores Republican acquiescence in the use of regulars as the tipping point for a permanent American army and notes Jefferson's efforts to rationalize the role of militia in that context (290–301). For the army's extension farther west after the Louisiana Purchase, see Prucha, *Sword of the Republic*, chaps. 4 and 5.

380 *the only humane way*: To look deeply into the Jeffersonian future that follows the action here, see Sheehan, *Seeds of Extinction*.

381 *"even to their extermination"*: Grant, *Papers*, 422.

381 *Blue Jacket moved*: Incidents in the late career of Blue Jacket mentioned here are based on Sugden, *Blue Jacket*, chaps. 11–17, detailing the connection to Tecumseh's attempted reboot of the western Indian confederation. For Little Turtle's later years and efforts, see Carter, *Life and Times of Little Turtle*, chaps. 14–19.

382 *Washington sent him a ceremonial sword*: Heath, *William Wells and the Struggle for the Old Northeast*, 242, dissents from the commonly told story of Little Turtle and Washington's meeting personally, citing the record of Wells's trip to Philadelphia.

382 *a liar, a drunk, and a fool*: The story told here of Wayne's activities after the Treaty of Greeneville is drawn from Paul David Nelson, *Anthony Wayne*, 275–77, and Linklater, *Artist in Treason*, chaps. 14 and 15. For Wilkinson's explicit plan, made with Spain, to destroy Wayne and diminish the size of the U.S. Army, see Linklater, *Artist in Treason*, 158.

384 *it was rumored that they planned to be married*: Paul David Nelson, *Anthony Wayne*, 293, documents the rumor; Tucker, *Mad Anthony Wayne and the New Nation*, 253–55, reports the engagement as fact, with much romantic embellishment.

384 *Theodore Roosevelt, looking back*: Roosevelt, *Winning of the West*, 225–30, 264–65.

385 *John Wayne*: Moss, *Raoul Walsh*, 122–24.

BIBLIOGRAPHY

Alder, Jonathan. *Captivity of Jonathan Alder by the Indians in 1782.* David Webb, 1904.

Alvord, Clarence Wadsworth. *The Illinois Country, 1673–1818.* 1920. Reprint, Loyola University Press, 1965.

———. *The Mississippi Valley in British Politics.* Arthur H. Clark, 1917.

———. "Virginia and the West." *Mississippi Valley Historical Review* 3, no. 1 (June 1916).

American State Papers: Indian Affairs. Vol. 1. Gales and Seaton, 1832.

Ames, Fisher. *Works.* Edited by Seth Ames. Little, Brown, 1854.

Annals of Congress. http://memory.loc.gov/ammem/amlaw/lwaclink.html.

Anson, Bert. *The Miami Indians.* University of Oklahoma Press, 1970.

Aupaumut, Hendrick. *A Narrative of an Embassy to the Western Indians.* Edited by Benjamin Coates. Memoirs of the Historical Society of Pennsylvania, 1827.

Bailey, Kenneth P. *The Ohio Company of Virginia and the Westward Movement, 1748–1792: A Chapter in the History of the Colonial Frontier.* Arthur H. Clark, 1939.

Barnhart, John D. "A New Evaluation of Henry Hamilton and George Rogers Clark." *Mississippi Valley Historical Review* 37, no. 4 (March 1951).

Barnhart, John D., and Dorothy L. Riker. *Indiana to 1816: The Colonial Period.* Indiana Historical Bureau & Indiana Historical Society, 1971.

Bartoloni-Tuazon, Kathleen. *For Fear of an Elective King: George Washington and the Presidential Title Controversy of 1789.* Cornell University Press, 2014.

"Biographical Memoir of Major General Anthony Wayne." *Casket: Flowers of Literature, Wit, and Sentiment,* May 1829.

Boston 1775. http://boston1775.blogspot.com/.

Boyd, Julian P. *Number 7: Alexander Hamilton's Secret Attempts to Control American Foreign Policy.* Princeton University Press, 1964.

———. Review of *The Ohio Company,* by Kenneth P. Bailey. *Pennsylvania Magazine of History and Biography,* Jan. 1940.

Brown, Alan S. "The Role of the Army in Western Settlement: Josiah Harmar's Command, 1785–1790." *Pennsylvania Magazine of History and Biography*, April 1969.

Burton, C. M., ed. *The Journal of Pontiac's Conspiracy, 1763*. Michigan Society of the Colonial Wars, 1912.

Butler, W. D., J. C. Butler, and J. M. Butler. *The Butler Family in America*. 1909. Reprint, Higginson, 1989.

Calloway, Colin. *The American Revolution in Indian Country*. Cambridge University Press, 1995.

———. *The Shawnees and the War for America*. Viking Penguin, 2007.

———. *The Victory with No Name: The Native American Defeat of the First American Army*. Oxford University Press, 2015.

Carlos, Ann M., and Frank D. Lewis. *The Economic History of the Fur Trade, 1670 to 1870*. https://eh.net/encyclopedia/the-economic-history-of-the-fur-trade-1670 -to-1870/.

Carroll, John M., and Colin F. Baxter, eds. *The American Military Tradition: From Colonial Times to the Present*. Rowman & Littlefield, 2007.

Carter, Harvey Lewis. *The Life and Times of Little Turtle: First Sagamore of the Wabash*. University of Illinois Press, 1986.

Chalmers, George. *Queries of George Chalmers, with the Answers of General Gage, in Relation to Braddock's Expedition, the Stamp Act, and Gage's Administration of the Government of Massachusetts*. Massachusetts Historical Society Collections, 4th ser., 4 (1858).

Clary, David A. *George Washington's First War: His Early Military Adventures*. Simon & Schuster, 2011.

Clifton, James A., ed. *Being and Becoming Indian: Biographical Studies of the North American Frontiers*. Dorsey Press, 1989.

"The Constitutional Act, 1791." http://www.solon.org/Constitutions/Canada/English /PreConfederation/ca_1791.html.

Cook, Bernard A., ed. *Women and War: A Historical Encyclopedia from Antiquity to the Present*. Vol. 2. ABC-CLIO, 2006.

Crean, J. F. "Hats and the Fur Trade." *Canadian Journal of Economics and Political Science* 28, no. 3 (Aug. 1962).

Curtis, Christopher Michael. *Jefferson's Freeholders*. Cambridge University Press, 2012.

"Definitive Treaty of Peace Between the United States of America and His Britannic Majesty." https://memory.loc.gov/cgi-bin/ampage?collId=llsl&fileName=008 /llsl008.db&recNum=93.

Del Papa, Eugene M. "The Royal Proclamation of 1763: Its Effect upon Virginia Land Companies." *Virginia Magazine of History and Biography*, Oct. 1975.

Denny, Ebenezer. *Military Journal of Major Ebenezer Denny, an Officer in the Revolutionary and Indian Wars*. Historical Society of Pennsylvania, 1859.

Denny's Vocabulary of Shawnee. 1860. Reprint, Arx, 2005.

Dowd, Gregory Evans. *A Spirited Resistance: The North American Indian Struggle for Unity, 1745–1815*. Johns Hopkins University Press, 1992.

Downes, Randolph C. *Council Fires on the Upper Ohio: A Narrative of Indian Affairs in the Upper Ohio Valley Until 1795*. University of Pittsburgh Press, 1940.

Egnal, Marc. *A Mighty Empire: The Origins of the American Revolution*. Cornell University Press, 1988.

Eid, Leroy. "American Indian Military Leadership: St. Clair's 1791 Defeat." *Journal of Military History* 57, no. 1 (Jan. 1993).

Farrand, Max, ed. *The Records of the Federal Convention of 1787*. Yale University Press, 1911.

Feinstein, Kelly. *Fashionable Felted Fur: The Beaver Hat in 17th Century English Society*. Center for World History, University of California at Santa Cruz, 2006. http://cwh.ucsc.edu/feinstein/Main%20Page.html.

Ferguson, E. J. *The Power of the Purse: A History of American Public Finance, 1776–1790*. University of North Carolina Press, 1961.

Ferling, John E. *The Ascent of George Washington: The Hidden Political Genius of an American Icon*. Bloomsbury Press, 2010.

Flexner, James Thomas. *Washington: The Indispensable Man*. Little, Brown, 1974.

Ford, Paul Leicester. *The True George Washington*. Lippincott, 1911.

Founders Online, National Archives. http://founders.archives.gov/.

Freeman, Douglas Southall. *Washington: A Biography*. Vol. 1. Scribner, 1966.

Fryer, Mary Beacock, and Christopher Dracott. *John Graves Simcoe: A Biography*. Dundurn Press, 1998.

Gaff, Alan D. *Bayonets in the Wilderness: Anthony Wayne's Legion in the Old Northwest*. University of Oklahoma Press, 2004.

Gist, Christopher. *Christopher Gist's Journals: With Historical Geographical and Ethnological Notes and Biographies of His Contemporaries*. Edited by William Darlington. William McCullough, 1889.

Grant, Ulysses S. *The Papers of Ulysses S. Grant*. Vol. 16. Edited by John Y. Simon. Southern Illinois University Press, 1988.

Greiert, Steven G. "The Board of Trade and Defense of the Ohio Valley, 1748–1753." *Western Pennsylvania Historical Magazine*, Jan. 1981.

Hawke, David Freeman. *In the Midst of a Revolution*. University of Pennsylvania Press, 1961.

Heath, William. *William Wells and the Struggle for the Old Northwest*. University of Oklahoma Press, 2015.

Heckewelder, John. *History, Manners, and Customs of the Indian Nations Who Once Inhabited Pennsylvania and the Neighbouring States*. Historical Society of Pennsylvania, 1881.

Henry, Patrick. "Speech Before the Virginia Ratifying Committee." http://www.let.rug.nl/usa/documents/1786-1800/the-anti-federalist-papers/speech-of-patrick-henry-(june-5-1788).php.

Higgonet, Patrice Louis-René. "The Origins of the Seven Years' War." *Journal of Modern History* 40, no. 1 (March 1968).

Hill, Christopher. *Intellectual Origins of the English Revolution—Revisited*. Clarendon Press, 1997.

Hinderaker, Eric. *Elusive Empires: Constructing Colonialism in the Ohio Valley, 1673–1800*. Cambridge University Press, 1997.

Hogeland, William. *Declaration*. Simon & Schuster, 2010.

———. *Founding Finance*. University of Texas Press, 2012.

———. *The Whiskey Rebellion*. Scribner, 2006.

Holton, Woody. *Forced Founders: Indians, Debtors, Slaves, and the Making of the American Revolution in Virginia*. University of North Carolina Press, 1999.

———. "The Ohio Indians and the Coming of the American Revolution in Virginia." *Journal of Southern History* 60, no. 3 (Aug. 1994).

Horsman, Reginald. "The British Indian Department and the Resistance to General Anthony Wayne, 1793–1795." *Mississippi Valley Historical Review* 49, no. 2 (September 1962).

Howe, Henry. *Historical Collections of Ohio: An Encyclopedia of the State*. Vol. 1. State of Ohio, 1907.

Hutchinson, William Thomas. "The Bounty Lands of the Revolution in Ohio." Ph.D. diss., University of Chicago, 1927.

James, Alfred P. *The Ohio Company: Its Inner History*. University of Pittsburgh Press, 1959.

Jefferson, Thomas. *The Papers of Thomas Jefferson*. Vol. 3. Edited by Julian P. Boyd. Princeton University Press, 1951.

———. "A Summary View of the Rights of British America." http://avalon.law.yale.edu /18th_century/jeffsumm.asp.

Jortner, Adam. *The Gods of Prophetstown: The Battle of Tippecanoe and the Holy War for the American Frontier*. Oxford University Press, 2012.

Journal of the Military Service Institution of the United States 40 (1907).

Kelsay, Isabel Thompson. *Joseph Brant, 1743–1807: Man of Two Worlds*. Syracuse University Press, 1984.

Ketcham, Ralph. *James Madison: A Biography*. Macmillan, 1971.

Knollenberg, Bernhard. *George Washington, the Virginia Period, 1732–1775*. Duke University Press, 1964.

Knopf, Richard C., ed. *Anthony Wayne: A Name in Arms*. University of Pittsburgh Press, 1960.

Kohn, Richard H. *Eagle and Sword: The Federalists and the Creation of the Military Establishment in America, 1783–1802*. Free Press, 1975.

Kopper, Kevin Patrick. "Arthur St. Clair and the Struggle for Power in the Old Northwest, 1763–1803." Ph.D. diss., Kent State University, 2005.

Lincoln, Benjamin. *Journal of a Treaty Held in 1793 with the Indian Tribes North-West of the Ohio, by Commissioners of the United States*. Massachusetts Historical Society Collections, ser. 3, 5 (1836).

Linklater, Andro. *An Artist in Treason: The Extraordinary Double Life of General James Wilkinson*. Walker, 2009.

Littlefield, Daniel C. "The Varieties of Slave Labor." National Humanities Center, TeacherServe. http://nationalhumanitiescenter.org/tserve/freedom/1609-1865 /essays/slavelabor.htm.

Loudon, Archibald. *A Selection of Some of the Most Interesting Narratives of Outrages Committed by the Indians in Their Wars with the White People*, Vol. 1. Harrisburg Publishing Company, 1888.

Lynd, Staughton. "The Compromise of 1787." *Political Science Quarterly* 81, no. 2 (June 1966).

Lytle, Richard M. *The Soldiers of America's First Army, 1791*. Scarecrow Press, 2004.

Maier, Pauline. *Ratification: The People Debate the Constitution, 1787–1788*. Simon & Schuster, 2010.

Mann, Barbara Alice. *George Washington's War on Native America*. Praeger, 2005.

Maurer, Maurer. "Military Justice Under General Washington." *Military Affairs* 28, no. 1 (Spring 1964).

Mayer, Henry. *A Son of Thunder: Patrick Henry and the American Republic*. F. Watts, 1986.

McGaughy, J. Kent. *Richard Henry Lee of Virginia: A Portrait of an American Revolutionary*. Rowman & Littlefield, 2003.

Michigan Historical Collections. Vol. 17 (with Jacob Lindley, "Expedition to Detroit"). Vol. 24 (with transcriptions of Canadian Colonial Record Office documents). Vol. 34 (with General Wayne's Orderly Book). Michigan Pioneer Historical Society, 1895.

"Minutes of Debates in Council on the Banks of the Ottawa River (Commonly Called the Miamia of the Lake), November——, 1791." William Young, 1792.

Moore, George H. *Libels on Washington, with a Critical Examination Thereof*. Privately printed, 1889.

Moore, H. N. *The Life and Services of Gen. Anthony Wayne*. J. B. Perry, 1845.

Morrow, George. T. *"We Must Fight!": The Private War between Patrick Henry and Lord Dunmore*. Tetford Publications, 2012.

Moss, Marilyn. *Raoul Walsh: The True Adventures of Hollywood's Legendary Director*. University Press of Kentucky, 2011.

The National Cyclopaedia of American Biography: Being the History of the United States as Illustrated in the Lives of the Founders, Builders, and Defenders of the Republic and of the Men and Women Who Are Doing the Work and Moulding the Thought of the Present Time. Vol. 8. James White, 1898.

Nelson, Larry L. *A Man of Distinction Among Them*. Kent State University Press, 1999.

———. "Never Have They Done So Little: The Battle of Fort Recovery." *Northwest Ohio Quarterly* 64, no. 2 (Spring 1992).

Nelson, Paul David. *Anthony Wayne, Soldier of the Early Republic*. Indiana University Press, 1985.

Onuf, Peter S. *Statehood and Union: A History of the Northwest Ordinance*. Indiana University Press, 1987.

Parkman, Francis. *The Conspiracy of Pontiac and the Indian War After the Conquest of Canada*. Macmillan, 1885.

———. *Montcalm and Wolfe*. Vol. 1. Little, Brown, 1914.

Parsons, Joseph, Jr. "Civilizing the Indians of the Old Northwest, 1800–1810." *Indiana Magazine of History*, Sept. 1960.

Philyaw, L. Scott. *Virginia's Western Vision: Political and Cultural Expansions on the Early American Frontier*. University of Tennessee Press, 2004.

Pound, Merritt. *Benjamin Hawkins, Indian Agent*. University of Georgia Press, 2009.

A Precise Journal of General Wayne's Last Campaign. Proceedings of the American Antiquarian Society, Oct. 1954. http://www.americanantiquarian.org/proceedings/44524998.pdf.

"Proclamation by Lord Dunmore." American Archives, Northern Illinois University Libraries. http://amarch.lib.niu.edu/islandora/object/niu-amarch%3A78658.

Prucha, Francis Paul. *The Sword of the Republic: The United States Army on the Frontier, 1783–1846*. University of Nebraska Press, 1969.

Putnam, Rufus. *The Memoirs of Rufus Putnam and Certain Official Papers and Correspondence.* Houghton Mifflin, 1903.

Quaife, M. M. "General James Wilkinson's Narrative of the Fallen Timbers Campaign." *Mississippi Valley Historical Review* 16, no. 1 (June 1929).

Rashid, Mahrub. "The Plan Is the Program: Thomas Jefferson's Plan for the Rectilinear Survey of 1784." Paper presented at the Annual Meeting of the Association of Collegiate Schools of Architecture, 1996.

Reuter, T. "'Petty Spy' or Effective Diplomat: The Role of George Beckwith." *Journal of the Early Republic* 10, no. 4 (Winter 1990).

Richter, Daniel K. *Facing East from Indian Country: A Native History of Early America.* Harvard University Press, 2001.

Riddell, William Renwick. *The Life of John Graves Simcoe: First Lieutenant-Governor of the Province of Upper Canada, 1792–96.* McClelland and Stewart, 1926.

Ritcheson, C. R. "The Earl of Shelbourne and Peace with America, 1782–1783: Vision and Reality." *International History Review* 5, no. 3 (Aug. 1983).

Roosevelt, Theodore. *The Winning of the West.* Vol. 5. Charles Scribner's Sons, 1906.

Rush, Richard. *Washington in Domestic Life: From Original Letters and Manuscripts.* J. B. Lippincott, 1857.

Salmon, Emily Jones, and John Salmon. "Tobacco in Colonial Virginia." In *Encyclopedia Virginia.* Virginia Foundation for the Humanities, 2013. http://www.encyclopediavirginia.org/Tobacco_in_Colonial_Virginia.

Sargent, Winthrop. *Diary of Colonel Winthrop Sargent, Adjutant General of the United States' Army, During the Campaign of 1791.* Wormsloe, 1851.

Sheehan, Bernard W. Review of *A Spirited Resistance: The North American Indian Struggle for Unity, 1745–1815,* by Gregory Evans Dowd. *Georgia Historical Quarterly* 76, no. 4 (Winter 1992).

———. *Seeds of Extinction: Jeffersonian Philanthropy and the American Indian.* University of North Carolina Press, for the Omohundro Institute of Early American History and Culture, 2011.

Shriver, Philip B. "America's Other Bicentennial." *Old Northwest: A Journal of Regional Life and Letters,* no. 9 (Autumn 1983).

Shy, John. "A New Look at Colonial Militia." *William and Mary Quarterly* 20, no. 2 (April 1963).

Simcoe, Elizabeth. *The Diary of Mrs. John Graves Simcoe, Wife of the First Lieutenant-Governor of the Province of Upper Canada, 1792–6: With Notes and a Biography.* Edited by Ross Robertson. William Briggs, 1911.

Simcoe, John. *The Correspondence of John Simcoe.* Edited by E. A. Cruikshank. Vols. 1–3. Ontario Historical Society, 1923.

———. *Remarks on the Travels of the Marquis de Chastellux in North America.* G. and T. Wilkie, 1787.

Skaggs, David Curtis. Review of *Tecumseh: A Life,* by John Sugden. *Indiana Magazine of History,* March 1999.

Skaggs, David Curtis, and Larry Nelson, eds. *The Sixty Years' War for the Great Lakes, 1754–1814.* Michigan State University Press, 2001.

"Sketch of Career of Joseph G. Butler, Jr." *Blast Furnace and Steel Plant,* Jan. 1922.

Sosin, Jack M. "The Yorke-Camden Opinion and American Land Speculators." *Pennsylvania Magazine of History and Biography,* Jan. 1961.

Spencer, Oliver M. *The Indian Captivity of O. M. Spencer.* R. R. Donnelly & Sons, 1917.

St. Clair, Arthur. *A Narrative of the Manner in Which the Campaign Against the Indians, in the Year One Thousand Seven Hundred and Ninety-One, Was Conducted, Under the Command of Major General St. Clair: Together with His Observations on the Statements of the Secretary of War and the Quarter Master General, Relative Thereto, and the Reports of the Committees Appointed to Inquire into the Causes of the Failure Thereof: Taken from the Files of the House of Representatives in Congress.* Jane Aitken, 1812.

———. *The St. Clair Papers.* Edited by William Henry Smith. Robert Clarke, 1882.

Sugden, John. *Blue Jacket: Warrior of the Shawnees.* University of Nebraska Press, 2003.

Sword, Wiley. *President Washington's Indian War: The Struggle for the Old Northwest, 1790–1795.* University of Oklahoma Press, 1985.

Tanner, Helen Hornbeck. "The Glaize in 1792: A Composite Indian Community." *Ethnohistory* 25, no. 1 (Winter 1978).

Taylor, Alan. *American Revolutions: A Continental History, 1750–1804.* W. W. Norton and Company, 2016.

———. *The Divided Ground: Indians, Settlers, and the Northern Borderland of the American Revolution.* Alfred A. Knopf, 2006.

Tucker, Glenn. *Mad Anthony Wayne and the New Nation: The Story of Washington's Front-Line General.* Stackpole Books, 1973.

The United States Songster: A Choice Selection of About One Hundred and Seventy of the Most Popular Songs. P. James, 1836.

Virginia Revolutionary War Records. Library of Virginia. http://www.lva.virginia.gov /public/guides/rn8_varev.pdf.

Ward, Harry M. *George Washington's Enforcers: Policing the Continental Army.* Southern Illinois University Press, 2006.

———. *When Fate Summons: A Biography of General Richard Butler, 1743–1791.* Academica Press, 2014.

Warner, Michael S. "General Josiah Harmar's Campaign Reconsidered: How the Americans Lost the Battle of Kekionga." *Indiana Magazine of History,* March 1987.

Washington, George. *The Journal of Major George Washington.* T. Jefferys, 1754.

Wharton, Thomas. "Selections from the Letter-Books of Thomas Wharton, of Philadelphia, 1773–1783." *Pennsylvania Magazine of History and Biography* 33, no. 4 (1909).

"What's in an H?" *Popular Pittsburgh.* http://popularpittsburgh.com/whatsinanh/.

Whitaker, Arthur Preston. "Wilkinson's First Descent to New Orleans in 1787." *Hispanic American Historical Review* 8, no. 1 (Feb. 1928).

White, Edmund J. "Pantisocracy and Pennsylvania: Plans of Coleridge and Southey and of Cooper and Priestley." *Bulletin for the History of Chemistry* 30, no. 2 (2005).

Wildes, Harry Emerson. *Anthony Wayne, Troubleshooter of the American Revolution.* Greenwood Press, 1970.

Williams, Robert A. *The American Indian in Western Legal Thought: The Discourses of Conquest.* Oxford University Press, 1990.

Wills, Garry. *Cincinnatus: George Washington and the Enlightenment.* Doubleday, 1984.

Winkler, John. *Fallen Timbers: The US Army's First Victory.* Osprey, 2013.

———. *Wabash 1791: St. Clair's Defeat.* Osprey, 2011.

ACKNOWLEDGMENTS

Thanks to Eric Lupfer for sticking with this idea when I was ready to give up, and for adroit representation for, I'm amazed to realize, almost ten years. Thanks to Alex Star, whose unfailing judgment, close reading, literary simpatico, and reserves of patience enabled me to go further here than I had before; and to everybody else at Farrar, Straus and Giroux, whose taste, creativity, and diligence have transformed my sentences into this book and helped get the word out.

I'm always grateful for archives and libraries and those who work at them, in this case especially the New York Public Library, and especially its Milstein Division; the Historical Society of Pennsylvania; the Clements Library of the University of Michigan; and the Internet Archive. Museums and historic sites and replicas have been important to this project: their range may be suggested by mentioning the National Park Service site at Fallen Timbers and Fort Miamis, the Great Law of Peace Center, Her Majesty's Royal Chapel of the Mohawks, Shawnee Lookout County Park, and the Fort Recovery State Museum. But there are too many to list, and I'm at least as grateful for the less official, barely maintained plaques, markers, and ruins, often hard to find along booming suburban strips and empty back roads, among abandoned industrial buildings, and, once, on a busy golf course.

The involvement of my family, friends, colleagues, and competitors has served as a critical source of support. Close friends, other writers and historians, and faithful readers alike have raised questions, exchanged information and ideas, and encouraged my progress. For this book, each of my brothers accompanied me in a phase of research travel, one to Stony Point, one to the Ohio River sites. My wife provided, along with more than I can say here, navigation for a last-minute, time-pressured spin down the lakeshores on the wrong side of the contested border with Canada. My efforts rely as well on the enthusiastic interest of my stepdaughter, son-in-law, grandchild, and grandchild-in-law. The dedication is to the memory of my mother.

INDEX

324, 350, 363, 364; Simcoe and,
172–73, 316
Doughty, John, 96
Duer, William, 236, 239
Dunmore, 286, 289
Dunmore, John Murray, Lord, 71–77;
Henry and, 76
Dunmore's War, 75–76, 107
Duquesne, Marquis, 37, 40

Eel River, 87, 88, 115, 381
Elliott, Matthew, 143, 172, 289–92, 318,
322, 348
England: Anglo-Saxon, 65–66; *see also*
Great Britain, British
England, Colonel, 324, 337, 362
Eyer's Hill, 236

Fairfax, Thomas, 29
Fairfax, William, 23, 29, 31
Fallen Timbers, Battle of, 337–51, 354,
361, 362, 366, 367, 375, 385
Fauquier, Francis, 58
Federal, 281
Federalist Party, 277–80
Forbes, John, 54–55, 140
Fort Canandaigua, 224
Fort Clinton, 199
Fort Defiance, 334–35, 351, 354–55,
364, 365
Fort Detroit, 49, 52, 82, 87–89, 102,
113, 138, 139, 147, 161, 164–65, 173,
176, 219, 225, 228, 239, 246–47,
289–90, 299, 316–17, 324, 330, 337,
338, 342, 351, 362, 364, 381, 384;
conference at, 104; McKee at, 140,
143, 145–46, 164, 166; Wayne's army
and, 317, 324, 327
Fort Duquesne, 37–42, 49, 54–55, 125,
279
Fort Erie, 286, 289
Fort Fayette, 231, 232, 236, 237, 241,
246, 253, 255, 281, 312, 356–58
Fort Finney, 101
Fort Finney Treaty, 101–103, 113, 146

Fort Greene Ville, 303–304, 313, 316,
318–20, 322, 323, 325–26, 328, 334,
336, 355, 356, 358, 363–66; Blue
Jacket at, 364–66; Greeneville Treaty,
365–66, 368–76
Fort Hamilton, 118, 150, 151, 166, 232,
255, 262, 263, 265, 281, 284, 302;
Wayne's army at, 301
Fort Harmar, 108–10, 162, 231, 240,
243, 281, 353; meeting at, 108,
110–14, 227; Treaty of, 113, 114, 138,
157–58, 179, 227–28, 230, 241, 243,
250, 256, 258, 259, 277, 278, 353,
363, 365–68, 370–72
Fort Jefferson, 117–18, 150, 151, 165,
166, 232, 247–48, 255, 262, 263, 284;
Indian attack on hay cutters at, 239,
243–44, 263, 267; Little Turtle's army
and, 265; Wayne's army at, 286–87,
298, 300–303, 304, 314
Fort McIntosh, 100–101
Fort Miamis, 316–18, 323–24, 326–30,
337, 339, 348–51, 352, 356, 362–65;
Fallen Timbers and, 348; Indians
refused refuge at, 348–49, 369;
refugees from the Glaize at, 330, 362;
Wayne's army and, 329, 334, 349–51,
354
Fort Necessity, 40–42; Battle of the
Great Meadows, 38–43, 53
Fort Niagara, 49, 57, 82, 112, 143, 175,
218, 219, 222, 223, 225, 226, 246–47,
268, 269, 274–76, 316, 352
Fort Pitt, 49, 52, 56, 69, 75, 83, 96, 97,
107, 118, 141, 143, 153, 231
Fort Recovery, 299–300, 303–304,
313–14, 318, 328–30, 352, 370; Blue
Jacket's attack on, 313, 318–24, 326,
328–30, 374; Little Turtle and, 324
Fort Recovery, Ohio, 352; Monument
Park in, 385
Fort St. Clair, 151, 232, 263, 265, 302,
311; Little Turtle's attack on Kentucky
volunteers at, 265, 266, 270, 272
Fort St. Louis, 308, 309
Fort Stanwix treaties, 61–64, 68,
97–101, 104, 142, 161, 226, 257, 291

Jackson, Andrew, 380–81

Jackson, James, 216–17

Jay, John, 136, 326

Jay Treaty, 326, 334, 363, 371, 376

Jefferson, Thomas, 58, 64–66, 70, 74, 136, 154–57, 161, 164, 169, 183, 220, 253, 274, 276, 282, 358, 382; article on army plan by, 169–70; and assimilation of Indians, 380; British as viewed by, 156; Declaration of Independence drafted by, 79–80; Hamilton and, 154, 178, 224, 225; Indians as viewed by, 155–56; Knox and, 157; Louisiana Purchase of, 379; militia as viewed by, 156, 224, 379; as minister to France, 156; Monticello home of, 154; national military establishment and, 378–80; Norman Yoke theory and, 65–66; Pond-Steedman report and, 224–25; presidency of, 378–80; slaves and, 155; standing army policy and, 224; "A Summary View of the Rights of British America," 79, 80; in Washington's cabinet, 154–56; western expansion and, 154–56; Whiggism of, 64–65

Jimmy the Drover, 201–202

Johnson, John, 90, 98, 166–67, 173, 218

Johnson, William, 61

Jumonville, Joseph Coulon de Villiers, Sieur de, 39–40, 42–43, 69

Kanawha River, 239

Kaskaskia, 87, 96–97

Kekionga, 86–89, 103–104, 113–15, 117, 138–39, 145–47, 151, 166, 231, 241, 259, 352, 355, 382; Blue Jacket at, 113–15, 138, 146–47; Fort Wayne built at, 355–56; Glaize settlement of, see Glaize settlement; Harmar's flying strike mission against, 22, 114–15, 119, 125, 137, 229, 230, 311, 313; Little Turtle at, 113–15, 138, 146–47, 229; McKee and, 144, 146–47; resettlement of inhabitants of,

146–47; St. Clair's defeat at, see St. Clair's defeat; Wayne's army and, 328

Kenton, Simon, 88, 103

Kentucky, 61–64, 74, 75, 79, 82, 84, 87, 91, 102–104, 108, 134, 142, 144, 312, 383; Blue Licks battle in, 84, 91, 103; Fort Stanwix Treaty and, 61–64, 68, 97–101, 104; new settlers in, 307; secession from U.S., 310–12; secession from Virginia, 306–308, 310, 312; statehood of, 312; Wilkinson in, 305–308

Kentucky militia: at Fort St. Clair, Little Turtle's attack on, 265, 266, 270, 272; in Wayne's army, 299–300, 302, 303, 325, 334, 339–44, 346, 356

Kew, 211

Kickapoo, 64, 81, 164

King, Rufus, 180

Kirkland, Samuel, 224, 227

Knox, Henry, 96, 106, 117, 119, 126, 134, 137, 152–53, 157, 186, 196, 225, 236, 239, 253, 260, 266–67, 277, 278, 286–87, 293, 357, 358, 366, 368, 378; article on army plan by, 169–70; as bookseller, 189; Brant and, 227; congressional report of, 266–67; in Continental army, 189; Duer and, 236; Hamilton and, 157, 225; Indians as viewed by, 157–59; and investigation of St. Clair's defeat, 182–83; Kekionga and, 114; militia system and, 158, 170–71, 177; plan for national army, 161–64, 168–70, 224; Pond and Steedman's expedition and, 222–24; Putnam and, 243–46; resignation of, 366–67; Sandusky meeting and, 272–73; Washington and, 157, 189, 244–45, 274; in Washington's cabinet, 154, 157–58; Wayne and, 214, 217, 231, 333, 355; Wayne's army and, 231–33, 238, 242, 245, 253–55, 264, 269–71, 281, 283–84, 302, 303, 326, 327, 334, 335, 354, 358; Wayne's letter to, after orders to withdraw and delay operations,